A VOYCE FROM
THE WATCH TOWER

Part Five: 1660–1662

EDMUND LUDLOW

A VOYCE FROM
THE WATCH TOWER

Part Five: 1660–1662

edited by
A. B. WORDEN

CAMDEN FOURTH SERIES
Volume 21

LONDON
OFFICES OF THE ROYAL HISTORICAL SOCIETY
UNIVERSITY COLLEGE LONDON,
GOWER STREET LONDON WC1E 6BT
1978

ISBN 0 901050 43 1

Printed in Great Britain by Butler & Tanner Ltd
Frome and London

CONTENTS

ABBREVIATIONS

'Voyce'	Edmund Ludlow, 'A Voyce from the Watch Tower'
Darby	*Memoirs of Edmund Ludlow Esq.* (3 vols., 1698–9)
Firth	C. H. Firth (ed.), *The Memoirs of Edmund Ludlow* (2 vols., Oxford, 1894)

B.L.	British Library (formerly British Museum)
H.M.C.R.	*Historical Manuscripts Commission Report*
P.R.O., SP	Public Record Office, State Papers
P.R.O., 30/24	Public Record Office, Shaftesbury Papers

PREFACE

W H E N Charles II was restored in 1660, the regicide Edmund Ludlow fled to Switzerland. During the Puritan Revolution he had had an influential career, as an army officer, as a member of the Long Parliament, as a parliamentary commissioner to Ireland, as an opponent of the Cromwellian Protectorate, and as one of the leading republicans of 1658–60. After the Restoration, an exile at Vevey on Lake Geneva, he composed a manuscript narrative which was to form the basis of one of the best-known sources for the study of the Civil Wars and Interregnum, the *Memoirs of Edmund Ludlow*. He died in November 1692. The *Memoirs* were published six years later, in 1698–9.

After their publication, Ludlow's manuscript disappeared. C. H. Firth, while preparing the standard edition of the *Memoirs* which he produced in 1894, searched for it in vain, and until recently it seemed irretrievably lost. In 1970, however, there was sold at Sotheby's a large manuscript volume written by Ludlow and entitled 'A Voyce from the Watch Tower'.[1] It was acquired by the Bodleian Library, where it has the classmark MS. Eng. hist. c. 487. Alas, it is only a part of the manuscript on which Ludlow's *Memoirs* were based. The remaining sections of 'A Voyce from the Watch Tower', from which it became artificially separated at some time after Ludlow had completed his text, remain undiscovered. The portion in the Bodleian, which will be referred to as the Bodleian manuscript, is the second of three sections of Ludlow's narrative. It covers the period from February 1660 to the spring of 1677. The first section, the one we would most like to possess, ended in February 1660. The third section covered the years 1677 to 1685, and we are able to form, from a table of contents written by Ludlow and bound into the Bodleian manuscript, some idea of the material we would be likely to find in it.

The differences between the Bodleian manuscript and the corresponding section of the *Memoirs* are striking. They show that, when the *Memoirs* were prepared for publication, Ludlow's text was radically altered and abridged. On this point, Firth, who accepted the *Memoirs* as authentic, made an understandable but fundamental error of judgement. The error led him to further errors, and the mistakes of a great historian can offer a useful cautionary tale. It is a mark of Firth's stature that his edition of the *Memoirs* will nevertheless remain a work of immeasurable value. His editorial apparatus—the

[1] Sotheby's sale catalogue, 23 June 1970, p. 123.

introduction, the footnotes, the appendices—is an enduring monument to his exact and penetrating scholarship. The present volume is designed not to replace Firth's work, but to supplement it. I have therefore registered my indebtedness to and disagreements with Firth, and have reproduced information available in his edition, only when my argument has made it necessary or helpful to do so. Inevitably I have emphasised the differences between the manuscript and the *Memoirs*, for the contrasts are the *raison d'être* of the present volume. The surprise afforded by the differences should not blind us to the similarities. If we return to the *Memoirs* armed with the information which the present volume provides, and read them in the critical spirit which that information impels, we shall find that they are still a major source for the study of the Puritan Revolution. We shall also find that the *Memoirs* are an unexpectedly useful source for the study of the politics of the period of the late 1690s in which they were first published.

The Bodleian manuscript—which begins on p. 721 of 'A Voyce from the Watch Tower', and ends on p. 1454—is about 400,000 words long. Only a part of it is reproduced here. This volume thus contains only a portion of a document which is itself only a portion of 'A Voyce from the Watch Tower'. At some time when the composition of his manuscript had neared or achieved completion, Ludlow, evidently sensing the need to impose organisation on his text, divided the narrative into parts, and the parts into chapters. Part five, the portion chosen here, begins on the first page of the Bodleian manuscript, and occupies about two-sevenths of it (ending on p. 934). Had the Bodleian manuscript remained wholly unpublished, part five is probably the portion which scholars would have consulted most frequently. Because it has been affected by damp, it is the portion which they would have found hardest to use. The choice of part five leaves the way open for the publication of later portions of the Bodleian manuscript, if that should ever seem desirable and practicable. In my introduction I have considered the character of the Bodleian manuscript as a whole, rather than merely of part five (and have left the reader to discover many of the pleasures of part five for himself). Ludlow's table of contents for the complete Bodleian manuscript has been reproduced, in Appendix A.

The Bodleian manuscript reached Sotheby's from Warwick Castle. When and why it arrived at the castle we cannot say. In 1763 the Scottish historian William Robertson transcribed at the castle 'An Account of the Family and Descendants of Oliver Cromwell', which had recently been left there, 'with other papers', by the antiquarian Robert Symmar.[2] It is conceivable that the Bodleian manuscript was

[2] National Library of Scotland, MS. 3942, fos. 52–3.

among the 'papers' brought by Symmar to the castle, where a number
of mid-seventeenth-century pamphlets are still to be found. The
acquisition of the manuscript can be more plausibly attributed, however, to Henry Greville, third Earl of Warwick of the Greville descent,
who held the title from 1816 to 1853. The third Earl took pains to
build up the castle library, and the Bodleian manuscript contains his
signature. There remains at the castle a hitherto unknown manuscript
by Algernon Sidney, which will be considered in connection both with
the writing of Ludlow's manuscript and with the publication of
Ludlow's *Memoirs*. It is a fair guess that the Ludlow and the Sidney
manuscripts reached Warwick Castle together.[3] The castle library has
had a colourfully confused history, and the surviving catalogues do
not enable us to say whether the missing sections of 'A Voyce from
the Watch Tower' were ever there. Firth recorded that 'a manuscript
copy was some years ago in the possession of a member of the Ludlow
family; but whether it was the original or simply a transcript from
which the Memoirs were printed I have been unable to ascertain,
for it has been appropriated by a person to whom the owner lent it'.[4]
The trails I have followed in pursuit of the missing sections have all—
for the present anyway—petered out.[5]

It is a pleasure to record my indebtedness to the many scholars whose
help and advice have made the preparation of this book possible. Let
me particularly thank Reg Alton, Eric Bagnall, Molly Barratt,
Giancarlo Carabelli, Jeremy Cater, Patricia Crawford, David Foxon,
Mark Goldie, Geoffrey Holmes, Charles Hoover, Michael Hunter,
Ronald Hutton, Philip Long, Valerie Pearl, John Pocock, Ian Roy,
Quentin Skinner, Henry Snyder, Bill Speck, Keith Thomas, Michael
Treadwell, Hugh Trevor-Roper and Anne Whiteman. The list is
long, and as I look over it I realise how extensive the generosity of
my colleagues has been, and how fortunate I have been to benefit
from it. I have profited too from the expertise and kindness of archiv-
ists at the Bodleian Library, Warwick Castle, the Warwickshire and
Wiltshire Record Offices, the History of Parliament Trust, the Sheffield and Leeds City Libraries, the Library of Manchester College,
Oxford, the Folger Library, the Staatsarchiv des Kantons Bern, the
Stadt- und Universitätsbibliothek Bern, the Burgerbibliothek Bern,
and the Archives Cantonales et Vaudoises in Lausanne. I am glad
to thank Lord Brooke and Earl Fitzwilliam, for permission to make
use of manuscripts in their ownership; the Faculty Board of Modern
History at Oxford, for granting me financial assistance; and the *Times*

[3] See below, p. 15. Algernon Sidney's *Discourses concerning Government* is among the
books at the castle which contain the third Earl's signature.
[4] Firth, i. x.
[5] See also the pessimistic reflection below, p. 3, n. 8.

Literary Supplement, for allowing me to reproduce material from my essay 'Edmund Ludlow: the Puritan and the Whig', published in the *T.L.S.* on 7 January 1977.

In so far as the book is mine to dedicate, I dedicate it to my father, lovingly and with deep gratitude.

AN EXPLANATORY NOTE

THE editorial conventions adopted in the reproduction of Ludlow's text in this volume are described below, pp. 81–3. The same conventions have been used in quotations from 'A Voyce from the Watch Tower' in the Introduction (with the single exception of the long passage reproduced on pp. 54–5). In quotations from seventeenth- and early eighteenth-century printed sources, the use of capital letters has been modernised, and (for the sake of clarity) punctuation has occasionally been modernised too. In references to printed works, the place of publication is given only when the work cited was not published at London.

When Ludlow's *Memoirs* are cited, references are normally given both to the 1698–9 edition and to Firth's; but on subjects in which attention is drawn to Firth's footnotes, reference is made only to Firth's edition. Firth amended the punctuation of the 1698–9 edition, modernised the use of capital letters, and corrected obvious misprints.

When comparisons are drawn between Ludlow's manuscript and Ludlow's *Memoirs*, references are normally given only to the manuscript. The means by which passages in the two documents may be compared with each other are described below, p. 81.

INTRODUCTION

1. THE MEMOIRS AND THE MANUSCRIPT

FOR nearly forty years after the Restoration of Charles II, men who argued about the Civil Wars and Interregnum were largely dependent for their supporting evidence on works which were essentially documentary compilations. The chief histories of the Puritan Revolution published in the Restoration period—Heath, Dugdale, Nalson, Rushworth, Whitelocke—were often animated by party zeal or adorned by commentary, but they drew principally upon official publications and newspapers. Informal evidence, contained in diaries and journals, remained hidden from public view. The history which most resembled an autobiography, Whitelocke's *Memorials*, was deprived by cautious editors of the most revealing passages of personal narrative in Whitelocke's manuscript. By the end of the seventeenth century, the dry diet of Restoration histories had become unsatisfying. The rights and wrongs of the Civil War period remained as controversial, and seemed as relevant to contemporary politics, as ever, but the passage of time had made it harder for readers to enter into the minds of politicians who had participated in the events of 1640–60. Time, too, had begun to enable historians of the Civil Wars to depict light and shade where their predecessors had offered only white and black.

Early in 1698, the opportunity to supply a new genre of Civil War history was taken. It was then, possibly in January but probably in February, that the *Memoirs of Edmund Ludlow*, covering the period from the accession of Charles I to the Restoration, were published in two volumes. They sold unexpectedly well, and caused a considerable stir. Their vivid narrative provided fresh information which could only have been available to a leading politician who had seen the events of the Puritan Revolution from the inside. Those events were presented, for the first time, through the eyes of a fully rounded personality.[1] The publishers brought the *Memoirs* to a close in 1660

[1] For the date of the publication of the first two volumes, see Bodleian Library, Ballard MS. xxiv, fo. 65 (Sloane to Charlett, 19 February 1698), and B.L., Add. MS. 17677SS, fo. 171 (letter of Dutch envoys, 7 March 1698). For their reception, see also *A Just Defence of the Royal Martyr King Charles I from . . . . Ludlow's Memoirs* (1699), p. 12, and *Regicides no Saints or Martyrs* (1700), p. 9. There seems to have been a series of fresh impressions of the *Memoirs* between 1698 and 1700: E. Arber (ed.), *The Term Catalogues 1688–1709* (3 vols., 1903–6), iii. 77, 108, 179. The *Memoirs* were translated into French: *Les Mémoires d'Edmond Ludlow* (2 vols., Amsterdam, 1699) and *Nouveaux Mémoires d'Edmond Ludlow* (i.e. vol. iii: Amsterdam, 1707); cf. J. Bernard (ed.), *Nouvelles de la République*, February 1699, pp. 145ff., and E.S. de Beer, 'Edmund Ludlow in Exile',

because Ludlow had thereafter been removed from the centre of political action.[2] In the spring of 1699, however, the publishers were emboldened by the success of the first two volumes to bring out a third, which took the story from 1660 to 1672. To boost the sales of the third volume they padded it with documents concerning events described in the first two, and with an index covering all three. Although the third volume seems to have made less impact than its predecessors, the genre which had been launched by the first two volumes—'that allamode way of Memoirs', a hostile observer called it[3]—soon caught on. The *Memoirs of Sir John Berkeley*, the *Memoirs of Denzil Lord Holles*, and the *Short Memorials of Thomas Lord Fairfax* all appeared in 1699. Like Ludlow's *Memoirs*, they were Whig publications. The Tory counter-offensive began in 1701 with the *Memoirs of Sir Philip Warwick*, which were followed in 1702 by Clarendon's *History of the Rebellion* and by the *Memoirs* of Sir Thomas Herbert. The publication of these Tory works was at least partly inspired by the desire to rival the success of the Whig memoirs.[4]

In 1699 and 1700, William Baron, chaplain to the second Earl of Clarendon, attacked the publishers of Ludlow's *Memoirs* in two substantial pamphlets whose length is in itself a tribute to the success the *Memoirs* enjoyed. One of Baron's charges was that the publishers had been unfaithful to Ludlow's manuscript. The *Memoirs*, he wrote, were 'but the abridgement of many more reams', which Ludlow's 'party, and printer, thought fit to lick into something of form, contract, and perhaps alter too, as might best serve the present design of promoting the Good Old Cause'. Ludlow had 'provided the ingredients', but it was the publishers who had 'composed the dish, from a confused heap'; they had 'cut off the superfluities of that fanciful Swiss dress' in which Ludlow's manuscript had reached them.[5] We do not know how widely Baron's suspicions were shared. The authenticity of the *Memoirs* was questioned at a dinner party at Lambeth Palace in 1705, and was to be challenged later in the eighteenth century by the literary historians Richard Rawlinson and Thomas Tyers.[6]

Notes and Queries, June 1962, p. 223. They also seem to have been translated into Dutch: W. H. Hull, *William Sewel of Amsterdam* (Swarthmore College, 1933), pp. 152, 209.

[2] Darby, iii, preface (or Firth, ii. 261n.).

[3] *Regicides no Saints*, pp. 3, 7; Firth, i. xi.

[4] This can be inferred from their prefaces; for Clarendon, see the edition by W. D. Macray (6 vols., Oxford, 1888), i. xix.

[5] *A Just Defence*, pp. 5–6; *Regicides no Saints*, pp. 4, 8. The traditional attribution of these anonymous pamphlets to William Baron is surely correct: see [Willia]m [Baro]n, *The Dutch Way of Toleration* (1698), pp. 2, 21. A copy of *A Just Defence* in the Cambridge University Library (classmark VIII. 30. 8) carries a manuscript ascription to John Baron, Fellow and later Master of Balliol, but although John Baron probably disliked Ludlow's *Memoirs* as much as William did, his known writings make the ascription implausible.

[6] Below, p. 18, n. 75; Firth, i. xi.

Nevertheless, the *Memoirs* seem to have been generally regarded as Ludlow's own. The three eighteenth-century editions (a reprint of 1720–22, and the handsome single-volume editions of 1751 and 1771), although correcting obvious misprints, otherwise faithfully reproduced the text of 1698–9.

When C. H. Firth came to publish the standard edition of 1894, a little evidence had come to light about the relationship between Ludlow's manuscript and the *Memoirs*. In the middle of the nineteenth century, W. D. Christie discovered that John Locke had made copies of a series of passages in Ludlow's manuscript which contained hostile references to Locke's patron, Anthony Ashley Cooper, first Earl of Shaftesbury. None of these passages was to be found in Ludlow's *Memoirs*.[7] Firth duly incorporated them into his edition of the *Memoirs*, but that is the only respect in which the wording of his text differs from that of the earlier editions. He did not pursue Christie's suggestion that other passages of Ludlow's manuscript might have been suppressed. Ludlow's *Memoirs*, Firth decided, 'have every internal sign of genuineness, and stand every test which can be applied to their contents'.[8] The thoroughness and reputation of Firth's scholarship have inhibited further speculation about the relationship between the manuscript and the printed text. H. N. Brailsford, in a perceptive note in his book on the Levellers, questioned Firth's judgement, but his appears to have been a solitary voice.[9]

[7] Christie printed them first in his edition of the *Memoirs, Letters, and Speeches of Anthony Ashley Cooper, First Earl of Shaftesbury* (1859), pp. 108–29, and later in his *A Life of Anthony Ashley Cooper, First Earl of Shaftesbury* (2 vols., 1871), i, appendix iii. Locke's copies are now in the Bodleian, Locke MS. b. 4, fos. 1 & ^{v}.

[8] Firth, i. xii, ii. 528. We do not know how accurately Locke transcribed Ludlow's manuscript. Christie made errors of transcription when he copied Locke's text, and these, with two fresh errors, appear in Firth's text of the *Memoirs*. Christie amended the punctuation when he first reproduced Locke's copies, and amended it further in the second publication, from which Firth took the Ashley Cooper material. Firth amended Christie's punctuation. The cumulative effect of these changes was to reduce the discrepancies of style between the passages copied by Locke and the main body of the *Memoirs*. Even so, discrepancies remain: see the four departures into the present tense on Firth, i. 389, the use of the future tense on Firth, ii. 85, and the absent main verb on Firth, ii. 205. Firth noted (ii. 217n.) that one passage copied by Locke 'cannot be conveniently placed in the text': it is, in fact, not the only passage which does not fit, as a comparison between Christie's transcriptions and Firth's insertions reveals.

Locke's extracts—which his notes show to have been made at some time after the publication of the first two volumes of the *Memoirs*—all come from the missing, pre-1660 section of 'A Voyce from the Watch Tower'. His papers do not contain copies of the many hostile references to Ashley Cooper in the Bodleian manuscript which were omitted from the *Memoirs* ('Voyce', pp. 738, 740–1, 747, 752, 1117, 1264, 1332, 1337, 1364, 1368, 1443). Perhaps he took them down on a separate, and now missing, piece of paper; perhaps he saw no purpose in copying them. But the possibility also has to be considered that the pre-1660 section of the manuscript became divorced from the later sections during Locke's lifetime, and that Locke consequently never saw the post-1660 sections. If that is the explanation, our chances of recovering the missing portions of the manuscript seem thin.

[9] *The Levellers and the English Revolution* (ed. C. Hill, 1961), p. 165.

The emergence of the Bodleian manuscript puts the *Memoirs* in a very different light from that in which Firth presented them, and confirms the claims made by William Baron and his eighteenth-century successors. In the first place, it shows that the 1698–9 publishers cut Ludlow's text very heavily. The page numbers and the table of contents of the Bodleian manuscript enable us to calculate that the complete text of 'A Voyce from the Watch Tower' must have been nearly a million words long, almost four times the length of the *Memoirs*. The portion in the Bodleian is more than five times as long as the corresponding section of the *Memoirs*, while Ludlow's narrative from 1672 to 1685, which must have been about 70,000 words long, is wholly omitted from the printed version. The publishers, aware that the chief interest of Ludlow's account lies in his narrative of events before 1660, become increasingly ruthless the farther the manuscript moves beyond the Restoration. Thousands of words are transformed into a single brief paragraph; clauses and sentences are inserted by the publishers to give shape to the story; incidents far removed from each other in the manuscript are stitched together; details are impishly invented to enliven the narrative. The abbreviation and reorganisation of Ludlow's material is, despite occasional signs of haste, an impressively nimble and ingenious performance.

The publishers did not merely cut and reorder the manuscript. They completely rewrote it. There is not a single sentence in the *Memoirs*—indeed, it is relatively unusual to find a sequence of more than four or five words—in which Ludlow's text is accurately reproduced. The publishers, presenting prose acceptable to late seventeenth-century tastes, altered Ludlow's style quite beyond recognition. It would be inaccurate to describe Ludlow as a bad writer, for his prose has an urgency which can occasionally yield eloquent and even memorable phraseology, while his vivid account of his escape and flight in 1660 conveys considerable suspense. For the most part, however, Ludlow's narrative is cumbersome and disorganised. Engagingly aware of his own literary deficiencies, he produces vast, shapeless, breathless, anarchically punctuated sentences. By contrast, the *Memoirs* have a stylistic ease and polish which were much admired in the eighteenth century, and which can be admired today.[10]

The abbreviation of Ludlow's manuscript by the 1698–9 publishers, an exercise for which there were obvious commercial incentives, has deprived us of much information. For the period covered by the Bodleian manuscript, that information is now recoverable. It

[10] For Ludlow's literary self-criticism, see 'Voyce', p. 1214, and below, p. 55. For eighteenth-century literary enthusiasm for the *Memoirs*, see e.g. J. Oldmixon, *Clarendon and Whitlocke Compared* (1727), p. 108, and W. Coxe, *Travels in Switzerland* (3 vols., 1789), ii. 77.

could not be adequately summarised here, for the new information has no common characteristic save that the 1698–9 publishers omitted it. There is fresh material concerning a number of individuals who are well known to students of the Puritan Revolution; there are retrospective accounts of, and comments on, events of the Civil Wars and Interregnum; there is novel material about developments in the months preceding the Restoration and in the years following it; and there is a wealth of information about the exiled regicides and their relations with the Swiss and Dutch governments. Yet the fresh factual evidence, cumulatively very valuable as it is, is never revolutionary. The chief interest of the Bodleian manuscript lies less in the new details to be found in Ludlow's narrative of events than in the light thrown by the document on Ludlow's personality and beliefs. It lies, in particular, in the evidence which the manuscript supplies about his religious convictions.

The *Memoirs* do not suggest that religion entered frequently into Ludlow's political calculations. We find, it is true, recurrent grumbles about the 'corrupt interest' of the clergy.[11] Occasionally we find references to the Bible. There are the citations of Samuel and Numbers in the justification of the 'Commonwealthsmen' of the later 1640s; there is the account of Ludlow's conversation with Cromwell in 1650 about the 110th Psalm; there is the record of Ludlow's discussion with Harrison in 1656 about the political implications of the Book of Daniel.[12] Yet such allusions are so rare as to be surprising, indeed jarring, when they occur. The principal subjects of religious controversy in the 1640s and 1650s, toleration and church government, are rarely mentioned. In the words of a nineteenth-century ecclesiastical historian, the Ludlow who emerges from the pages of the *Memoirs* is 'a man of Roman rather than Christian virtue'.[13] The tone of the *Memoirs* is predominantly secular.

The tone of the Bodleian manuscript could hardly be more different. Spiritual intensity and apocalyptic prophecy are closely woven into the narrative, and give it its guiding purpose. Political events, inseparable in Ludlow's mind from their millenarian context, are to him the workings of the God who, throughout Europe, 'shakes nations', 'levels mountains', 'overturns, overturns', and prepares for the destruction of the Beast.[14] The manuscript is swamped with

[11] Darby, i. 5, 7, 41, 188, 319, ii. 449, 472, 476, 744, 751, 758, 808, 833: Firth, i. 12–13, 37, 147, 246, 345, 365, 368, ii. 156, 161, 166, 204, 225.

[12] Darby, i. 238, 267, 319, ii. 565–6: Firth, i. 185, 207, 246, ii. 7–8. Other biblical allusions or professions of godliness in the *Memoirs* are usually attributed to Ludlow's enemies, to demonstrate their hypocrisy: Darby, i. 214, 282–3, ii. 612, 726–7: Firth, i. 167, 219, ii. 45, 140–1.

[13] W. Orme, *The Life and Times of Richard Baxter* (2 vols., 1820), i. 180n.

[14] 'Voyce', pp. 1138–9, 1196–1200, 1206, 1209, 1224, 1248, 1256–7, 1274, 1310, 1315.

biblical references, a high proportion of them to the Book of Revelation. The biblical texts with which Ludlow prefaces each section of his table of contents illustrate his persistent search for the pattern of providence both in his own life and in public events.[15]

The contrast between the Ludlow of the *Memoirs* and the Ludlow of the manuscript is nowhere more vividly displayed than in the treatment by the two documents of the execution of Charles I's judges in 1660 and 1662. In the *Memoirs*, the regicides die like Romans: in the manuscript, 'those poor innocent lambs of Christ' meet their deaths like early Christian martyrs. 'The destruction and butchery of the faithfull witnesses' occupy thousands of words in 'A Voyce from the Watch Tower'.[16] At times, the blood of the regicides almost seems to run from Ludlow's pages. Describing the execution of Miles Corbet, Ludlow recalls that in January 1649, 'having many tentations upon him', Corbet 'forbore to appeare' in the regicide court

> till the day the sentence was pronounced, at which tyme that word in Revelation 21. 8, viz. the fearefull and unbeleeving shall have their parte in the lake that burnes with fire and brimstone, being set upon his heart by the Lord, did so worke upon him and powerfully prevayle with him that he durst not any longer absent himselfe, but made haste to come and sit amongst them, least the threatned punishment of the fearefull should be his portion.[17]

In the *Memoirs*, the passage becomes:

> he appeared not among the judges by reason of some scruples he had entertained, till the day that sentence was pronounced. But upon more mature deliberation finding them to be of no weight, he durst no longer absent himself, coming early on that day into the Court, that he might give a publick testimony of his satisfaction and concurrence with their proceedings.

In the manuscript, Ludlow treats the execution of his fellow regicide John Barkstead thus:

> When the Lord called him forth to witness to the justice of that act for which he suffered, he did it with much cheerefulness and satisfaction, declaring himselfe ready and willing to be offred up, as being very cleare in his conscience that what he was accused of and condemned for was done by him in obedience to the call of God, and the authority of the nation; and was often heard to

---

[15] Ludlow seems normally to have used the Authorised Version (often quoting it, not always accurately, from memory), but his copy was possibly one of the seventeenth-century editions which incorporated the marginal notes of the Geneva Bible: see the discussion of 1 Corinthians ii. 15 on 'Voyce', p. 1208.

[16] These quotations come from 'Voyce', pp. 804, 823; cf. pp. 1005, 1228.

[17] 'Voyce', p. 919.

say, and particcularly the day before his execution to an emynent minister, that his great burthen then was that he ever lifted up a finger against any of the people of God who were of a contrary opinion to him; and desired them to love the image of Jesus Christ wheresoever they found it.[18]

We turn to the corresponding passage of the *Memoirs*:

When he was brought forth to confirm with the testimony of his blood that cause for which he had fought, he performed that part with chearfulness and courage, no way derogating from the character of a soldier and a true Englishman.

A long account in the manuscript of the spiritual exclamations with which John Jones and Adrian Scrope prepared themselves for death is reduced in the *Memoirs* to the remark that 'the gravity and gracefull meen of these ancient gentlemen' was 'accompanied with visible marks of fortitude and internal satisfaction'.[19]

The Bodleian manuscript surprises us not only by its religious intensity but by its religious radicalism. In long passages, Ludlow argues for complete religious toleration and for the total separation of church from state. Intolerance is 'the cause of all the confusions and disorders that are in the civill governments of the world .... The church in the primitive tymes consisted only of the willing .... till Antichrist began to prevayle'. Antichrist's progress began with the conversion of Constantine, when the church 'came to be countenanced by worldly authority'. 'God's spirit is as the wynd that bloweth where it listeth .... the Jewish church seemes to me to be pulled up by the roote, and consequently all other national churches'. Insistence on outward forms is a remnant of the Jewish law, preserved solely by the 'carnall, violent and imposing spirit' of the clergy. The magistrate should encourage a godly ministry, but is entitled to no authority in ecclesiastical matters. Churches possess the right of excommunication 'in such doctrinall points as are absolutely necessary to salvation', but only as a final sanction, after gentle persuasion and free discussion have failed.[20]

Ludlow's ecclesiastical principles created difficulties for him in Switzerland. Just as, in England, the purification of the church had been checked by Henry VIII, 'that monster of mankinde', so in Geneva Ludlow found that

though I dare not as guiltless cast a stone against this citty, yet .... neither in doctrine or discipline, principle or practice, they

[18] 'Voyce', p. 920.
[19] 'Voyce', pp. 871–3.
[20] 'Voyce', pp. 1194, 1196, 1200, 1209.

have made such progress since the tyme of the first Reformation
as might have been hoped for .... but .... have rather gone backward, and brought forth sower grapes.[21]

Ludlow allied himself with the separatist minister Jean de Labadie,
who became a centre of disturbance in Switzerland and later in the
United Provinces.[22] With his fellow exiles, Ludlow refused to take
communion in Swiss churches. We had not, he explains,

> a freedome to communicate with any in that holy ordinance of the
> Lord's Supper, of whom we had not a particcular satisfaction of
> a worke of grace in their hearts, and that their conversation was
> suitable thereto, a vissible church consisting of living stones, to wit
> of beleevers .... By communicating with such in this ordinance who
> in our judgement eate or drinke unworthily, we should contribute
> to their sin and consequently to their punishment, such eating and
> drinking their own damnation.[23]

The vocabulary of Ludlow's manuscript—like its title—reflects his
sectarian mentality. Saints are described not as dying, but as 'falling
asleep' or 'ending their pilgrimages'.[24] Except when quoting his
enemies, Ludlow avoids the pagan names of the days of the week,
and describes churches as 'meeting-places'.[25] On his journey to Switzerland in 1660, Ludlow was asked by some German travellers
'whether I were a Lutheran or a Calvinist; I telling them I was for
both as farr as they agreed with the word of God, and for neither
any further'. One of the Germans 'cryed out, He is a Quaker, a
Quaker; to whom I replyed, I was one who desired to tremble at
God's word'.[26] The context suggests that Ludlow's admiration for
the Quakers stopped short of complete acceptance of their beliefs,
but he followed their sufferings in England after 1660 with close
sympathy.[27]

Ludlow scornfully rejects infant baptism, and proclaims that 'nothing bee more express in Scripture then that none but believers were
subjects of water baptisme'.[28] He abhors the distinction between

[21] 'Voyce', pp. 962, 1237.

[22] 'Voyce', pp. 923, 995, 1224–5, 1237–9, 1242–3, 1258, 1277–8, 1301, 1310, 1376ff.,
1450. Milton had corresponded with de Labadie in 1659: D. Masson, *The Life of Milton*
(6 vols., 1859–90), v. 591–5.

[23] 'Voyce', pp. 1184–5; cf. pp. 1424–32.

[24] 'Voyce', pp. 996, 1096, 1165, 1274, 1423–4, 1427.

[25] 'Voyce', pp. 1000, 1028, 1030, 1036, 1149. The *Memoirs* normally restore the con-
ventional phraseology.

[26] 'Voyce', p. 820.

[27] 'Voyce', pp. 1042, 1049, 1063, 1078, 1246. Ludlow's feelings about Quakers probably resembled those of his brother-in-law and close friend Nicholas Kempson, who
had protected a Quaker colony in Ireland in the 1650s: Firth, ii. 444; 'Voyce', p. 1096.

[28] 'Voyce', pp. 1129, 1286–7.

clergy and laity, and thinks 'that all men even artizans might prophecy one by one, as the spirit moves them'.[29] Like William Dell,
whose writings he warmly admires, he detests the Universities—
especially Restoration Oxford, 'that nurssery at present of Baal's
priests'.[30] Only on predestination and the Trinity does Ludlow preserve a stern orthodoxy. He views with dismay 'the growth of that
opinion touching universall grace, of Christ's dying for all', a doctrine
'which would have man's salvation depend on the sandy foundations
of his own merits'. Socinianism, 'striking at the mistery of the Trinity',
is another symptom of an alarming Pelagian revival. Equally distress-
ing Pelagian notions are 'that we are to take the history of the holy
Scriptures as those of Titus Livius or Polibius; that to interpret them,
there is nothing needfull but the knowledge of words; that reason
ought to be the judge of the Scriptures'.[31]

When we reflect on the religious dimension of Ludlow's manuscript, we must be prepared to make certain allowances. Possibly
Ludlow—like the Marian exiles before him—experienced some
deepening of spiritual introspection and radicalism in Switzerland.
Nonconformists in England exercised a control over the information
sent out to him which may have given his interpretation of Restoration politics a heavier sectarian bias than it might otherwise have had.
Certainly, in his martyrology of the regicides and in his accounts of
the sufferings of the dissenters under Charles II, Ludlow allowed himself to overlook divisions in the 1640s and 1650s between men who
were able to make common cause after 1660. Yet even when these
allowances have been made, we are left with a picture of the Ludlow
of the Puritan Revolution profoundly different from the Ludlow we
meet in the *Memoirs*.[32]

Ludlow is not the only personality of whom the Bodleian manuscript requires us to revise our impression, for he incorporated into
his text letters and papers of other Puritan politicians—most notably
John Lisle and Sir Richard Lucy[33]—in which we likewise find an un-
expected spiritual urgency. The voice which clamours from Ludlow's
watch-tower may be unusual in its volume and in its stridency, but
it is by no means a solitary one. The letters written in the 1650s
by Ludlow's fellow parliamentary commissioners in Ireland,[34] the

---

[29] 'Voyce', pp. 1192, 1212–13, 1224ff.

[30] 'Voyce', pp. 1200–03, 1264, 1301; cf. Darby, i. 102: Firth, i. 81–2.

[31] 'Voyce', pp. 1225, 1238.

[32] Unfortunately, few of Ludlow's letters of the 1640s and 1650s survive, and those
which do are largely of a formal nature: Firth, i. 481, 486ff. For a glimpse of Ludlow's
religious affiliations in the 1650s see T. C. Barnard, *Cromwellian Ireland* (Oxford, 1975),
p. 101.

[33] 'Voyce', pp. 1082–6.

[34] J. Mayer, 'Inedited Letters of Cromwell, Colonel Jones, Bradshaw and other Regicides', *Transactions of the Historical Society of Lancashire and Cheshire*, new series, i (1860–2).

correspondence between leading politicians in Nickolls's collection of Milton's papers,[35] the theological treatises of Sir Henry Vane and of Ludlow's fellow regicide Robert Tichborne—these are merely random examples of documents which remind us that there is nothing anomalous about the Bodleian manuscript. Historians will always disagree about the explanations, and about the attractiveness, of Puritan spiritual intensity, but our image of Puritan politics is gravely distorted when we neglect it.

In exile, Ludlow maintained close links with, and displayed strong concern for, the nonconformists in England, whose network in London had sheltered him and enabled him to escape in 1660.[36] Among the dissenters whom Ludlow held in admiration and affection were Vavasour Powell, Nicholas Lockyer, Ralph Venning, Thomas Brooks, William Bridge, Edward Bagshaw, Henry Jessey, Henry Wilkinson, Praisegod Barebone and Walter Thimelton.[37] 'A Voyce from the Watch Tower' was clearly written with a nonconformist audience in mind, and one of the principal themes of the Bodleian manuscript is Ludlow's concern to fortify and unite the godly in England during the period of Egyptian bondage under the 'Pharaoh', Charles II. His attacks on the 'vipers' and 'confederats with hell' who ruled England after 1660 are often extravagantly intemperate.[38] He brings out the entire providence detection-kit to show that the destruction of the Antichristian regime is inevitable: storms, comets, plagues, fires, ghost armies fighting in the sky, huge whales washed up on beaches, children born with two heads and four arms, millions of whitings swarming on dry land, and so on.[39] Although 'Charles Steward', as Ludlow always calls 'the present usurper', fails to recognise in these 'prodigies' God's summons to repentance and His wrath at the slaughter of the regicides, Ludlow is confident that the King is powerless

> to suppress the worke the Lord is carrying on, and will carry on, be the earth never so quiet and the confederacy and uniting of powers never so strong against it .... Surely the measure of the

---

[35] J. Nickolls (ed.), *Original Letters and Papers of State* .... *addressed to Oliver Cromwell* (1743).

[36] Compare 'Voyce', pp. 750, 785, 787, 815, with 'Williamson's Spy Book', *Transactions of the Congregational History Society*, 1911–12, pp. 304–7, 315, 347, and P.R.O., SP 9/26, fos. 44, 52ᵛ, 69, 139.

[37] 'Voyce', pp. 808, 905, 996, 1042–3, 1077–9, 1094, 1096, 1111, 1115ff., 1123, 1165, 1223, 1258, 1274.

[38] The phrases are from 'Voyce', pp. 1006–7.

[39] 'Voyce', pp. 911–14, 925–6, 947, 977, 1049–50, 1061, 1073–4, 1100–01, 1128, 1140, 1147, 1161, 1249, 1261, 1264, 1308, 1387–8, 1395, 1413. Some of Ludlow's information about 'prodigies' was derived from pamphlet literature which is described by C. E. Whiting, *Studies in English Puritanism* (1931), pp. 546–52; see also K. V. Thomas, *Religion and the Decline of Magic* (1971), pp. 95–6, 204.

worm's [Charles's] iniquity fills apace, for though the hand of the
Lord is stretched out, he will not see it, but is laying his hands on
the prophets and people of the Lord, for meeting together to seeke
His face and to speake in His name.

At one time Ludlow suspects that 'the houre of his judgement is neare
at hand, Rev. 14. 7'; at another he detects an 'omen of the sufferings
of the witnesses drawing to an end', in 'answer to the cry of the soules
under the alter'; at another he thinks that 'the time .... is even at
the doore when we shall have judges as at the first and counsellors
as at the beginning, Isaiah 1. 26, when there shall be no difference
between the priviledge of the Jew and Gentile'.[40]

Such expressions of millenarian optimism are, however, relatively
rare. For the most part Ludlow is much less sanguine about the immediate political future. He repeatedly emphasises that 'the Lord's tyme
is not yet come', and that 'there is more of the bitter cupp behinde
for his people to drinke of'. Anxious as Ludlow is to raise and to
sustain the morale of the Saints in England, he is careful not to
excite them by the prospect of imminent apocalyptic deliverance. On
the contrary, he argues that the dissenters must learn to bear their
tribulations calmly, for their sufferings are largely self-inflicted. Their
persecution by 'the Nymrods of the earth who are hunters of the lives
and libertyes of mankind, Gen. 10. 9, feeding on the blood of the
Saints, Rev. 17. 6' is a punishment for the divisions and self-interest
which had resulted in the needless collapse of the Commonwealth in
1660. 'This is the day of the patience of the Lord and his Saints':
the strength of the Lord's people 'sometymes consists in quietness and
confidence, Isaiah 30. 15'. They can comfort themselves with the
knowledge that 'when the Lord hath humbled a people and fitted
them for Himselfe, making them willing to be abused for Him, He
will certeinly lift them up and bringe them to honour'. The patience
of the Saints will be rewarded in God's own time, for 'the Lord will
certeinly rayse up a generation that shall have eares to heare and
hearts to understand the thinges that concerne their peace. In the
meanetyme He seemes to permit the scales to continue.' Persecution
is not to be taken as an excuse for insurrection against the Restoration
government. Rather, the Saints should 'hide themselves as it were
for a little moment, untill the indignation be overpast'.[41]

The virtues of patience are expounded with growing frequency
in the later stages of the Bodleian manuscript, when Ludlow becomes

---

[40] 'Voyce', pp. 1016, 1079, 1090, 1104–5, 1237; cf. pp. 841, 843, 892, 918, 1026,
1049, 1061, 1071, 1214, 1249, 1261, 1278, 1410, and Firth, ii. 508.
[41] 'Voyce', pp. 940, 1019, 1041, 1082, 1121, 1134, 1140, 1171–2, 1192, 1260, 1423–
4; cf. pp. 750, 752, 853, 864, 994, 1035, 1095, 1101, 1161, 1174, 1255, 1274, 1300,
1400.

increasingly pessimistic about events in England, but it is a persistent theme of the whole volume. Its prominence is partly to be accounted for by Ludlow's need to explain to his readers, and perhaps to himself, his repeated refusals to assist those of his fellow exiles who were plotting against the Restoration regime. In particular he had to justify his decision, reached after much heart-searching, not to join the English conspirators in Holland, who saw in the Anglo-Dutch war of 1665–7—'this fire between the howses of Abimalech and Sechem', as Ludlow repeatedly calls it[42]—an opportunity to overthrow the English government. The sacrifice by the Dutch government of the blood of the regicides Corbet, Barkstead and Okey, who were handed over for trial in England in 1662, seemed to Ludlow an insuperable argument against compliance with the United Provinces. He feared, too, the ambitions of the House of Orange, whose 'usurpation' in 1672 he was to regard as analogous to Cromwell's usurpation in 1653.

There was also, as Ludlow admitted, a 'prudentiall' motive for his inaction. He was loath to leave Switzerland, where he enjoyed the benevolent protection of the Bern government. Yet Ludlow was not a coward. He would surely have joined the plotters, who were anxious for his help, had he believed them to enjoy a reasonable chance of success. Premature rebellion, on the other hand, could only have ended in disaster. Ludlow was determined to preserve himself as an instrument of the Lord until the time was ripe, and he urged the Saints in England to do the same.[43] He was therefore anxious to counter the influence of those who delivered prophecies of immediate release from the Egyptian bondage. Besides, he mistrusted their motives. He was always uneasy about the pretensions of Fifth Monarchists and other sectaries who based claims to a monopoly of political power on the certainty of their own salvation.[44] Radical as he was in his sympathies, Ludlow was never narrow in his allegiances. He could admire and befriend politicians who differed from him in religion, like the libertine Henry Marten and the presbyterians Philip Skippon and John Bradshaw.[45] In 1659 Ludlow had striven consistently to preserve the unity of the good old cause and to mediate between the conflicting factions within it. After the Restoration he pursued the same policy. The expressions in the Bodleian manuscript of concern for the unity of the cause remind us of the writings of Sir Henry Vane, whose role as the leading spirit among the Commonwealthsmen after 1653

[42] 'Voyce', pp. 1056, 1071, 1190, 1342.
[43] 'Voyce', pp. 744, 748–9, 761, 797, 822, 825–6, 834, 838, 863–4, 921, 924, 928, 931, 1049–50, 1056ff., 1066–7, 1105, 1113–15, 1147–8, 1153–4, 1277, 1282, 1315–19, 1400, 1423–4.
[44] E.g. 'Voyce', pp. 900, 927–8.
[45] 'Voyce', pp. 779, 1102; Firth, i. 241.

emerges strongly from Ludlow's text. So do Ludlow's intimacy with and reverence for him.[46]

From the dissenters in England, Ludlow and his fellow exiles received an almost continuous supply of news, much of which was incorporated into the Bodleian manuscript.[47] In 1669 Ludlow wrote that 'our usual way of correspondency with our friends at London' had been 'wholy interrupted' for '4 or 5 monthes, whereas, before, we usually received from them, and they from us, every fortnight or three weeks'.[48] Other references to information supplied by 'friends at London' abound in the manuscript. Slingsby Bethel, a powerful figure in the London dissenting community, visited Ludlow in Switzerland in 1662 and thereafter remained in close touch with him.[49] Ludlow's most regular contact in London was 'my good friend and correspondent' Walter Thimelton, the ally of Morgan Lloyd and Hugh Courteney. As the government knew, Ludlow was regularly in touch with 'Mr. Thomas Gardiner, a fringemaker at the White Horse in the Poultry, my very good friend'.[50] Tracts, newspapers, declarations, records of parliamentary proceedings, gossip about court politics, and accounts of the activities and sufferings of the dissenters, contributed extensively to Ludlow's narrative of the Restoration period.[51] Ludlow's wife, who visited him with the Bethels in 1662 and who later came to settle at Vevey, wrote to him frequently while she was in England and provided him with a constant stream of information—and, apparently, with a regular income.[52] Some of her knowledge of English politics was probably derived from connections which she succeeded in

[46] 'Voyce', pp. 757, 794, 802, 926ff., 976, 1055, 1063; cf. pp. 781, 930; P.R.O., SP 9/26, fos. 69, 139; *Trans. Congreg. Hist. Soc.*, 1911–12, p. 307. Vane's religious beliefs, and his role as a religious leader, have not been adequately explored. There are interesting sermons by him in the Victoria and Albert Museum, Forster MS. 48D. 41.
[47] 'Voyce', pp. 802–3, 805 (cf. p. 939), 1020, 1061, 1064–5, 1073–4, 1079, 1096, 1100, 1111–14, 1122ff., 1139, 1150, 1180, 1183, 1186, 1263, 1270.
[48] 'Voyce', p. 1222.
[49] 'Voyce', pp. 964, 1080, 1246; P.R.O., SP 29/81, no. 43. Cf. Bethel's *The Interest of Princes* (1681), pp. 171ff., 197ff.
[50] 'Voyce', pp. 1096, 1443; P.R.O., SP 29/31, no. 100; cf. 'Voyce', pp. 1132, 1348, and Firth, ii. 489–92, 504, 508.
[51] Tracts: 'Voyce', pp. 800, 891, 903, 914 (cf. p. 935), 1166, 1170, 1217, 1241, 1250, 1254–7, 1294; newspapers: pp. 822 (cf. *Mercurius Publicus* no. 39, 20–27 September 1660), 824 (cf. *Mercurius Publicus* no. 42, 11–18 October 1660, and *Parliamentary Intelligencer* no. 43, 15–22 October 1660), 911 (cf. *Mercurius Publicus* nos. 48–9, 52–3, 21 November 1661–2 January 1662), 1005–6 (cf. *The Newes* no. 4, 14 January 1663–4), 1042 (cf. B.L., Burney collection, no. 62a, p. 583), 1121 (cf. *London Gazette*, 4–7 June 1666), and Firth, ii. 489–91; declarations: pp. 958–61, 1053–4, 1119, 1130; parliamentary proceedings: pp. 866, 914, 955–7, 970, 974, 1017, 1162, 1231, 1308, 1364, 1368ff., 1411ff., 1440.
[52] 'Voyce', pp. 801, 822, 897, 926, 941, 993–4, 1059, 1063, 1143, 1176–8, 1424 (cf. p. 1261); de Beer, *Notes and Queries*, 1962, p. 223; P.R.O., SP 29/81, no. 43. Some passages of the manuscript are clearly written for the eyes of Ludlow's wife.

establishing at Charles II's court.[53] John Lisle's wife Alice, and
Bulstrode Whitelocke's son James, may have provided Ludlow with
further material about court politics.[54] Ludlow, despite his passionate
antipathy to the Restoration regime, displayed a scrupulous refusal
to bend the evidence which reached him, and took pains to verify it
where possible.[55]

The principal route of intelligence from England to Switzerland
seems to have been through Paris and Lyons.[56] In both cities Ludlow
had his own contacts with merchants and messengers.[57] He acquired
French and Dutch newspapers and letters of intelligence,[58] and received regular supplies of information from Savoy and Germany.[59]
He was helped in his search for information by those of his Swiss
friends, particularly the minister Jean Hummel and Ludlow's landlord at Geneva, Charles Perrot, who had connections in England.[60]
John Dury may have kept him informed about the movement for the
unity of European Protestantism.[61] Holland was a major source of
intelligence, especially during the Anglo-Dutch war of 1665–7.
Slingsby Bethel's journey to Switzerland in 1662, and a visit by Algernon Sidney in 1663, seem to have strengthened Ludlow's English and
continental contacts. For the first two years after his flight in 1660,
his narrative is relatively uninformative about events in England, and
the portion of the Bodleian manuscript reproduced in the present
volume thus pays a less impressive tribute to Ludlow's sources of intelligence than do some of the later ones.

We cannot say when Ludlow began to write 'A Voyce from the
Watch Tower'. As Firth noted, a story was published in 1698 that
Colonel Thomas Blood had visited Switzerland in Charles II's reign
and had found that Ludlow 'was writing a history as he called it,
which he told the colonel would be as true as the gospel'. The Bodleian

[53] 'Voyce', pp. 1178, 1332–3; and see the references to Henry Wilkinson on pp. 808,
905, 935, 938–9, 991, 1094.

[54] 'Voyce', pp. 1040, 1083, 1180–1, 1333, 1348; for the Whitelockes see also below,
p. 67.

[55] 'Voyce', pp. 754, 784, 977, 1270, 1274–5, 1284, 1301, 1326, 1349.

[56] 'Voyce', pp. 817, 819–22, 1051–2, 1124; Peter Fraser, *The Intelligence of the Secretaries
of State and their monopoly of Licensed News 1660–1688*, map facing p. 64.

[57] 'Voyce', pp. 908, 916, 1249, 1329 (cf. p. 1114); Firth, ii. 491.

[58] French: 'Voyce', pp. 893, 945, 950, 1050, 1089, 1106, 1133, 1137, 1179, 1189,
1246, 1260, 1263, 1314, 1316, 1348, 1383 (cf. pp. 1108, 1118, 1125–6); Dutch: pp.
1263, 1389, and Firth, ii. 491.

[59] 'Voyce', pp. 1060, 1063, 1108 (cf. pp. 1124, 1222). For Ludlow's continental
sources see also pp. 1059, 1109, 1111, 1129, 1145, 1168, 1266.

[60] For Hummel, see 'Voyce', pp. 978ff., 993, 1001, 1060, 1062, 1181, 1184–7, 1192,
1216, 1221, 1223, 1363, 1378, 1425; cf. R. Vaughan (ed.), *The Protectorate of Oliver
Cromwell* (2 vols., 1839), i. 196, 204, 217, 323. For Perrot, see 'Voyce', pp. 822, 923,
1181, 1186–7.

[61] 'Voyce', p. 891; cf. pp. 903, 990–1, 1037–8 (and see Baron F. de Schickler, *Les
Eglises du Refuge en Angleterre* (3 vols., Paris, 1892), ii. 208, 223). Hummel figured prominently in the ecumenical movement.

manuscript confirms that Blood met Ludlow in Switzerland, and shows that the encounter took place in 1666.[62] By the time of Blood's visit, the composition of 'A Voyce from the Watch Tower' was probably well advanced. In Ludlow's narrative of the previous year, 1665, we find passages which suggest that he is writing not more than a year or so after the events he is describing. Similar hints are present in the narrative of 1666 and 1667,[63] and in 1668 the picture becomes clear when Ludlow suddenly looks forward to an episode which occurred 'this summer 1669'.[64] From 1669 there are a number of passages which were clearly written within months of the events described in them.[65] Before the mid-1660s, the Bodleian manuscript provides no indications that Ludlow is writing so soon after events.[66] Had he been, such indications would almost certainly survive. It seems likely, then, that Ludlow had written the section reproduced in this volume, as well as the missing pre-1660 section, by 1665 or 1666.

Ludlow was not the only opponent of Charles II writing in the mid-1660s. There was Slingsby Bethel, author of *The World's Mistake in Oliver Cromwell* (1668). There was the exile Algernon Sidney, who composed three manuscript works which survive: 'The Character of Sir Henry Vane'; a 'prophecy' of 1666 which was subsequently printed;[67] and a document which is now at Warwick Castle, 'Court

[62] Firth, i. ix; 'Voyce', pp. 1111, 1113–14, 1265 (cf. pp. 960–1, 1234, 1268, 1274).

[63] For 1665–7, see e.g. Ludlow's correction of 'hope' to 'hoped', and his insertion concerning the death of William Cawley, on 'Voyce', p. 1107; and observe how far his narrative proceeds before he discovers the identity of the men responsible for John Lisle's murder and for the attempts on his own life in 1664–5: pp. 993–5, 998, 1000–01, 1010, 1027, 1029–35, 1038–9, 1043–4, 1059, 1067, 1090, 1109, 1126, 1149, 1179, 1181–3, 1252–3.

[64] 'Voyce', p. 1178.

[65] The evidence is to be found in (i) changes of tense in Ludlow's corrections of his text, (ii) the occasions on which he gives the day and the month of an event but omits, or only adds subsequently, the year, (iii) corrections of errors which have come to Ludlow's attention after the composition of the narrative, (iv) references to the length of time which has passed since the occurrence of particular events, and (v) remarks about present and future contingencies: 'Voyce', pp. 1192, 1230, 1233–5, 1245, 1249, 1254, 1260–1, 1266, 1268, 1270–1, 1276, 1278–9, 1289, 1293–4, 1310, 1319, 1321, 1362, 1370, 1424, 1436, 1438, 1440. The point is confirmed by references to living individuals who died shortly after the episodes in which their roles are described (pp. 1077 (Edward Bagshaw: cf. p. 1274), 1093 (Montague: cf. p. 1300)) and to the recent deaths of regicides (pp. 1250 (Walton and Wogan), 1378 (Say), 1267–8, 1285–6 (Holland; cf. p. 964)).

[66] Ludlow's narrative provides some false trails here. In particular, his dependence on newsletters and newspapers sometimes leads him to describe events which must have taken place long in the past as if they have occurred very recently. And in a passage printed in this volume ('Voyce', p. 923), the reader will find a potentially misleading reference to the appointment of a new Lieutenant Bailiff of Lausanne 'this very yeare'. By 'this', Ludlow means 'that': Jean-François Gaudard, the Lieutenant Bailiff whose death created the vacancy (and whom Ludlow calls 'Mr. Godward'), died (as the Lausanne archives show) in January 1662—the year which the narrative is describing, not the year in which Ludlow is writing. Cf. 'Voyce', p. 914.

[67] The first of these manuscripts is preserved, in the hand of a copyist, in the Hertfordshire Record Office (MS. D/EP/F 45), and is published as an appendix to V. A. Rowe,

Maxims', written in or about 1665. From 'Court Maxims' and from *The World's Mistake in Oliver Cromwell*, it appears that Sidney and Bethel both exchanged ideas with Ludlow.[68] 'Court Maxims', like 'A Voyce from the Watch Tower', vividly portrays the sufferings of dissenters and Quakers in Restoration England—although Sidney, like Bethel, was less preoccupied than Ludlow with the dispensations of providence.[69] In form and in theme, 'Court Maxims' much resembles Henry Nevile's *Plato Redivivus* (1681), and Nevile is likely to have co-operated with other anti-government propagandists in the 1660s.[70] It was probably in the 1660s, too, that the exiled regicide Valentine Walton composed the history of the Civil War period which was extant in 1733 but which subsequently disappeared.[71] Gradually the picture emerges of a coordinated literary campaign against the Restoration regime, to which 'A Voyce from the Watch Tower' was designed as a contribution. It is a subject to which we shall return.

Except for the last hundred pages, which are in Ludlow's own hand, the Bodleian manuscript was written by a scribe. Ludlow went over the scribe's text and made numerous corrections of fact and presentation. Probably Ludlow dictated his narrative to his amanuensis, who improvised the punctuation as best he could.[72] The scribe's contribu-

Sir Henry Vane the Younger (1970). The second is in the Bodleian, MS. Eng. letters c. 200, fos. 24–5. For Sidney and Vane see also 'The Trial of A. Sydney', in *The Works of Algernon Sydney* (1772), pp. 5, 10, and, in the same volume, Sidney's 'Apology', pp. 6, 13–14.

[68] The resemblances between 'Court Maxims' and the Bodleian manuscript are numerous. Some are to be found in the illustrations, especially the biblical illustrations, with which the two authors justify their republicanism. Others lie in their treatments of contemporary political themes, such as the deaths of Corbet, Barkstead, Okey and Vane, the sale of Dunkirk, and the need to repair the divisions within the parliamentary party which had brought about its fall in 1660. Comments in 'Court Maxims' about the glorious achievements of the Rump, about the rule of Cromwell, and about the destruction of the balance of power in Europe as a result of the rise of France remind us of pre-1660 passages in Ludlow's *Memoirs*. 'Court Maxims', pp. 16, 70, 148, 150ff., 158, 168–9, 172, 188–9, 196. (The pagination of 'Court Maxims' expires mid-way through the document: I have here supplied the missing pagination.) For Sidney's relations with Ludlow in exile, see 'Voyce', pp. 977–8, 1004, 1056, 1063–6, 1081–3, 1111–15, 1123, 1127, 1188, 1265; cf. p. 990, and Firth, ii. 486. 'Court Maxims' also contains reminders of Bethel's writings, not only *The World's Mistake* but *The Interest of Princes* and *The Providences of God* (1691). The approximate dating of 'Court Maxims' can be determined from internal evidence: pp. 2, 23, 55, 61, 77–8, 96, 149, 155, 161–4, 166, 173. For Ludlow and *The World's Mistake* see below, pp. 76–7; for the context of the publication of *The World's Mistake* see *A Free Conference touching the present State of England* (1668).

[69] 'Court Maxims', pp. 86ff., 108, 192, 195–6.

[70] 'Voyce', pp. 1003, 1013; cf. Caroline Robbins (ed.), *Two Republican Tracts* (Cambridge, 1969), pp. 12–13.

[71] *Dictionary of National Biography*, Walton.

[72] Both the punctuation and the spelling of the section of the manuscript which is in the scribe's hand differ significantly from Ludlow's own, and some of the corrections made by Ludlow to the scribe's text suggest that the scribe is likely to have misheard oral instructions rather than inaccurately transcribed written ones: for example,

tion ends on p. 1354, when the story has reached June 1673. There
follows an unpaginated 'Conclusion' of about 8,000 words, in which
Ludlow reproduces and reflects on a letter of theological condolence
sent him by a minister at Lausanne after the murder of John Lisle
in 1664. On the final page of the 'Conclusion' Ludlow adds, in his
own hand, a note dated November 1674 giving instructions concerning the publication of 'A Voyce from the Watch Tower'. After the
'Conclusion' we have exactly a hundred pages (pp. 1354–1454)
written in Ludlow's own hand. Their presence in the Bodleian manuscript is probably to be explained by a binder's error.

Towards the end of the Bodleian manuscript, Ludlow's narrative
becomes fuller but duller. His connections in England become less
dependable, and he draws increasingly on dry accounts provided by
newspapers and newsletters. Events in England come to form only
a part of a voluminous but arid chronicle dominated by European
battles and diplomacy. Describing the recent past, the narrative loses
the perspective which the passage of time had given to the composition
of earlier parts of the story. One can see why the 1698–9 publishers
brought the *Memoirs* to an end in 1672. After that year, in which the
assassination of the de Witt brothers and the French invasion of the
United Provinces inflicted grievous blows on the causes of republicanism and European Protestantism, much of the life goes out of Ludlow's
narrative. It is hard to imagine that the disappearance of the section
of the manuscript which covered the years 1677 to 1685 is a grave
loss.

2. THE EDITOR

How, why and by whom was 'A Voyce from the Watch Tower' transformed into Ludlow's *Memoirs*? Perhaps the story began in 1689,
when, after nearly thirty years in exile, Ludlow made a brief and unhappy return to England.[73] Apparently he saw in the accession of
William III the long-awaited hour of deliverance, but he found himself swiftly deported, and spent the last three years of his life in exile
again. Did he take 'A Voyce from the Watch Tower' with him to
England in 1689, and leave it there? In 1700 William Baron, whose
challenge to the authenticity of the *Memoirs* we noted earlier, wrote
of Ludlow that it was 'generally presumed the last of his acquaintance
and confidants was S[lingsby] B[ethel], with whom those many reams

---

'accepted' is twice corrected to 'excepted' ('Voyce', pp. 788, 907; cf. p. 878 ('course')
and p. 903 ('too')). See also the idiosyncratic spellings on pp. 783 and 1242 of 'Mews'
as 'Muse' and 'Baxter' as 'Backster'. The scribe wrote in an impersonal hand. Was
he perhaps Edward Dendy, a fellow exile of Ludlow who died in April 1674? See
'Voyce', pp. 1065, 1378–9; Darby, ii, 574–5: Firth, ii. 14–15.
[73] Firth, ii. 509–11.

of paper he had, whilst grumbling in Swisserland, emptied his galls
into, were entrusted'.[74] Archbishop Tenison also thought that Bethel
had acquired Ludlow's manuscript.[75] In 1674 Ludlow had asked that
'A Voyce from the Watch Tower' should be bequeathed to his wife,
who was to supervise arrangements for its publication.[76] If she ever
possessed it, it would have been natural for her to hand it to Bethel,
with whose family she, like her husband, had long been on close terms.

During the exclusion crisis, Bethel—immortalised by Dryden as the
Shimei of *Absalom and Achitophel*—had been Sheriff of London and
a leader of the radical wing of Shaftesbury's Whig party. The fall
of Shaftesbury and the Rye House executions crushed the radical
cause. After 1688, Bethel sought to revive it. Among his allies were
two fellow survivors from the dark days of the early 1680s, the
publishers Richard Baldwin and John Darby, both of whom play important parts in the story surrounding the publication of Ludlow's
Memoirs. Baldwin, who published the first two editions of Bethel's *The
Providences of God* (1691 and 1694), was perhaps the most prominent
of the radical Whig publishers of William III's reign. On his death
in 1698 his business was taken over by his widow Anne, who retained
her husband's political affiliations.[77] Darby, who was very close to
the Baldwins, was almost as influential as they in radical Whig circles.
His firm, like theirs, was a family concern. By the late 1690s he was
sharing much of the work with his son, John Darby junior, who
after his father's death in 1704 expanded the business with a series
of publishing successes which included the *State Tracts* of 1705–6,
the abridged version of Rushworth's *Historical Collections* (1703–8),
Shaftesbury's *Characteristicks* (1711), and that grand feat of Whig
historical confection, the *State Trials* (1719).[78] A close collaborator
both with the Baldwins and with the Darbys was another publisher,

---

[74] Firth, i. x.

[75] An entry in Bishop Nicolson's diary for 29 October 1705 reads: 'I dined at Lambeth, together with the Archdeacon of Dublin, Sir Gustavus Hume, Mr. Archdeacon
Kennett, Dr. Fuller of Hatfield, etc. The impudent forgery of the History of Formosa
occasioned the mentioning of the counterfeit Petronius, Caesar's Commentaries, and
others; and the Archbishop of Dublin confidently averred that Ludlow's Memoirs are
of that kind. *No*, saies my Lord of Canterbury. *Ludlow indeed left his works, in Slingsby
Bethel's hand, much larger than they are; but nothing was cut of f, save his long citations out
of Scripture and some canting digressions.*' Tullie House MS., Carlisle, vol. vi: transcript
by Geoffrey Holmes at the History of Parliament Trust.

[76] Below, p. 55.

[77] Eleanor Rostenberg, 'English "Rights and Liberties": Richard and Anne Baldwin,
Whig Patriot Publishers', in her *Literary, Political, Scientific, Religious and Legal Publishing
in England* (2 vols., New York, 1965), ii. 369–415. Staunchly Whig as the Baldwins
were, they were capable of backing more than one Whig horse at once. I refer to Mrs.
Baldwin by the name by which she was commonly known, but her Christian name
was in fact Abigail: see Michael Treadwell's notes on the bookseller James Roberts
in the John Johnson collection in the Bodleian (Room 132).

[78] J. G. Muddiman, *State Trials. The need for a new and revised edition* (Edinburgh, 1920).

Andrew Bell, who married the elder Darby's daughter Elizabeth in 1696,[79] and among whose numerous Whig publications was the third edition of Bethel's *The Providences of God* (1697).[80]

The cooperation of these publishers, who sold and advertised each other's productions, provides a key to the composition and behaviour of that secretive and elusive group which was known to its enemies as the 'Calves-Head Club', and which was renowned for its republicanism and for its deist and Socinian leanings. Some of the accusations levelled at the 'club' by contemporaries were absurdly far-fetched, and perhaps for that reason historians have rarely given detailed consideration to the club's activities. Affiliations within the group were certainly looser than its enemies liked to suggest. Yet there was fire amidst the smoke; and when all proper reservations have been made, we are left with a body of men whom we can confidently regard as among the chief 'Calves-Head' republicans of the 1690s. There was Bethel. There were Milton's nephews Edward and John Phillips. There was Isaac Littlebury, translator and a friend of the Darbys. There were the historians James Tyrell, Roger Coke and David Jones, all of whom published with Bell and the Baldwins. There were the pamphleteers John Tutchin and Matthew Tindal. There were the clergymen Samuel Johnson and William Stephens. And there was a figure of whom we shall hear much more, John Toland.[81]

Bethel died in February 1697, a year before the *Memoirs* were published. It is conceivable that he set in motion the process by which the manuscript was turned into the *Memoirs*;[82] but if he did so, then any text which he may have prepared must have been scrapped or extensively revised. Bethel was an able writer, but his known works nowhere display the inventiveness and lightness of touch

---

[79] Register of St. Michael's, Cornhill, 14 July 1696.

[80] For introductions to these publishers, see H. R. Plomer, *A Dictionary of the Printers and Booksellers .... from 1688 to 1725* (Oxford, 1922), pp. 15–17, 28, 97; cf. Lois Schwoerer, '*No Standing Armies!*' (Baltimore, 1974), p. 198.

[81] Most of these figures will be discussed in due course. The political views of the Phillips brothers were flexible. For the stature in the group of Samuel Johnson, see especially *King Charles I no such Saint, Martyr or Good Protestant as commonly reputed* (1698), p. 22. Other radicals of the 1690s whose careers and affiliations would repay closer examination than they have received include Sir Robert Howard, Charles Blount and Charles Gildon; for Howard, compare the present introduction with H. G. Oliver, *Sir Robert Howard* (North Carolina, 1963), pp. 115, 126n., 154.

[82] There are two hints in the *Memoirs* that the manuscript may have been perused, prior to publication, by someone who had been well acquainted with Ludlow in the 1660s but whose memory had faded. In the manuscript ('Voyce', p. 964) Ludlow correctly states that Bethel visited Lausanne in 1662: the *Memoirs* surprisingly leave the date blank. In the manuscript ('Voyce', pp. 1218–19) Ludlow refers to a French officer, who allegedly plotted against the exiles in 1668, as 'Marrell'. The *Memoirs*, recognising an error, change the name to 'Martell': it should, apparently, have been 'Mazel' (see *Nouveaux Mémoires d'Edmond Ludlow*, preface; cf. M. C. Jacob, *The Newtonians and the English Revolution* (1976), p. 258).

manifest in the revision of Ludlow's manuscript. Baron, after recording Bethel's acquisition of Ludlow's papers, observed:

> report speaks that he was tricked of them by a republican confident
> who best understood to make the best of them, as well for the Good
> Old Cause as his own advantage; which 'tis further said the same
> churlish Nabal was very angry at, and would have resented accord-
> ingly, had not death interposed and put an end to that dispute.
> The usurper of the copy, having now got quiet and sole possession,
> consulted more than once the whole Calves-head fraternity, not
> without some representatives, as to the most creditable way of
> publishing ....[83]

Who, then, gained access to the manuscript after Bethel's death?
On the title pages of the *Memoirs*, the pretence is made that the work
was printed at Vevey; but the blind fooled no one.[84] Baron com-
mented: 'had they said at Darby it might have been nigher home,
and nigher truth too; nay certainly so, by a little quibling transition
from place to person.'[85] A pamphlet of 1698 sometimes attributed to
Daniel Defoe, *A Brief Reply to the History of Standing Armies*, included
Ludlow's *Memoirs* in a list of works which had been 'hammered from
the same forge': all the other works in the list are known to have been
published by the elder Darby.[86] They included anti-standing army
tracts and the first edition of Algernon Sidney's *Discourses concerning
Government* (1698), publications whose connection with the appearance of Ludlow's *Memoirs* will become apparent. Other works produced by the elder Darby will likewise be seen to have formed part
of a series to which Ludlow's *Memoirs* belonged. One of them was
Milton's Historical and Political Works, a three-volume production of
1698 edited by John Toland. It contained the biography of Milton
by Toland which was also published separately by Darby in 1699 as
The Life of John Milton. Others were Toland's *Amyntor: or a Defence
of Milton's Life* (1699), and Toland's edition of the first collected *Works*
of James Harrington (1700).[87] In 1699 Darby and Anne Baldwin produced the *Memoirs of Sir John Berkeley*,[88] parts of which had been incorporated, in abbreviated form, into the first volume of Ludlow's

[83] Firth, i. x–xi.
[84] See B.L., Add. MS. 17677SS, fo. 171; *Nouvelles de la République*, February 1700,
p. 180n.
[85] Firth, i. xiii; cf. *Regicides no Saints*, p. 134.
[86] *Brief Reply*, pp. 24–6.
[87] All these books either bear Darby's name on their title-pages or are frequently
advertised in his publications. That he published Sidney's *Discourses*, Milton's *Works*
and Harrington's *Works* is confirmed by: *A Transcript of the Registers of the Worshipful
Company of Stationers from 1640 to 1708* (3 vols., 1913–14), iii. 484, 492; the title-page
of the 1704 edition of Sidney's *Discourses*; *The Post Boy*, 9–11 August 1698; *The Post
Man* no. 559, 5–7 January 1699, and no. 628, 15–17 June 1699.
[88] Title-page. The volume probably appeared at the beginning of the year: *The Flying
Post*, 24–26 and 26–28 January 1699.

Memoirs.[89] That the elder Darby published Ludlow's *Memoirs* seems beyond reasonable doubt.

If Darby published the *Memoirs*, who rewrote Ludlow's manuscript? Firth—unaware, of course, that the manuscript had been rewritten—thought that the editor of the *Memoirs* had been Isaac Littlebury. In 1697 Littlebury carried to the press an anti-standing army pamphlet published by Darby. Later, as a translator, he was to be responsible for an English version of Fénelon's *Télémache* and for the 'lame Herodotus' which was eagerly read by the young Gibbon.[90] Firth's suggestion sprang from the handwritten insertion of Littlebury's name by the eighteenth-century republican Thomas Hollis at the conclusion of the preface in a copy of the 1751 edition of Ludlow's *Memoirs*.[91] Hollis's opinion, which his knowledge of Whig literature entitles to respect, is supported by an observation of Thomas Tyers in 1780–1, who wrote that after Ludlow's death his manuscript had been 'placed in the hands of Littlebury, the translator of Herodotus; who fabricated or prepared the Memoirs, from those materials, for the press'.[92] Littlebury's name has also been inserted, by a hand which is hard to date, at the conclusion of the preface in a copy of the 1704 edition of Sidney's *Discourses*,[93] a work whose first publication in 1698 had been connected with the appearance of Ludlow's *Memoirs*. Sentiments in the preface to Littlebury's Herodotus[94] suggest that he would have approved warmly of the publication of the *Memoirs*, and there is no reason to doubt that, like other members of the 'Calves-head fraternity' whose role in the publication Baron noted, Littlebury was well informed about the revision of Ludlow's manuscript and exercised an influence on the contents of the *Memoirs*. It is not difficult to envisage him helping to compose the prefaces to the *Memoirs* and to Sidney's *Discourses*, the publications in copies of which his name has been found. It is only the prefaces, we notice, which the manuscript ascriptions attribute to him; and the composition of the prefaces may of course have been an exercise separate from the preparation of the texts. Even so, if there were not a more plausible candidate than Littlebury, we would have to conclude that it is he who is likely to have rewritten Ludlow's manuscript.

---

[89] Below, p. 57.

[90] I. Littlebury and A. Boyer, *The Adventures of Telemachus* (1721); *The History o Herodotus* (1709: reprinted in 1720 by Bell and Darby junior); G. Birkbeck Hill (ed.), *The Memoirs of the Life of Edward Gibbon* (1900), p. 44.

[91] Firth, i. xi–xiii; Alfred Stern, *Briefe englische Flüchtlinge in der Schweiz* (Göttingen, 1874), p. xi.

[92] Firth, i. xi–xii. The tradition reached Tyers 'many years ago from an oracle in history to whom it was communicated by the late Mr. Andrew Stone, who derived his intelligence from Buckley, the splendid editor of Thuanus'.

[93] B.L., classmark 521 m. 15.

[94] pp. iii–vi.

We would, however, reach the conclusion with reluctance. The problem is the literary 'lameness' of which Gibbon complained. It is easier to see Littlebury as one of the men who—if Baron was right—were 'consulted' about the publication of the *Memoirs* than as the 'quiet and sole possessor' who rewrote the manuscript. For the operation carried out on 'A Voyce from the Watch Tower' showed remarkable qualities of nimbleness, energy and wit, of which Littlebury's known writings afford no trace. And it displayed something more. To create, and to inhabit, a personality which was so different from Ludlow's own, and which has carried conviction across the centuries, required exceptional powers of imagination, one might even say of fantasy. Who could have supplied those gifts?

There is one candidate who possessed them in abundance. Firth, having settled for Isaac Littlebury as the editor, acknowledged in a footnote:

> The name of John Toland has also been coupled with the Memoirs; and in the Bodleian Catalogue the editorship of the third volume is ascribed to him. The views expressed in the preface agree very well with those of Toland, but so far as I am aware there is no good evidence for this ascription. The author of 'Regicides no Saints' [Baron] however certainly ascribes to Toland the selection of the papers printed at the end of volume three. He does not mention him by name, but refers to him as 'aspiteful young fellow', whom he terms 'Amyntor', 'Milton junior', and the 'son of a potato'.[95]

It is true that Baron never specifically states that Toland was the editor of Ludlow's *Memoirs*. The two pamphlets in which Baron attacks the *Memoirs* show that he has not been able to identify their editor with certainty, and his failure is a tribute to the effectiveness with which the 'Calves-head fraternity' has covered its tracks. Yet the preface to the first of Baron's pamphlets, and the whole of the second (from its title-page onwards), suggest strongly where his suspicions lie.[96] Firth's reference to 'the papers printed at the end of volume three' (most of them taken from *The King's Cabinet Opened* (1645), to which Toland explicitly refers in 1699 in his *Amyntor*)[97] is misleading, for Baron's technique of association and innuendo is directed at the *Memoirs* as a whole, not merely at their appendix. Throughout, Baron makes it clear that he believes the publication of the *Memoirs* to have been intimately associated with Toland's Milton publications of 1698–9.

The connection in Baron's mind between the *Memoirs* and the 'son

[95] Firth, i. xiiin.
[96] Cf. the references to Toland and Ludlow in *The Secret History of the Calves-Head Club* (1704), pp. 6–7.
[97] *Amyntor*, p. 134.

of a potato' (a reference to Toland's Irish nationality) becomes particularly interesting when we find Baron attributing to Toland two anonymous pamphlets of 1698, *A Defence of the Parliament of 1640* and *King Charles I no such Saint, Martyr, or Good Protestant as commonly reputed.*[98] Internal evidence in both pamphlets shows that Baron was almost certainly correct;[99] and if he was right about the pamphlets, then the hints he drops about Ludlow's *Memoirs* deserve to be pursued. The ascription to Toland of volume 3 of the *Memoirs* in the Bodleian catalogue, which puzzled Firth, is presumably to be explained by the flyleaf of a copy in the Bodleian of volume 3 of the 1699 edition, where there are inscribed, in an eighteenth-century hand, the words 'Written by Toland'.[100] If Toland did edit volume 3, he must have edited the first two volumes as well, for the three volumes are unmistakably the product of the same pen.

John Toland is known to history primarily as one of the fathers of deism. His political and historiographical significance awaits proper recognition.[101] We shall examine in a moment the evidence which supports Baron's hints, but before we do so we may observe that Toland, who was twenty-seven when the first two volumes of the *Memoirs* appeared, possessed three qualities which the editor of the *Memoirs*, whoever he was, would have found invaluable. First, he could write very quickly, very energetically, and very enjoyably.

---

[98] *Just Defence*, pp. 12–13, 126–9, part ii pp. 207–8; *Regicides no Saints*, p. 123.

[99] Compare the treatment of the question of the authorship of *Eikon Basilike* in *Amyntor*, pp. 156ff., with the discussion in *A Defence*, pp. 15–27; and compare the autobiographical passage in *King Charles I* . . . . (a work which is explicitly a sequel to *A Defence*), pp. 23–4, with the passage about Holland in P. Desmaizeaux (ed.), *A Collection of Several Pieces of Mr. John Toland* (2 vols., 1726), ii. 106–7. *King Charles I* . . . . is signed 'D.J.', i.e., presumably, [Tolan]d J[ohn] (a device characteristic of Toland, who signed a later work 'Londat'). It may well be, however, that D[avid] J[ones], whose career the autobiographical passage would also fit, assisted Toland in the composition of the pamphlet. Jones is a shadowy figure. Baron does not mention him, and I have found nothing to connect him directly with the rewriting of Ludlow's manuscript. Had there been such a connection, it would almost certainly have left some trace. The style of the *Memoirs* does not seem to me to be Jones's. At the same time, Jones must have known all about the preparation of the *Memoirs*, and his expertise is likely to have been drawn upon during their composition: cf. below, p. 38.

[100] Classmark Godwin 674. The hand seems more likely to belong to the first than to any other quarter of the century, but certainty is impossible.

[101] Perhaps the most influential study of Toland in English has been Leslie Stephen's *History of English Thought in the Eighteenth Century* (2 vols., 1876), i. ch. iii. F. H. Heinemann wrote a series of valuable pioneering essays on Toland between 1943 and 1950, and there is a bold and informative study of Toland in Jacob, *The Newtonians and the English Revolution*, pp. 201ff. Other useful surveys are by W. Dienemann (1953), H. F. Nicholl (1965), E. Twynam (1968: privately printed by David Low), and J. G. Simms (1969): for full details, see G. Carabelli, *Tolandiana* (Florence, 1975), a very substantial bibliography which is now the indispensable companion to all studies of Toland. I became aware of Professor Carabelli's book too late for me to make use of it here, but my approach to Toland has in any case been rather different from (and much narrower than) his. Professor Carabelli has deposited extensive lists of additions and corrections to *Tolandiana* in the British Library, the Bodleian and other major libraries.

Toland is one of the great posturers of Anglo-Irish literature. Different stances and different styles come easily to him. He can be solemn and responsible: he can be outrageously funny; but always the strength lies in the conviction (and no doubt the self-conviction) with which he carries off the pose. Beneath the surface lay violent passions. We need no great psychological insight to detect, in Toland's writings, the memory of some grievous childhood cruelty or insecurity, for which his rejection of his parents' Catholicism in adolescence afforded revenge.[102] Wherever we follow his varied career, we find him embroiled in scandalous—and from the safe distance of the twentieth century often hilarious—episodes: street brawls, coffee-house quarrels, embarrassing brushes with England's ambassadors abroad. His vanity and dishonesty were notorious.[103] Yet he could project an earnestness and a charm which captivated the great philosophers of the age. Leibniz, Le Clerc, Spanheim, Locke, Shaftesbury—all at first warmed to him, and attributed his excesses to youthful and curable exuberance. All in the end wearied of his charlatanism, his untrustworthiness, and what seemed to them the shallowness and ethical bankruptcy of his ideas.

Toland's second gift was green fingers with manuscripts. On seemingly any subject he could locate them with uncanny ease: the early church, primitive Ireland, Renaissance France, seventeenth-century England.[104] Once he had gained access to manuscripts he had no scruples about appropriating them or tampering with them. He extracted a 'manuscript book of Servetus' from Thomas Firmin and passed it off as his own;[105] he apparently stole a manuscript translation of Giordano Bruno's *Spaccio della Bestia Trionfante* from Anthony Collins's library[106] (and certainly defied Collins's attempt to recover books he had borrowed from him);[107] he intercepted a private letter from one of his Tory enemies and doctored it with a view to publishing

---

[102] B.L., Add. MS. 4295 (Toland papers), fo. 39ᵛ; R. Huddleston (ed.), *Toland's History of the Druids* (Montrose, 1814), p. 187; Toland, *Letters to Serena* (1704), pp. 2–8. Toland assiduously spread confusion about the year of his birth.

[103] Jacques Bernard told Pierre Desmaizeaux that Toland had imbibed the 'Socinian' doctrine 'qu'il est permis de mentir à certaines occasions', but his explanation of Toland's conduct seems needlessly sophisticated. B.L., Add. MS. 4286 (Desmaizeaux papers), fo. 100.

[104] *Toland's History of the Druids*, pp. 84, 92–3, 228; *Amyntor*, p. 32; *Complete Prose Works of John Milton* (Yale), e.g. i. 618, vii. 189, 322, 389; Toland, *Nazarenus* (1718), p. ii; Toland, *A Philippick Oration* (1707), p. 1; *Somers Tracts* (13 vols., 1809–15), xii. 565; Desmaizeaux, *Toland*, i. lxi, 404, 448–9; B. Rand (ed.), *The Life, unpublished Letters, and philosophical Regimen of Anthony, Earl of Shaftesbury* (1900), p. xxx; Toland (ed.), *Letters from the Right Honourable the late Earl of Shaftesbury to Robert Molesworth* (1721), pp. v–vi; B.L., Add. MS. 4465 (Toland papers), fo. 19; B.L., Harleian MS. catalogue, ii. 230ff.

[105] Lambeth MS. 933, no. 74, Simpson to Toland, 20 April 1697.

[106] Samuel Paterson (ed.), *Bibliotheca Westiana* (1773), p. 44; flyleaf of James Martineau's copy of the translated *Spaccio* in the library of Manchester College, Oxford (cf. R. Watt (ed.), *Bibliotheca Britannica* (4 vols., Edinburgh, 1824), i. 162).

[107] B.L., Add. MS. 4282 (Desmaizeaux papers), fos. 118, 190.

it;[108] and he possessed an extraordinary talent for hoodwinking ecclesiastical dignitaries into providing him with documents which he then exploited to his own advantage and in opposition to theirs.[109] If, as will come to seem likely, Toland was the 'republican confident' who, according to Baron, 'tricked' Slingsby Bethel of Ludlow's manuscript, the action was entirely in character.

Thirdly, Toland, who as a historian had wide interests and considerable abilities, was very well informed about seventeenth-century English politics, and identified himself strongly with the 'Commonwealthsmen' of the Puritan Revolution. In 1695 he was expelled from Oxford for 'comending Commonwealths', railing against priests, and 'justifying the murder of K[ing] C[harles] 1st'.[110] Cromwell's 'usurpation' of 1653, a theme which will be familiar to readers of Ludlow's *Memoirs*, was a *motif* of Toland's own writings.[111] His *The Life of John Milton* and *Amyntor* display his extensive knowledge of Puritan politics and of the sources available for their study. He was to demonstrate the same expertise still more impressively in two pamphlets of 1714: *The Art of Restoring* (which drew an inspired parallel between Robert Harley's conduct at the end of Anne's reign and George Monck's actions in 1660), and a collection of Monck's letters. The two tracts show that Toland had thought hard about the genesis and reliability of the available evidence concerning the Restoration of Charles II. They also show that he had thought about Edmund Ludlow.[112]

In January 1697 Toland, in debt as usual, signed a contract with John Darby. In February he secured an advance from Richard Baldwin.[113]

[108] Ballard MS. vii, fos. 94, 96, Kennett to Charlett, 29 March and 2 April 1701, xxi, fo. 17, Bishop to Charlett, 2 April 1701, xxiv, fo. 54, Birch to Charlett, 4 April 1701.

[109] T. Sharp, *The Life of John Sharp* (2 vols., 1925), i. 273ff.; J. H. Kemble (ed.), *European State Papers and Correspondence* (1857), pp. 459–60; Desmaizeaux, *Toland*, i. v–vi; cf. Ballard MS. v, fos. 46, 58, Gibson to Charlett, 13 June, 20 July 1694. For Toland's tactics see also *Cato's Letters* (4 vols., 1733), i. xviii; Bodleian Library, MS. Eng. letters c. 200, fo. 21.

[110] Lambeth MS. 942, no. 110, Charlett to Tenison, 25 October 1695; *Notes and Queries*, 4 January 1862. Cf. Ballard MS. v, fo. 27; J. G. Simms, 'John Toland (1670–1722), A Donegal Heretic', *Irish Historical Studies*, 1969, p. 305; Toland, *Clito* (a work which may have been doctored by Toland's enemies before publication, but which was clearly based on a text of Toland: compare it with the sentiments in Toland's *Anglia Libera* (1701), p. 188, and in *An Apology for Mr. Toland* (1702), p. 10).

[111] Toland, *Vindicius Liberius* (1702), p. 146; *Toland's History of the Druids*, p. 153; Toland, *High Church Displayed* (1711), p. 13; *Somers Tracts*, xii. 573; *The Liberties of England Asserted* (1714), p. 12. (This last, anonymous, work can be plausibly attributed to Toland on the basis of internal evidence: e.g. compare the page cited with *Amyntor*, p. 100, and see Toland's *The Grand Mystery Laid Open* (1714: published, like *The Liberties of England Asserted*, by James Roberts, who, with Andrew Bell's partner Bernard Lintott, was Toland's most regular publisher in Anne's reign).

[112] *The Art of Restoring*, p. 37; *A Collection of General Monck's Letters*, esp. pp. viii ff. Milton's influence on Toland was, I suspect, considerable.

[113] B.L., Add. MS. 4295, fos. 4, 6&ᵛ, 10&ᵛ.

The precise nature of the obligations laid on Toland by the Darby contract are not clear, and in any case Toland's literary career was temporarily interrupted in the summer of 1697 by a disastrous visit to Dublin, an enterprise which culminated in the public burning of his most famous work, *Christianity not Mysterious* (1696), and which left him more heavily in debt than ever.[114] He was back in England by September, however,[115] and his partnership with Darby was soon resumed. Early in 1698, the time of the appearance of the first two volumes of Ludlow's *Memoirs*, Darby published Toland's *The Militia Reformed*.[116] Toland's edition of the *Works* of Milton followed later in the year.

Also in 1698, probably in August,[117] Darby published Algernon Sidney's *Discourses concerning Government*. They may not have been the only work by Sidney planned for publication in that year, when there was much talk about 'Sidney's maxims'.[118] 'Court Maxims', the manuscript by Sidney which is likely to have reached Warwick Castle in the company of 'A Voyce from the Watch Tower', is in the handwriting of two copyists, whose notes suggest that the manuscript was being prepared for the press. The notes also show that Sidney's original manuscript was reorganised and abbreviated, either by the copyists or by their employers. The manuscript of Sidney's *Discourses*, too, seems likely to have undergone revision. The passages read from it at Sidney's trial in 1683 are hard to reconcile with the 1698 publication,[119] the preface to which neatly sidesteps the question whether the manuscript has been faithfully reproduced.[120] At his trial, Sidney had said that he had drafted the treatise only in a 'crude and undigested form'. The sheets were full of 'confusions and errors', which 'showed that they had never so much as bin reviewed' and which rendered them 'not fit for the press'.[121]

---

[114] Desmaizeaux, *Toland*, i. xxv.

[115] *The Works of John Locke* (9 vols., 1824), viii. 434; *H.M.C.R. Portland*, iii. 486.

[116] For the timing, see Lois Schwoerer, 'Chronology and Authorship of the Standing Army Tracts', *Notes and Queries*, 1966, p. 387; *The Post Boy*, 1–3 February 1698.

[117] *Stationers Company Register*, iii. 384; *The Post Boy*, 9–11 and 23–25 August 1698.

[118] Caroline Robbins, *The Eighteenth Century Commonwealthman* (Cambridge, Mass., 1959), p. 6; cf. *Regicides no Saints*, p. 24.

[119] Caroline Robbins, 'Algernon Sidney's Discourses concerning Government: Textbook of Revolution', *William and Mary Quarterly*, 1947, p. 281n.

[120] See particularly its concluding paragraph.

[121] 'The Trial of A. Sydney', pp. 21–44, and Sidney's 'Apology', pp. 11–12, 17, 22, 26, both in Sidney's *Works* (1772). The problem of the date of the composition of the *Discourses* (discussed by Z. S. Fink, *The Classical Republicans* (Evanston, Illinois, 1945), p. 149n.) could profitably be considered afresh. The gaps in the *Discourses* (listed by Robbins, *William and Mary Quarterly*, 1947, p. 281n.) may reflect the bafflement of the publishers, but they could alternatively be an attempt to strengthen the impression of authenticity. Even so, if Sidney's text was pruned before publication, it is surprising that it was not pruned more extensively. A discussion of the question of the fidelity of the publishers to Sidney's manuscript might also take account of the references in the *Discourses* to the classic work of Bartolomeo de las Casas (Robbins, *William and*

Sidney's prose style is likely to have required less revision than Ludlow's, but a comparison between the opening sentence of the *Discourses* and the opening passage of Ludlow's *Memoirs* leads us to suspect that the manuscripts of the two authors have been amended by the same hand. The similarities may be heightened by the use of italics. The text of the *Discourses* begins:

> *Having* lately *seen* a book intituled 'Patriarcha', written by Sir Robert Filmer, concerning the universal and undistinguished right of all kings, *I thought* a time of *leisure* might be well *employed in* examining his doctrine ....

Ludlow's *Memoirs* begin:

> *Having seen* our cause betrayed, and the most solemn promises that could be made to the asserters of it openly violated, I departed from my native country. And hoping that my retirement may protect me from the rage and malice of my enemies, *I* cannot *think* it a mispending of some part of my *leisure*, to *employ* it *in* setting down the most remarkable counsels and actions....

It seems a fair inference that the editor of the *Discourses* was using a formula which had already served him well in the *Memoirs*.[122]

The name of the editor of the *Discourses* was not published until 1763. Then a new edition, prepared by Thomas Hollis, attributed them to Toland; and the attribution, belated as it was, is persuasive. One of the distinctive features of Toland's writings lies in the frequency with which he provides gratuitous publicity for his own works, and *The Life of John Milton* (dated 3 September 1698, and probably finished very shortly after Sidney's *Discourses* had appeared) contains a shameless reference to 'the incomparable and golden Discourses of that heroic patron of liberty, Algernon Sidney'. Later in the same work, Toland, who was probably already preparing his edition of Harrington's *Works*, contrived to insert a reference to 'Harrington's *Oceana*, which for the practicableness, equality, and completeness of it, is the most perfect form of such a government that ever was delineated by any antient or modern pen'.[123] The Sidney and

---

Mary Quarterly, 1947, p. 283n.), which was published by Darby in the spring of 1698 (Arber, *Term Catalogues*, iii. 476), and to the political wisdom of Sir Walter Ralegh. *The Cabinet Counsel*, a work which was supposed to have been written by Ralegh, and whose publication in 1658 had apparently been sponsored by Milton, was republished in 1697, probably by the Darby–Toland circle (see *The Life of John Milton*, p. 142). Andrew Bell published an abridged version of Ralegh's *History of the World* in 1698. See also Bethel, *The Interest of Princes*, sig. A5 and pp. 20, 36, 57.

[122] If the opening sentence of the *Memoirs* was a fabrication, the inspiration for it could have come from a passage on 'Voyce', p. 963.

[123] *The Life of John Milton*, pp. 62, 122; cf. *Anglia Libera*, p. 59. Harrington was much quoted in the pamphlet debates of the later 1690s.

Harrington publications were widely advertised as a pair, and were regarded as such by contemporaries,[124] who were also quick to associate the printing of Sidney's *Discourses* both with Ludlow's *Memoirs* and with Toland's Milton publications of 1698–9.[125]

We can say, then, that whoever edited Sidney's *Discourses* is likely to have edited Ludlow's *Memoirs*, and that Toland is likely to have edited Sidney's *Discourses*. However, we do not need to rest the case for Toland as the editor of Ludlow's *Memoirs* on the Sidney publication, for two works printed in 1699 connect Toland still more closely with the preparation of the *Memoirs*. The first, printed by Andrew Bell and sold by the Darbys, was *An Inquiry concerning Virtue*, written by Toland's patron the third Earl of Shaftesbury. Toland revised Shaftesbury's text extensively before its publication,[126] and the deft stylistic devices he adopted repeatedly call to mind the rewriting of 'A Voyce from the Watch Tower'.

The second publication was the *Memoirs of Denzil Lord Holles*. Holles's manuscript survives, and for the most part the editor faithfully reproduced it.[127] Although Toland's name does not appear in Holles's

[124] See e.g. the advertisements in the 1700 edition of Harrington's *Works*, in the 1704 edition of Sidney's *Discourses*, and in the 1705–6 edition of *State Tracts*, vol. ii; O. Klopp (ed.), *Correspondence de Leibniz* (3 vols., 1894), ii. 209. Toland inserted fresh manuscript material into the Harrington edition. He gained access to the Harrington family papers, and claimed to have drawn from them part of the biographical account of Harrington which prefaces the *Works*. He also published in the *Works* two treatises by Harrington which previously existed only in manuscript. J. G. A. Pocock, our leading authority on Harrington, considers that Toland probably reproduced the treatises faithfully, but that the biographical sketch of Harrington must be treated with caution.

[125] E.g. *A Brief Reply to the History of Standing Armies*, p. 24; *A Just Defence of the Royal Martyr*, preface; *Regicides no Saints*, pp. 12–13, 16, 18–19, 44–5, 47. See also *The Post Man* no. 628, 15–17 June 1699.

[126] Confusion has arisen about this work, partly because the 1699 version was for long hard to obtain, and so eluded the searches of Stephen and others. An impression may have appeared before the end of 1698 (*The Flying Post*, 26–29 November 1698). For the version later owned by Shaftesbury, see his *Characticks* (3 vols., 1711), ii. 5–176; for Toland's responsibility for the revision see Rand, *Shaftesbury*, pp. xxiii–xxiv. See also *The Post Man* no. 610, 4–6 May 1699, and below, p. 44.

[127] The manuscript, which is in Holles's own hand, is in the Sheffield City Library, Wentworth Woodhouse Muniments, Strafford papers, MS. 12. It differs from the printed version in only two significant (although in many insignificant) respects. It is entitled, not 'Memoirs', but 'Some Observations of the Designes and Proceedings of the Independents in, by and upon the Parliament and Kingdome, since the beginning of our unnaturall Warr in the yeare 1642, unto this present Time, the ending of the yeare 1647'; and Holles's dedication is dated 14 February 1647–8 rather than 14 February 1648–9. In the same collection (Strafford papers, MS. 15) is another manuscript in Holles's hand, called 'The Grand Question concerning the Prorogation of this Parliament for a Yeare and Three Months Stated and Discussed'. A 'part of' this treatise seems to have been published in 1676–7: see *Journals of the House of Lords*, 1 March 1676–7. It was evidently related to, but should be distinguished from, two other works of approximately the same date: *The Long Parliament Dissolved*, and *Some Considerations upon the Question whether the Parliament is dissolved by its Prorogation for 15 Months* (cf. B.L., Harleian MS. 6810, fos. 102–5; W. Hamper (ed.), *The Life, Diary, and Correspondence of Sir William Dugdale* (1827), pp. 404–5). A further bibliographical problem concerning Holles is discussed below, p. 38.

Memoirs, their preparation for the press is attributed to him in the dependable biography of Toland published in 1726 by the Huguenot *émigré* Pierre Desmaizeaux.[128] Having arrived in England in 1699, Desmaizeaux was soon taken up, on the recommendation of Pierre Bayle, by the third Earl of Shaftesbury, who commissioned him to translate Toland's version of *An Inquiry concerning Virtue* into French. Desmaizeaux knew Toland well enough to be aware of the defects of his character.[129] His attribution of Holles's *Memoirs* to Toland is supported by a contemporary manuscript ascription in a copy of the work in the Bodleian.[130] According to Desmaizeaux, the publication was commissioned by Shaftesbury's friend and Holles's kinsman the Duke of Newcastle. The editor's dedication is addressed to Newcastle, and contains the remark that 'the following papers of the famous Lord Holles, your great uncle, happened to fall into my hands': the dedication of Toland's *Anglia Libera* (1701) is likewise addressed to Newcastle, and congratulates the Duke on 'having bin the darling, and (as it were) the pupil, of the famous Lord Holles your great uncle'.[131] Toland certainly possessed advance knowledge of the publication of Holles's *Memoirs*, for he refers to them in *Amyntor*, the preface to which is dated only two days later than the editor's dedication in the Holles volume. In the same passage of *Amyntor*, Toland also mentions the 'Memorial' of Thomas Fairfax, which had yet to be published.[132] The preface to Holles's *Memoirs* announces the editor's intention of publishing Fairfax's 'Memorial', a copy of which he has somehow pirated. In the event, the threat was narrowly averted by Bryan Fairfax, who managed to get into print first with his own version.[133]

It can scarcely be doubted, then, that Toland edited Holles's *Memoirs*. Holles had been a presbyterian, whose views and actions in the Civil War had been very different from Ludlow's, but no one who has studied Toland's political career would expect to find him putting ideological consistency before the inducements of fame and

[128] Desmaizeaux, *Toland*, i. lxii–lxiii.

[129] For Shaftesbury and Desmaizeaux, see Rand, *Shaftesbury*, pp. 395–6; *A Concise Catalogue of the Library of Anthony Collins* (1731), part i, p. 79; below, p. 44 n. For Toland and Desmaizeaux, see e.g. B.L., Add. MS. 4282, fos. 139^v, 141, 143, 190, 192, 235, Add. MS. 4465, fos. 19, 36^v. Desmaizeaux was a friend of Jacques Bernard and a contributor to Bernard's *Nouvelles de la République*, which made its disapproval of Toland plain in its issue of July 1699, pp. 224–5. Cf. above, p. 24, n. 103.

[130] Classmark 8°. T. 40 Med. As a number of flyleaf ascriptions are cited in this introduction, it is perhaps worth mentioning that they are all in different hands.

[131] Manuscripts were always happening to fall into Toland's hands. For Toland's relations with Newcastle see also Desmaizeaux, *Toland*, ii. 343, 348; *Somers Tracts*, xii. 558; *H.M.C.R. Portland*, v. 259; cf. Toland, *The State-Anatomy of Great Britain* (1717), p. 96. See also below, p. 45.

[132] *Amyntor*, p. 135. For the connection between *Amyntor* and Holles's *Memoirs* see also *Nouvelles de la République*, July 1699, pp. 223–5.

[133] *Memoirs of Denzil Lord Holles*, pp. xi–xiii; *Short Memorials of Thomas Lord Fairfax* (1699), pp. iii–iv; B.L., Harleian MS. 1786, fos. 1, 48, and Harleian MS. 6390, fos. 1–4 (letters of Bryan Fairfax). See also *The Post Man*, 15–17 June 1699.

fortune. Holles's *Memoirs* were, in fact, clearly designed as a companion to Ludlow's. They contain an engraving of Holles by R. White which instantly recalls White's engraving of Ludlow in volume 1 of Ludlow's *Memoirs*; the dedication is dated 28 March 1699, two days later than the preface to volume 3 of Ludlow's *Memoirs*; and the preface to Holles's *Memoirs* begins:

> Such as really desire to know the naked truth, and propose for their chiefest aim the common good (which are certainly the best, tho not the greatest part of mankind) have ever exprest a desire in their writings of seeing the Memoirs of all parties made public as the most effectual means of framing a true General History .... Without consulting therefore the particular interest or reputation of any faction, but only the interest of England in general, these Memoirs of the Great Lord Holles are communicated to the world, *that by comparing them with those of Ludlow, and such as appeared before, or will be published hereafter relating to the same times, they may afford mutual light to each other* [my italics]; and, after distinguishing the personal resentments or private biasses of every one of 'em, the truth wherein they are all found to agree (tho drest by them in different garbs) may by som impartial and skilful hand be related with more candour, clearness, and uniformity.

The passage is an obvious echo of a statement in *The Life of John Milton*, in which Toland approvingly quotes Sir William Temple's complaint that no Englishman has yet 'produced one good or approved general History of England' and applauds James Tyrell's progress with the composition of his *General History of England.*[134] It also echoes Toland's frequently iterated belief that, within the broad Whig spectrum, diversity of opinion and interpretation would have the beneficial effect of preventing political and intellectual 'stagnation'.[135] The

---

[134] *The Life of John Milton*, pp. 139–41; cf. Rand, *Shaftesbury*, pp. 325–6, and J. M. Levine, 'Ancients, Moderns, and History', in P. J. Korshin (ed.), *Studies in Change and Revolution* (Scolar Press, 1972), pp. 54ff. For Tyrell see also Kemble, *European State Papers*, pp. 230–1, 240.

[135] Desmaizeaux, *Toland*, ii. 106; Toland, *The Art of Governing by Partys* (1701), p. 7; Toland, *Socinianism truly Stated* (1705), pp. 5, 7; *The State-Anatomy of Great Britain*, preface and p. 28; Toland, *Tetradymus* (1720), p. 182; cf. *Somers Tracts*, xii. 549. Cf. also Toland's 'inclination for paradoxes': Desmaizeaux, *Toland*, i. xii, lvii; *Christianity not Mysterious*, p. iv; *Anglia Libera*, p. 145; *Letters to Serena*, sig. c; *State-Anatomy*, p. 33; *Toland's History of the Druids*, p. 80. Holles's *Memoirs* were published not by Darby but by Timothy Goodwin, who was a friend of Darby but who had a rather more reputable clientele—a consideration which would no doubt have appealed to Newcastle. Molesworth's *An Account of Denmark* was among Goodwin's publications. Anne Baldwin advertised Holles's *Memoirs*: *The Post Man*, 11–14 April 1699. The remark in the preface to Holles's *Memoirs* that Holles may have 'guided his pencil to draw the lines of Cromwel's face too strong, and the shadows too many' could have been elicited by the hostile reception provoked in some quarters by the characterisation of Cromwell in the first two volumes of Ludlow's *Memoirs*: see *Somers Tracts*, vi. 416ff.

conviction accorded conveniently with the diversity of Toland's political allegiances.

In 1705, Toland recalled that he had 'published the lives and works of Harrington and Milton, with some other authors'; that these publications had been part of a concerted political campaign with influential political backing; and that they had all been distinguished by 'their democratical schemes of government'.[136] It is hard to believe that Ludlow's *Memoirs* were not among them.

Of course, we cannot prove that Toland edited Ludlow's *Memoirs*. The evidence which has been adduced, however pressing it may seem, must in the last resort be described as circumstantial. Circumstantial or not, however, it seems as persuasive as any which a historian could reasonably expect to find. In any case, it is not the only evidence. The evidence which has been considered so far is external to the text of the *Memoirs*. It has been described separately from the internal evidence of the *Memoirs*, for the reader is in a position to weigh the external evidence for himself. An assessment of the internal evidence requires an acquaintance not only with Ludlow's *Memoirs* but with Toland's own writings. The judgements on which it calls are often bound to be intuitive. They are also likely to be risky, for Toland is so versatile a writer that we might deceive ourselves into finding echoes of his prose wherever we looked for them. There are some points in the *Memoirs*, however, at which his presence seems unmistakable.

We have seen Firth observing that the views expressed in the preface to volume 3 'agree very well with those of Toland'. The same can be said of the preface to the first two volumes. In its final paragraph, for example, our attention is caught by the remark, which accords with one of Toland's strongest obsessions and which we find echoed again and again in his writings, that 'it can never be expected that all men should be of the same mind'.[137] Many writers, it may be felt, could have penned that sentiment. But who, other than Toland, would have followed it with the observation that when, in 1689, the republicans proposed that William III should send Ludlow to reconquer Ireland, 'the whole Kingdom of Ireland, London-derry only excepted, was unhappily fallen into the hands of the Irish papists'? The reference to Londonderry is gratuitous. Toland, proud to have been brought up in the Londonderry peninsula, rarely misses an opportunity to parade his affection for his birthplace, his patriotism, or his dismay at the baneful influence of popery on Irish history.[138]

---

[136] Desmaizeaux, *Toland*, ii. 338–9.
[137] Cf. the sources cited above, p. 30, n. 135.
[138] Desmaizeaux, *Toland*, i. v–vi; *An Apology for Mr. Toland*, p. 15; *Tetradymus*, pp.

The preface, it seems reasonable to assume, gave him just such an opportunity.[139]

It is not merely in the prefaces to the *Memoirs*, however, that the internal evidence points to Toland. The text of the *Memoirs* themselves contains frequent affinities of style, sentiment and even wording with Toland's own writings. Many of the resemblances are ones of rhythm and stylistic device, which could not be adequately conveyed by selective quotation. In some passages, however, Toland's influence can be clearly pinpointed. We shall see that the editor of the *Memoirs* inserted passages about the study of history, and about the evils of standing armies, which had no foundation in 'A Voyce from the Watch Tower'. All these passages are closely paralleled in Toland's own writings.[140] Then there are the impish inventions which enliven the *Memoirs*. When Ludlow recalls in the Bodleian manuscript that one of his enemies in Switzerland was obliged, after being captured, 'to call for somethinge to recover his spirits',[141] the *Memoirs* tell us that the same man 'recovered his spirits by drinking brandy'. When Ludlow tells us that the impressive arsenal at Bern contained 'arms as I guessed for about fifteene thousand footmen',[142] the *Memoirs* raise the figure to 20,000. The *Memoirs* take frequent liberties with Ludlow's figures—sometimes, it seems, for the sole purpose of relieving the editor's boredom.[143] When deletions and revisions in the manuscript make Ludlow's account of Charles II's reception in London at the Restoration very hard to read, the *Memoirs* have Ludlow say that Charles was entertained 'with much more empty pageantry, which I purposely omit'.[144] We read the solemn works of other possible contenders for the role of editor of Ludlow's *Memoirs*, like Slingsby Bethel and Isaac Littlebury, and try in vain to imagine those authors indulging in such frivolities.[145] It is hard to imagine Toland resisting them. At its most humdrum, the rewriting of Ludlow's manuscript reminds us of a seasoned and slightly mischievous copy editor revising an eager and verbose contribution by a novice reporter. At its best,

---

174–6; *Nazarenus*, p. x; Toland, *An Account of an Irish Manuscript* (1718), pp. 2, 16ff., 29; *Toland's History of the Druids*, pp. 52, 126, 142–3. Toland may have pressed the point about Londonderry on John Aubrey when he cooperated with him (and learned a good deal from him) in 1694–5: see Aubrey's *Miscellanies* (1890), pp. 28–9, and cf. Michael Hunter, *John Aubrey and the World of Learning* (1975), pp. 59–60. Perhaps Toland was introduced to Aubrey by Milton's nephews Edward and John Phillips, who knew Aubrey well; cf. Helen Darbishire (ed.), *The Early Lives of Milton* (1932).

[139] Isaac Littlebury, as we have already seen, may also have had a hand in the prefaces. Baron refers to the 'prefacers' of volume 3 of the *Memoirs* (*Regicides no Saints*, pp. 3–4).

[140] Below, pp. 41, 48–50, 62.

[141] 'Voyce', p. 1068.

[142] 'Voyce', p. 983.

[143] 'Voyce', pp. 749, 985, 1022, 1067, 1096, 1141, 1149, 1219.

[144] 'Voyce', p. 786.

[145] The same objection can be made against David Jones (cf. above, p. 23, n. 99).

it is a work of art, of a kind which no one in late seventeenth-century England was better equipped to create than Toland.

That it was indeed Toland who created it is suggested, finally, by three pieces of internal evidence which take us back to the connection between Ludlow's *Memoirs* and the other publications of 1698–9 which have been discussed. Normally, passages in the Bodleian manuscript which provide information about the careers of individual politicians are heavily compressed in the *Memoirs*. Very occasionally, however, the printed version expands biographical material given in the manuscript; and the three pieces of internal evidence to be considered are among the rare instances of biographical elaboration.

The first concerns Ludlow's close friend John Cook. The Bodleian manuscript tells us that Cook had, as a young man, spent 'some monthes at Geneve, at the howse of Mr. Deodat'.[146] In the *Memoirs*, this becomes: 'he resided some months in the house of Signior Gio. Diodati, minister of the Italian church in that city'. Toland, of course, knew about Diodati from his research for *The Life of John Milton*, where he records that in 1639 Milton travelled from Italy 'to Geneva, where he contracted an intimat familiarity with Giovanni Diodati, a noted Professor of Divinity'.[147]

The second passage concerns Algernon Sidney. In the Bodleian manuscript, Ludlow tells us that after the Restoration Sidney had 'chosen Rome for his retirement': the *Memoirs* inform us that Sidney 'had resided in Rome and other parts of Italy'. The Bodleian manuscript then records that when Sidney visited Ludlow in 1663, he 'as a marque of his favour was pleased to bestow on me a paire of silver pistols, the barrells whereof he had brought with him from a noted place in Italy':[148] the *Memoirs* tell us that 'He .... at his departure presented me with a paire of pistols, the barrils of which were made at Brescia in Lombardy by old Lazzarino Cominazzo.'[149]

The third instance concerns Denzil Holles. Recording, in the Bodleian manuscript, Holles's championship of the Lords against the Commons in the case of Skinner *versus* the East India Company, Ludlow recalls that 'whilest the said Holles was of the Howse of Commons, there was none who trampled underfoote the priviledge of the

---

[146] 'Voyce', p. 853.

[147] *The Life of John Milton*, p. 22; cf. Darbishire, *The Early Lives of Milton*, pp. 2, 38, 59. For Cook, Diodati and Milton, see also *A true Relation of Mr. Justice Cook's Passage* (1650), p. 16, and C. H. Firth (ed.), 'Papers relating to Thomas Wentworth', *Camden Miscellany*, ix (1895), 19.

[148] 'Voyce', p. 977.

[149] How did Toland acquire—or how did it occur to him to invent—so arcane a piece of information? One slight possibility will perhaps suggest itself to the reader who consults: Firth, ii, 346n.; Hunter, *John Aubrey*, p. 103n.; the reference to John Evelyn in the life of Edward Phillips in the *Dictionary of National Biography*; and above, p. 32, n. 138.

Lords Howse more then he'.[150] Once more the *Memoirs* fill in a detail which the manuscript omits: we learn that when Holles

> was a member of the House of Commons, he had so far despised the priviledges of the Lords, that at a conference between the two Houses, in which the Lords shewd themselves unwilling to comply with the Commons, he had openly said, that if they persisted to refuse their concurrence, the Commons would do the thing in dispute without them.

Whatever the editor's source for this episode (presumably the occasion in December 1641 when Holles carried a stiff message to the Lords about the impressment bill),[151] it seems fair to suppose that he was bringing to the writing of Ludlow's *Memoirs* a depth of knowledge about Holles's career comparable to that which he displayed about the careers of John Milton and Algernon Sidney.[152] As an expert on all three men, Toland had excellent credentials.

The reader will decide for himself whether the evidence which has been presented allows him to assume that Toland edited Ludlow's *Memoirs*. But to spare him wearisome qualifications in the pages which follow, I shall proceed on the assumption to which the evidence seems to me firmly to point, that 'A Voyce from the Watch Tower' was rewritten by Toland. The reader can then make any mental reservations he thinks appropriate. The story of Toland's involvement in the preparation of the *Memoirs*, however, has not yet been fully told. So far, the preparation of the *Memoirs* has been viewed chiefly in the light of Toland's other editorial activities of 1698–1700. It is now time to cast the net a little wider.

Between 1691 and 1693, four pamphlets had been published in the name of Edmund Ludlow.[153] Concentrating on the misrule of Charles

---

[150] 'Voyce', p. 1230.

[151] S. R. Gardiner, *The History of England* (10 vols., 1886), x. 103; W. H. Coates (ed.), *The Journal of Sir Simonds D'Ewes* (New Haven, 1942), p. 315.

[152] The episode is not mentioned in Holles's *Memoirs*, and it seems likely that the editor of Ludlow's *Memoirs* was alerted to it by Ludlow. There is a brief discussion of the incident earlier in Ludlow's manuscript ('Voyce', p. 800), where Ludlow notes that it had been mentioned in a pamphlet attack on Richard Baxter published in 1660. By locating the attack, which is to be found in *The Rebels Plea* (1660), p. 30, the editor would have seen that *The Rebels Plea* had drawn its information from Edward Husbands's *An Exact Collection* (1642), p. 548; and from Husbands's account (but not from Ludlow's or from *The Rebels Plea*) the editor could, with a little licence, have produced the story as it appears in Ludlow's *Memoirs*. He would surely have gone to such lengths only if he had been eager to arouse his readers' interest in Holles. A second possible explanation for the appearance of the episode in Ludlow's *Memoirs* is that Ludlow had mentioned it in the missing, pre-1660 section of his manuscript, but the reference on 'Voyce', p. 800, does not lead one to suppose that he had done so.

[153] The first three (whose full titles are given by Firth, i. lvi–lvii) were reprinted by Francis Maseres in 1812 as *Three Tracts published at Amsterdam, in the years 1691 and 1692, under the name of Letters of General Ludlow*. The fourth was *Truth Brought to Light* (1693). We do not know who printed the tracts, but it is a fair guess that Richard Baldwin

I, they had been contributions to the debates which attended the anniversaries of Charles I's execution and to the controversy over the authorship of *Eikon Basilike*. As the fourth of the pamphlets admitted, they were plainly not written by Ludlow.[154] The adoption of the pseudonym was an inspired move. Since 1660, Ludlow's name had been a rallying cry for dissenters and republicans. In Charles II's reign there had flourished persistent (and baseless) rumours, often believed by the government, that Ludlow was in England, plotting against the regime and preparing to lead a rebel army.[155] Ludlow's visit to England in 1689 had made him, to radical Whigs, a symbol of deliverance: his deportation had become a symbol of government betrayal.[156] The decision to present the pamphlets as compositions by Ludlow, written in the first person, gave a historical dimension to the Calves-Head views which they propagated. The tracts were able to portray those views as the logical lessons to be derived not merely from the immediate circumstances of the early 1690s but from the whole seventeenth-century constitutional struggle in which the regicide Ludlow had figured.

Who wrote the Ludlow pamphlets? They have often been attributed to Slingsby Bethel, whose *The Providences of God* (1691) indeed bears a number of resemblances to them of content, although not of style.[157] Anthony Wood noted that they were 'commonly reported' to have been written by Milton's nephew John Phillips,[158] while Andrew Bell attributed them to 'Thomas Percival', under whose name there had appeared *The Rye House Travesties* (1696).[159] All these men are likely to have been involved in the preparation of the pamphlets. They are not, however, the only candidates for their authorship, and they do not include the most convincing candidate. In a brief article in *Notes and Queries* on 16 December 1933, G. W. Whiting claimed that the Ludlow tracts had been written by John Toland. Unfortunately Whiting's note, intended as a prelude to a more substantial study which in the event he does not seem to have published, scarcely proceeds beyond assertion to argument, but it is not difficult to see where his thoughts were leading.

---

was involved; cf. the history of James I's reign reprinted from a 1651 pamphlet by Baldwin in 1692 as *Truth Brought to Light*.

[154] *Truth Brought to Light* (1693), p. 4.

[155] Firth, ii. 329n. The *Memoirs* discreetly play down Ludlow's capacity for conspiracy: see 'Voyce', pp. 726–8, 731–2.

[156] See the references to the recovery of Ireland in Maseres, *Three Tracts*, pp. 63, 65. See also *The History of the King-Killers* (2 vols., 1720), i. 44ff.

[157] See especially *Providences*, pp. 8ff. (Compare for example the references on p. 9 to Scotland and to Vittorio Siri with Maseres, *Three Tracts*, pp. 36, 112; and see Toland, *State-Anatomy*, p. 5.)

[158] Flyleaf to Bodleian Library, Wood pamphlets 363.

[159] Advertisement in the 1697 edition of *The Providences of God*. For further support for Percival see *Notes and Queries*, 21 October 1933.

His claim was based partly on stylistic evidence. The dangers inherent in the search for echoes of Toland's style have already been noted: even so, it may be worth recording that the present writer, approaching the Ludlow pamphlets from an angle very different from Whiting's, had come to suspect that they were Toland's before he became aware of Whiting's article. The obvious strength of Whiting's suggestion, however, lies in the close continuity and similarity which he noticed between the material in the Ludlow pamphlets concerning the authorship of *Eikon Basilike* and Toland's discussions of the same subject in *The Life of John Milton* and *Amyntor*. It is conceivable that in the 1698–9 Milton publications Toland was plagiarising material which had been used in the Ludlow pamphlets, but it seems much more likely that he was reworking his own texts.[160] Whiting's attribution receives support from a copy in the Bodleian of Richard Hollingworth's *The Character of King Charles I* (1692), which was written as a reply to the third of the Ludlow pamphlets, *Ludlow no Lyar*. A note on the title-page, in a contemporary hand, states that *Ludlow no Lyar* had been written by Toland.[161] Not only do the Ludlow pamphlets of 1691–3 contain much material which was to be reproduced or reworked in the 1698–9 Milton publications. They include equally distinctive material which we find reused in two anonymous pamphlets of 1698 whose persuasive attribution to Toland by William Baron we have already observed, *A Defence of the Parliament of 1640* and *King Charles I no such Saint*.....[162]

Toland was twenty-one when the Ludlow pamphlets appeared. He had recently moved south from Scotland, where he had received his university education. No doubt Scotland was glad to see the back of him. At Glasgow, where he had delivered harangues against priests and magistrates and had 'pretended to work wonders by some secret arts', he had led a rabble in a pope-burning ceremony round the market-place. His subsequent visit to Edinburgh, where he 'set up for a Rosacrucian', was no doubt similarly eventful.[163] Yet in England, to

---

[160] For the resemblances between the Ludlow pamphlets and the Milton publications, compare: *Three Tracts*, pp. 19–20, with *Amyntor*, pp. 155ff.; *Three Tracts*, pp. 86ff., and *Truth Brought to Light*, p. 6, with *The Life of John Milton*, pp. 86ff.; *Three Tracts*, pp. 111–12, and *Truth Brought to Light*, p. 6, with *Amyntor*, p. 171; *Three Tracts*, pp. 141–2, with *Amyntor*, p. 129; and *Three Tracts*, p. 144, with *The Life of John Milton*, p. 123. See also the reference to *Truth Brought to Light* in *Amyntor*, p. 85, and F. Madan, *A New Bibliography of Eikon Basilike* (1950), pp. 126, 142–5.

[161] Classmark Bodl. C. 6. 12. Linc. (2).

[162] Compare *Three Tracts*, p. 120, with *A Defence*, pp. 55–6; the passages in the Ludlow pamphlets concerning *Eikon Basilike* cited above, n. 160, with *A Defence*, pp' 15–17; and *Three Tracts*, p. 10 (marginal reference to Fleta and Bracton), with *King Charles I* ...., p. 7.

[163] F. H. Heinemann, 'John Toland and the Age of Enlightenment', *Review of English Studies*, 1944, pp. 127–8, and 'John Toland, France, Holland, and Dr. Williams', *Review of English Studies*, 1949, pp. 346–7. These stories, which we owe to Toland's enemies

the puzzlement of his enemies, he rapidly acquired distinguished patronage. He was taken up by a presbyterian alderman at Clapham, and soon enjoyed the favour of that doyen of the London dissenting community, Daniel Williams. In such circles, it would have been natural for Toland to be introduced to the Bethel–Phillips group, whose connection with the Ludlow pamphlets of 1691–3 has already been noted. Much of the material in the pamphlets was a contribution to the London parish warfare between Anglicans and presbyterians, and the dissenters were said to have greeted their appearance with acclamation.[164]

The Ludlow pamphlets drew heavily, without acknowledgement, on Milton's *Eikonoklastes*;[165] and the abbreviation and reordering of Milton's text remind us forcibly of the rewriting of 'A Voyce from the Watch Tower'. Perhaps the earlier operation did not display quite the flair of the later one—it hardly needed to, since it was Milton rather than Ludlow who provided the material—but the similarity of technique is unmistakable. Should the publication of Ludlow's *Memoirs* be seen, then, not as a sudden initiative of the late 1690s but as the continuation of an enterprise which had begun early in the decade? It will become clear that the content of Ludlow's *Memoirs* was partly determined by the particular political circumstances of 1697–9, but it is quite conceivable that the revision of the manuscript had begun at an earlier stage. The possibility is strengthened by close similarities in the choice and arrangement of subject matter between, on the one hand, certain passages of the Ludlow pamphlets and, on the other, comparable passages both in the Bodleian manuscript and in the early pages of Ludlow's *Memoirs*.[166] It may well be that use was made of 'A Voyce from the Watch Tower' in the composition of the 1691–3 tracts. There are passages, too, in the 1697 edition of *A Detection of the Court and State of England*—a work published (by

---

in the Church and the Universities, may have grown a little, but probably did not grow much, in the telling.

[164] *Three Tracts*, pp. 71–2, 85ff., 102, 143, 146; *Truth Brought to Light*, pp. 4–5; *A Second Defence of King Charles I* (1692), dedication.

[165] G. W. Whiting, 'A Late Seventeenth-Century Milton Plagiarism', *Studies in Philology*, 1934, pp. 37–50; G. F. Sensabaugh, *That Grand Whig Milton* (New York, 1952), pp. 144ff.

[166] *Three Tracts*, pp. 8–9, 15–16, 41, 55, 66, 77, 131–2; Darby, i. 1–39: Firth, i. 9–36; *Truth Brought to Light*, p. 4; 'Voyce', pp. 762ff. We may also note the similarity between the curious chronology of Charles I's reign in the first of the Ludlow pamphlets (*Three Tracts*, p. 7) and the parallel chronological approach in the *Memoirs*. We may observe too the use of the words 'digress' and 'digression' in the Ludlow pamphlets (*Three Tracts*, pp. 41, 103, 123), which, if it was Toland's, was very characteristic of him: *The Life of John Milton*, p. 139; *Letters to Serena*, p. 186; *Socinianism truly Stated*, pp. 6, 10–15; *The Liberties of England Asserted*, p. 20; *The Art of Restoring*, p. 6; *Nazarenus*, p. 76; *Tetradymus*, pp. 20, 113; *Toland's History of the Druids*, pp. 62, 226; cf. *Anglia Libera*, pp. 62–3. See also Darby, iii. 698: Firth, ii. 118.

Andrew Bell) in the name of Roger Coke, but at least partly written by David Jones[167]—which suggest that the Calves-Head group made use of Ludlow's manuscript, or of a draft of the *Memoirs*, before the *Memoirs* were published.[168]

Others of Toland's publications of the late 1690s may also have been planned earlier in the decade. G. W. Whiting, who observed the resemblances between the Ludlow pamphlets and *Amyntor*, also noticed Toland's statement at the beginning of *The Life of John Milton* that he had 'at length' produced a work which he had been 'often and earnestly solicited to write'. References in the Ludlow pamphlets to 'the great Lord Holles', which we find echoed in Toland's dedication of the *Memoirs of Denzil Lord Holles*, raise the possibility that the publication of Holles's *Memoirs* had been projected well before 1699.[169] Indeed, it is probable that Holles's name had become closely associated with Ludlow's in radical Whig minds by the early 1690s. In 1691 there appeared a pamphlet entitled *A Letter to Monsieur van B[euningen] de M——, at Amsterdam, written 1676, by Denzil Lord Holles.* The tract is an exposition of favourite radical Whig themes, above all the Harringtonian interpretation of Tudor and Stuart history and the destruction of the balance of Europe consequent upon the rise of France. Holles's 'letter' is an obvious parallel to the 'letters' of 1691 which constituted the first two Ludlow pamphlets, *A Letter from Major General Ludlow to Sir Edward Seymour* and *A Letter from Major General Ludlow to Dr. Hollingworth.* There is scarcely more reason to suppose that Holles (who died in 1680) had written the tract published in his name in 1691 than there is to imagine that Ludlow wrote the Ludlow pamphlets of 1691–3.[170]

[167] B.L., Loan MS. 29/90 (Harley papers, Portland Collection), fo. 157; *Dictionary of National Biography*, Jones.

[168] See the distinctively inaccurate observations that 'The Victory at Worcester swelled the sails of Cromwel's ambition brimfull, so that he began to entertain thoughts of setting up himself' (cf. below, p. 75), and that 'The Dutch above all things dreading the Rump, animated Cromwell to dissolve it'. The remark that Cromwell 'felt the pulse of the lawyers and soldiers' also sounds like an echo of Ludlow: the metaphor (like 'taking off the masque') appears frequently both in the Bodleian manuscript and in the *Memoirs. A Detection*, pp. 348, 359, 361; Firth, i. 282, 344, 355 and n.

[169] *Three Tracts*, pp. 18, 55; above, p. 29. On 'Voyce', p. 962, Ludlow has a passage concerning 'Mr. Denzil Hollis': Toland, revising the passage in Ludlow's *Memoirs*, inserts the information that Holles was 'since the late Revolution called the Lord Hollis'.

[170] Holles's 'letter' is usually supposed to have been published in 1676, but of the many variant pre-1700 editions of the pamphlet which I have seen, only one (in the Bodleian, with the title *The Danger of Europe, from the growing power of France foretold*) gives (on p. 8) a date of publication: 1691. The document had been printed as a folio sheet in the 1689 *State Tracts* (and reappeared in later editions), but the prefaces to the *State Tracts* leave open the question whether the pamphlet had been in print earlier than 1689. I can find no reference to the tract in Van Beuningen's correspondence (B.L., Add. MS. 17677CC and DD; and the words 'at Amsterdam' in the title are a puzzle). Radical Whigs were to make further use of Holles in publications of Anne's reign.

So it may be that when Toland, in his dedication of the *Memoirs of Denzil Lord Holles* in 1699, urged his readers to compare them with Ludlow's *Memoirs*,[171] he was pursuing a tactic which he had helped to develop at the beginning of the 1690s. But whether or not the series of Darby–Toland publications which appeared between 1698 and 1700 had been planned earlier in the decade, the political circumstances of the last years of the century made Toland's editions much more marketable, and much more influential, than they could have been earlier. It is to those circumstances that we shall now turn; for it is in them that the explanation of the differences between Ludlow's manuscript and Ludlow's *Memoirs* is largely to be found.

3. THE MEMOIRS AND THE STANDING ARMY CONTROVERSY

In 1697 the pattern of political allegiances in England was profoundly affected by the Treaty of Ryswick. Despite the return of peace, William III was determined to retain the bulk of the land forces which had been used against France. His resolve provoked the 'standing army controversy' which raged from 1697 to 1699. The debate cut across Whig–Tory divisions and—as Toland was quick to point out—made possible the creation of an effective 'country', or anti-court, alliance.[172] The controversy revealed the extent of the mistrust of William's constitutional intentions held by backbench M.P.s, and showed how widespread was the anxiety about the uses to which a standing army might be put by William's successors. It also brought into the open tensions within the Whig party which had been growing since 1693–4. The Whigs were held together before 1697, and were to be held together again after 1699, by fear of France. In the interim, however, the support given by Somers and his fellow 'junto' Whigs to the retention of William's land forces seemed to 'country' Whigs a final confirmation of the junto's apostasy from the revolutionary principles of 1688–9.

Opponents of standing armies were able to exploit ignorance, irrational fears, and resentment against high taxation. Yet the opposition to standing armies had an intellectual as well as a political purpose. Indeed, the debate is a critical episode in English intellectual history. To Calves-Head Whigs, the standing army debate presented an opportunity to create a respectable ideological and historical pedigree for the cause which had fallen with the first Earl of Shaftesbury and which, they believed, had been betrayed since 1688–9 by the junto. The Darby–Toland publications were partly designed to seize

[171] Above, p. 30.
[172] *The Militia Reformed*, pp. 7, 32.

that opportunity and to broaden the appeal of republicanism by an appeal to country party sentiment. The initiative behind them cannot, however, be attributed to the Calves-Head republicans alone.

There has been no detailed study of the ideology of the country Whigs of the late 1690s. In the absence of such an examination, we can perhaps best approach the subject by adopting categories which, although they will inevitably conceal subtleties and if pressed too hard would become artificial and misleading, may at least draw attention to significant differences of philosophy among the country Whig apologists. In that cautious spirit we shall make a distinction between the 'Calves-head fraternity' and a group which can best be described as the 'aristocratic' or 'Roman' Whigs. The latter group, drawing much of its inspiration from Robert Molesworth and from Molesworth's *An Account of Denmark* (1694), included among its other leaders Lord Ashley (third Earl of Shaftesbury from 1699), to whom Molesworth was an 'oracle',[173] and the chief worthies of the Grecian Club, John Trenchard and Walter Moyle. Like the Calves-Head republicans, these men believed that the predominant political characteristics of the 1690s were apostasy and corruption. Like them, too, they admired the virtues which had been displayed by the Long Parliament, and were keenly interested in the constitutional struggles of the seventeenth century. Their horizons, however, were broader than those of their Calves-Head allies. In their view, the solution to England's problems lay in that 'ancient prudence' of republican Rome which had been rediscovered and celebrated by Machiavelli and by Harrington. The preservation of the Machiavelli–Harrington tradition in the later seventeenth century was achieved largely through the efforts of the father-figure of the Grecian Club, Henry Nevile, who died in 1694, and whose Harringtonian tract *Plato Redivivus* (1681) was republished by Anne Baldwin in 1698.[174] Whereas Calves-Head republicans had merely flirted with the tradition, the Roman Whigs played a major role in its development, and gave it a central place in the development of the anti-standing army ideology.[175]

---

[173] *Letters from* .... *Shaftesbury to Robert Molesworth*, p. ix.

[174] With the title *Discourses concerning Government*—the title of the Sidney publication of the same year.

[175] On the ideology and the tradition, see Robbins, *The Eighteenth-Century Commonwealthsman* and *Two Republican Tracts*; Fink, *The Classical Republicans*; H. T. Colbourn, *The Lamp of Experience* (North Carolina, 1965); Felix Raab, *The English Face of Machiavelli* (1964); J. G. A. Pocock, *Politics, Language and Time* (New York, 1971), ch. iv, and *The Machiavellian Moment* (Princeton, 1975), ch. xii; Quentin Skinner, 'The Principles and Practice of Opposition', in N. McKendrick (ed.), *Historical Perspectives* (1974), pp. 93ff. Schwoerer, '*No Standing Armies!*', is the best recent introduction to the controversy of 1697–9, although it is still hard to resist Macaulay's discussion in ch. xxiii of his *History of England*. The most eloquent testimony to the influence of the anti-standing army ideology in eighteenth-century England seems to me to be Gibbon's *Decline and Fall*: see Everyman edition (6 vols., 1974), e.g. i. 56–7, 59, 101–3, 120, 133, 153–4,

Between 1697 and 1699 the Calves-Head republicans and the Roman Whigs were able to join forces, and the Roman Whigs brought to the alliance an intellectual depth and a political respectability which the Calves-Head group could not have achieved on its own. The differences between the two groups must not be exaggerated. The Calves-Head republicans appear to have viewed the settlement of 1689 with grave mistrust: the Roman Whigs, although deeply dismayed by the abuses of the constitution, protested that the constitution itself was compatible with the ideals of ancient prudence; but both sides were prepared to modify their positions in times of crisis. It would be a mistake to suppose a contrast between intemperate pamphleteers on the one hand and lofty patrician theorists on the other. The Calves-Head republicans were not mere subversive extremists. Equally, the Roman Whigs were fully willing to dirty their political knees. Their collaboration with John Toland sufficiently illustrates the point. *An Argument, shewing that a Standing Army is inconsistent with a Free Government* (1697) was probably the fruit of co-operation between Trenchard, Moyle and Toland, and the same trio is likely to have been responsible in the autumn of 1698 for *A Short History of Standing Armies*,[176] which drew very heavily on Ludlow's *Memoirs*[177] and which was cynically dishonest in its estimates of the strength and cost of William's army.[178] Toland's own writings contain some of the most thoughtful contributions to the standing army debate, and he shared the enthusiasm for Roman republican virtue which his edition of Harrington's *Works* helped to foster. Yet his posi-

---

162, 188–9, 227, ii. 109–10, 217, 326, 378 and n. 2, iii. 177, 194, 217–19, 286, 427 (and it is interesting to notice Gibbon's debt to Walter Moyle: *ibid.*, e.g. i. 191n., 491n., ii. 39n., 40n., 41n., iii. 119n., 122n.). See also (e.g.) Duncan Forbes, *The Political Philosophy of Hume* (Cambridge, 1975), p. 212 and n.; *The Works of William Robertson* (1831), p. 439b; Pope's *Iliad*, xix. line 145n.

[176] Two relatively well-informed replies to pamphlets against standing armies suggest that *An Argument*, which is normally attributed to Walter Moyle and John Trenchard, was written by the author of *A Short History*, and one of them claims that the author of both pamphlets was the author of *The Militia Reformed*, i.e. Toland: *A True Account of the Land Forces in England* (1699), pp. 7–8, 14–15, 67; *An Argument proving, that a small number of regulated Forces established during the present Parliament* .... (1698), preface (and see p. 24). Toland apparently claimed to have written *A Short History*: see *Remarks on the Life of Mr. Milton* (1699), p. 14. Compare too the reference to 'surly patriots' on pp. 38–9 of *A Short History* with Toland's remark about 'surly Whigs' in *The Art of Governing by Partys*, pp. 47–8. *An Argument* is attributed to Toland in Watt's *Bibliotheca Britiannica*. It may have drawn on Ludlow's manuscript: *An Argument*, p. 10. The posthumous edition of the *Works* of Walter Moyle (2 vols., 1726, published by John Darby jr.) is worth comparing with Desmaizeaux's edition of Toland's posthumous works in the same year. It is interesting, too, to read Moyle's writings—especially 'An Essay upon the Roman Government'—with Toland in mind.

[177] *A Short History*, pp. 2, 5, 8–9.

[178] B.L., Add. MS. 40072, fo. 357ᵛ, Vernon to King, 29 November 1698, and Add. MS. 17677SS, fos. 415 &ᵛ, report of Dutch envoys, 12 December 1698; *A True Account of the Land Forces*, p. 44.

tion, which gave him a foot in both the Calves-Head and the Roman camps, was an uncomfortable one. It is arguable that the content of Ludlow's *Memoirs* reflects the tension between his two loyalties. It is also arguable that the impact made by the *Memoirs* is likely to have pleased Roman Whigs more than Calves-Head republicans.

In April 1699 the government, convinced that Toland was an 'incendiary', was anxiously seeking to identify his 'encouragers'.[179] He had many clandestine contacts in high places. There was Robert Harley, the chief architect and the chief beneficiary of the country alliance of 1697–9, who encouraged Toland to edit Harrington's *Works* and to compose *The Art of Governing by Partys* (1701). Later Harley employed him to write other pamphlets, and may have used him as a spy in European capitals.[180] There was the Whig London alderman Sir Robert Clayton, who tried to persuade the City government to pay Toland for editing Harrington's *Works*.[181] There was Lord Methuen, who may have been behind Toland's visit to Ireland in 1697. There was the hotheaded Charles, Lord Spencer (son and heir of the Earl of Sunderland, and brother-in-law of Newcastle), who shared Toland's interest in Socinianism, republicanism and Roman history.[182] Most revealing for our purposes, however, is Toland's relationship with the third Earl of Shaftesbury. That relationship has been obscured by the subsequent estrangement between the two men, and by the fourth Earl's attempt to write the story out of his father's life.[183] Most people who befriended Toland soon learned to regret it, but

---

[179] B.L., Add. MS. 40773, fo. 333, Vernon to Portland, 29 April 1699.

[180] Desmaizeaux, *Toland*, i. lix–lxi, ii. 217–18, 345, 349–50; *The Art of Restoring*, dedication; Kemble, *European State Papers*, pp. 463–5; *The Wentworth Papers* (1882), pp. 132, 136 (cf. Angus Macinnes, 'The Political Ideas of Robert Harley', *History*, 1965, p. 321n.); *Somers Tracts*, xii. 557; *H.M.C.R. Portland*, iv. 408–10, 491, 572, v. 4, 120, 126, 258–60, viii. 279, ix. 289–90; F. H. Heinemann, 'A Prolegomena to a Bibliography of John Toland', *Notes and Queries*, 25 September 1943, and *Review of English Studies*, 1944, pp. 136–7; H. L. Snyder (ed.), *The Marlborough–Godolphin Correspondence* (3 vols., Oxford, 1975), ii. 1059, 1165, 1171; Jonathan Swift, *A Discourse of the Contests between the Nobles and the Commons in Athens and Rome*, ed. F. H. Ellis (Oxford, 1967), pp. 36–42. Toland proclaimed throughout Europe that he was Harley's agent, and was consequently disbelieved, but there may have been something in it—although Snyder's normally exemplary work has a misleading footnote on the subject (ii. 1059). I have found nothing to connect Harley with Ludlow's *Memoirs*. It is likely that Harley was not involved in the publication of Holles's *Memoirs* (see B.L., Loan MS. 29/189, fo. 84), but he could have been involved in Toland's plan for an edition of Fairfax's *Memorials*: Harley had inherited a copy of Fairfax's manuscript (now B.L., Harleian MS. 1786) from his father.

[181] Ballard MS. iv, fo. 53ᵛ, Tanner to Charlett, 6 May 1700; Harrington's *Works*, p. v; *The Life of John Sharp*, pp. 273–4; Lambeth MS. 933, no. 74; Jacob, *The Newtonians and the English Revolution*, pp. 220–2, 226.

[182] Lambeth MS. 933, no. 74; A. D. Francis, *The Methuens and Portugal* (Cambridge, 1966), pp. 357–8; *Anglia Libera*, pp. 164–5; cf. *The State-Anatomy*, p. 96.

[183] Rand, *Shaftesbury*, pp. xxiii–xxiv; cf. T. Fowler, *Shaftesbury and Hutcheson* (1882), p. 1. The draft of the fourth Earl's statement is revealing: P.R.O., 30/24/21, no. 225.

Shaftesbury, who was a year younger than Toland, took longer than most to see through him. One undated letter from Shaftesbury to Toland, probably belonging to the later 1690s, exudes devotion and dependence. Even in 1701, when Shaftesbury had become aware of at least some of Toland's failings, he called himself 'your best and truest friend'.[184]

Shaftesbury's political career was dominated by what he called 'the much injured memory' of his grandfather, Anthony Ashley Cooper, the first Earl.[185] Here Toland saw his opportunity. In 1695 he 'boasted much of the young Lord Ashley, how he had framed him, and that he should outdo his grandfather'.[186] Ten years later, the third Earl could reflect on his grandfather's contribution to 'the history of those times, when the foundation was laying for the present glorious ones and for the happy revolution that gave birth to them'; but the Shaftesbury of Anne's reign, whom we meet as a relatively mellow and contented philosopher, was a changed man from the nervous, impetuous politician of William's last years. In Europe, the very survival of Protestantism and liberty had then appeared to hang in the balance. At home, the 'happy revolution' had seemed dangerously insecure and incomplete. In the late 1690s, the instruments of tyranny remained to hand. There were the 'mercenary soldiers' retained by William after Ryswick; and there were 'mercenary parliaments', their independence corrupted by an unreformed electoral system, by placemen, by profiteers, and by the Whig junto's 'compliance with the court'. Shaftesbury was convinced that the 'total reform' for which he called, and which he believed to have been unforgivably deflected after 1688, could be achieved only when parliaments were reduced 'solely and wholly upon the country bottom'.[187]

In 1698, when he wrote despairingly to his old tutor and close friend John Locke about the 'shipwrecks' of English political life,[188] Shaftesbury was willing to adopt radical courses. It was now that his friendship with Toland developed into a close literary partnership—so close that it is often hard to distinguish, in their collaborative ventures, between Shaftesbury's contributions and Toland's. Shaftesbury probably encouraged Toland to write the anti-standing army pamphlet

---

[184] B.L., Add. MS. 4295, fo. 57; P.R.O., 30/24/21, no. 231.

[185] Rand, *Shaftesbury*, pp. 325–6.

[186] Lambeth MS. 942, no. 110; *Notes and Queries*, 4 January 1892. (Cf. *Tetradymus*, p. 94.)

[187] T. Forster (ed.), *Original Letters of Locke, Algernon Sidney, and Anthony, Lord Shaftesbury* (1847), pp. 75–7, 82–3, 92, 110–11; P.R.O., 30/24/21, no 231, 30/24/45, part i, fo. 73ᵛ; *Letters from . . . . Shaftesbury to Robert Molesworth*, pp. vii–viii, xv ff. To Shaftesbury—as to Toland—there was a natural connection between 'mercenary' politics and the prevalent 'mercenary' morality; see A. O. Aldridge, 'Shaftesbury and the Deist Manifesto', *Transactions of the American Philosophical Society*, 1951, pp. 297ff.

[188] MS. Locke c. 7, fo. 120.

which appeared early in 1698, *The Militia Reformed*.[189] In the same year the two men produced *The Danger of Mercenary Parliaments*.[190] Toland's version of Shaftesbury's *An Inquiry concerning Virtue*, although repudiated by Shaftesbury in a letter written ten years afterwards,[191] enjoyed his warm approval at the time.[192] It was in 1699, too, that Toland began to share lodgings with another of Shaftesbury's literary *protégés*, William Stephens, whose republican sermon before the Commons on 30 January 1700 (printed by Anne Baldwin) caused a minor sensation.[193] 'Many paragraphs' of Stephens's sermon were 'said to be given him by [John] Trenchard'.[194] Only later did Shaftesbury learn, painfully, of Stephens's capacity for 'forgery and abuse',[195] a trait which must have given Stephens and Toland ample scope for conversation—and perhaps gave them scope for literary cooperation, too.

In 1700 Shaftesbury, who had many friends among the group he thought of as 'the Holland Whig party', helped to organise the distribution of Harrington's *Works* in Holland.[196] In 1701, when the Earl

[189] Dedication; P.R.O., 30/24/30, fos. 135–6 (with which compare Toland, *An Account of the Courts of Prussia and Hanover* (1705), pp. 38–41; see also Toland, *A Philippick Oration*, p. 23).

[190] Heinemann (*Notes and Queries*, 25 September 1943) suggested that Shaftesbury was the sole or at least the principal author, but neither the internal nor the external evidence seems to me to support his view. Desmaizeaux, *Toland*, i. lxxxvii; *Letters from .... Shaftesbury to Robert Molesworth*, p. xxi; *The Art of Governing by Partys*, p. 69; 'Bibliotheca Collinsiana' (library of King's College, Cambridge: photocopy in the Bodleian, MS. Facs. c. 43), p. 468. Shaftesbury's clandestine support of pamphlets was probably widespread (Rand, *Shaftesbury*, p. 307; Forster, *Letters*, pp. 121, 188), but he was often accused of writing tracts for which he was not in fact responsible (B.L., Add. MS. 4288 (Desmaizeaux papers), fo. 95ᵛ). *The Danger of Mercenary Parliaments* is sometimes dated earlier than 1698; but, in the form in which we have it, it can be seen from internal evidence to have been an election manifesto of that year; see also *The True Englishman's Choice of Parliament-Men* (1698).

[191] In the letter Shaftesbury gave expression to his revulsion from the philosophy (although not from the personality) of Locke—an indication of the profound change in Shaftesbury's views since 1699.

[192] It was in Toland's version that Shaftesbury encouraged Desmaizeaux—and probably continued to encourage him at least until 1705—to translate it into French: P.R.O., 30/24/21, no. 227, 30/24/27, 17, i–iv, 30/24/30, fos. 383&ᵛ; B.L., Add. MS. 4288, fos. 95–9. The fourth Earl claimed that his father had so resented the publication of Toland's version that he had bought up all the available copies in circulation. In reality, Toland's version was being advertised by John Darby jr. as late as 1706 (*State Tracts*, iii; see also the advertisements in the 1704 edition of Sidney's *Discourses*)—although it is possible that Shaftesbury was uneasy about this publicity: see P.R.O., 30/24/27/7, p. 16.

[193] Jacob, *The Newtonians and the English Revolution*, p. 24; *Reflections upon Mr. Stephens's Sermon* (n.d.: 1700?), esp. p. 33. For Stephens's connection with Toland and Darby see also *Regicides no Saints*, p. 134, and Snyder, *Marlborough–Godolphin Correspondence*, ii. 1165. For evidence of support for Anne Baldwin in Parliament, see *Journals of the House of Commons*, 20 December 1699, 17–24 January, 6, 12 February, 1 March 1700. For Shaftesbury and Stephens see also Rand, *Shaftesbury*, p. 314.

[194] Manuscript annotation (evidently written in 1700) in a copy of the sermon in the Cambridge University Library, classmark 6. 21. 11³.

[195] P.R.O., 30/24/22/2, fo. 178, 30/24/22/3, pp. 57–8.

[196] P.R.O., 30/24/45, part i, fo. 42; Forster, *Letters*, pp. 71, 120 (and see *ibid.*, p. 88).

of Macclesfield was sent on a delicate mission to Hanover to guarantee the Protestant succession, Toland somehow managed to obtain a place on the party, despite Macclesfield's sensible opposition. For years afterwards Toland was to boast of the leading role he had played on the embassy. In reality, his preposterous antics must have come close to ruining it.[197] Leibniz thought that Toland might have been sent as a spy. If so, Harley may have been involved in Toland's appointment.[198] Yet it was Shaftesbury who felt obliged to apologise to Macclesfield for Toland's diplomatic improprieties.[199] Shaftesbury kept a close watch on Toland's behaviour during the embassy, and no doubt approved of the presentation of Toland's pamphlet in defence of the Act of Settlement, *Anglia Libera*, to the Hanoverian court. The work was dedicated, as we have seen, to Shaftesbury's friend the Duke of Newcastle, who shared Shaftesbury's keen desire to establish close links with the Hanoverian family.[200] After Toland's return from Hanover, Shaftesbury and Toland collaborated once more to produce *Paradoxes of State* (1702).[201]

The intimacy of Toland's friendship with Shaftesbury, and the extent of their literary cooperation, make it inconceivable that Toland would have edited Ludlow's *Memoirs* without Shaftesbury's approval. How strongly Shaftesbury approved of the venture, and how closely he involved himself in it, we cannot say, but there is one piece of evidence to suggest that he may have played a direct role in the enterprise. Shaftesbury longed to 'vindicate' his grandfather's reputation by commissioning a biography, and John Locke began work on it.[202] It was probably in this connection that Locke, at some time after the publication of the first two volumes of the *Memoirs*, gained access to

[197] P.R.O., 30/24/45, part i, fos. 41, 52–3, 60, 73&ᵛ, 90ᵛ, 304; Hertfordshire Record Office, D/EP/F 29 (Diary of Sarah Cowper), pp. 152–3; *Anglia Libera, passim*.; *Vindicius Liberius*, pp. 155–7; *An Account of the Courts of Prussia and Hanover*, pp. 58–9, 63–5, 69: cf. *Poems on Affairs of State* (7 vols., 1963–75), engraving opposite vi (ed. F. H. Ellis), 659.

[198] Klopp, *Correspondence de Leibniz*, ii. 333–4; *Anglia Libera*, pp. 50–1; but cf. *Some Queries which Deserve no Consideration, Answered* (n.d.: 1701?), p. 5.

[199] Forster, *Letters*, pp. 105–6; and see P.R.O., 30/24/21, no. 231.

[200] Klopp, *Correspondence de Leibniz*, ii. 403; Rand, *Shaftesbury*, pp. 318–20, 322–3, 335 (and see p. 279); Kemble, *European State Papers*, p. 377. Given Shaftesbury's friendship with the Electress Sophia and her daughter Sophia Charlotte, and the contacts established in England by their adviser Leibniz, it seems unlikely that Shaftesbury and Leibniz, whose views about the Protestant succession in England and about European diplomacy were so similar, were not in touch by 1701. The only direct evidence we seem to have about their relationship concerns Leibniz's view of Shaftesbury's philosophy: see Leibniz's 'Remarques sur un . . . . "Lettre sur L'Enthusiasme"', in *Recueil des diverses Pièces*, tom. xii (Amsterdam, 1720); P. Riley (ed.), *The Political Writings of Leibniz* (Cambridge, 1972), pp. 192–8.

[201] Forster, *Letters*, pp. 122, 147; 'Bibliotheca Collinsiana', p. 469; Desmaizeaux, *Toland*, i. liv; [E. Curll?], *An Historical Account of . . . . John Toland* (1722), p. 98; Klopp, *Correspondence de Leibniz*, ii. 341–2; advertisement page (evidently of works by Toland) in *Vindicius Liberius*; P.R.O., 30/24/20, no. 68.

[202] Rand, *Shaftesbury*, pp. 345–6; cf. Locke MS. c. 7, fo. 124.

Ludlow's manuscript and copied from it the passages hostile to the
third Earl's grandfather. Locke knew Toland well. He had established
contact with him at least as early as January 1694,[203] and in January
1695 we find Toland acting, in conjunction with James Tyrell, as a
political agent on Locke's behalf.[204] By 1698, however, relations
between Locke and Toland had cooled.[205] The man most likely to
have provided Locke with access to Ludlow's manuscript is Shaftesbury. Similarly, the omission from the *Memoirs* of all the passages in
which Ludlow had criticised the first Earl, although conceivably attri-
butable to veneration for the first Earl's memory among the Calves-
Head group from which the manuscript emerged, can be more simply
explained by the wishes of the grandson.

We have described Shaftesbury as a Roman Whig. The story of
his relationship with Toland shows how close the Roman Whig
and the Calves-Head positions could be to each other in the
last years of the century, and helps to explain why the two groups
were able to cooperate and to overlap during the standing army controversy. Yet beneath their agreement, a fundamental difference of
political style and political belief can be discerned. We have located
the genesis of the publication of Ludlow's *Memoirs* in the aims of the
'Calves-head fraternity'. Now we must examine the influence of the
Roman Whig philosophy on the content of the *Memoirs*.

The programme of Shaftesbury and his fellow Roman Whigs,
although dependent for its success on the wise conduct of the monarch
whose powers the Calves-Head group so mistrusted, was primarily
concerned with the behaviour not of the Crown but of Members of
Parliament. At Westminster, Shaftesbury and his friends hoped,
M.P.s would model themselves on Roman senators. Resisting the
temptations of fear and favour, and rigorously subordinating private
to public interest, they would vigilantly guard the ancient constitution
against the encroachments of prerogative. In their localities, they
would train and lead the county militias. If the militias could be
reformed, and if the administration of the navy could be purged of
corruption, then standing armies, which had destroyed Rome's
liberties and which now threatened England's, would become superfluous. In its pure form, the Roman ideal was as politically impractic-
able as it was militarily anachronistic. If reinforced by the anti-court
prejudices of M.P.s, however, it might make a telling impact.
Ludlow's *Memoirs* assisted the process of reinforcement.

Toland's strategy as editor of the *Memoirs* will perhaps emerge the

---

[203] Locke MS. f. 29 (notebook), p. 14.
[204] Ballard MS. xxxvii, fo. 4, Hinton to Charlett, 31 January 1694–5; see also Jacob,
The Newtonians and the English Revolution, p. 214n.
[205] *The Works of John Locke*, viii. 422, 425–6.

more clearly if we recall the Harringtonian tract of 1681 which Anne Baldwin reprinted in 1698, Henry Nevile's *Plato Redivivus*. Attempting to graft the classical republican ideal on to country Whig prejudices, Nevile had built, in his concluding pages, a remarkable prototype of an incorruptible country gentleman who had resisted the courtly temptations of the Stuarts and of Cromwell alike. On this proto- type Nevile had urged members of the Oxford Parliament to model themselves.[206]

Toland's Ludlow, too, is a prototype. If the 'fanciful Swiss dress' to which Baron referred has been removed, respectable Whig clothes have taken its place. The reference in the preface to volume 1 of the *Memoirs* to 'the vertues of Scipio and Cato', and to Ludlow's endeavours 'to imitate those great examples', gives the Whig clothes Roman trimmings. The Ludlow of the *Memoirs* invites M.P.s to view themselves in a flattering mirror, which highlights their good manners and integrity and which dignifies their opinions and prejudices. The reader who takes any section of the text printed in the present volume, and compares it with the corresponding portion of the *Memoirs*, can watch Toland time after time replacing Ludlow's blunt and at times splenetic wording with polite, measured, almost stately phraseology. The language of the *Memoirs* is language which country Whigs would have been proud to hear themselves deliver in the House of Com- mons.[207] It was, indeed, delivered almost *verbatim* by the country Whig Sir Richard Cocks, whose maiden speech in the Commons in January 1699, an eloquent attack on standing armies, drew heavily on Ludlow's *Memoirs*.[208]

The literary technique which Toland adopted, cumulatively very effective, is for the most part gently deployed. Sometimes, however, the liberties he takes are striking. By inserting clauses and sentences which have no foundation in the manuscript, he gives Ludlow an earnest modesty which has little connection with the personality we meet in 'A Voyce from the Watch Tower' (and still less with the Ludlow of the 1691–3 pamphlets): 'For my own part, if I may be permitted to deliver my opinion'; 'if I may be permitted to deliver my sense'; 'I hope a man in my condition may mention, without incurring the charge of ostentation'.[209] The text of the *Memoirs*

[206] Robbins, *Two Republican Tracts*, pp. 196–8. I suspect that Toland may also have been influenced by Burnet's life of Matthew Hale, published in 1682 and popularised in an abridged form in the 1690s.

[207] Ludlow possessed most of the accoutrements of a gentleman, but Toland adds a few (such as an interest in horse-breeding: Darby, iii. 9–10: Firth, ii. 267). To take another obvious—although by itself relatively minor—example of Toland's technique: the *Memoirs* normally refer to Ludlow's fellow country gentlemen by their full names and ranks, whereas in the manuscript Ludlow tends to provide only their surnames.

[208] Bodleian Library, MS. Eng. hist. b. 209, fos. 87ᵛ, 93ᵛ.

[209] Darby, ii. 674–5, 816, iii. 118: Firth, ii. 99, 212, 345.

credits Ludlow with a decorous platitude about the function of historical writing which a 1690s backbench M.P. might have been pleased to have committed to his commonplace book, but to which no corresponding passage can be found in Ludlow's manuscript:

> As the memory of those men whose lives have been remarkable for great and generous actions, ought to be transmitted to posterity with the praises they have deserved, that others may be excited to the imitation of their virtues: 'tis as just that the names of those who have rendered themselves detestable by the baseness of their crimes, should be recorded, that men may be deterred from treading in their steps, lest they draw upon themselves the same infamy.[210]

It was to the 'imitation' of Ludlow's 'virtues' that Toland wished M.P.s to be 'excited'. Polite and thoughtful, Ludlow is shown to be politically incorruptible: as resolute in his subordination of private to public interest, and as scornful of the luxury and servility of courtly life, as the hero of *Plato Redivivus*.[211]

Toland does not invent Ludlow's antipathy to courtly corruption. His pure inventions, delightful as they are, are comparatively rare. His usual technique, as we can study it in the revision of the Bodleian manuscript, is to select and to heighten those aspects of Ludlow's personality which he can make attractive to country Whigs, and to remove those which he cannot. We shall consider in due course some of the liberties which Toland may have taken with the missing, pre-1660 section of the manuscript. For the moment it is enough to notice that there are passages in the pre-1660 section of the *Memoirs* where, even without possessing the corresponding section of the manuscript, we can safely assume that he has used the techniques of selection and emphasis familiar from his revision of the Bodleian portion. The villains on the Puritan side on whom Toland concentrates in the pre-1660 *Memoirs* would have been instantly recognisable to country Whigs of the late 1690s: sycophantic politicians who betrayed the revolution which had brought them to power (Cromwell's courtiers in the 1650s, junto Whigs in the 1690s), embezzling courtiers and office-holders, janizaries, corrupt lawyers, excise-men, electoral managers, place-seeking clergymen who flattered despots.[212]

The Ludlow who wore country Whig clothes could make acceptable, as the Ludlow of the manuscript could never have done, the

---

[210] Darby, iii. 235: Firth, ii. 427. Compare Darbishire, *The Early Lives of Milton*, pp. 17, 49; and see Desmaizeaux, *Toland*, i. 15: 'As the fundamental law of a historian is, daring to say whatever is true .... so he ought of course to be a man of no time or country ....' (see also *ibid.*, p. 18, and *A Philippick Oration*, p. vii). Compare too the passage from *The Life of John Milton* qupted below, p. 62.

[211] Cf. Darby, i. 4: Firth, i. 5.

[212] Below, pp. 72–4. See too the passage, inserted by Toland, about the corruption prevalent 'since the late Revolution': Darby, iii. 402: Firth, ii. 332.

historical lessons which the *Memoirs* conveyed. It was difficult for politicians, however suspicious they might be of William III, to criticise openly the deliverer of 1688. They could, however, disguise their criticisms in historical parallels. That is one reason why so much political controversy in the 1690s was conducted as a debate about the 1640s. Toland was fond of historical parallels; and, as Firth observed, the preface to volume 3 of the *Memoirs* hints strongly at one particular parallel.[213] Cromwell's tyranny, made possible in the first place by the Long Parliament's fatal decision to keep up a standing army at the expense of the county militias in 1651, had not merely destroyed the parliament's glorious achievements: by splitting the Puritan cause, it had led men to turn back to the Stuarts. The apostasy of the junto Whigs did not merely threaten the constitutional achievements of 1688–9: it opened the door to the Jacobites. In the last years of William's reign, that fear was widely held.[214]

'Men may learn from the issue of the Cromwellian tyranny', runs the preface to volume 3 of the *Memoirs*, 'that liberty and a standing mercenary army are incompatible.' In case Ludlow's own descriptions of military intervention in politics, as rewritten by Toland, should fail to establish the point, Toland inserts into the text of volume 3 passages about standing armies which have no basis in 'A Voyce from the Watch Tower'. Thus, when New Model cavalry regiments welcome Charles II's return in 1660, Toland gives Ludlow the words:

> And, I confess, it was a strange sight to me, to see the horse that had formerly belonged to our army, now put upon an employment so different from that which they had at first undertaken; especially, when I considered that for the most part they had not been raised out of the meanest of the people, and without distinction, as other armies had been; but that they consisted of such as had engaged themselves from a spirit of liberty in the defence of their rights and religion: but having been corrupted under the tyranny of Cromwel, and kept up as a standing force against the people, they had forgotten their first engagements, and were become as mercenary as other troops are accustomed to be.[215]

And when Toland comes to the disbandment of the New Model by Charles II, he inserts the statement that their dispersal

> was not caused by the King's aversion to a standing army; for the whole course of his life demonstrates the contrary; but being persuaded that they [the New Model] who had already made so many changes in England, were able to bring about another, and to turn

[213] Firth, i. xii–xiii.
[214] Not least by Shaftesbury: e.g. Forster, *Letters*, pp. 76, 110–11.
[215] Darby, iii. 20–1: Firth, ii. 274–5.

him out again with as little consideration as they had brought him in, he thought it most safe and necessary to free himself at once from such dangerous companions.[216]

Of course, points made in volume 3 of the *Memoirs* were not necessarily those which the first two volumes, published a year earlier, had been designed to illustrate. The creation of Ludlow the country Whig, which was Toland's achievement, may not have corresponded exactly to his intention. Ludlow, after all, was a regicide. The first volume of the *Memoirs* contains an uncompromising justification of the execution of Charles I. In William III's reign it still required courage to argue that the regicides had been right, and the evidence does not tell us how courageous the Roman Whigs were prepared to be on this subject between 1697 and 1699. There is no sign that they regarded Charles's execution with enthusiasm. The Calves-Head republicans, on the other hand, the men with whom Ludlow's name had been firmly associated since the appearance of the Ludlow pamphlets of 1691–3, seem to have been convinced that the tyrant's death had been justified. It may be that Toland's aims, when he began work on the *Memoirs*, were exclusively 'Calves-Head', or at any rate as close to the wishes of the Calves-Head group as his friendship with Shaftesbury permitted. It may be that he saw in the emergence of the country party of 1697–9 an opportunity to convert country Whigs to Calves-Head republicanism, and that he gave Ludlow his country Whig features in order to sweeten the bait. It may be that he wanted to show that no honourable, incorruptible country gentleman of the Puritan Revolution could have failed to support the execution of the King, or to realise that liberty was incompatible with the rule of a single person.

Yet if those were his aims, the outcome was different. Jacques Bernard told Desmaizeaux in 1703 that the popularity of the *Memoirs* had at first seemed to him evidence of the existence of widespread republican feeling in England, and admitted that he had been wrong.[217] Regicide was the theme of the *Memoirs* which Tory propagandists found it convenient to emphasise, but it was not necessarily the theme which most interested those who derived instruction from them. It was plainly not the theme which most interested Sir Richard Cocks—devout, soul-searching, interested in the political lessons of history, loyal to the institutions of church and state yet critical of their abuses—to whom the *Memoirs* seemed of such pressing political relevance in the late 1690s.[218] And it is unlikely to have been the theme

[216] Darby, iii. 94: Firth, ii. 326.
[217] B.L., Add. MS. 4289 (Desmaizeaux papers), fo. 130ᵛ.
[218] Above, p. 47; below, p. 73.

which most interested the numerous country gentlemen who bought elegant editions of the *Memoirs* for their libraries in the eighteenth century, or which aroused the admiration displayed for the *Memoirs* by the elder Pitt.[219]

Perhaps the country Whig clothes with which Toland adorned the Ludlow of the *Memoirs*—so much more respectable than the Calves-Head garments worn by the Ludlow of the 1691–3 pamphlets—proved more alluring than Toland anticipated. Far from converting country Whigs to republicanism, Toland helped to adapt republicanism to country Whig ends. The Calves-Head message of the *Memoirs* proved detachable. Why that was so it is hard to say. Perhaps we have been misled by the Tory propaganda of the 1690s into exaggerating the embarrassment suffered by the Whig cause from the memory of 1649. William III, after all, was not Charles I. Perhaps the Roman Whigs themselves, whatever they thought about the execution of Charles I, helped to remove its political sting by their willingness to interpret seventeenth-century English history in classical terms.[220] At all events, it is clear that the *Memoirs* made their impact not as an incitement to republicanism but as a country party manifesto, which was to take its place, with the other works in the Darby–Toland series, in the aristocratic constitutionalist tradition of the eighteenth century.

In the creation of Ludlow the country Whig, however, one problem remained: religion. To provide occasional biblical references, as Toland did in the *Memoirs*, was in keeping with the proprieties of Whig publications in the late 1690s.[221] It would have been quite a different matter to reproduce from 'A Voyce from the Watch Tower' passages which, by the end of the seventeenth century, would have seemed dangerously seditious cant. The retention of the spiritual dimension of the manuscript would have wrecked the *Memoirs'* chances of political success. Toland, in any case, would have been glad to discard it. Ludlow's theology had placed providence in the centre of the political stage: Toland's banished it to the wings. Toland, whose career had been launched by dissenters, had broken with them by the mid-1690s, and he was never a man to leave a feeding hand unbitten. Toland's own views, however, were probably of secondary importance. The contrast between the Puritan Ludlow whom we meet in 'A Voyce from the Watch Tower', and the Whig Ludlow whom we meet in the *Memoirs*, is a powerful reminder of the changes in belief and feeling

[219] Robbins, *The Eighteenth-Century Commonwealthsman*, p. 274.
[220] In the American colonies, in particular, the classical aura in which the execution of Charles I was placed may have dignified the event and reduced its horror. Colbourn, *The Lamp of Experience*, has interesting information about the reception of Ludlow's *Memoirs* in eighteenth-century America; see also Bailyn, *The Ideological Origins of the American Revolution*, pp. 118n., 140n.
[221] See e.g. the title-page of *King Charles I no such Saint* . . . . .

which affected English society in the second half of the seventeenth century.

By 1699, the country alliance against standing armies had begun to crack. A series of events in the last years of William's reign gave country Whigs frightening reminders of the menace of France and of the precariousness of the Protestant succession. Opposition to standing armies appeared untimely, if not irresponsible. The impeachment of Somers brought home to Shaftesbury the need for a united Whig front. Toland now eagerly disowned his republican past and repeatedly assured his readers that the ideals of the 'Commonwealthsmen', far from tending to democracy, were fully compatible with the existing mixed constitution. Nevertheless William's death left Toland in the political cold, and he spent the first two years of Anne's reign abroad. As so often, his political career seemed in ruins. Yet he never sank. In 1704 he bobbed up again, now as a propagandist for Harley, Marlborough and Godolphin. The promise of a salaried post which Toland claimed to have received from Harley never materialised, however, and by the last years of Anne's reign Toland and Harley had finally parted company.[222]

Most of Toland's energies in Anne's reign were devoted to the cultivation of the Hanoverians at Brunswick and Berlin. The two courts seemed powerless to prevent his unsolicited visits. Tactful suggestions that his arrivals might be better postponed fell on deaf ears. Messages intended to forestall him reached their destinations—it is a recurrent pattern in Toland's life—just after he had moved a stage nearer. We find him strutting in the gardens of the royal palaces, passing himself off as the *éminence grise* of the English ministry or as the agent of the Archbishop of York, pressing his charms upon the ladies, and bombarding the Electress Sophia with hints about the qualities which would make him the ideal tutor for the future George II.[223] Sophia and her family took it all with a resigned politeness which Toland interpreted as a mark of high favour. Was he wholly oblivious to the sniggers behind his back? Possibly; for beneath all his airs and ambitions, beneath all his absurd fantasies, there lay an incorrigible, and in its way enchanting, innocence.

There were limits, however, to the protection which innocence could provide. In 1708 Toland's association with Berlin was abruptly terminated. For a time the English ambassador, Lord Raby, had enjoyed playing him off against the clergymen on his staff. But when

[222] For their relations see the sources cited above, p. 42, n. 180.

[223] Klopp, *Correspondence de Leibniz*, ii. 118, 333, 365–6, 379; *An Account of the Courts of Prussia and Hanover*, pp. 34–5, 73. Cf. *An Answer to Mr. Toland's Reasons* (1702), p. 3; *The Life of John Sharp*, p. 275. See also Toland's *Letters to Serena*, his *Reasons for addressing His Majesty*, and his *The Funeral Elegy .... of .... Sophia* (1714).

Toland began to interfere in carefully laid plans for the reunification of European Protestantism, Raby had him booted out 'with the threatning of a bastinado'.[224] Still, Toland had fish to fry elsewhere. There was Utrecht, where in 1703 he had been beaten up in the street, possibly by ruffians employed by the Duke of Marlborough.[225] There was Prague, where he obtained from the Irish Franciscans a document attesting his legitimate descent from an ancient and noble Londonderry family.[226] There was Vienna, and there was Holland: from both bases, Toland sought persistently to ingratiate himself with Prince Eugene of Savoy and with Eugene's cultural and literary adviser, Baron Hohendorf.[227]

Toland seems to have remained in England from 1710 until his death in 1722. After the accession of George I, he resumed his attempts to alert the Hanoverian dynasty to his merits. The lifelong champion of frequent elections now discovered overwhelming arguments in favour of septennial parliaments and of standing armies. But it was no use: Baron Bothmer, George I's Hanoverian adviser, on whom Toland had pinned his hopes, would not employ him.[228] Toland took his defeat well. His last years, although marred by poverty and illness, produced some of his most influential, exuberant and eccentric writing. And the great posturer discovered a new posture. No longer a celebrity in London, he professed himself weary of the 'tattling and busy citizens' who infested the metropolitan coffee-houses, and retreated to rural felicity in Surrey. He now preferred 'the innocent amusements of the country', with its 'frugal but salubrious diet', 'the purity of the air', 'the charms of the earth and water', and 'the tranquillity of all my walks, unconfined as my thoughts', to 'all the pomp and delicate entertainments of the court' and to 'all the wealth and splendid luxury of the city'. The preface to one of his last works, *Tetradymus* (1720), was composed 'from under an elm' by Wimbledon Common.[229] He died two years later, leaving behind him a mass of books and manuscripts stuffed into chests and heaped on chairs in

[224] Ballard MS. xxvii, fos. 37ᵛ–38, 41ᵛ, Ayerst to Charlett, 26 November 1707, 31 March 1708 (cf. Desmaizeaux, *Toland*, i. lxii); *H.M.C.R. Portland*, iv. 456, 491, ix. 289–90; Kemble, *European State Papers and Correspondence*, pp. 459–60, 462–3, 466–7.

[225] B.L., Add. MS. 4465, fo. 3; *H.M.C.R. Portland*, vii. 441.

[226] Desmaizeaux, *Toland*, i. v–vi, lxii.

[227] B.L., Add. MS. 4295, fo. 19; Desmaizeaux, *Toland*, i. lxv; *Tetradymus*, p. 194; F. Venturi, *Utopia and Reform in the Enlightenment* (Cambridge, 1971), pp. 60, 65–6; G. Ricuperati, 'Libertismo e deismo a Vienna: Spinoza, Toland e il "Triregno"', *Rivista Storica Italiana*, 1967, pp. 628ff.

[228] *State-Anatomy*, pp. 40, 57, 59; Toland, *The Second Part of the State Anatomy* (1717), p. 35; *An Argument proving that the Design of employing and enobling Foreigners* .... (1717), pp. 52ff., 97; *The Life and Errors of John Dunton* (1705), p. 8.

[229] *Tetradymus*, pp. xx, xxii; *Letters to Serena*, pp. 131–2; P.R.O., 30/24/20, no. 105; *Second Part of the State Anatomy*, p. 8. Perhaps Toland drew—consciously or unconsciously—on a reference by Sir William Temple to 'the pleasures of the air, and the earth, and the water' at an earlier rural retreat in Surrey: see Swift's edition of Temple's

a carpenter's shop in Putney.[230] We can only wonder what secrets they contained.

Toland's writings, and many of his actions, testify to his abundant talent for self-advertisement. In England, and still more on the Continent, the vigour and iconoclasm of his prose made his name into a symbol. But beside the blustering Toland there is always the secretive Toland, who moves in a world of surreptitious allegiances and of *incognito* backdoor assignations in furtive alleys. Toland survived because, for all the wildness of his tongue, he knew how to hold it when he needed to. Just as his self-promotion advanced his philosophical reputation, so his capacity for concealment has obscured his political and historiographical importance. In 1705 he wrote of his editions of Harrington, Milton 'and some other authors' that 'in general they greatly contributed to beget in the minds of men, as the effect has shown, an ardent love of liberty, and an extreme aversion to arbitrary power'.[231] The boast was more profoundly warranted than he could have known. The chief publications of the Toland–Darby–Baldwin series of 1698–1700—the works of Sidney, Ludlow, Milton, Nevile and Harrington—were to be among the most central and widely-read texts of eighteenth-century Whig doctrine in England and America,[232] and their influence was not to be confined to the English-speaking world.[233] It was the temporary political alignments of 1697–9, and the inspired editorial enterprise which took advantage of them, which made the texts accessible. Many of them might otherwise have remained in obscurity, or have disappeared from circulation.[234] For better or worse, the Whig intellectual tradition might have been stillborn.

What would Ludlow's response to the rewriting of his manuscript have been? We can provide at least part of the answer. In 1674, when he had temporarily resolved to bring his manuscript to a conclusion, he ended with a note which deserves to be printed in full, with Ludlow's punctuation intact.

> If the Lord please to put a period to my pilgrimage, before I have brought this narrative to its perfection, it's my desier, that my deare wife, if liveing, if not, those of my deare friends, and relations,

---

Letters (2 vols., 1700), i. 59. (For Toland and Temple cf. above, p. 30, and below, p. 58, n. 242.)

[230] B.L., Add. MS. 4295, fos. 41–42^v.

[231] Desmaizeaux, *Toland*, ii. 338–9.

[232] See above, pp. 40, 51n.

[233] Cf. Robert Shackleton, 'Montesquieu and Machiavelli: A Reappraisal', *Comparative Literature Studies*, 1964, at pp. 8–10.

[234] A publisher's note at the beginning of the 1698 reprint of *Plato Redivivus* suggests that the work had previously existed only in manuscript—a ruse which surely would have been risked only if the two editions of 1681 had been forgotten.

into whose hands by providence it shall fall, will take care that if it, or any part of it, bee thought of use unto others, it may not bee made publique, before it hath ben perused, rectifyed, and amended by some one, or more judicious friends, who have a fluent style, and of the same principle with mee, as to civill, and spirituall government, the liberty of men, and Christians, and well acquainted with the transactions of the late times, to whome I give full power to deface what hee, or they conceive to be superfluous, or impertinent, or what they know to bee false, to change and alter what they find misplaced in respect of time, or other circumstances, to adde what they conceive to bee deficient, or may conduce to render it more usefull, and agreable, and to that end to cloth it with a more full, and liquid stile, and to illustrate what is therein asserted with such reasons, similes, examples, and testimonys, as they shall thinke fit. Provided that in the maine, they make it speake noe other then my principle (which as I judge is according to the minde of the Lord) in relation to the gouvernement of church, and state, and Christ's ruleing, yea ruleing alone by his spirit in the hearts of his people, and carrying on his worke in them by his owne weapons, which are spirituall, mighty through his blessing for the beating downe of the strongholds of sin, and Sathan, and bringing into captivity every thought to the obedience of Christ. In testimony heereof I have heereunto set my hand this 27th of November 1674. Edmund Ludlowe.[235]

Between this call from the heart of the ageing Ludlow, and the rural poses of the ageing Toland, lay a chasm of human experience. Perhaps Ludlow would have regarded the style of the *Memoirs* as 'more full, and liquid' than his own. It was his misfortune that the man who rewrote his manuscript, although he may have shared much of Ludlow's 'civill principle', did not subscribe to his 'spirituall' one.

4. THE MISSING MANUSCRIPT

Now that we have considered the character of the Bodleian manuscript and the circumstances in which Ludlow's *Memoirs* were published, we are in a position to address ourselves to a question which students of the Puritan Revolution will obviously wish to ask. If we were to discover the missing sections of the Bodleian manuscript, what would we find in them? As they may conceivably somewhere survive, we cannot speculate about their contents without risking red faces. The risk seems worth taking. We have found reason to doubt whether the post-1677 section would be a particularly inviting or interesting

[235] 'Voyce', immediately prior to p. 1355.

document.[236] But what of the pre-1660 portion, the first four parts of 'A Voyce from the Watch Tower', which would clearly tell us a great deal?

About two things, at least, we can be confident. First, the general character of the pre-1660 section would not differ radically from that of the Bodleian manuscript. The Bodleian manuscript presumably begins where it does, *viz.* on p. 721, because it is on that page—two-fifths of the way down it—that part four of the narrative ends and part five begins, and because the binder found in the opening of part five a convenient point at which to begin a new volume. It is evident from the rest of the Bodleian manuscript that Ludlow's division of his text into parts and chapters, which was effected long after he had completed part five (and which was wisely ignored by Darby and Toland, who presented an uninterrupted text), was a somewhat arbitrary exercise. The divisions, although for the most part sensibly positioned, do not correspond to any significant changes of direction or style. We may take it, then, that both the prose and the preoccupations of the pre-1660 section were similar to those which we find in the Bodleian manuscript.[237] And although we cannot say whether the entire pre-1660 section was in the hand of Ludlow's scribe, it seems unlikely that we shall go far wrong if we assume, when we estimate the length of the pre-1660 section, that it contained approximately the same number of words on an average page as the Bodleian manuscript.

Secondly, there are some passages which we know we would find in the pre-1660 section: the extracts, hostile to the first Earl of Shaftesbury, which John Locke copied. Locke wrote down the page numbers of the manuscript from which the passages were taken, and made very brief notes about some of the intervening material. The first extract copied by Locke, which concerns Anthony Ashley Cooper's role in the Wiltshire election of 1654, was taken from p. 344 of 'A Voyce from the Watch Tower'. The period from 1654 to February 1660 (the date at which part five begins) must thus have been covered by 376 pages. If the pre-1660 section contained roughly the same number of words on a page as the Bodleian manuscript, then the portion of 'A Voyce from the Watch Tower' which covered the events of 1654 to 1660 must have been approximately twice the length of the corresponding section of the *Memoirs*. Locke's notes also suggest that Toland spread the process of abbreviation fairly evenly over the 1654–

---

[236] Above, p. 17.

[237] It is true that (as the reader who consults Appendix A will see) Ludlow gives the title of his manuscript afresh at the beginning of his table of contents for part five (which may be why the binder began a new volume at p. 721). The explanation, however, must be that Ludlow either paused after drawing up the table of contents for part four, or had completed it in a separate bundle of papers.

60 section, and that, whatever liberties Toland may have taken and whatever subjects he may have omitted, he at least followed the main outline of the narrative. Confidence in this view is strengthened by cross-references in the Bodleian manuscript to accounts in the pre-1660 section of two episodes which appear in the *Memoirs*: Ludlow's conversation with Harrison in 1656, and Thomas Venner's rising in 1657.[238]

The years 1654 to 1660, however, were probably those which presented Toland's editorial abilities with their least demanding challenge. When we turn to the pre-1654 section of the *Memoirs*, matters become more complicated. At first sight, Toland seems to have been more generous to Ludlow in his allocation of space in the *Memoirs* before 1654, for the pre-1654 part of the *Memoirs* is about three-fifths as long as the corresponding pages of the manuscript are likely to have been. As we shall see, however, the appearance of liberality may be deceptive.

Let us begin with the long section in the *Memoirs* which describes the peace negotiations with Charles I in 1647. The Ludlow of the *Memoirs* states that he has derived some of his information from an account which 'I have seen in a manuscript written by Sir John Berkeley himself, and left in the hands of a merchant at Geneva'. He does not acknowledge, however, what Firth noted, that the whole passage is based very closely on Sir John Berkeley's account.[239] If Ludlow did use Berkeley's manuscript, he cannot merely have 'seen' it: he must have acquired or copied it. It is not inconceivable that he did so, for Berkeley's manuscript was on the Continent in the 1650s,[240] and there is nothing to prove that it did not remain there when Berkeley returned from exile to England in 1660. None of the references in the Bodleian manuscript to Berkeley's political activities under Charles II suggest that Ludlow was acquainted with Berkeley's manuscript or with the light it threw on Berkeley's personality,[241] but that negative evidence cannot be regarded as conclusive.

Even so, when we remember that Darby printed Berkeley's

---

[238] 'Voyce', pp. 898, 900. For other references in the Bodleian manuscript to events before 1660, see the two passages cited below, pp. 62–3, and: pp. 731 (the Rump's 'engagement'); 741, 790, 967, 1148 (Ludlow's activities in Ireland, and opposition to Cromwell, during the Protectorate); 774 (Solemn League and Covenant); 779 (presbyterian plot of 1651); 795 (December 1648–January 1649); 800, 890 (Christopher Love and the Uxbridge negotiations); 831 (membership of the Rump); 1025, 1104, 1229–30 (Irish massacre of 1641); 1077 (Westminster College); 1135 (Ludlow at the outbreak of the Civil War); 1169 (events of 1659); 1177 (Henry Manning); 1222–3 (James I); 1230 (death of Cromwell); 1251 (Cornet Joyce); 1274 (Robert Overton). See also pp. 1131, 1282.

[239] Firth, i. 153 and n., 157, 168, 182n.

[240] Firth, i. 153n.

[241] 'Voyce', pp. 801, 1237, 1244, 1270, 1408, 1442.

Memoirs in 1699, and when we recall Toland's skill in laying hold of manuscripts, a suspicion is bound to arise in our minds. Might Toland not simply have invented the story that Ludlow had 'seen' a manuscript left with a merchant at Geneva? Might he not have acquired Berkeley's manuscript from another source, inserted the passage which is based on it into Ludlow's *Memoirs*, and then, after the success of Ludlow's *Memoirs*, aimed at another publishing coup by printing Berkeley's? He would have been fully capable of such an exercise, and would greatly have enjoyed it.[242]

Whether or not Toland took the Berkeley material from 'A Voyce from the Watch Tower', it is easy to see what he did with it. The passage in Ludlow's *Memoirs* which is based on Berkeley is an abbreviated and reorganised version of the document published in 1699 as the *Memoirs of Sir John Berkeley*. The process of abbreviation and reorganisation is exactly reminiscent of the rewriting of the Bodleian manuscript.[243] It is the technique we have also observed in the use of Milton's *Eikonoklastes* in the Ludlow pamphlets of the early 1690s, and in Toland's revision of Shaftesbury's *An Inquiry concerning Virtue*.

There are other problems about the sources from which the pre-1660 section of 'A Voyce from the Watch Tower' was compiled. For Berkeley's is not the only document we may suspect Toland of culling for material to insert into Ludlow's *Memoirs*. Firth thought that Ludlow had compiled his narrative with little or no help from manuscript or printed sources. He suggested that even where—as at certain points in the account of the 1650s—Ludlow's information appears to be derived from pamphlet material, Ludlow 'was probably drawing on his reminiscences of past reading, not summarising or quoting books which he had before him'.[244] Even if we did not have the Bodleian manuscript, we would need to regard Firth's tribute to Ludlow's

[242] Compare the use of volume 3 of Ludlow's *Memoirs* and of Holles's *Memoirs* to advertise each other in 1699 (above, pp. 30, 33–4). Did Toland and his friends perhaps acquire the Berkeley manuscript, directly or indirectly, from Sir William Temple, whom they assiduously cultivated in the 1690s? Berkeley had accompanied Temple to the negotiations at Nymeugen in 1675, and one of Berkeley's letters from Nymeugen is printed at the end of a work edited by David Jones and published by Anne Baldwin in 1699, *Letters written by Sir William Temple . . . . to the Earl of Arlington*. At the conclusion of the passage in Ludlow's *Memoirs* which is based on Berkeley, the narrative turns almost immediately to the Vote of No Addresses, in the account of which Toland's hand is probably busily at work.

[243] On only one point do Ludlow's *Memoirs* elaborate on the Berkeley text: they refer (twice) to the letter left 'on the table' by Charles I at his flight from Hampton Court in November 1647 (Darby, i. 216, 221 : Firth, i. 168, 171). The detail had been used in the debate over the 1691–3 Ludlow pamphlets (Hollingworth, *Defence of King Charles I*, p. 29). The relationship between Berkeley's manuscript and Berkeley's *Memoirs* is unknown. It is possible that Berkeley wrote his narrative in Latin, and that a Latin edition was published in 1699: W. T. Lowndes, *The Bibliographer's Manual* (4 vols., 1858–64), i. 161.

[244] Firth, i. lxvi.

memory as excessively generous, for Firth's own footnotes bear ample testimony to the dependence of the *Memoirs* on pamphlet and newspaper sources of the 1650s. Further, the *Memoirs* contain a number of passages which are clearly derived from printed sources of the 1640s. The Nineteen Propositions are reproduced with almost complete accuracy, while other passages of the *Memoirs* include, in amended form, the 'three votes' of 20 May 1642, the Four Bills of 1647, the document handed in to parliament by the army on the morning of Pride's Purge, and passages from the published accounts of the trial of Charles I. There are a number of points, too, at which the narrative is obviously based on parliamentary ordinances, declarations and protestations, including the Grand Remonstrance and the Vote of No Addresses.[245]

To the reader who has studied the rewriting of the Bodleian manuscript, there is no difficulty in explaining the differences between the pre-1660 documents which appear in revised form in the *Memoirs* and the passages in the *Memoirs* which are based on them. Toland's technique, once again, is unmistakable. The passages in the *Memoirs* differ from the originals simply and solely because Toland has rewritten them. The question we have to consider is whether Ludlow had incorporated the originals into 'A Voyce from the Watch Tower', or whether they were inserted into the *Memoirs* by Toland. We cannot provide a decisive answer; but the attempt to provide one will alert us to some of Toland's more ingenious tactics.

Clearly Ludlow can only have reproduced pre-1660 publications if he had them before him as he composed his narrative. That he possessed some pre-1660 documents in exile is clear. The Bodleian manuscript shows that he possessed the 'three votes' of 20 May 1642. It also shows that he had copies of, and borrowed (without acknowledgement) from, Milton's *Defensio* of 1651 and his *Defensio Secunda* of 1654. He quoted extensively, too, from Salmasius's *Defensio Regia* (1649).[246] Some private papers belonging to Ludlow were seized in England

---

[245] Darby, i. 13–14, 22–5, 31–7, 39, 155, 224, 232–3, 236, 271–2, 275ff., 326: Firth, i. 17–18, 24–6, 29–34, 36, 121–2, 174, 179, 182, 210–11, 213ff., 251–2. See also Firth, i. 12n.

[246] 'Voyce', p. 764; and compare 'Voyce', pp. 766–8, 779, 830, with *The Works of John Milton* (18 vols., New York, 1931–8), vii. 326–7, 441–7, viii. 196–8, and Salmasius, *Defensio Regia* (1649), pp. 258–9 (also (e.g.) Husbands, *Exact Collection*, pp. 263ff.; *His Majesty's Reasons against the Pretended Court of Justice* (1649); *Putney Projects* (1647), p. 44; S. L. Wolff, 'Milton's "Advocatum Nescio Quem": Milton, Salmasius, and John Cook', *Modern Language Quarterly*, 1941, pp. 559–600; Sensabaugh, *That Grand Whig Milton*, pp. 14, 19, 80–82, 87–8, 101–3, 133–4). Latin editions of Milton's two 'Defences' were, of course, widely available on the Continent. However, those who know Milton's *Eikonoklastes* and who read the text of the present volume may think it likely that Ludlow also had a copy of *Eikonoklastes*. There seem to me to be clear echoes of *Eikonoklastes* in the account in Ludlow's *Memoirs* of the years 1640–2, but it is hard to say whether the explanation of their presence lies with Ludlow or with Toland.

after the Restoration,[247] but others must have accompanied him into exile or have been smuggled out to him, for the *Memoirs* contain letters (rewritten by Toland) which had been exchanged between Ludlow and the Earl of Clanricarde in 1652, and which even Toland can hardly be suspected of acquiring from any source other than Ludlow. It seems safe to assume that Ludlow also possessed in exile a collection of ephemeral tracts and newspapers of the 1650s. A few of the passages in the *Memoirs* which are derived from such publications present problems to which we shall have to return. Of the rest, however, we may say that although Toland could have laid his hands on the 1650s pamphlet material from sources other than Ludlow's manuscript had he wanted to, there is nothing in the passages in the *Memoirs* which are based on it to suggest either that he would have had any incentive to do so, or that the flow of Ludlow's narrative has been interrupted by editorial interpolations.[248]

Ludlow may, indeed, have had a wealth of documentary evidence from the Puritan Revolution to help him. We have seen that his friends in England sent him numerous publications printed after 1660. Much of it was reproduced in the Bodleian manuscript. Once Ludlow was known to be writing a history, he could easily have been sent pre-1660 printed material as well, and this, too, could obviously have been incorporated into his narrative. On one occasion Ludlow asked his contacts in England to try to secure papers containing speeches delivered by his father in the early stages of the Long Parliament.[249] He may have acquired printed sources from the papers of John Lisle after Lisle's death in 1664, or have borrowed them from Lisle earlier.[250] John Phelps is another exile from whom Ludlow may have acquired documents concerning events before 1660.[251]

On the basis of the evidence we have considered, we might feel justified in assuming that Ludlow had access to all the pre-1660 publications which reappeared in revised form in the *Memoirs*, and that

[247] 'Voyce', p. 897; cf. p. 749.
[248] Compare Firth, i. 264, 268–9, 296, 302, 306, with *A Perfect Diurnal of . . . . the Armies*, 1651–2, pp. 1058, 1189, 1840, 1850, 1879–80; and see Firth, ii. 34n., 45n., 62n., 148n., 172n., 176n., 184n., 228n., and the numerous citations of newspapers in Firth's footnotes to the passages of the *Memoirs* which cover Ludlow's service in Ireland. Ludlow evidently drew on Cromwell's speeches: Firth, i. 334 and n., 350–1, 359, 365, 391–2, 399–400. The Ludlow–Clanricarde letters were published in the newspapers (*Perfect Diurnal*, 1652, pp. 1777–9, has the versions which most closely resemble those in the newspapers), but the dates of the printed versions are different from those given them in the *Memoirs*, and the only plausible explanation of the differences is that Ludlow incorporated his own manuscript copies into 'A Voyce from the Watch Tower'. Cf. Firth, i. 341.
[249] 'Voyce', p. 1333.
[250] 'Voyce', p. 1083.
[251] In 1660 the government was anxious to seize (and *claimed* to have seized) papers in Phelps's possession: *Parliamentary Intelligencer*, 14–21 May 1660. Phelps figures regularly in the Bodleian manuscript; see especially p. 924.

he incorporated them into 'A Voyce from the Watch Tower'. That would be a tidy conclusion and, since it would reduce the area in which we could suspect Toland of editorial intervention, a reassuring one. Further investigation, alas, renders it untenable.

All but one of the pre-Restoration documents which we have shown Ludlow to have almost certainly possessed were written after the execution of Charles I, and most of them were written after 1650. It was in December 1650 that Ludlow left England to take up his appointment as a parliamentary commissioner to Ireland. Newspapers and pamphlets were regularly shipped over to Ireland, and a possibility we must consider is that Ludlow began to collect such documents after his arrival there. The vivid account in the *Memoirs* of his military exploits in Ireland suggests that he may have begun, while there, to keep some sort of diary or record. Perhaps—we can only speculate—he even began work on a first version of 'A Voyce from the Watch Tower'. In the course of the 1650s, the *Memoirs* acquire markedly greater coherence and control, an improvement which becomes readily explicable if Ludlow did compile an autobiographical or historical record in Ireland. Here, too, may lie the explanation of the disproportionate space given in the *Memoirs* to relatively insignificant events in Ireland in the 1640s, about which Ludlow could have learned from men who had witnessed them.[252] The reader of part five may suspect that Ludlow kept a record of some kind in the months preceding his flight in 1660. The *Memoirs* give the impression that during the 1650s—particularly, perhaps, during his exclusion from power after 1653—Ludlow became increasingly anxious to discover backstage information about English politics. To that end he evidently sounded a number of men who included Richard Salwey, William Allen, John Vernon, Thomas Harrison and Hugh Peter.[253] Either in or after the 1650s his information about Interregnum politics was probably supplemented by knowledge gleaned from Nicholas Love, William Cawley and Algernon Sidney.[254]

Before 1650, the Ludlow whom we meet in the *Memoirs* seems, for the most part, a much less inquisitive man. If we look only at the autobiographical passages of the pre-1650 part of the *Memoirs*, we find, it is true, a vigour and an immediacy which, however much they may owe to Toland's rewriting, must have sprung initially from the manuscript. By contrast, the accounts of public events before 1650

[252] Firth, i. 22–3 (cf. *ibid.*, i. 191). For Ludlow's Irish sources, cf. *ibid.*, i. 127, 129, 261–2, 341. Perhaps we should also allow something for Toland's interest in Ireland.
[253] Firth, i. 344, 347, 351–2, 354, 356, 358, 380, 406, ii. 5–9. Sir Peter Wentworth and Sir William Masham may also have given Ludlow information incorporated into his manuscript: see Firth, i. 352–3, 372, 380, 413–14, ii. 139.
[254] Firth, i. 134, 357, ii. 83, 118, 299, 337, 343, 347; cf. 'Voyce', pp. 895, 902.

in which Ludlow was not directly involved are limp and confused. They draw heavily on published documents, but they rarely embellish them with telling detail. How is the contrast to be explained? There is one possible explanation which becomes increasingly persuasive the farther we explore. It is that the section of 'A Voyce from the Watch Tower' which covered events prior to Ludlow's arrival in Ireland in 1650 was predominantly an autobiographical document; that the accounts which it contained of public affairs in and before the 1640s were even feebler than the corresponding accounts in the *Memoirs*; and that the balance between autobiography and history achieved in the *Memoirs* was attained by editorial tactics similar to those which we have already found cause to suspect Toland of employing in the passages based on the recollections of Sir John Berkeley.

In *The Life of John Milton*,[255] Toland resolved

> not to be too minute in relating the ordinary circumstances of his life, and which are common to him with all other men. Writings of this nature should in my opinion be designed to recommend virtue, and to expose vice; or to illustrate history, and to preserve the memory of extraordinary things. That a man, for example, was sick at such a time, or well at another, should never be mentioned; except in the causes or effects, cure or continuance, there happens something remarkable, and for the benefit of mankind to know.

The Puritan conception of autobiography as a witness to the patterns of providence had no appeal to Toland. In the Bodleian manuscript, Ludlow dwells at length on the significance of a childhood dream, and later refers to a passage in the pre-1660 section of his manuscript in which he has described the circumstances of his marriage.[256] These episodes are omitted from the *Memoirs*, where Toland adheres firmly to the policy adopted in *The Life of John Milton*. The frequent but brief references to Ludlow's father which Toland permits to appear in the *Memoirs* probably point to another theme on which Ludlow had dwelled at length in the manuscript.[257]

If 'A Voyce from the Watch Tower' is likely to have contained much information about Ludlow's youth which is omitted from the *Memoirs*, there is an equal likelihood that the earlier part of the political narrative in the manuscript was much thinner than the *Memoirs* might lead us to suppose. There are two passages in the Bodleian manuscript, written in the 1660s, which lend weight to this suggestion. Together they lead us to doubt whether, when Ludlow came to write

[255] pp. 6–7.
[256] 'Voyce', pp. 741–2, 1176–7.
[257] Firth, i. 56, 62, 65, 131, 145, 435. Cf. 'Voyce', p. 1077.

about the origins and course of the Civil War, his memory was strong enough to enable him to compose a narrative comparable to the account (in itself unsatisfactory enough) in the *Memoirs*. The first passage comes when Ludlow unexpectedly embarks on a *résumé* of those events of Charles I's reign which he believed to have justified the King's execution. The account contains many echoes of the early pages of the *Memoirs*, and (we may suppose) of the early section of 'A Voyce from the Watch Tower'. Compared with the early pages of the *Memoirs*, however, it is curiously patchy and disorganised.[258]

The second passage is to be found in Ludlow's account of the occasion in 1663 when, at a feast given for the exiles by the Senators of Bern, he was invited by his hosts to explain the collapse of the Commonwealth in 1660. He replied with a narrative of the events of 1640 to 1660 which is reproduced in 'A Voyce from the Watch Tower'. His account is chaotic.[259] In the version of the speech given in the *Memoirs*, Toland reduces the confusion by inserting passages which provide information essential to an understanding of Ludlow's narrative and which give it a semblance of coherence. Toland also invents for Ludlow the face-saving remark that he had delivered his account to the Senators 'with all the brevity I could', and inserts the observation, which likewise has no basis in the manuscript, that

> though the brevity of this account would not admit of that clearness and perspicuity which I could have wished; yet our generous friends were not only willing to forgive the imperfections, but gave me thanks for the information they said I had given them of their affairs, expressing themselves deeply sensible of the troubles that had befallen us and the honest interest by so base a treachery.[260]

We shall now see how Toland turned to sources other than 'A Voyce from the Watch Tower' to give Ludlow's narrative of the Puritan Revolution more 'clearness and perspicuity' than was to be found in the manuscript.

Although we cannot establish for certain whether the major public documents of the 1640s which appear in revised form in the *Memoirs*— the Nineteen Propositions, the Four Bills, and so on—were available to Toland in Ludlow's manuscript, there is one thing we can say. They were available to him, if he needed them, in one or other (where not in both) of the two standard Whig histories on which radical publicists

[258] 'Voyce', pp. 762ff.

[259] 'Voyce', pp. 986–7. The problem raised by the chaos would not be resolved even if it could be established that Ludlow began to write 'A Voyce from the Watch Tower' before 1660. For if he possessed in exile a clear account of the 1640s which he had drawn up in the 1650s, why did he not make use of it in the two passages in the Bodleian manuscript which we are considering?

[260] Darby, iii. 133–6: Firth, ii. 355–7.

drew so frequently in the 1690s—and an impressive command of which had, indeed, been displayed in the composition of the Ludlow pamphlets of the early 1690s: Rushworth's *Collections* (of which the volumes which would have been most useful to Toland were printed in 1680 and 1692), and Bulstrode Whitelocke's *Memorials* (published in 1682).[261] If the resemblances between Rushworth and Whitelocke on the one hand, and Ludlow's *Memoirs* on the other, extended only to the 'set piece' public documents which appear in revised form in the *Memoirs*, we would not need to pay any attention to them. However weak Ludlow's memory, he could obviously have incorporated the documents into his manuscript if they were in his possession; and although it may seem strange that all of them belong to the 1640s and none of them to the 1650s, there is no *prima facie* reason to suppose that Toland took them from Rushworth and Whitelocke rather than from Ludlow: indeed we have already seen that Ludlow certainly possessed one of them, the 'three votes' of 20 May 1642. There are, however, strong echoes of Rushworth and Whitelocke at points in the *Memoirs* where the text presents not, as in the passages we have considered so far, revised versions of public documents, but a political narrative which appears at first sight to be based on Ludlow's own prose.

The similarities between the narratives of the *Memoirs* and of Whitelocke's *Memorials* are especially striking. Now Whitelocke's narrative, like most seventeenth-century histories of the Puritan Revolution, draws heavily on pamphlets and newspapers. If we allow that the exiled Ludlow could have had access to a mass of printed material from the 1640s, then we can contemplate the possibility that the resemblances between the *Memoirs* and the *Memorials* are all to be explained by the common dependence of Ludlow and Whitelocke on pamphlet and newspaper sources. The explanation strains credulity, for two reasons. First, Ludlow's supply of 1640s printed material would have had to be at least as large as, and probably far larger than, that which he is likely to have possessed for the 1650s. If it was, then it is curious that his account of the politics of the 1640s, as rewritten by Toland, is frequently so feeble. Secondly, we would be crediting Ludlow and Whitelocke not merely with dependence on the same sources but with an extraordinary propensity to select the same passages from them. Fortunately we do not need to weigh the claims of coincidence, for there are two occasions on which the explanation breaks down.

---

[261] The only exceptions were the published accounts of the trial of Charles I, which were in any case widely available in the 1690s. For the sole original contribution of the *Memoirs* to the evidence concerning the trial, see C. V. Wedgwood, *The Trial of Charles I* (1964), pp. 159, 238.

Heavily dependent as Whitelocke is on tracts and newspapers, he often rewrites or summarises material to be found in them, or provides information which is not to be found in them. The two occasions which we are to consider, the first concerning 1644 and the second concerning 1651, exemplify Whitelocke's ability to break free of his printed sources. The first is a passage in Whitelocke's *Memorials* about the conversion of Royalists to the parliamentary cause early in 1644:

> Sir Edward Deering came from Oxford into the Parliament; and upon his examination said, that since the Cessation in Ireland, and seeing so many papists and Irish rebels in the King's army, and the Anti-Parliament set up at Oxford, and the King's counsels wholly governed by the popish party, his conscience would not permit him to stay longer with them, but he came to throw himself upon the mercy of the Parliament, and according to their Declaration, to compound for his Delinquency. To which he was admitted, and order given for all others that would come in after him, who was the first.

The account does not correspond to material in any tracts or newspapers which describe Dering's change of sides. The words are Whitelocke's own. So is the sentence on a similar subject which we find a page later:

> The Earl of Westmorland, and divers others delinquents came in to the Parliament, desiring the benefit of the Declaration of both Kingdoms for composition.

We turn to the description of these episodes in Ludlow's *Memoirs*:

> Sir Edward Deering came from the King's quarters at Oxford, and surrendered himself at Westminster; where being examined in the House of Commons, he said, that since the Cessation made with the rebels in Ireland, seeing so many papists and Irish in the King's army, and his councils wholly governed by them, his conscience would not permit him to remain any longer with the King, and therefore he was come to throw himself upon the mercy of the Parliament, and in conformity to their Declaration, to compound for his delinquency. Accordingly he was admitted to composition, and an order made to proceed in like manner towards such as should come in after him. Whereupon the Earl of Westmorland, and divers others, came in to the Parliament, and desired the benefit of their Declaration for composition.

Obviously Toland took the passage not from Ludlow's manuscript but from Whitelocke's *Memorials*.[262]

[262] Whitelocke, *Memorials of the English Affairs* (1682), pp. 77–8; Darby, i. 106–7:

Toland clearly turned to Whitelocke, too, when preparing the account in the *Memoirs* of the Worcester campaign of 1651. In that account, as frequently happens in the descriptions in the *Memoirs* of battles in which Ludlow had not fought, the resemblances between the *Memoirs* and the *Memorials* are very strong. Almost all of Whitelocke's narrative of the campaign is taken from newspapers; but when Whitelocke comes to enumerate the Scottish prisoners taken at Worcester, he departs from the newspapers and provides his own mathematics: 'Prisoners taken, three English Earls, seven Scotch Lords, of .... officers about 640'. At exactly the same point in the story, Ludlow's *Memoirs* depart from the newspaper material also reproduced by Whitelocke, and inform us that among the prisoners were 'three English Earls, seven Scots Lords, and above six hundred officers'.[263]

In neither of these instances had Toland any discernible ideological reason for turning to Whitelocke. His aim must simply have been to flesh out and to give shape to Ludlow's narrative. How extensively Toland used the tactic it seems impossible to say. There are passages in the *Memoirs* where the political narrative of Charles I's reign has an idiosyncratic flavour which suggests that Toland was working exclusively from Ludlow's manuscript. There are others where political narrative and autobiography are so closely woven into each other that 'A Voyce from the Watch Tower' again seems Toland's only plausible source. Again, relatively little of the material in the *Memoirs* which is derived from pamphlets and newspapers of the 1650s was available to Toland in Whitelocke, Rushworth, or any other text published after 1660; the passage concerning the battle of Worcester is one of the exceptions. In the 1640s, however, the echoes of Rushworth and Whitelocke in the *Memoirs* are frequent. It seems most unlikely that the two instances when Toland can be shown to have plagiarised Whitelocke are the only two when he did so. Whitelocke and Rushworth, in any case, are probably not the only printed sources to which Toland turned for aid, any more than they were the only printed sources on which the Ludlow pamphlets of 1691–3 had drawn. It seems likely, for example, that the frequent references in the *Memoirs* to the letters of Charles I which were seized at Naseby[264] were inserted by Toland, who printed the letters from *The King's Cabinet Opened* at the back of volume 3 of the *Memoirs*. At all events, when we work through the accounts in the pre-1660 section of the *Memoirs* of military and political events in which Ludlow was not involved, we are clearly inspecting

Firth, i. 85–6. Whitelocke seems to have made a little use, but did not make much, of Dering's *Declaration* of 1644.

[263] Whitelocke, *Memorials*, p. 484; Darby, i. 364: Firth, i. 281.

[264] Darby, i. 67, 153–6, 186, 267: Firth, i. 56, 121–3, 145–6, 207.

a text which derives from more than one source. And once we have seen the lengths to which Toland was prepared to go in order to produce a fluent narrative, we are bound to suspect that some of the 'set piece' public documents of the 1640s which appear in the *Memoirs* were taken from sources other than 'A Voyce from the Watch Tower'.

In one sense, it might be argued, Toland's insertion of printed material into the *Memoirs* does not matter very much. The passages in the *Memoirs* which reproduce information available in documents printed during Charles I's reign are the sections least valuable to a historian. It is in the autobiographical passages, which describe Ludlow's military and political activities, that the chief value of the *Memoirs* as a source for the Puritan Revolution has always lain, and it is there, even when we allow for Toland's rewriting, that it still lies.

As far as it goes, this argument is correct. Unfortunately, Toland may not have confined his raids on Whitelocke's *Memorials* to occasions when he needed to flesh out Ludlow's narrative. At this point, however, the attempt to distinguish between the contributions of Ludlow, Whitelocke and Toland becomes beset by an intriguing, but at moments an acute, complication.

Reference has been made to a coordinated literary campaign against the government in the 1660s, to which Ludlow, Sidney, Bethel and Nevile should probably be regarded as among the leading contributors.[265] There may have been other contributors, too. In 1660 Whitelocke moved to Coleman Street,[266] one of the chief centres of the dissenting community with which the exiled Ludlow remained in close touch. Whitelocke's *Memorials*, published posthumously in 1682, were based on manuscript 'Annals' which he appears to have drawn together in the decade between the Restoration and his death in 1670. During that period Whitelocke's son James visited Ludlow in Switzerland, and it was James who later tried to obtain the papers of Ludlow's father which Ludlow wanted to use in 'A Voyce from the Watch Tower'.[267] Was material by Bulstrode Whitelocke smuggled out to Ludlow? It is unlikely to have been smuggled out in bulk. Had it been, Ludlow would surely have been better informed about the 1640s than he evidently was. It would therefore be unpersuasive to suggest that the passages in Ludlow's *Memoirs* which we have already seen to bear strong resemblances to Whitelocke's *Memorials* had passed first from Whitelocke to Ludlow and then from

[265] Above, p. 15–16.
[266] Ruth Spalding, *The Improbable Puritan* (1975), p. 229.
[267] 'Voyce', pp. 1180–1, 1333.

Ludlow's manuscript to Toland. In any case, the skill with which Whig publicists of the 1690s habitually wove material from White-locke into their writings makes the suggestion superfluous. That Ludlow received some material from Whitelocke, however, seems distinctly possible.

The possibility can be best explored by a consideration of the famous passage in Ludlow's *Memoirs* which lauds the glorious achievements of the Long Parliament and laments its forcible dissolution by Cromwell in April 1653. Here we must distinguish between the narrative of Cromwell's coup and the comments which are passed on it. The narrative bears many similarities to the description of the dissolution recorded by Algernon Sidney, from whom either Ludlow or Toland seems likely to have borrowed a number of details.[268] It is in the comments on the dissolution that the resemblances between the *Memoirs* and Whitelocke's *Memorials* become more suggestive. Both documents recall the accusations of corruption, self-seeking and delay brought by Cromwell and the army officers against the Rump before the dissolution. Whitelocke then relates that 'with these and many others the like censures they endeavoured to calumniate the Parliament': Ludlow's *Memoirs* tell us that Cromwell reproached the Rump with 'these and other calumnies'. Whitelocke says that the Long Parliament was dissolved 'having subdued all their enemies': Ludlow's *Memoirs* state that the parliament was dissolved 'having subdued their enemies'. Whitelocke refers to 'this great parliament, which had done so great things': Ludlow's *Memoirs* praise 'this parliament that had performed such great things'. The *Memorials* and the *Memoirs* resemble each other, too, in their accounts of the naval preparations and achievements of the Rump's last months; and they agree in blaming Cromwell's ambition for the expulsion of the M.P.s, who, in Whitelocke's words, were 'ruined by their servants'.[269]

The explanation of the similarities which immediately suggests itself is that Toland has once more simply plagiarised Whitelocke. Certainly it seems unlikely that Toland did not have Whitelocke's *Memorials* beside him when he drew up the passage in Ludlow's *Memoirs* which concerns the dissolution of the Rump. Yet there is a passage in the Bodleian manuscript which shows that in the 1660s Ludlow himself entertained sentiments about the expulsion of the parliament, and used words with which to lament it, very similar to some of those to be found both in the *Memoirs* and in the *Memorials*:

---

[268] W. C. Abbott, *Writings and Speeches of Oliver Cromwell* (4 vols., Cambridge, Mass., 1937–47), ii. 641–2. Ludlow was also able to draw (apparently) on a description of the dissolution given him by Harrison in 1656, and (certainly) on the account delivered by Harrison in 1660: Firth, i. 354n., ii. 6.

[269] Darby, ii. 446–58: Firth, i. 343–55; Whitelocke, *Memorials*, pp. 526–9.

so unhappy were they, when by the blessing of the Lord on their councells and forces they had subdued the enemy's armyes, and after many rebellions and insurrections reduced all to their intire obedience in the three nations, as also the Low Countryes to a resolution of a full complying with them for the preservation of religion and civill liberty, then were they betrayed by their owne servant Cromwell, who having formed the most parte of the army to his interest, and cousening others of them, by their assistance, together with the interest of the corrupt lawyers and clergy, thrusts the Parlament out of their places, usurpes their authority, and by severall indirect courses endeavours to destroy such as were faithfull to the interest of the Commonwealth, advancing such as would sacrifice their conscience to his lust ....[270]

It seems, then, that if we must allow something for Toland's use of Whitelocke in the comments in the *Memoirs* on the demise of the Rump, we must also be prepared to allow something for the possible collaboration between Whitelocke and Ludlow.

There is, however, one aspect of the treatment in the *Memoirs* of the coup of April 1653 which suggests that Toland is likely to have inserted material of his own in order to distort Ludlow's opinions. Ludlow's admiration for the naval achievements of the Rump, his belief that after 1653 the Long Parliament was the only legitimate authority still in being, and his obsession with Cromwell's 'usurpation' of 1653, are almost as strongly expressed in the Bodleian manuscript as they are in the *Memoirs*.[271] What we do not find in the Bodleian manuscript is the uninhibited adulation of the Long Parliament which the *Memoirs* attribute to Ludlow. From where did the adulation come?

Toland and his fellow radical Whigs saw in the Long Parliament the assembly on which they wished late seventeenth-century parliaments to model themselves. We have seen that Toland almost certainly wrote *A Defence of the Parliament of 1640*. In *Amyntor*, Toland identified himself with those men who 'cannot endure to hear the Members of the Parliament of 40 ... infamously branded'.[272] The title-page of the second of the Ludlow pamphlets of 1691–3 had proclaimed the tract's aim of 'vindicating the conduct of the Parliament which began in November, 1640': the third of the pamphlets was described on its title-page as 'a further Vindication of the Parliament of the 3d of November, 1640'. On the title-page of the *Memoirs*, we are reminded that Ludlow was 'a Member of the Parliament which

[270] 'Voyce', p. 987.
[271] Navy: 'Voyce', p. 1044 (cf. p. 1055); Long Parliament's authority: pp. 780, 791, 816, 831, 874, 919; Cromwell's usurpation: pp. 726, 789–90, 802, 826, 893, 933, 987, 1005–6, 1064, 1079, 1131, 1166, 1241, 1250, 1274, 1300, 1389–90, 1400, 1408, 1448.
[272] *Amyntor*, p. 166. Cf. *A Short History of Standing Armies in England*, p. 2.

began on November 3, 1640'. We should be on our guard, then, when we reach the eulogy of the Long Parliament which follows the account of the dissolution of the Rump in the *Memoirs*. At the climax of the passage, Ludlow is given the words: 'however the malice of their enemies may endeavour to deprive them of the glory which they justly merited, yet it will appear to unprejudiced posterity, that they were a disinterested and impartial Parliament'.[273] References to the judgement of posterity can usually be taken as likely indications of Toland's editorial intervention,[274] and the passage seems more likely to have been invented by Toland than to have been taken from Ludlow's manuscript.

For Ludlow's conduct in 1653, as it is presented in the *Memoirs*, presents a puzzle which is resolved once we allow for the possibility that Toland has distorted Ludlow's opinions. The *Memoirs* pass with curious haste over Ludlow's failure to break with Cromwell in April 1653.[275] The breach came, not in April, but after the dissolution of Barebone's Parliament and the inauguration of the Protectorate. Ludlow's fellow commissioners in Ireland, as their surviving letters show,[276] welcomed the Barebone's experiment, and it is probable, from what we have seen of Ludlow's religious convictions, that he welcomed it too. There are signs, too, even in passages which Toland has allowed to appear in the *Memoirs*, that Ludlow had been dismayed by the Rump's failure to produce a speedy reformation between 1650 and 1653.[277] After 1653 it was natural for Ludlow to feel, as others felt, that the dissolution of the Rump had been a critical moment in Cromwell's apostasy. It was also natural for him to recall with pride the achievements of the regime in which he had played an important part, and to regard the defunct Long Parliament as the sole repository of the good old cause. Ludlow could, however, have entertained all those sentiments without subscribing to the eulogistic view of the Long Parliament which is presented in the *Memoirs*.

We are left, then, with the impression that the account of the dissolution of the Rump in the *Memoirs* is a *pot-pourri* whose ingredients were supplied by Ludlow, Sidney, Whitelocke and Toland. The questions raised by the relationships between these authors lead us to wider questions which might repay investigation. We have seen that either Ludlow or Toland probably turned to Sidney for information about

[273] Darby, i. 453: Firth, i. 349. Cf. the distorting emphasis in the account of Cromwell's speech of January 1655 on the virtues of the Long Parliament: Darby, ii. 510: Firth, i. 399.
[274] Below, p. 73.
[275] Darby, ii. 460-1: Firth, i. 356-7.
[276] Mayer, *Transactions of the Historical Society of Lancashire and Cheshire*, 1860-2.
[277] Darby, i. 329, 430: Firth, i. 254, 333-4.

the dissolution of the Rump. It is equally probable that Sidney's writings provided either Ludlow or Toland with material used in Ludlow's *Memoirs* concerning the Rump's naval achievements, and that either Ludlow or Toland took from Sidney the argument, which was to prove so useful in the standing army controversy and of which so much is made in Ludlow's *Memoirs*, that men who believe in the cause for which they fight are likely to make much better soldiers than will hired mercenaries.[278] Sidney could well have been in touch with Bulstrode Whitelocke after the Restoration;[279] and the whole question of Whitelocke's literary contacts merits fuller consideration. It is distinctly possible, for example, that manuscript material by Whitelocke was seen by Lucy Hutchinson, whose biography of her husband contains what look like a series of echoes of Whitelocke's writings.[280] Whitelocke certainly lent manuscripts to John Rushworth.[281] The circumstances in which Whitelocke's *Memorials* were published also deserve to be considered afresh. Henry Nevile had advance knowledge of their publication, and sought to whet the public's appetite for it.[282]

Of course, the authors whose literary collaboration we are considering included individuals between whom little love had been lost before the Restoration, and who did not always write politely about each other after it. The anti-Puritan reaction after 1660, however, produced some strange alliances among the defeated. In any case, men who entrust manuscripts to circulation are not necessarily in a position to confine their readership.

If Bulstrode Whitelocke would be one obvious focus for a study of the organisation and development of Whig historical writing in the later seventeenth century, Slingsby Bethel would be another. We have seen that the Ludlow pamphlets of the early 1690s are very likely to have owed something to collaboration between Bethel and Milton's nephews Edward and John Phillips. We have also seen that the Bodleian manuscript, like the Ludlow pamphlets, makes unacknowledged use of Milton's political writings of the Interregnum. When

---

[278] Sidney, *Discourses* (1698), pp. 220–2; Darby, i. 10, 309–10, 496: Firth, i. 15–16, 239, 385–6.

[279] Cf. Victoria and Albert Museum, Forster MS. 48. G. 26, Sidney to Whitelocke, 4 March 1660.

[280] Cf. B. Worden, *The Rump Parliament 1648–1653* (Cambridge, 1974), pp. 45–7, 51. See also C. H. Firth (ed.), *Memoirs of the Life of Colonel Hutchinson* (1906), pp. 272–3.

[281] *Dictionary of National Biography*, Rushworth; Whitelocke, *Memorials*, p. 666.

[282] Robbins, *Two Republican Tracts*, p. 148 and n. We might also ask what became of Whitelocke's papers between the publication of the first edition of the *Memorials* in 1682 and the appearance of the second, expanded edition of 1732. Perhaps the papers included the material concerning James Nayler which was published for the first time in the younger Darby's edition of the *State Trials* (1719), ii. 265ff., and which included a speech by Whitelocke. The publishers of Whitelocke's *Memorials of the English Affairs, from the supposed Expedition of Brute to this Island, to the Reign of King James I* (1709) included Edmund Curll, to whom the first biography of Toland is normally attributed.

were Bethel's links with the Milton household forged? If they were established by the 1660s, Ludlow's use of Milton in 'A Voyce from the Watch Tower' becomes easily explicable. In the early 1660s Edward Phillips completed the account of the Interregnum and of the Restoration which appeared in Sir Richard Baker's *Chronicle*.[283] In 1694 Phillips produced the biography of Milton on which Toland was to build in the life published in 1698. Perhaps, in the story of the emergence of Whig historiography, there lies yet another of the seventeenth-century roads which lead us back to Milton.[284]

A consideration of the sources available to Ludlow and to Toland is one way of trying to detect Toland's editorial interventions in the *Memoirs*, but not the only one. We have already noted that, in rewriting the Bodleian manuscript, Toland selected and heightened passages concerning the evils of courtiers and politicians who could be made to resemble the bogeymen of country Whigs in the 1690s. Let us take some instances where we may suppose him to have used the same technique in rewriting the pre-1660 section of 'A Voyce from the Watch Tower'.

It seems unlikely, for example, that Ludlow gave as much emphasis as Toland does to the relatively unimportant episode in 1651 when the Rump expelled the embezzling office-holder Lord Howard of Escrick for accepting bribes. The *Memoirs* relate that

> notwithstanding all the art of counsel learned in the law, who are very skilful at putting a good appearance on a bad cause, and all the friends the Lord Howard could make, so just and equitable a spirit then governed, that the committee having represented the matter to the Parliament as they found it to be, they discharged him from being a member of Parliament, sent him to the Tower, and fined him ten thousand pounds.[285]

---

[283] Phillips worked from Monck's papers; cf. Toland's works on Monck cited above, p. 25. See also W. R. Parker, *Milton. A Biography* (2 vols., Oxford, 1968), ii. 1073. Phillips had a strong reputation for plagiarism. Another historian whose narrative of the Puritan Revolution was written in the mid-1660s is Richard Baxter. In 1662 Baxter moved to Moorfields, where he would have found it difficult to remain ignorant of the political and literary plans laid against the government by the dissenters. One of the surprises of Baxter's narrative arises on a subject about which Ludlow's *Memoirs* agree with him. Arguing (like Ludlow, Whitelocke, Bethel and Sidney) that the political history of the 1650s was profoundly affected by Cromwell's ambition, Baxter claims that Cromwell had called Barebone's Parliament in order to give the radicals enough rope to hang themselves, and so to pave the way for his personal supremacy (*Reliquiae Baxterianae* (1696, ed. M. Sylvester), p. 70). On the text of Baxter's narrative see G. F. Nuttall, 'The Manuscript of Reliquiae Baxterianae', Dr. Williams's Library Occasional Paper no. 1 (1954).

[284] It is interesting to compare Ludlow's movements and affiliations in hiding in 1660 with what is known of Milton's.

[285] Darby, i. 334–6: Firth, i. 258–9.

The reference to the 'just and equitable spirit' which 'then governed' would not have been lost on, and seems likely to have been designed for, country Whigs of the 1690s, who were provided in the *Memoirs* with frequent reminders of the evils of courtly corruption and luxury, of bribery, and of sycophantic courtiers.[286] Another lesson offered them was the long account in the *Memoirs* of the action brought by Henry Nevile against a sheriff who had obstructed Nevile's election to the 1656 parliament. Attempts had been made by the Court 'to take off Mr. Nevil, by compounding the business, but he preferring the advantage of the Commonwealth before his private interest, refused to hearken to any overtures, till the judgement was recorded for an example to posterity'.[287] Sir Richard Cocks, whom we have found quoting Ludlow's *Memoirs* in the Commons against standing armies, noted Nevile's 'example to posterity' in his commonplace book. He also took notes on the schemes described in the *Memoirs* for the redistribution of constituencies in the 1650s,[288] and one wonders whether the issue of electoral corruption and reform, which so concerned Toland and the third Earl of Shaftesbury,[289] figured as prominently in Ludlow's own account of the parliamentary history of the Interregnum as the *Memoirs* suggest.[290] Other preoccupations of Toland and Shaftesbury, such as the need to purge the navy of corruption and the responsibility of experienced backbench M.P.s to alert young members to the dangers of corruption, may also help to explain some of the emphases of the *Memoirs*.[291] And when we remember the broad political strategy behind the *Memoirs*, we might ask whether Toland did not simply invent the remark attributed to Ludlow about Penruddock's rising of 1655:

But certainly it can never be esteemed by a wise man to be worth

[286] Darby, i. 42, 384, ii. 444–5, 512–13, 582, 672: Firth, i. 38, 295–6, 342, 401, ii. 20, 97.

[287] Darby, ii. 600–02: Firth, ii. 35–6. Cf. the incident described on Darby, ii. 559–60: Firth, ii. 3.

[288] Bodleian Library, MS. Eng. hist. b. 209, fos. 90, 93.

[289] Forster, *Letters*, pp. 82, 128; Fowler, *Shaftesbury and Hutcheson*, pp. 9–10; *The Danger of Mercenary Parliaments*.

[290] Darby, ii. 435–6, 497, 615: Firth, i. 384, 386, ii. 48. (We may note, too, the tribute to the ideal of the independent country gentleman displayed by the transformation of the observation in the Bodleian manuscript ('Voyce', p. 932) that Sir Henry Vane had been elected to the Long Parliament 'without his seeking' into the statement in the *Memoirs* that Vane had been elected 'without the least application on his part to that end'.) The Ludlow of the *Memoirs*, like Toland and Shaftesbury, shows considerable interest in the redistribution of seats, and none in the franchise. Can 'levelling Ludlow' have omitted to mention the franchise in his manuscript? Again, perhaps we should allow something for Toland's elaboration or invention in the interest in neo-Harringtonian ideas attributed to Ludlow in the *Memoirs* (Darby, ii. 628–9, 674–5, 766–7: Firth, ii. 59–60, 99, 172).

[291] Forster, *Letters*, pp. 99, 162; Darby, ii. 439, 465–71, 500, 625: Firth, i. 337, 361–5, 391, ii. 55–6.

the scratch of a finger to remove a single person acting by an arbitrary power, in order to set up another with the same un-limited authority.[292]

The content of volume 3 of the *Memoirs* has been seen to have been influenced by the standing army controversy. The content of the first two volumes seems likely to have been affected by it, too. Toland and his friends, we recall, were anxious to show that reformed, properly trained county militias, led by courageous country gentlemen, would prove amply adequate to meet England's military needs of the 1690s. The qualities which country gentlemen would need are all personified by the Ludlow presented in the *Memoirs*. The picture of Ludlow as the valiant, skilful leader of his county forces, who spurns 'mercenary' military values, is subtly built up by the use of phrases very different from the language we meet in the Bodleian manuscript and, we may assume, equally different from the language of the pre-1660 section of 'A Voyce from the Watch Tower'. In 1642, the Ludlow of the *Memoirs* tells us, 'I thought it my duty, upon consideration of my age and vigorous constitution, as an English-man, and an invitation to that purpose from my father, to enter into the service of my country'.[293] Accordingly, Ludlow and 'many young gentlemen of the Inns of Court' assembled

in order to be instructed together in the use of arms, to render our-selves fit and capable of acting in case there should be occasion to make use of us. To this end we procured a person experienced in military affairs to instruct us in the use of arms; and for some time we frequently met to exercise at the Artillery-Ground in London.

In the early stages of the war, Ludlow's inexperience leads to military setbacks, but he is quick to learn from his mistakes. His bravery, his powers of leadership, his capacity for self-sacrifice and his rapidly acquired military expertise enable him to overcome all obstacles, both in the England of the 1640s and in the Ireland of the 1650s. The pre-face to volume 1 of the *Memoirs* tells us 'how great a progress he made ... in the science of war', and reminds us of 'the military honours he received in a time when rewards were not blindly bestowed'. The text of the *Memoirs*, by illustrating those claims, provides an attractive model for country gentlemen of the 1690s.[294]

[292] Darby, ii. 518: Firth, i. 405.

[293] For Toland's strategic use of the word 'Englishman' later in the *Memoirs*, cf. above, p. 7.

[294] Darby, i. 42ff.: Firth, i. 38ff. Cf. *Persecutio Undecima* (1648), p. 56; Darby, i. 85ff., 111ff., 135ff., 346ff.: Firth, i. 70ff., 89ff., 107ff., 268ff. (and the reference to Ludlow's expenses on Darby, ii. 465: Firth, i. 361). The text also supports the Calves-Head view that Ludlow would have been an ideal commander in Ireland in 1689.

There is another way, too, in which the standing army controversy may have affected the content of the *Memoirs*. We have seen that Toland inserted into volume 3 passages about standing armies which had no basis in the manuscript. Two passages in volume 1 must arouse suspicion on the same score. They concern Cromwell's behaviour after the battle of Worcester in 1651. The *Memoirs* emphatically tell us, in the face of a wealth of contemporary evidence to the contrary, that, after the victory, Cromwell 'dismissed' the county militias 'with anger and contempt'—an accusation repeated *verbatim* in *A Short History of Standing Armies*,[295] the Roman Whig tract of 1698 which drew so heavily on Ludlow's *Memoirs*. Cromwell, the *Memoirs* observe, knew that the militia regiments 'had deserved as much honour as himself and the standing army': nevertheless he had disbanded them, 'well knowing, that a useful and experienced militia was more likely to obstruct than to second him in his ambitious designs'.[296] The passage is reminiscent of the sentence, quoted earlier, which Toland inserted into volume 3 of the *Memoirs* to explain Charles II's decision to disband the New Model.[297] The preface to volume 3 asserts that the Long Parliament's decision to keep up the standing army after Worcester, at the expense of the county militias, had proved fatal to the Commonwealth. It seems a fair guess that in volume 1 Toland had taken editorial liberties to prove the point.[298]

Whenever religion is allowed to raise its head in the *Memoirs*, we must allow for a much fuller treatment in the manuscript. There is a reference in the Bodleian manuscript to a theological discussion in the pre-1660 section of 'A Voyce from the Watch Tower' to which no corresponding passage is to be found in the *Memoirs*,[299] and there must have been many similar passages which Toland excised. There are occasions in the pre-1660 *Memoirs*, too, when Toland's policy of softening Ludlow's spiritual enthusiasms—a policy adopted so efficiently in the revision of the Bodleian manuscript—has clearly been implemented. Thus when we are told that in 1642 the Long Parliament had 'the laws of God, nature and reason, as well as those of the land on their side'; when we read that the reformers in Barebone's Parliament 'manifested a good affection to the publick cause' and sought to 'reduce the clergy to a more evangelical constitution'; when

[295] p. 8.
[296] Darby, i. 365–6, ii. 447: Firth, i. 282, 344. The word 'dismissed' may have been taken from Whitelocke (*Memorials*, p. 484), but Whitelocke does not use the word to criticise Cromwell.
[297] Above, pp. 49–50.
[298] The preface to volume 3 also refers to the tyranny of the Major-Generals, and the treatment of their rule in the text of the *Memoirs* clearly needs to be studied with a critical eye.
[299] 'Voyce', p. 1214.

we learn that the Fifth Monarchists rose in 1657 'expecting extraordinary assistance from heaven'; when we are informed that Ludlow and John Cook (whom we know from the Bodleian manuscript to have been united by intimate spiritual bonds) 'took leave of each other with mutual recommendations to the direction and protection of Almighty God':[300] in these and many other instances Toland's capacity for eschatological euphemism has obviously made its mark. Ludlow's conversations with Cromwell, too, which must have closely resembled Cromwell's other recorded discussions with 'saints', take on a new character when we have met the Ludlow of the manuscript.

Just as there are times when we can detect the impact of Toland's political purposes on the content of the pre-1660 *Memoirs*, so there are occasions when we can recognise, from a comparison of the Bodleian manuscript with the corresponding section of the *Memoirs*, the influence in the pre-1660 section of the *Memoirs* of Toland's techniques of abbreviation and reorganisation. Toland's use of the words 'divers' and 'others' usually signifies that abbreviation has been effected. Thus when the *Memoirs* record a decision taken in 1659 by 'divers persons' at Sir Henry Vane's house 'after mature deliberation', we can be sure that Ludlow would have named the persons (and described the deliberation).[301] Toland often uses the phrases 'about this time' and 'in the meantime' (especially at the beginnings of paragraphs) when he has omitted passages of the manuscript or stitched separate sections together. As Ludlow sometimes uses these phrases himself in the Bodleian manuscript, their presence in the *Memoirs* need not always indicate Toland's intervention, but it can at least alert us to the possibility of it.

If the *Memoirs* need to be read with Toland's tactics in mind, we also need to recall the purposes of Slingsby Bethel. Perhaps we should detect Bethel's influence—probably during the composition of the manuscript in the 1660s, but possibly during the preparation of the *Memoirs* in the 1690s—in the unexpectedly long and sympathetic account of the fate of Sir Henry Slingsby, executed by Cromwell as a royalist plotter.[302] Slingsby was Bethel's uncle, and Bethel had bought some of Slingsby's estates in order to preserve them from sequestration.[303] Bethel's writings, particularly *The World's Mistake in Oliver Cromwell* (1668), repay close comparison with the *Memoirs*.

[300] Darby, i. 43, ii. 463, 471, 604, 709: Firth, i. 38, 359, 365, ii. 38, 127. For Ludlow and Cook see also 'Voyce', pp. 723–4, and compare Firth, i. 246–7, with E. MacLysaght, *Irish Life in the Seventeenth Century* (Oxford, 1950), p. 444.
[301] Darby, ii. 617–18: Firth, ii. 50. Compare the use of the phrase 'mature deliberation' in the passage cited above, p. 6.
[302] Darby, ii. 605–7: Firth, ii. 39–41.
[303] G. Ridsdill Smith, *Without Touch of Dishonour* (Kineton, 1968), pp. 107–8.

In his account of Cromwell's tyranny in *The World's Mistake*, Bethel concentrates, as the *Memoirs* do, on the persecution of Vane, Cony and Lilburne. The treatment of Lilburne's case by the two documents is especially interesting. Both subtly avoid reference to the banishment of Lilburne by the Long Parliament in 1652. The *Memoirs* manage to imply that Cromwell, rather than parliament, was responsible for Lilburne's banishment, and claim that the punishment had been 'contrary to all law': *The World's Mistake* states that Lilburne had been imprisoned 'contrary to law'.[304]

More significant, perhaps, is the similarity between the treatments by the two publications of Cromwell's foreign policy. The diplomacy of the Protectorate, they claim, had disastrously raised the power of France at the expense of Spain, and so had destroyed that balance of power in Europe which it had been England's interest to maintain. Bethel observes that, thanks to the wise neutrality of the Long Parliament,

> the ballance betwixt the two crownes of France and Spain was preserved, untill Cromwell imprudently broke it, not knowing (I suppose) that our interest was changed, but thinking it was still the same, and as popular as it had formerly been, to be against Spain.

Ludlow's *Memoirs* assert that Cromwell's 'confederacy' with France

> was dearly purchased on our part; for by it the balance of the two crowns of Spain and France was destroyed, and a foundation laid for the future greatness of the French, to the unspeakable prejudice of all Europe in general, and of this nation in particular, whose interest it had been to that time to maintain that equality as near as might be.[305]

Ludlow's own account of European diplomacy in the Bodleian manuscript suggests that he would have been incapable of formulating such a view on his own. Bethel probably supplied him with it. If he did so, however, it is likely that Bethel's formulation was recast by Toland. The reference in the passage in the *Memoirs* to France's 'future greatness', the use of the pluperfect tense ('had been to that time to maintain'), and the comment about the consequences of France's rise for all Europe, indicate that the passage as it appears in the *Memoirs* has been composed with an eye firmly on the 1690s, when the destruction of the balance of power by the rise of France was a favourite theme

---

[304] *World's Mistake*, pp. 12–13; Darby, ii. 533: Firth, i. 417–18. Compare also Bethel's 'Brief Narrative' of Richard Cromwell's parliament (Bethel, *The Interest of Princes*, pp. 349–51) with Darby, ii. 626–7: Firth, ii. 57–8.

[305] *World's Mistake* (Rota edition, 1972), preface and pp. 3, 11; Darby, ii. 559: Firth, ii. 2–3. Cf. Bethel, *The Interest of Princes*, pp. 56, 159, 187–8, 321–2.

of Whig writers. It was, indeed, a persistent theme in the writings of Toland himself.[306]

In the concluding pages of the *Memoirs*, Toland appears to take a number of liberties with Ludlow's account of European diplomacy, presumably in order to prove a contemporary political point.[307] In the same way, the description in the *Memoirs* of the enthusiasm with which the Scots received the Commonwealth's proposals for an Act of Union may well have been designed to illustrate Whig views about Anglo-Scottish relations in the late 1690s.[308] On the subject of England's relations with the United Provinces, however, Whigs had to tread more carefully. Hence, perhaps, the gingerly treatment of the Navigation Act in the *Memoirs*.[309] Toland and his friends had no love for William III's Dutch followers, and the *Memoirs* contain a few hits at Dutch politicians; but they do not reveal the bitterness of anti-Dutch—and anti-Orange—sentiment which is to be found in the Bodleian manuscript.

We have selected for discussion some of the ways in which Toland's influence is discernible in the pre-1660 section of the *Memoirs*. Numerous other examples of Toland's editorial intervention will suggest themselves to the reader who has compared the prose of the *Memoirs* with the text of the present volume. Once we have learned to recognise Toland's tactics, we have to ask two obvious questions of any passage in the pre-1660 *Memoirs* which arouses our suspicion. First, were sources other than Ludlow's manuscript available to Toland? Secondly, what advantages could have accrued to Toland's political cause from the appearance of the passage in the *Memoirs*? The first question can rarely be answered quickly. The second brings us up against a problem which will frequently have nagged the reader who has persisted through our discussion of the missing manuscript. We may be able to see why Toland might have chosen to present a passage of the pre-1660 *Memoirs* in a particular way: we do not know the contents of the manuscript he was rewriting. It is often impossible

---

[306] *Anglia Libera*, pp. 148–50, 160, 166; *Reasons for addressing His Majesty*, pp. 6, 13; *The Art of Restoring*, p. 5; *State-Anatomy*, pp. 53–4. Cf. the Darby–Baldwin publication *A Letter to his Most Excellent Majesty King William III* (1699), p. 15. Toland shared much of the dismay expressed by Bethel and in Ludlow's *Memoirs* about the sale of Dunkirk in 1662: see Toland, *Dunkirk or Dover* (1713), p. 16; *The Liberties of England Asserted*, p. 32; *The Second Part of the State Anatomy*, p. 35; cf. *Truth Brought to Light*, p. 4, and above, p. 16, n. 68.

[307] See particularly the surprising, grudging praise of Sir George Downing, for which I can find no basis in the Bodleian manuscript, on Darby, iii. 237: Firth, ii. 428.

[308] Compare Darby, i. 388, 401–2: Firth, i. 298, 310, with *The Argument against a Standing Army Rectified* (1697), p. 28. See also *Memoirs of Denzil Lord Holles*, p. xii.

[309] Darby, i. 345–6: Firth, i. 267. It seems possible that Toland turned to James Heath's *A Chronicle of the Late Intestine War* (1676 edn., pp. 286–7) in drawing up the account in the *Memoirs* of the Anglo-Dutch negotiations of 1651.

to guess—let alone to decide—whether Toland was drawing on Ludlow's manuscript or resorting to pure invention.

There is no point in pretending that, at such moments, the challenge to the reader of the pre-1660 *Memoirs* is less taxing than it is. It would be an equally unfortunate mistake to exaggerate the difficulties. To say, as we are bound to say, that after the emergence of the Bodleian manuscript Ludlow's *Memoirs* can never be seen in the same light again is not to suggest that they can no longer be profitably read at all. Far from it. Toland's role, after all, must be seen in proportion. Emphasis has been laid on the ways in which he is likely to have revised Ludlow's manuscript for political purposes. Yet the insertions and deletions which we discover when we compare the post-1660 *Memoirs* with the Bodleian manuscript, important and revealing as they are, occupied a small proportion of Toland's editorial labours. The adoption of the same tactics in the pre-1660 *Memoirs* can likewise be safely said to have constituted a secondary activity.

For if the *Memoirs* were a tract for the times, they were also a narrative; and a narrative, whatever political needs it may be intended to meet, can meet them only if it can be easily read. Toland's prime task, which he performed admirably, was to produce a fluent, readable and marketable text. For all his embellishments, deletions and distortions, it was Ludlow's narrative which enabled him to produce it. Lament as we must the disappearance of the material in the pre-1660 section of the manuscript which Toland left out, we can cheer ourselves with the reflection that there were limits to the liberties which even he could take with the material which was left in. Once we have absorbed the differences between the Ludlow of the Bodleian manuscript and the Ludlow of the *Memoirs*, we can profitably remind ourselves of the similarities which survive. At the core of the *Memoirs* lies an autobiography which, however radically it has been attenuated and however ruthlessly it has been rewritten, is in essence unmistakably Ludlow's own. The voice from the watch tower has been emasculated, muted and refined; but it survives.

With that consoling thought, we can return to the *Memoirs* afresh. If we shall need to read them in a more critical spirit, that will be no bad thing, for the consistency with which their authenticity has been accepted shows that hitherto we have not read them critically enough. The rhythm, the style and the wording of historical documents, which so often provide the keys to their authors' minds, are rarely given the attention they deserve. The evidence of Toland's editorial tactics which has been presented shows that Ludlow's *Memoirs* are not the only late seventeenth-century text which we shall need to re-examine. The re-examination will take us closer to those aspects of mid-seventeenth-century minds which Toland so successfully sought to hide. It will also beckon us towards a marvellous subject which has been touched on here and tentatively explored by others, but which still awaits its historian: the relationship between Whig politics and Whig ideas in the later seventeenth century.[310]

[310] Since this introduction was written, the picture of late seventeenth-century studies has been changed by the appearance of three works: Henry Horwitz, *Parliament, Policy and Politics in the Reign of William III* (Manchester, 1977); J. P. Kenyon, *Revolution Principles* (Cambridge, 1977); and J. G. A. Pocock (ed.), *Political Works of James Harrington* (Cambridge, 1977). Material which complements my argument can be found in Andrew Sharp, 'The Manuscript Versions of Harrington's *Oceana*', *Historical Journal*, 1973, pp. 227–39, in the manuscript volumes there discussed, and in Douglas Greene, 'The Authenticity of the Earl of Anglesey's *Memoirs*', *Bodleian Library Record*, January 1978, pp. 351–7. There is a new edition of Shaftesbury's *Inquiry concerning Virtue*, edited by David Walford (Manchester, 1977).

EDITORIAL CHOICES AND CONVENTIONS

THE problems of providing a text which is both faithful to Ludlow's original and tolerably easy to read are considerable, and I have had throughout to choose between a variety of unsatisfying compromises. The character of the Bodleian manuscript—as of most manuscripts—can only be fully appreciated in the original, and some nuances are inevitably lost in print.

Numbers in bold print

The numbers inserted into the text in bold print are the page numbers of 'A Voyce from the Watch Tower'. They are placed at the points where the pages concerned begin.

Page numbers of Ludlow's Memoirs

In the headings of the pages of the text printed below, there will normally be found three page numbers. The first (VOYCE) is the number of the page of the manuscript from which the first word on the printed page is reproduced. The second and third page numbers are of the 1698–9 edition of Ludlow's *Memoirs* (DARBY) and of the 1894 edition (FIRTH) respectively. They are provided to help the reader to compare the manuscript with the *Memoirs*. The page numbers of the *Memoirs* refer to the opening words on the page beneath, or to the first passage on that page to which a passage in the *Memoirs* corresponds. Pages which are headed only by a page number of the manuscript are those which contain no passages to which there are corresponding passages in the *Memoirs*. I have deposited in the Bodleian Library a guide (MS. Eng. hist. c. 966) designed to facilitate a comparison between the *Memoirs* and those portions of the Bodleian manuscript which are not reproduced in the present volume.

Italics

Passages in italics are those added or substituted by Ludlow when he revised the scribe's text. I have recorded such corrections only when they tell us something about Ludlow's views, about his sources, or about the process by which the manuscript was composed. I have not recorded them when they involved only changes of grammar or improvements of presentation: in those cases I have merely reproduced the wording in the form in which Ludlow finally left it. Where names are italicised, it can be taken that Ludlow has filled in spaces in the manuscript previously left blank. Sometimes he had left them blank because he had not yet discovered or checked the names concerned: at other times, when the names eventually inserted belonged to his friends or contacts, his initial decision to omit them had evidently sprung from a fear lest his manuscript should be seized by his enemies.

Spelling

The spelling of the manuscript has been retained (except that 'i' has been modernised to 'j', and 'u' to 'v'), but the abbreviations used by Ludlow and his scribe have been extended (except in the case of biblical references, which have been extended only in the table of contents in Appendix A).

Punctuation

Punctuation has proved the most difficult textual problem. To have reproduced the punctuation of the original would have been to present the reader with a dauntingly and at times impenetrably deterrent text. No author who ends paragraphs with semi-colons, as Ludlow does, can expect his punctuation to be faithfully reproduced. Indeed Ludlow, as we have seen (above, p. 55), wished his text to be amended so that it should be made suitable for publication. On the other hand, to impose twentieth-century punctuation on Ludlow's enormous sentences would have been impossible. Even if it had been possible, the exercise would have distorted the rhythms (uneven as they are) of the original. In revising Ludlow's punctuation I have tried to present a text of which I think Ludlow would have approved, and which at the same time is as easy as possible to follow. The result is the least unsatisfactory of the various solutions which have suggested themselves, but I have been able to think of no solution which would merit enthusiasm. I have usually succeeded in ensuring that sentences have main verbs, but there are a few points at which one can only echo the insertion which Carlyle was wont to place in Cromwell's speeches: 'sentence gone'. I have employed more parentheses than Ludlow does, and have used them to try to make some of his longer sentences navigable. Passages thus confined to parentheses are all subordinate or explanatory, but Ludlow would not have regarded any of them as insignificant. As all editors who amend punctuation know, and as one of the most distinguished of them has remarked in the Latham–Matthews edition of Pepys's *Diary* (i. lxii), 'punctuation involves interpretation'. I have endeavoured to preserve as far as possible the pace and the emphases of Ludlow's manuscript. When, as sometimes happens, his punctuation makes his meaning ambiguous, I have preserved the ambiguity.

I have modernised the use of capital letters, although I have left in capital letters passages which in the manuscript are emphasised by large handwriting.

Paragraphs

It is not always possible to identify the points in the manuscript where Ludlow wished new paragraphs to begin. Where he clearly wanted one, I have always provided it. But I have also very frequently broken down long paragraphs into shorter ones.

Dots and square brackets

Especially in the earlier pages and in the table of contents, damp at the top outside corner of the Bodleian manuscript has rendered some passages irretrievable. Where I have provided three dots, there is probably or certainly one missing word which cannot be reclaimed. Four dots indicate that more than one word is missing. I have placed in square brackets readings which I believe to be almost certainly correct, but about which the damp makes complete confidence impossible. In the early pages the missing passages often consist of several words, and the text can consequently be difficult to follow, but thereafter the problem gradually diminishes.

Blanks

Blanks in the printed text correspond to passages left void in the manuscript.

Chapter headings

Ludlow indicates in his table of contents, but not in the main body of the manuscript, the points at which he wants new chapters to begin. Sometimes he makes errors, and the first chapter of part five cannot begin at the precise point Ludlow indicates. I have opened the chapter at the point which I think Ludlow had in mind.

Corrections

In a few instances, all of them trivial, I have silently corrected obvious errors of wording which Ludlow failed to notice when he checked the scribe's text.

Ludlow's sources

The text of part five is likely to be consulted for a variety of purposes, most of them specialist ones, and it would have been difficult (and costly) to provide explanatory footnotes on a useful scale. The reader who is sufficiently interested in one of Ludlow's statements to wish to follow it up in other works will know where to look. I have preferred not to burden the text with editorial apparatus. One subject on which readers may welcome guidance, however, is Ludlow's use of his sources. His resort to newspapers, tracts and declarations has already been discussed (above, pp. 13, 59–60, 64). His references to such documents rarely present problems, but a word of explanation about a few of them may be helpful. Some of Ludlow's additions to the scribe's text are taken from Thomas Gumble's *The Life of General Monck* (1671): compare 'Voyce', pp. 721, 731, 733, 786, 796, 892, 911,

1095, 1236, with Gumble, pp. 265, 268, 275–7, 383, 387–97, 401–2, 407–10, 453, 476. The reference to parliamentary records on 'Voyce', p. 810, can be compared with *Journals of the House of Commons*, 13 September 1660. I have not identified the 'Quaeries' and the 'Answer' to which Ludlow refers on p. 811.

The printed works of which Ludlow makes most use in part five are the tracts which concern the trials and executions of the regicides, above all *An Exact and most Impartial Accompt of the* .... *Trial* .... *of Nine and Twenty Regicides* (1660) and *The Speeches and Prayers of some of the late King's Judges* (1660). Ludlow borrows very extensively from these works, and it is interesting to watch him working through them, selecting the passages he thinks most deserving of reproduction, and interspersing them with his own comments (e.g. 'Voyce', pp. 838–9, 854, 857, 859, 889). We learn from the Bodleian manuscript (pp. 948–50, 993) that it was Ludlow who organised the French translation (*Les Juges Jugez*, Geneva, 1663) of *The Speeches and Prayers*—an operation in which he encountered many difficulties with his printers. At the back of the translation Ludlow inserted material about the death of Sir Henry Vane which appears in English in 'A Voyce from the Watch Tower'. At some points in the manuscript Ludlow quotes the anti-regicide tract *A Compleat Collection of the Lives* .... *of those Persons lately Executed* (1661): compare 'Voyce', pp. 863–4, 869, with *A Compleat Collection*, pp. 77, 117–18, 120, 133–4. Ludlow makes considerable use, too, of the martyrological tracts *The Speeches, Discourses and Prayers of Col. John Barkstead, Col. John Okey, and Mr. Miles Corbet* (1662) and *The Life and Death of Sir Henry Vane Kt.* (1662). At the end of part five he draws on the tracts of 1661–2 which record the sufferings of John James.

J. G. Muddiman, in *The King's Journalist* (1923), pp. 141n., 169–70, and in a series of contributions to *Notes and Queries*—written under the name J. B. Williams—between May and September 1913, attempted to show that the martyrological works of 1660–2, which he regarded as 'a mass of horribly blasphemous lies', were 'forgeries'; see also Whiting, *Studies in English Puritanism*, p. 544. Obviously the accounts of the dying speeches and prayers of the regicides owed a great deal to the imagination and to the propagandist aims of their partisan reporters. Even so, the similarities between the accounts given by the friends of the regicides and those written by their enemies are at least as striking as the differences. Muddiman and Whiting had no difficulty in exposing the manufacture of the 'prodigy' literature on which Ludlow drew (above, p. 10 and n. 39). Ludlow's decision to reproduce material from martyrological tracts and from prodigy literature in 'A Voyce from the Watch Tower' was either naive or disingenuous.

CHAPTER ONE

721 But it was not yet tyme for Monke to pull off his last hood, though it was so thin that every one might see through it that had a minde so to doe. For he now takes away Colonell Walton's regiment of horse, one of those generals appointed by the Parlament, who had all alonge declared with him, and gives it to Colonell Howard, who had bin a papist in armes for the King and stood very faire for popery againe. *And haveing made choyse of a packed party of 200 horse for his guard, hee appoints Captaine Phillip Howard, his brother, and [theire?] .... papist to have the command of them.* He disposeth of Colonell Rich his regiment to Colonell Ingoldsby. But before the order was put in execution, Colonell Rich, hoping he should prevaile with his regiment to declare as he formerly had done for the lawfull authority, repaires to them, though before he went I told him I thought he would have no success in his enterprise had he not some garrison for them to retire into. Colonell Ingoldsby, with some of Monke's guard and other ruffian-like fellowes, were sent downe to take posession of the regiment; which together with his old interest in those of it (having bin under his command the greatest parte of Cromwel's usurpation), but principally because the torrent of the usurped authority and power ranne that way, did so overballance Colonell Rich his interest that, though before Ingoldsby's going downe they promissed to be faithfull to him, now the third parte remained not with him; who finding himselfe thus deserted, upon Colonell Ingoldsby's letter sent to him, delivered up the rest, declaring his resolution to desist.

Captaine Walcot also, an honest and faithfull officer of the Irish brigade, having gained an interest in the officers and souldiers by his sincere deportement and good conduct, finding all thinges turned upside downe, and supposing **722** .... officers of that brigade had shewed to the good old [cause?] .... to the Parlament whom the Lord had bin .... carrying of it on, during the time they were .... Major Generall Lambert was with an army to.... had bin still to have bin found amongst them, ... towards them, who at that tyme were quartered at Chester, ... [the borders?] of Wales, and being come within twelve myles .... he sends a letter to Major *Woodard*, acquainting [him?] of his being there, and with his intentions of coming thither; supposing, by what he had found him in the late dispute betweene Lambert and Monke, that he was the most faithfull of the officers of that brigade to the interest of the Parlament. But such an alteration had this great turne wrought in most men, and in him in particcular, that instead of promoting the business he writ about, he gives the letter to Colonell Redman, who (being appointed by Monke to comand the brigade) sends forthwith a party of horse to seize Captaine Walcot; which they did rather to obey their order then out of any desire they had so to doe, as might appeare by their permitting him to escape, which with ease he did, making his way towards South Wales. But being pursued for forme sake by those horse, whether he was taken, or delivered himselfe to an officer that commanded in those partes, I cannot say; but being in his hands, he tooke his word for his forthcomming, and on that account gave him his liberty; whereupon he went to the howse of my brother Thomas, where he was very kindly received, and afterwards went to London, and attended on Monke. And speaking his minde freely to him, upon the account of what related to the publique, and likewise as to what he was accused, Monke began to breake forth into choller against him; but recollecting himselfe, thought fit to treat him after a better sorte, giving him liberty and his pass to retorne into Ireland, where his familly and estate lay, supposing (as affaires were) he could doe less hurte there then in England.

He was put out of his command in Cromwell's tyme because he had relation to my regiment, though knowne to be an officer without all exception for his valour, experience, good conduct and piety. When the Parlament sent me over into Ireland to comand in chief there, soone after, upon the rising of Sir George Booth, receiving an order to send into England a brigade of horse and foote, finding one troope to want his captaine (to wit the son of Colonell Jepson, a schollar in Oxford, whom Oliver gratified for his father's sake, in moving in the Convention that he might be king), I put this worthy person Captaine Walcot in the head of the sayd troope. Whereupon afterwards meeting with Colonell Norton in Westminster, who was a great friend of Colonell Jepson's, and an opposer of any thinge or person that obstructed his absolute soveraignty, he upbraides me for not continuing Captaine Jepson in his command, saying he should now be restored whether I would or no; to whom I replyed that I had rather it should be done by another hand then myne, for that I durst not be so prodigall of the publique purse, nor so negligent of their service, as to continue such in commands as did no duty. **723** Colonell Edmund Temple who sollicited me .... in his owne, having an hand in the last turne .... mee in Westminster Hall, and apprehending .... England, complained of the selfishness .... in that they preferred none but those of their owne .... and confessed to me that had not Monke .... underhand against me, I should have ....

The secluded members, having put a period to the [sitting of the?] Councell of State, choose one of their owne number, in the [choosing?] of which they observed the like method for the ..., as wee had

done in the choyce of ours formerly .... chosen of it, Mr. Hollis, Sir
Gilbert Gerrard, Mr. Crew, Mr. Swinfen, Sir William Lewis, Sir
William Waller, Colonell Birch, Monke, Sir Anthony Cooper,
Colonell Norton, Mr. Knightly, Colonell Morley, Sir Harbottle
Grimstone, Mr. Annesle, Sir Richard Onsloe, Chiefe Justice St.
Johns, Serjeant Browne, Colonell Browne etc. This Councell of State
had vast powers given them for the committing of persons, and such
like thinges relating to the securing of their interest. Sir Hardress Waller had so much interest there, by reason of his kinsman Sir William
Waller, that he was sent for by them out of Ireland, that so he might
get out of the hands of Coote, whose cruelty encreased with his power.
He was sent over by a guard, and by them brought to the Councell,
but upon the engagement subscribed by him not to doe anythinge
to their disturbance, and to appeare before them upon summons, his
guard was dischardged. But Coote, being acquainted with the bottome of Monke's designe (by reason of the opposition he had made
to the King's freinds in Ireland, not only in constantly fighting against
that party which the King favoured, for which he had received much
pay, and a vast proportion of land for his arreares, and a thousand
pounds per annum as a gratuity, but also in hanging one Steward,
who was Charles Steward's kinsman, and putting to death the Lord
Mayo and severall others who acted by the King's comission), thinkes
he never can doe acts horrid enough to those of his own party for
the reconciling of himselfe to the other. And to give them assurance
that he was wicked enough to be imployed and trusted by them, two
dayes after Justice Cooke retorned to Monketowne from Waterford,
and the day after he was to wayte upon him at Dublin to present
his service to him, the sayd Coote sends a party of horse, and takes
this poore single-hearted man into custody, that he might have this
lamb to offer up to the fury of his sacred Majestie, he having had
the honour to be an instrument in that eminent act of justice upon
the late King.

For though Justice Cooke, out of the sense he had how much I was
callumniated and aspersed by the letter published by the officers at
Dublin, and knowing how little ground there was for the same, supposing me altogether destitute of an opportunity for the clearing of
myselfe (for the want of a press), writes an answer thereto, which he
intitled my Vindication, and **724** .... and gave order for the printing and publishing of it, ... of severall coppyes of it to the members
of .... I never heard that it was knowne by any .... my enemyes
that it was written by him, neither .... charged with this, or with
his having done anythinge [in?] opposition to Coote when he was
seized by him; so [that the?] ... who had bin all alonge for the Parlament, ... [rewarded?], so highly entrusted by them, is now the [first

that?] imbrues his hands in the blood of those who had bin faithfull
to their cause (and upon the same account, for I know of no other
except what I before mentioned). I have heard it from a very good
hand, he protested that either he must dye for it or I should (and
by the way, it's worth the notice that the principle instruments in
this horrid treachery were those whom Cromwell and his sonne made
their greatest confidents, as Monke, Howard, Ingoldsby, Coote, Jones
etc., which plainly demonstrats it to be the designe of Cromwell to
ruyne our cause, and theirs to be the ruining of him, they knowing
well that his familly could not keepe that which he had advanced
them to).

But to retorne: Monke being told, by a plaine-dealing member of
parliament, that he gave great distaste to the honest party in turning
out Colonell Walton (who had alwayes declared for them), he replyed
he was sorry it was done, but he could not now helpe it. He gets a
declaration drawne, in the name of the officers about London, to the
rest of the officers throughout the three nations, declaring it their duty
and resolution to submit to the authority that was now over them,
and to obey such orders as they should receive from them. This was
subscribed by most of the officers about the towne, even by those
whom the Parlament had preferred, as Colonell William Eyres,
Colonell Fleetwood, Colonell Evelin, Colonell Stretter and the rest.
Some generall wordes theire were in the declaration looking towards
a Comonwealth, which they were willing to cousen themselves with.
But when, upon the importunity of their old freinds, who upbrayded
them with the betraying of the publique cause, the officers would have
met about the signifying of their sense, as well for the uniting of themselves to one another as for the satisfying of others (touching their
intentions) that it was their resolution to live and dye in the maintenance of the interest of the Comonwealth, Monke (being warned of
their designe) takes upon him to interrupt their counsels, and to disperse them to their commands; which they, notwithstanding the bigg
words they spake without doores, tamely submit unto.

And Sir Arthur Haslerigg, being suspected by the secluded
members to have a principall hand in the raysing of this spirit in the
officers of the army, was sent unto by them to take his place amongst
them,   **725** which to that time he had not done. He [submitting?]
. . . . the day appointed procures severall members to [be?] . . . . the
Howse where the Parlament ought to sit . . . . gone in but upon that
occasion. And as I have heard by [some that?] were then in the
Howse, he did not behave [himselfe?] in [answering?] that with
which they chardged him with such couradge and resolution as he
used to doe, but pleaded the reverence he alwayes . . . to the parlamentary authority, and justifying . . . . any violation that had bin, or was

endeavoured to be made . . . ., intimating his resolution to yeild obedience [thereunto?]; so that it was too vissible we began to be now
deserted by all our champions. For those who were willing to helpe
us, could not; those whom we had some hope of, durst not; and those
who could, were so farr from doing it that they imploy all their
endeavours for the destroying of us. Yet doth Sir Arthur and Mr. Scot
apply themselves to Monke. But sure it was rather out of hopes to
make their own tearmes then to get any on behalfe of the Comonwealth; though I well remember they pretended otherwise when they
went to him at James's Howse, after they had dyned in King Street
with Mr. Wallop, Mr. Nevill, Mr. Love, Sir James Harrington, and
some others well-wishers to the Comonwealth; they both expressing
the hopes they had of success, Sir Arthur saying it was his happ
alwayes to be putt upon an aftergame. But that which I thought most
strange at this meeting was that, when we saw what a nose of wax
the sword made of the Parlament's priviledges (pleading for them or
against them as they served the promoting of their owne interest),
one of that number, who had owned the Howse of Commons as the
Parlament of England, declared *with a great deale of confidence* that he
would never give his consent to the imploying of any who should in
any case dispute their commands; as if that authority was the patterne
seene in the Mount. From these and such like passadges I became
more and more convinced of the hand of the Lord in this confusion
of languages amongst us, seeing that those whose interest it was to
unite had still such principles of divission raigning in them, most of
those from whom we could probably expect any succour being such
as, in this gentleman's oppinion, were never to be imployed more.

Major Generall Lambert, who to this tyme had lyen private wayting for an opportunity to head a party for the opposing of Monke's
designe, finding that those who assumed the authority were submitted
to by those of the army, and hoping it may be to have better tearmes
from this Councell of State then from the former (the force that hee
had imposed upon the Parlament having occasioned the restoring of
them to the exercise of their authourity), and without doubt having
assurance from some persons of the Councell of all civillity, renders
himselfe. But they insisting upon his giving his engagement or security
that he would not doe anything to their disturbance, upon his refusall
so to doe comitted him to the Tower. Though the army were
obstructed by Monke to make their declaration for **726** . . . ., yet
in their particcular addresses to him . . . . made, as that which Leiftenant Colonell Farley . . . . and that of Colonell Moss and others, they
. . . . thereunto, and Monke thought not fit as yet to . : . . them, ...
being willing they should please themselves [with the?] expectation
thereof.

The secluded members having .... Committee for Plundered
Ministers, a way being now ... for the ... of mynisters into such places
as were [voyd?] .... act to impower and constitute certeine ... therein
named to institute and induct; I having in my despose, by the death
of Deane Wren, the parsonage of East Knoyle, which amounted to
the vallue of £350 by the yeare, but was kept from the [presenting?]
thereunto by Cromwell and his creatures during the tyme of his
usurpation. I thought it my duty, as soone as I was permitted, to make
provission of the ablest minister I could finde for the benifit of the
people, according to the trust reposed in me, and accordingly made
choyce of Mr. Enoch Grey, who I judged well quallified for that
worke, and who was also driven out of Ireland by those who had
usurped the power. The conditions on which I proposed it to him,
and on which he was pleased to accept thereof, were, that he should
have two hundred pounds by the yeare payd him; that the minister
of Hinden, a market towne within the said mannour, should have
his salary made up a hundred pounds by the yeare, which was now
but thirty; that forty pounds yearely should be payd to him who had
officiated there, till he could be supplyed with a chardge elsewhere;
and then that that forty pounds a yeare should goe towards the maintenance of a schoolmaster to live at Knoyle; and what upon the account
should remaine as an overplus at the year's end should goe to the
minister of Knoyle. This good man, having for the fortifying of himselfe
heerein got the testimoniall of three neighbouring ministers, as the act
which the secluded members made directed, he got the order of those
intrusted for the investiture of him. The Commissioners for the Seale
were sollicited by another, who wayted for such an advantagious
place, though accomodated with one before, looking more at the
fleece then the flock, pretending that by reason of the elapse of six
monthes it was in their hands. But they were so civill that they would
not take the advantadge against me for such a thinge, might they
in justice have done it.

Most of the freinds of the Commonwealth begin to be sensible of
their condition, but there was none who could advice them to helpe
themselves. Great hopes were conceived that, if any considerable
party were drawne together, they would soone encrease. Mr. Scot
poore man, as high as he was with me upon the last day of the Parlament's sitting, now thought fit to conferr with me about some
expedient, finding himselfe wholy deserted by Monke. Mr. Say, he
and I meete together. I proposed to them that, were there but a resolution to put in practice what might be advised, I supposed they might
yet put faire to recover all, for that without doubt the lawfull authority
was on our side, and so were ten to one of the souldiers.

That which I proposed was,   **727** that for the authorizing and

carrying on of the [designe?] .... expedition, all orders for the putting
of it [into effect?] .... ready drawne, and then signed by seaven of
the [Councell of State?], or three of the generals, either of which were
a quorum .... the doing thereof by authority of Parlament, [the
designe?] ....; that the regiment of Colonell Moss, which lay neere
London .... which lay in Southwarke commanded by Leiftenant
[Colonell Farley?] ... of above two thousand old souldiers, and of
.... affection there was very good assurance, ... Tower of London,
to have joyned with Colonell [Morley's regiment which?] was already
there, and from the chiefe feild officers .... who had the entire comand
of that regiment, which for some tyme belonged to me, I had a messadge sent by a sure freind that the Tower was at my command when-
soever I pleased to desire it; that the respective comanders should
be authourized to take in with them six monthes' provission for each
souldier, at the meale mens, cheesmongers and elsewhere, giving
tickets for the quantity so taken, with engagement to pay for the same;
that those fower or five thousand militia forces in the citty of London,
which had bin listed during the Parliament, and who were all armed,
and knew each their officers and souldiers, should be authourized to
draw together, to be assistant to those in the Tower of London as
there should be occation; that fower or five randevouzes should be
appointed of the forces of the army, both horse and foote, that lay
scattred up and downe throughout the nation, and that persons
should be agreed upon to head them at their severall places of rende-
vouz; that horse and foote should have liberty to follow either their
old officers or new, and those officers who had most of their souldiers
following of them should continue their command of them, and those
officers that appeared to owne heartily this designe, though they had
the less number of souldiers following of them, yet should have provissions made for them suitable to their conditions; that the militia
troopes and companyes in their respective countryes should be authorized to draw together, and impowred to seize all such persons within
their said countyes as they knew to be enemyes to the Comonwealth
interest, as also their horse and armes, those forces beeing not yet dis-
armed who were of the militia, but ready to appeare at a day's warning, which would have made a very considerable body if each county
were as well furnished as my owne country of Wiltshire, where were
listed fower troopes of horse conteyning three hundred, and as many
more might soon have bin got together, besides foote; that the fleete
should be ordred to declare at the same tyme; and, if they could spare
them, that a thousand or two of the marryners might be sent to assist
those in the Tower of London, which they might the better doe
because the enemy we were to contest with was intestine and not from
abroade.

The grounds we had to hope why the fleete would joyne with us was because Vice Admirall Lawson, who had the command and a great interest **728** ...., was he who lately had declared for the ...., and being of the Councell of State had taken [oath for the?] abjuration of the King's familly, and by an honest man .... from the fleete, who had bin with them to perswade .... I was assured hee resolved so to doe; and .... to them to the same end, I accompanyed him .... to Vice Admirall Lawson to encouradge him in .... of his resolution, laying open to him his .... and what I apprehended his duty to be. Montague .... at that tyme by the new Councell of State to have the comand of the fleete, and Hull a considerable place for his retreat, in case he should fayle of success at London, it being as yet in the hands of Major Generall Overton, a hearty and affectionate person to our interest. And Captaine Aldworth, who transported me into Ireland, being of the Vice Admiral's squadron, I hastned to the fleete from London, where he was solliciting for his arreares; whom I assured, that the readiest way for the having of his desires answered was to procure the restitution of his old freinds the Parlament, who only were the lawfull authority; and that all persons who should act by their authority or for their service would be justifyed in their so doing; that the governours of garrisons should be required to yeild obedience to no authority but that which was derived from the lawfull authority, which the secluded members (who now usurped it) were not; that a declaration should be prepared to shew the grounds and reasons, together with the necessity of these proceedings; that a quorum of the Councell of State, or the three generalls, should meete to signe and seale orders, and appoint them to be put in execution on a certeine day; and then they to disperse themselves to their severall posts for the acting of their partes. Mr. Scot promisseth to advise with some of the Counsell of State about this, and hoped that a quorum of them might be found to put thinges in execution that should be agreed on. But wee being ripe for the Lord's rod, nothing could prevent it, for our enemyes thrived in all their undertakings, and all ours proved abortive.

Monke he is enterteyned by most of the companyes of London; the end of which was, to ratify and confirme the bargaine they had made with him, and to express their desires of having the King brought in, by the representing of someone speaking in verse or prose in a disguise, whilest they were carrousing it (he seldome parting from thise enterteyments before he was as drunke as a beast, and giving ear to those harranges without reproving them). And yet at this tyme, when Colonell Okey repayred to his command and tooke his leave of him, desiring him to assure him against Charles Steward, he gave him his hand before all the officers, that he would oppose his comming in to the utmost. The secluded members goe on in preparing an act for the setling of the militia in such hands as they could trust,   **729** knowing that their sword was the best title they .... they consider how to settle the thousand pounds .... that the Parlament had given him, and which he to .... asleepe with, had desired might be given to him .... at Hampton Court, the dispute was now, [whether?] .... or in ready mony, those in the Howse who [were?] .... were for the making good of their former [order?] .... divers of the secluded members also, though [they hated the treason,?] yet hating the traytour, concurred with them, [that?] .... useless to him, and some others withdrew, not willing .... one way or other. But yet their party was still stronge enough to carry it the worst way for the Commonwealth, which was, first that it should not be out of the lands at Hampton Courte, and in the next place that in leiu thereof he should have twenty thousand pounds payd him out of the publique treasury; which was done accordingly.

The Irish officers who now exercised both civill and military power, as a testimony of their acceptance of his good service in betraying the publique cause, present him with a gold embroydred belt, a hatband, spurrs, and hilt of a sword of pure gold; a poore recompence for so prodigious treachery. But the greatest parte of his wages is behynde. He sets at liberty the Lord Lotherdale, and the rest of the Scots which were taken at Worcester fight and kept prysoners since that tyme. The secluded members also order the dischardge of Sir George Booth out of prisson, upon his giving security to appeare when summoned. But he thinking himselfe injured in being required so to doe, in that his engagement was upon the same score they now acted, refused to accept of his dischardge upon those tearmes, whereupon as I remember that ceremony was dispensed with. I had some from severall partes who applyed themselves to me, assuring me that they had five hundred horse under Major Creed in one place and a thousand that were ready to draw together in another, wanting only someone to countenance and head them, which they desired me to doe. But I thought not fitt to hazzard them or myselfe upon such uncerteintyes. I was sollicited also by some of the Wallingford Howse party to the same effect, with assurance that mony would be raysed in the citty of London for that designe. But I understood it was much obstructed by Alderman Tichborne's insisting upon their declaration for the setting up of Richard againe, which the rest were averse to. Yea so much in love were that party with domination and power, that Colonell Zanchy, discoursing of publique affaires at my howse, hinted the like designe. But I told him I thought they had bin more sensible of their folly and wickedness in having attempted that thinge, and that for my parte I durst not adventure to scratch my finger for the promoting thereof, knowing that confusion, and consequently the bringing in of Charles Steward, would be the product of it. The **730** .... having a jelousy of some designe against .... their orders for summoning the old officers of the .... Colonell Cobbet, Major Creede and some others, Leiftenant Colonell .... with me whether his brother should appeare .... I told him if he were out of all hopes of .... opportunity by force to rescue the power out of the .... he had usurped the same, and were free .... to act against them, he might appeare, ... he would certeinly be imprysoned; whereupon he .... himselfe, lying privately, and Major Creed he did the like, so as no summons was served upon him.

The Councell of State having also some jealousy of me, and it being against the priviledge of parlament to seiz any member without their particcular order (which priviledge, notwithstanding the great and apparent violation made by them thereupon, they would seeme to be tender of), procures the members that sate in the Howse of Parlament to order, that the Councell of State might be authorized to seize any member of parlament which sate not since the day of the comming in of the secluded members, if there should be an occation; by which order very probably they aymed at me, no member refusing to sit with them whom they had cause to mistrust that I know of besides myselfe. Yea though they, who had ben excluded the Parlament by a lawfull authourity, had now (contrary to all presidents) signed a previous engagement, which they knew had no other tendency but the overthrowing of the priviledge of parlament, and the betraying of the liberty of the people, and the bringing in of tiranny upon us, yet they still pretend to be zealous for the Covenant, and give order that coppyes thereof should be fairely drawne, and one of them hung up in every parrish church throughout the nation. But if any of them had an intention to observe any parte thereof, yet was it very vissible they were but Monke's journymen to make up what worke he had cut out for them; he being a man voyd of all faith and honesty, that whilest he lived and contynued in power, no good could probably be effected by any other, he awing the officers and souldiers to act contrary to their interest and principle.

And therefore judging it to be the most probable way to prevent the ruine threatned to be the removing of him, and being satisfied that he, by his treachery and vyolence having made himselfe above law, had rendred himselfe lyable to have his throate cutt by any-one who had an opportunity so to doe (his life in my conscience threatning more of evill **731** to the nation, and oppression to the people of [God?] .... doe), I conferred with a colonell about a .... who found out an honest man that was .... of the act, and would freely sacrifice .... so as he could have had an assurance, ... should have had a subsistance after .... then I could undertake, not knowing but that .... be suddenly taken from me, as seemed .... this I was free to undertake, that .... left, they should have a share, and if I .... to supply them, they should not want. But this designe stuck heere. Yet hopeing that the officers and souldiers would have bin stirred up to doe it, when rightly informed of their interest and of the danger they were in to be deprived thereof, and being informed that many pamphlets were ready for the press to that end, I got a friend to lend twenty pounds to the said colonell towards the buying of a press and setting forward the worke, which accordingly was put in execution with much secrecy and dilligence. But the Lord's will was not that it should have its desired effect. The secluded members restore Dr. Reynolds to the Deanery of Christ Church Colledge in Oxford, out of which he was removed about ten yeares before for not taking the engagement to be true and faithfull to the Comonwealth (and Dr. Owen put in his place, though Dr. Reynolds, after the place was disposed of, did also signe the engagement). This was all the alteration that was made (to the best of my remembrance) of those which the Parlament had placed in the Universityes.

Those who were formerly of the Howse of Lords press Monke very earnestly that they might take their places in the Lords' Howse, alleadging that nothing was legall in the Howse of Comons without their approving thereof. But it not being seasonable as yet for him to act so directly opposite to the engagements he had made to the contrary, nor to discover so apparently the designe he was carrying on (the army not yet being fit for it, and the cavaleerish militia not yet setled), he not only gave them possitive denyals, but, to make his zeale therein the more publique, pretending least they should force themselves into the Howse, orders a guard of souldiers to prevent their so doing; which contynued daily during the sessions of the secluded members, as most proper for his present worke, which must be carryed on by deceit and force, not by law or justice. *But the secluded members being for the admission only of those Lords who sate in that Howse ... they were excluded, was the principal reason why Monke refused to consent to their admission. However the secluded members,* taking upon them the authority of Parlament, appoint Colonell Fairfax, unkle to him who was the Parlament's Generall, to be Governour of Hull in the place of Major Generall Overton (who had hitherto refused to yeild obedience to Monke, suspecting him to be an enemy to the publique interest), which **732** .... convinced of. Monke having obteyned .... [prevayles?] with Colonell Allured (one of those whom the Parlament .... one of their generals) to repaire to Hull to perswade [Major Generall?] Overton to a complyance, an imployment which seemed .... to all standers-by who wisht well to the publique, ... that he

would accept thereof, and the rather in .... he was to endeavour the
having of it done .... souldiers without him, and in opposition to him
.... to consent thereto, Hull being a towne of greate strength and
the first that opposed the late King. But it was delivered accordingly.
And Major Generall Overton coming to London, and giving me a
vissit, acquainted me with the trueth of that affaire, saying that there
being a civill authourity joyned with a power favouring the cavaleers,
the towne was so generally united against him, and the souldiery,
which were not above six or seaven hundred, so divided from him
and amongst themselves, that he had no hopes of keeping it, and that
Colonell Allured neither did or sayd anythinge to him but what
became a freind to him and the publique to say or doe. Yet was I
not satisfied that it was fit for him to undertake that imployment,
considering the trust which the contrary party had reposed in him.

A dispute began to be within and without doores whether this packt
authority should agree upon a settlement, or whether it should be
left to another parliament to doe. I have heard that Mr. Prinne was
for calling in of the Lords that sate in 1648, and that they and the
Commons might proceed in treaty with the King for the settlement
of the nation, according to the propositions that were made to the
King at the Isle of Weight, whose concessions the Comons had voted
as a ground for a future settlement. Cheife Justice St. Johns opposed
this as I have heard, declaring it as his judgement to be better to leave
it to a free parlament to doe. But what secret reason moved him
thereto (he seldome doing anythinge openly and clearely) I know not,
unlesse it were that, finding the current to be for the bringing in of
the King, he would helpe to doe it for the saving of his own stake,
with as much advantadge to him as might be, or that hoping in the
interim a party would strengthen themselves to set up Richard againe,
or some such like thinge, which those who knew him judged he most
aymed at. Some of those without doores who had purchassed lands
of the state were for the petitioning of the secluded members to make
some settlement before they rose, and not to leave it to the judgement
of another parlament; presuming that those who had bin engaged
in the publique cause, and had sold some of those lands, would have
bin more carefull to have made conditions for those who were therein
concerned, then strandgers. But what by reason of the unfreeness of
some to owne them as an authority,   **733** and the desire of others
that these secluded .... will be made sensible of their folly and [knav-
ery?] .... and the oppinion of a third sorte, that their .... enemy
was at his entrance, the more .... he would deporte himselfe, and
so consequently .... the more shorte, nothing was done therein ....
himselfe was against it, being resolved by .... Steward without conditions which he knew .... would doe, to lay the highest obligation upon

him, ... his wickedness and treachery so his reward might be
the ...

To this effect he declares himselfe to his correspondent Sir John Greenville,
who brought him a letter from the King to ... his endeavours for the [establish-
ment?], that though he had great [difficultyes?] to surmount, hee would either
loose his life in the [designe?], or establish the King according to his desier,
and [that the meanes to rendre?] his [returne ...?] agreable would bee, to
promise an act of oblivion [and?] indemnity; to confirme all publique sales;
to give liberty of conscience; and further, advises the King to quit the territorys
of Spaine, and desireth that hee may have time for the better ripening of this
affaire; wherein his knavish pollicy was so obvious, that many others
endeavoured to imitate him; as Mr. Crew for one, a member of the
Howse of Commons, who first engaged the nation in a warr, sent
horsses against the King to the Earle of Essex, and moved the Parlament that, seeing the Scots had shewed so much affection to our cause
and us as to march into our assistance through the snow to the middle,
that the Howse would shew so much love to them that some of their
number (with the then Committee of Safety) might make together
a Comittee of Both Kingdomes. And yet this Mr. Crew now moves
the secluded members that all those who had engaged in this warr
should be left to the pleasure of the King, in desiring that all the King's
party should be admitted to be the electours of members to the
succeeding Parliament; which to the great astonnishment of all was
consented to, though most apparently tending to destroy his owne
interest, as well as that of the Comonwealth.

Monke complaineing of breach of promise as to the putting of a
period to the sitting of the secluded members (it being about the
middle of March 1659), they prepare an act for the dissolving of themselves, and the election of a Parlament which was to meete on the
23th of Aprill following. They order writs to issue out in the name
of the Keepers of the Libertyes of England, and heerein assert the
authority of the Commonwealth, and exclude those who have bin for
the King to be chosen. But this was but to mainteyne the cheate which
Monke had engaged them in, for since they had given liberty to cavaleers to choose, it was not like that they would choose any of other
principles. And the honest party, finding the power and authority
against them, were discouraged to appeare. And if they contented
not themselves with choosing of cavaleers' sonnes, and such who had
bin secret enemyes, but would choose those who had bin in open
armes, they being chosen and having free liberty to sit in the Howse,
and to be judged only by the Howse, was it probable that in such
a tyme as this they would be ejected, when it was a difficult thinge
to cast out those who had bin in armes against us even in Richard's
Convention? The act for   **734** .... into the hands of those who were

enemyes to the .... for the disarming of their freinds was passed
by the .... and ordered by them to be prynted and published, ...
whereof were set so close upon the consideration .... were about
Monke, that though they had lost .... to the interest of the publique,
and had neither honesty [nor courage?] to propose anythinge to
Monke on that account .... that the erecting of such a militia would
prove .... of the army, it being entrusted in such commissioners'
hands as were disaffected to the publique interest, and might set up
.... opposition to the army, for the bringing in of Charles Steward,
without interruption, they make their application to Monke, desiring
that, for the preventing of his owne and their danger, he would
obstruct the putting of that act in execution; whereupon Monke
writes to the Parlament that, seeing as he understood the act for the
militia was entrusted in such hands as were disaffected to the publique
interest, and might set up a power in opposition to the army for the
bringing in of Charles Steward, he desired they would forbeare the
putting of it in execution.

This letter, being brought and read in the Howse, made most at
a stand what judgement to give thereof. Though for my parte I looked
on it as a blynd, yet a high cavaleere who was then with me was much
amazed thereat, expressing his feares lest Monke should deceive them
at last; upon the receipt of which letter, Mr. Prinne hastens to the
press, to quicken the printer to bringe the prynted coppyes of the said
act; which was done that morning, and delivered to the members,
and dispersed according to former order, they knowing well enough
Monke's desire was that they should bee so. But to correspond with
him in his deceit, they send to him Sir William Waller and one other,
to give him satisfaction in the particculars wherein he pretended to
be scrupled; to which end they acquainted him that though there
were many comissioners in the act who might be willing to doe as
was suspected, yet that by it none were to be permitted to act as
commissioners before they had, by a subscription to a paper to be
drawne to that purpose, owned the justice of the Parlament's cause
against the King to the yeare 1648. They acquainted him likewise
that, by the act, the said comissioners were not to appoint any colonels
or captaines to act in the said militia before they were approved of
by the Councell of State. Monke having obteined his end in sending
the letter, which was to answer the importunity of his officers, resolved
to be satisfyed with whatever was sayd to him, were it to the purpose
or not; as indeed it was but very little, for experience told us
how little conscience the cavaleere party made of signing a paper,
when at any tyme they could obteyne their owne ends, though
735 directly opposite to such a subscription, ... choose such
officers as would probably doe .... unlikely that a Counsell of State

of that [Parlament would?] .... those of the King's party should elect
in .... Parlament, would deny to confirme [such officers?] ....
commissioners they should nominate, though they .... armes for the
King.

The act for the militia .... and the command of all the forces and
garisons on Monke .... with Montague appointed Admiralls of the
fleete .... for the army and fleete, and impoured the Councell of State
.... authority for the providing of all emergencyes, and the dispose
of all affaires as they should thinke fit, till the meeting of the next
Parliament, having now no more to doe but the putting a period to
themselves, and to appoint another Parlament to meete, for both
which an act was prepared (as hath bin before mentioned). Though
by a former act of parliament it was declared by the King, Lords and
Commons, that there should be, to the dissolution of this Parlament,
the consent of King, Lords and Commons, yet, though King and
Lords were wanting, the secluded members ordred that the writs for
the summoning of a new Parlament should goe forth in the name of
the Keepers of the Liberty of England. Though no Lords were sitting
to aske or to give their consents, and therefore this dissolution could
not have any couler of law to justify it, yet (to make it the less vallid)
espetiall care was taken by the Comonwealth party, that at the passing
of this act of dissolution there should not be a quorum of forty of the
lawfull members of the Howse of Commons present. When the Howse
was ready to pass the act, Mr. Crew, that he might sufficiently express
his treachery and enmity towards those whom he and others had
engaged in the warr against the King, and his desire to obleidge and
become one of that corrupt interest which he had formerly so
eminently blasted, he takes an occation to move the Howse that,
before they dissolved themselves, they would beare their witness
against the horrid murder of the late King (as he was pleased to
tearme it), expressing himselfe therein with all the gall and venome
imaginable; most of those who spoake after him making it their scope
rather to cleare themselves then to reflect on others. Amongst the rest
Mr. Robert Reynolds, who had learned to swimme with the tyde,
makes a long harrange in his owne vindication, concluding that he
had neither hand nor heart in that affaire.

Whereunto Mr. Scot, being satisfied in the justness of that act,
could not but beare his publique testimony, saying that though as
thinges stood he knew not where to hide his hated head, yet he durst
not but owne that he had both a hand in it and a heart to it. And
speaking lardgely in the justifying thereof, as that which God and
all good men of the nation required of **736** [those who?] had authority and power in their hands, the late King [being?] a man of blood,
for which the judgement written by the .... spirit of God was that

such should be put to death, [as?] in Prov. 28. 17, A man that doth
violence to the blood of any person, shall flee to the pit, let no man
stay him, and that it was not good to have respect of persons in judgement, Prov. 24. 23, [concludes?] that he should desire no greater
honour in this world, after the Lord should call him out of it, then
to have this epitaph written on his tombe, Heere lyes one who had
a hand and a heart in the execution of Charles Steward, late King
of England. Whether this his great courage and resolution diverted
them from making any order thereupon, I cannot say; but everyone
having said what he thought fit, they contented themselves without
doing anythinge further thereupon, supposing I presume that by what
was said the King and his party would sufficiently understand their
meaning. As soone as Mr. Scot had thus spoken, he and most of the
members who had right to sit in Parlament (yea all to the number
of six or seaven as I have bin credibly informed) withdrew out of the
Howse, leaving the secluded members, who being voted out of the
Howse by a quorum of the Howse of Commons (if not by a parlament), and never restored againe but by Monke's treachery and force,
had no more right to sit there then any others never elected. And
yet they take upon them to dissolve this Parlament; the pollicy of
doing which so lamely I cannot discerne, unless it were that, after
they had acted as farr as mallice and revendge could carry them, they
might leave the foundation of that authority still in being (which
they could not demollish) for the good people of the nation to
build a reformation upon, in case the King and his party should exercise their accustomed tyranny and oppression. But I believe it to
be the overruling hand of God, rather then that this was in their
intentions.

Their face of authority being thus vanished, the mallignity of their
designe more discovered, and consequently the feares and cruelty of
the Counsell of State being like to encrease, though I continued my
course of passing sometymes through Westminster Hall, that they
might see I was not withdrawne upon any designe, yet not so frequently or publiquely as formerly, lodging sometymes at one freind's
howse and sometymes at another. And when I lodged at my owne
home, I tooke speciall care that the out-gates should be kept close
locked, and that he who attended at them should not permit any to
enter of whom he had the least suspition, before he had first given
me notice, that so if I saw cause I might withdraw myselfe, which
by reason of back doores I had opportunity to doe. The honest party
of the Citty, thinking it now a tyme to stirr or never, have their often
meetings, where they resolve upon many particculars, and principally
for the raising of money for the paying of those   **737** who should
draw together, to the [sumons?] of . . . . they also resolve that two of

them should .... thousand pounds, for the peaceable deportement of [Major Generall Lambert?] (being the some insisted on by the Counsell of State) .... his liberty; and if by the heading of any party the .... come to be forfeited, and those who were bound constreyned to pay it, the said some should be dischardged out of the publique stocke. Mr. Slingsby Bethell an honest and faithfull ... was imployed by his fellow cittizens to communicate these their [resolutions?] to Sir Arthur Haslerigg, and to engage him in the designe; who [attending?] him at his lodging to that end, found him in a very melancholy and dejected posture, leaning his head upon both his hands, and farr from resolving anythinge of that kinde, saying unto him, We are undone, we are undone. For that having bin with Monke that morning, and pressing him that he would give him some assurance of his care of the Comonwealth, or at least of himselfe, and urging his engagements and many other reasons to that end, he had this answer from him, with a bended brow, How can you expect anythinge from me, whom you would have made less then I was when I marched up to London? Sir Arthur having let goe many opportunityes in hopes of his favour, and finding himselfe wholy deprived of the one and the other, became overwhelmed with despair.

Mr. Scot also informes me that he was out of hopes of getting a number together, for the ordering of that to be put in execution which I proposed unto him. And within two or three dayes after, having notice that the Councell of State had an intention to send for him and secure him, he acquainted me that he would retire into the country, as well to secure himselfe from them, as to endeavour his election at one of his neighbour townes to serve in the next Convention that was to meete (which by the vote of the secluded members was to be called a Parlament); hoping thereby rather to have an opportunity to make the better tearmes for himselfe, then to put a stopp to the great torrent of mallignancy that was falling upon the honest interest, which ran so violently for the present. And I knowing how much it concerned me to keepe myselfe from being restrained by those who were in power, and also what a jealousy they had of me, I (doubting my safety) seldome lay at home during the tyme I remained in London, which was not many dayes after Mr. Scot's departure. For that seeing myselfe deprived of any opportunity of doing good (the usurped authourity and power being so united), and beleeving that the utmost extreamity which the devill and his instruments should be permitted to act against those who had bin faithfull to the publique cause would fall upon them, I resolved to repayre into the country, as well to withdraw myselfe from under the eyes of those in power, as for the raysing of what monyes I could amonge my tenants, it being probably the last tyme   **738** .... an opportunity so to doe. And to that end I gave my steward .... the keeping of my courts against a certeyne day.

But understanding from Mr. Dove that the day for the election of the knights of the sheire of Wiltshire was appointed to be on the third day of the weeke following, I declared to him my resolution to goe imediately downe, in order to the making good my engagement to Mr. Bainton; which was not also without some intention to oppose Sir Anthony Cooper, who had now most clearly discovered himselfe to be what I always suspected him to be. As soone as I was parted from him, I acquainted my wife with my intentions of going into the country on the morrow, and of the jealousy I had of Mr. Dove, least he, being a flatterer of Sir Anthony Cooper, should imparte unto him my intentions, and he thereupon gaine some order from the Councell of State for the seizing of me, that so he might obstruct me in my designe. My wife discovering a desire to goe with me, I objected we had no accomodation for such a journey, having but a couple of coach horsses in the stable, and two saddle ones. But nothing being hard to a willing mynde, she contrives that her mayde should follow her to Salisbury in the hackney coach which usually went every weeke, and that she and I would goe together in a small charriot I had with two horsses, and that she would borrow her father-in-law's horse, that so I might have a lead horse to mount upon any occasion. She then proposed (seeing there was ground to beleeve that Sir Anthony Cooper, being informed of my designe, would be as speedy as he could in preventing me therein), that therefore we should begin our journey this afternoone, least we might be obstructed before the morrow. The advice seemed very rationall. And as at all tymes the Lord made her a meete healpe to me, so particcularly was she at this, as will more clearely appeare by the consequence.

All thinges being in a readyness by fower of the clock, we set forwards, having sent the horsemen before to attend us on the roade. And going out as privately as we could to avoyd suspision, we hoped to reach Brainford, if not Hounsloe, supposing it enough if I removed from my lodging. But before it was quite darke we reached Egham, where we lay that night. And the next morning we began our journey very early, resolving that night to lodge with my couzen Wallop at Farley. We had not ridd above a myle before we observed one to ride very hard after us, who coming nearer we discovered to be one who wayted on my mother, and in discourse with him found that he was sent by our relations to bringe an account of what hapned after our departure; which was contained more particcularly in letters from my mother Oldsworth and my sister Kempson, wherein we was certified that about an hower and halfe after we went from London, a messenger from the Councell of State came to the howse where I lodged, **739** with an order from them, requiring me to appeare [before?] .... he had the like orders for the summoning of Mr. Myles Corbet, ... and Colonell Thomplinson, commissioners of the Parliament for .... to attend on the said Councell, and that the messenger .... whither I was gone, that he might give the [moneys?] .... to them who sent him, my sister Kempson .... this question, doubting they might send after me .... refused to satisfy him therein.

My mother Oldsworth [whom the?] Lord had raised up to be most industrious for my ... to prevent any evill that might befall me, fearing least the [doubtfull?] answer which my sister gave the messenger might encrease the jealousy of the Councell of State, and put them upon taking some extreame wayes against me, prevayled with my father Oldsworth to attend the Councell the next morning, for the informing of them, as soone as they should sit, whither I was gone, and the occation thereof; whereupon as soone as I received this account, concluding that either they had or would send speedily after me, I mounted my lead horse, that if any horse should be coming after me I might be in the better posture to make my escape. And least they should have waylayd me on the roade at Bagshot, or Hartford bridge, I divided my little company, directing my wife with her charriot, the servant who wayted on her, and the footeman, to take that roade. And I with my groome crossed Bagshot heath, declyning all publique roades, especially those which led to my native country, supposing that the great suspition of Monke and the Counsell would be that I had taken that way; so that my wife and I met not till towards evening, in a private ground which, after she had left the roade to Basing Stoake, it was necessary to pass for the going to my couzen Wallop's howse.

Mr. Nicolas Love, one of the judges of the late King, was newly come thither before us. And my couzen Wallop, who had bin at his mannour of Husbands, came home not long after; who according to his wounted bounty, and unparalleld generossity, received us with much civillity, expressing no less zeale for the publique interest then when it was in its highest prosperity. And though I acquainted him how it stood with the Councell of State and me, he seemed not himselfe at all apprehensive of the danger that might befall him should I have bin seized at his howse, but importuned me to stay longer with him, which I thought neither prudence nor honesty to doe, lest a mischeife should befall him on my account. And therefore after two nights Mr. Love and I tooke our leaves of him. And that night my wife and I lay at Sutton with what privacy we could, concealing our names, and the rather because we found the master of the howse passionately affected to the King, and against the electing of any to the Parlament who had bought publique lands, and to be a great enemy to my couzen

wallop. I understood afterwards that he had bin one of   **740** ....
From thence the next day we reached to my couzen William Ludlow's
howse at Claringdon; from whom, and other .... that came thither
to me, I understood that at a meeting of the gentlemen of the north
parte of the country, Mr. Bainton finding the ... of them engaged
for Sir Anthony Cooper, and one Mr. Earnley, resolved to desist,
yet that he intended to appeare [at the place of election?] with such
as would accompany him. I supposing that this might be given forth
by the contrary party, for the dischardge of my promise that I might
serve him what I could if there should be occasion, I dispatcht a letter
to him, acquainting him with my being in the country and the end
of my comming, desiring to know from him if he persisted in his resolutions of serving the county if they made choyce of him.

During this tyme I remained about Salisbury. And doubting least
the Councell of State should send to seize me, or at least to summon
me, I resolved to lodge in some howse where I might not be knowne
to be. And to that end, leaving my wife and servants at Clarington,
I went in the evening to Mr. Coles his house at Salisbury, that so
I might have notice sent me if any order came to be served upon me
at Clarington, and so to avoyd the having of it served upon me. But
it being objected that that would be a place where I would be as soone
searched for as any, and that already one had bin that evening to
enquire at Mr. Coles's (he being the steward of my courtes) whither I
was come thither (before he knew of my being in the country), I went to
the howse of Mr. Troughton, an honest godly minister of that citty,
where I lay the Lord's day. Leiftenant Feely also was now so civill
to me as to tender me a lodging at his house with all secrecy, which
I tooke kindly of him. On the second day of the weeke I received
a letter by the post, that my father Oldsworth having informed the
Councell of State that I was gone into the country with my wife, and
that the occation of my going was for the setling of our affaires, they
seemed well satisfied therewith; and that Mr. Corbet, Colonell Jones,
and Colonell Thomlinson, attending the Councell in obedience to
their summons, had an engagement tendred them to signe, whereby
they obleiged themselves not to doe anythinge to the disturbance of
the present power, on the subscribing whereof they were permitted
to departe; the consideration of which proceedings towards them
made me set the higher vallue on the deliverance the Lord gave me
out of their hands. For had not God put it into the heart of my wife
to leave the towne that evening, I had bin summoned; and if I had
not   **741** appeared, it would have bin taken as a contempt; I
must have also signed at least the said engagement .... like occation
I had refused in Cromwel's tyme .... certeinly bin imprysoned, and
so in all probabillity kept till the comming in of Charles Steward,

the consequences of which may easily be understood. But thus the
Lord at this tyme delivered me out of the Denne, and Lyon's Mouth.
Yet knowing the [subtilty and?] watchfulness of my enemyes, I suspected .... should be a designe to seize me at the place of election.
However I resolved not to declyne appearing there if I had a call
so to doe, but to endeavour to come with a party that would have
protected me from such a vyolence.

In expectation of Mr. Bainton's answer, I rode that day to Mr.
Phipps of *Chitterne*, neare to the place appointed for the election. I
imparted not the place where I intended to lodge to any, except the
messenger (who I knew to be very faithfull) that he might find me
there. And in my way thither I avoyded all publique roads and places.
Mr. Bainton, in his retorne to me, let me know that upon the desire
of the gentlemen of the country, who had a meeting at the Devises,
he resolved to declyne the putting of his freinds to the trouble of
appearing for his election for the county, but that he had taken up
two innes to enterteine such of his freinds as came to him; he intending
with them to be in the feild, and to present his voyces to Sir Anthony
Cooper, judging it adviseable, seeing the torrent was so vyolent, rather
to swim with the streame then to be borne downe by it, supposing
this course the most probable for him to be serviceable to the honest
interest.

Being thus discharged of my engagement, I set forward to Mayden
Bradly the next day, for the keeping of a court at *Yardenfield*, that I
might rayse what money I could amongst my tennants, by filling up
estates and chandging of lives. For the assisting me therein, Mr. *Berien*
(though prelaticall in his judgement, yet a morall honest man, and
a constant lover of our familly) being there present, put me in mynde
of a dreame I had when I was a schooleboy at Blandford, which I
related to him when I came from schoole (he living at that tyme (as
minister of the parrish of Mayden Bradley) in the howse with my
father, who being impropriatour of the sayd parrish was bound to
provide a minister for the same); saying he had often thought of it,
judging that there was more in it then ordinary, and particcularly
of late, when he observed it so emynently fulfilled, both King, Parliament and army, after their long and bloody contest one with another,
all as it were concentring in my ruyne. I never had made any such
application thereof; but so deepe **742** an impression had it upon
my spirits, I being then not above ten yeares old, that I shall never
forget the particculars of it, having dreemed of the same dreame often
since, and spoken of it to many persons. The dreame was this. I
apprehended that as I was walking up a street neare to the schoole,
I heard a great noyse in a howse; and that looking into the howse,
I observed two persons lying on the floore on their backs feete to feete,

wasshing their faces in blood; and that whilest I looked upon them,
without bending of their joyntes, they rose up, and appearing to be
of extraordinary stature, fought one with another in the ayre; and
that after they had so done a whyle, they both leaped towards me
to seize upon me, who stood at the doore. And though it seemed to
me I made my escape, yet awaking thereupon, I was so terrifyed,
that I desired a gentleman who lay in the chamber to come to bedd
to me; neither durst I lye alone for some nights after.

I know Solomon saith that a dreame comes through multitude of
business, and that naturall causes may be given for them. But seeing
the Lord disposeth of all naturall causes as he pleaseth, speakes oft
tymes by his providencyes to his people for their instruction, and particcularly in this manner, as saith Elihu, Job 33, 14, 15, 16, 17, God
speakes once yea twice, yet man perceiveth it not. In a dreame, in
a vission of the night, when deepe sleep falleth upon men, in slum-
brings upon the bed; then he openeth the eares of men, and seales their
instruction, that he may withdraw man from his purpose, and hide
pride from man. And seeing the subsequent passages of God's providence hath, in the judgement of others as well as myselfe, given an
interpretation of the said dreame, I esteeme it not only lawfull, but
my duty, to enquire and hearken after the instruction, that the spirit
of the Lord would seale unto me, agreeable to his word; which in
the generall I judge to be, that seeing the Lord hath engaged me in
a cause wherein his glory and the good of his people is concerned,
who at the beginning was but a spectatour, although those who were
engaged on the one side and the other for selfish and carnall ends,
and who had thereby imbrued their hands in the blood of each other,
should both conspire to ruyne me and others, who had through mercey bin enabled in some weak measure to promote the worke wee
undertooke for the service of the Lord in their generation in integrity
and simplicity of spirit, yet we should not be discouraged from the
doing of our dutyes, for that the Lord would deliver us from their
hands, or by their hands, from the fyer, or by the fyer, **743** but
should be carefull of having pride hid from our eyes .... and of giving
the Lord the glory of all, by an humble and holy [conversation?],
and wayting on him in faith and patience till the appointed tyme
of his deliverance come.

Having dispatched what I had to doe heere, I resolved to doe the
like at my mannour of Knoyle. And being importuned by those of
the burrough of Hynden (which is part of the sayd mannor) who had
thoughts to make choyce of me for one of their burghesses for the
assembly that was to meete at Westminster, that (for the refuting of
those reports which some who laboured with them to choose Mr.
Seymor, and some who canvassed for voyces on the behalfe of Sir

Thomas Thinne, had raysed concerning me, as if I were imprysoned by those in power, or fledd from them and durst not appeare) I would shew myselfe amongst them, I called there in my way to Knoyle, and stayd with them about an hower; from the generallity of whom I found much affection and heartyness, they expressing a high sense of the good offices I had done them in relation to their markets (which the Bisshop had claymed a right unto), and that in consideration thereof they resolved alwayes to manifest their thankfulness to me as they had an opportunity; some of them saying that Mr. Seymore had declared he would not desire their voyces in case I would serve for them.

Though I durst not desire any to conferr so great a trust on me, yet I could not but take it kindly that they manifested their respects to me at such a tyme as this, when the cavallier party, for the rendring of the King's judges odious (of which number I had the honour to be), had printed their names, with cautions to the people against choosing of them, and when Mr. Topp, Mr. Bennet and Mr. Marvin, three neighbouring gentlemen (who had formerly acknowledged themselves obleiged to me), improved their interest in the inhabitants of the burrough (which was not small) on the cavalleerish account against me; that interest getting ground and already uppermost, insomuch that the Lord Cottington's heyre, a papist and even a naturall foole, got partyes enough to seize by fraud, and to keepe by vyolence, the posession of Founthill Howse there adjacent, which the Parlament bestowed on President Bradshaw; the kinsman and heyre of whom was at that tyme at Hinden, endeavouring to reposess himselfe thereof, and made his complaint to me. But such were the tymes that I could doe him little service therein. At the election of the knights of the sheire, I understood that the cavalleere interest were so numerous that the principle persons of the presbyterian party, who used to beare sway at those meetings, were much affronted by the debauched party. Yet so desirous were some to worship the rising **744** .... our owne party outdid the others in their debauchery, ... their ground, that they must doe so, or else they [should?] yet be taken for reall converts.

I went that evening to Knoyle, where all that I could doe in relation to my owne particcular was to get in and secure *the best I could* those rents that were due to me. As to those leases which I proposed to fill up, I found the present tennants to dally with me, proposing a desire to agree ... for the prise, which they also beate very low, but reserving the day of payment to halfe a yeare after; in which tyme they hoped to have another landlord, more agreeable to their temper, to pay their fine to, or it may be from whom they hoped for a better bargaine. The principle thinge that was done at that court was upon the complaint of the poore of the parrish that, by reason of the enclosure of the common, they were deprived of fuell for their winter provission. Though, at the tyme of the enclosure, every poore man who had a howse in the parrish had fower acres of land set out to him for his proportion, and I had since parted with thirty acres of my allotment for the satisfaction of those who conceived themselves aggreived therein, yet, for the answering of everyone's complaint as farr as it was possible, I consented to signe a paper, chardging every acre which upon the enclosure was my allotment with 4d. per annum, which to my parte amounted to yearly two pounds sixteene shillings and eight pence, for the supply of the poore of the parrish with fuell (provided it should be looked upon as a free guift, and not be payable unless so many did subscribe as made up the sum to a considerable proportion in the paper mentioned; many of the principle persons, who were no less concerned then those who had subscribed, being then absent).

Having now finished the more publique parte of my private concernes, that which remayned being cheifely to conceale myselfe (that I might not fall into the hands of my enemyes, but be at liberty to improve what opportunity the Lord should give me for the serving of my generation, which in all probabillity would either suddenly be, or else to wayt the Lord's tyme), I was willing to have it beleeved I was gone to Salisbury, and to that end set forward that way. But when I had taken leave of those who would accompany me, and was got upon the open downes, I sent my charriot with Mr. Troughton (the aforesayd minister) to Salisbury, and on horsebacke coasted over the hills towards Somersetshire, declyning all great roades what I could; insomuch that that day I met **745** with none that I knew, except a tennant's daughter ...., whom I engaged not to discover that .... That evening, after it was darke, I went to my [brother Strangways'?] howse at East Charleton, where I lay for about [four?] dayes, not stirring by daylight out of his walls, my horse also being watered within doores, and the servants commanded not to speake of my being there.

During this tyme, the election for the knights of the sheire passed in Somerset, which I understood [were?] chosen intirely by the cavaleers; the Lord Pawle's interest having such sway that Colonell Stroud's son, though his father was one of the most vyolent of the secluded members for the closure with the King, because he had bin once in armes against him it was carryed against by a double number of voyces for Mr. Smyth, whose father dyed in the King's service, and Mr. Horner, who alwayes shewed himselfe affected to that interest. After this manner were the elections in generall. I tooke this opportunity of giving a vissit to Mr. Buckland, who marryed a kinswoman of myne, intending to spend some parte of my privacy with him, from whom I knew I should understand the state of affaires; he being a very honest and understanding gentleman, very well esteemed by the country, and usually chosen by them to serve for them before any other. But now there was so much solliciting to be chosen, that scarse any who were not free so to doe (which was his case) were chosen. I understood from him they would have chosen him at Wells, if he would have appeared to stand. But he refused so to doe, only answered them that if they made choyce of him, he would doe them the best service he could. He also acquainted me with the feares he had, lest the vyolence of a young hot-headed party should runne downe all before them; those who were named comissioners for the militia making nothing to swallow the subscribing to the justice of the Parlament's cause untill 1648 (which he as thinges stood would not doe), that so they might have an oppertunity to destroy what they subscribed to. I also understood from him that Colonell Robert Phillips (whose sister he marryed, and who had bin very active for the King, but alwayes very civill to me) had bin lately at his howse, having leave from Monke to come into England. It was twielight (as we call it) with us both: with me it was as that of the evening, when it darkens by reason of the departure of the sunne, but with him as that of the morning, when it vanisheth by reason of its rising; the said Colonell Phillips passing privately, because it was not yet time altogether to unmaske the designe.

I was informed by Mr. Buckland of a contest that was at Glocester betweene some of the townesmen, who appeared for the election of Colonell Massey, and the souldiers who quartered there, and who could not imagine that (considering the many engagements made by Monke against bringing in of the Kinge, and that the act enjoyned that none who were engaged for the King should be chosen) such **746** .... [should?] be owned by those in power .... I came to my cousen's howse. [Betweene two?] and three of the clock, a country fellow knocking at the gate with great importunity, considering what I had heard overnight of the difference at Glocester betweene the townesmen and souldiers, and how necessary it was that the [army?] should draw together, I concluded it was some messadge he had brought to that effect; but upon further .... that he was sent unto me by my wife, who being ... to my sister Strangeways' howse, writ that I should come to speake with her (as she pretended) upon earnest business, and therefore desired me to hasten to her, she being to retorne that day about noone; which I accordingly did, but found that her greatest business was to evidence her deare affection to me, and, by conferring together, somewhat to ease herselfe of the burthen that was upon her by reason of the thick clowd of confusion that was comming not only upon us but on all that feared God.

I understood by him who attended on her thither that Sir Thomas Thinn, by his agents, had procured the hackney sheriff of Wiltshire (formerly mentioned) to deliver the writ for the election of two burghesses by the burrough of Hinden to one entrusted by him; who, having packed a party (generally consisting of the scum and poore of the parrish, whom he had bribed by giving mony to, and promissing more, filling them with drinke, and engaging to the richer sorte that they should have the command of his brother Sir James Thinn's parke), would have had the bailiffe to have gone forthwith to the election; an action which savoured not of a gentleman of honour, and much less of a neighbour and a freind, as he professed himselfe to be, especially at such a tyme as this, when he perceived me going downe the wynde. But the bayliff, understanding the duty of his place, refused so to doe, alleadging that he was to give a competent warning, that all concerned in the election, as burghesses, might have due notice; who accordingly published that the election should be upon a certeine day; at which tyme, of about twenty sixe who had any right to give voyces, nineteene appeared for me, and the other for Sir Thomas Thinne, all agreeing in the choyce of Mr. How of Barwick; so that the baylife declared Mr. How and me to be chosen, and, having signed the indentures to that purpose, retorned the writ with the indentures to the sheriff, as is accustomed in such cases. But the agents of Sir Thomas Thinne (unwilling to loose all their chardge and labour, and ghessing upon very probable grounds that, could they but bring the business to a contest, the next assembly would consist of such judges as would favour any cause in opposition to that wherein I was concerned) signe another indenture for Mr. How and Sir Thomas Thynne,   747 making up in quantity what they wanted in quallity, taking the subscription of the rabble (who payd no chardge either to state, church or poore), yea even of those who received almes from the parrish; whom, to procure of their party, they made beleeve that I was already fledd, and that they would certeinly be destroyed by the King if they made choyce of me.

Before I went into Somersetshire, I left order with a tenant of myne, of whose integrity and faithfulness I had great assurance, that he should seeke me out some private howse with some howse man, where I might lye concealed till I might see more clearly what course to steere (not being willing to be at any place where I had bin accustomed to resorte, least the enemy should there seeke for me, nor where many did use to come, least I should be discovered). He gave me an account of severall that I might make choyce of, and came to me to conduct me to that I should resolve upon. That which I judged

most aggreable, in respect of the privacy of the person and situation
of the place, was not farr from Knoyle, which lay bordering upon
Somersetshire, Dorset and Wiltshire. I accompanyed my wife as farr
as Knoyle, where having dispatched what we had to doe, I seemed
to accompany her to Salisbury. But when we were past the veiu of
the people upon the downes, I left her, and loytered in the copices
till it grew darke. And then, being guided by my tennant Peter King,
I went the privatest way I could to the howse prepared for me, where
I was received with hearty affection, and for the space of a weeke
enjoyed much satisfaction in the converse I had with the good man
of the howse; he being one of a good understanding, well affected
to religion and the publique interest, of a competent estate of about
a hundred pounds a yeare free land. After I had lyen there about
a weeke, I thought I might without suspition give my wife a vissit,
seeing it was knowne I was not usually there. I came in thither after
it was darke. And the next day, being the Lord's day, newes was
brought to Salisbury that Major Generall Lambert had made his
escape out of the Tower, and that it was supposed he would draw
a considerable body of the army together speedily; upon consideration whereof, and in that it was by this tyme knowne at Salisbury
(where a troope of horse lay which was molded by Monke and Cooper
to their interest) that I was at Clarington, least I should have been
seized by them, as soone as it was darke I retyred towards my former
lodging, hoping to get thither before breake of day. But missing of
my way once or twice upon the downes, by reason of the darkness
of the night, the day was broake before I could get thither. And though
it was not above three a clock, yet did I finde one at worke not farr
from the howse where I was to goe.

Two or three dayes after, an honest man who helped to get the
Major Generall out of the ditch of the Tower (after he was got downe
into it from his chamber wyndow by a rope which was fastned thereto)
came to me from him, acquainting me, that severall officers repayred
to him about Staffordshire; that they had agreed upon two randevouzes of horse and foote, and had issued out orders and disperssed
themselves for the better effecting thereof **748** .... assurance that
a considerable party, if not the whole army, would joyne with them;
desiring that I would give order to those [forces in the West?], as
well of the army as of the militia, to draw [together, and?] that I
would meete him with them about Oxford ... I thought it not prudence to engage any of my freinds [publiquely?] till I understood
more clearely of the probabillity we [had?] .... [our?] designe; of
which I should be able to make some [ghesse by?] Major Generall
Lambert's first randevouz, *which was about Daventrey*; after which, if
he could [but for?] a while make good his ground, I had some hope

of [the success?]. In the meanetyme, by the assistance of the person who this messenger made use of to guide him to me and others, I sent to those who comanded the forces in Dorsset, Somerset and Wiltshire, to be in a readyness to draw together if there should be occation. I had very good assurance from a considerable party about Taunton, and that the castle there should be secured for the publique service. The like I had from the north and other partes of Wiltshire. The troope of horse which lay at Salisbury began to stagger in their resolutions, and would without doubt have bin honnest had they seene a power to protect them. A company of honest men, who were consulting together upon the borders of Somersetshire, were very earnest with me to come to them, but I judged it not seasonable to doe so.

I had taken order that, the night before our drawing together, a party of horse should have seized those gentry who were like to oppose our designe, together with their horse and armes. And having notice that the person whom I saw so early in the morning had traced me to my lodging, I removed in the night to an honest man's howse (about a myle from the other, which stood out of all roades, and whereunto very little company did resorte), where I lay five or six dayes, in expectation to heare the success which Major Generall Lambert had; in which tyme my deare wife makes me another vissit. Coming to the howse where I first lodged, not knowing of my removall, I had soone notice of her being there. And it was not long before I was with her; which whilest I was, *Major Whitbey*, a major of a regiment of foote which lay in the West, being sent by Major Generall Lambert to doe his endeavour to engage them in this designe, and to consult with me about it in his way, and to acquaint me with his condition, being conducted by some freind from Shaftsbury to the howse where I now lodged, he spake with much confidence that about a thousand horse were in a body with Major Generall Lambert, and that the whole army would come off to them; and made his desires to me to the same effect with the gentlemen who had bin before with me. I desired to know of him what Major Generall Lambert declared for; it being every man's duty, before he adventured his life, to know upon what account; it being a folly for one to engage **749** his life, if that for which he adventures be not of [much more worth?] then it. He answered that it was not now a tyme to say what we would be for, but what we would be against, which was that torrent of tyranny and popery which was breaking in upon us; to [which?] I replyed that the best way to oppose that was to agree upon something that might be contrary thereto, not so much in the name as in the nature of it, that being the most likely way for the uniting of religious and rationall men in opposition. The ..., [having bin?] so lately cheated by the advancing of a personall instead of [a?] publique interest, would not

easily be taken by the same baite againe. And truely, though the condition we were in required us to draw together to defend the publique
cause, wherein our religion, lives, libertyes, and estates were concerned, yet was I not free to engage against others till we had agreed
for what. My wife tooke it not well from him, that he told her, her
coming to me might be a meanes to discover me.

His horse being tyred, he having ridd very hard, I directed him
to my tennant, who furnished him with a fresh. And then my wife
retorning to Knoyle, and so to Clarington, I repaired to my retirement, where I had not bin two dayes before I had an account of the
dispersing of Major Generall Lambert's party, and of his being taken
prysoner; of which being fully assured, and finding that the Lord had
deprived me at present of an opportunity of appearing in the feild,
or indeed of being any way active for him, I resolved forthwith to
repaire to London, and there to wayte what the pleasure of the Lord
should be, in relation either to my doing or suffering for him. About
midnight I recovered to my wife at Clarington; where after I had
reposed myselfe three or fower howers (leaving her there, my couzen
Ludlow having sent her chariot to London for feare the horsses should
be seized), I set forward at the breake of day on my journey, crossing
all roades till I came to Odium; where whilest my horsses were bait-
ing, and something preparing for my dynner, I walking in the mea-
dows in the back side of the inn, observed a douzen or twenty coming
into the inn, which gave me cause to suspect that some of the towne
had discovered me and got a party to seize me. For the Councell of
State upon the escape of Major Generall Lambert, and gathering the
officers and souldiers together, had published a proclamation, and
sent it throughout England; wherein they declare Major Generall
Lambert and severall others mentioned therein traytours, and all
those who shall assist and joyne with him, commanding others therein
specified to render themselves by a certeine day, and requiring all
to seize upon them where ever they found them. And though my name
was not mentioned in the said proclamation, yet everyone endeavouring to doe some acceptable service to the rising party, and I being
looked upon as a favourer of Major Generall Lambert's designe, it
would without doubt have bin well taken. And had I bin seized upon
any account, I should have scarse ever got my liberty againe. Being
confirmed in this apprehension, I making an excuse to goe behinde
a hedge, did bury some papers I had about me, lest by search they
should by them have discovered more of me; which having done I
repayred to my chamber, where I understood that the occation
of **750** .... of people was the holding of a court barron ... the ...
which I was glad to understand.

That night I lodged at a [private?] inn upon the river that runnes

to Bagshot, fower miles above [it; and the next?] morning sent one of
my servants the direct roade to London, to acquaint my freinds of my
coming, and to prepare me [a lodging?] at an especiall freind's howse,
of whom I might have assurance. My [other servant?] and I, to
avoyd all places that might be layd for me, struck downe to Chesham,
and so past over the Thames by that bridge. And [desiring?] to
have it darke before I got to London, I called at [Hanworth?] to
spend some tyme there; where I found only a servant or two left to
keepe posession, attending daily some orders from the present powers
for their removall. And after two or three howers spent there, as the
more private way, I ferryed over the Thames at Twickenham; where
I perceived I was knowne by a brother of Mr. Asshe's, who lived by
the ferrey side, as also by Sir Thomas Not, who with his lady I met
in their coach upon the roade. But I was well provided to make my
escape, if I could not have kept my ground, should they have
attempted the seizing of me. But I hoped better, at least of one of
them, then that he would doe any such thinge. An hower within night
I arrived at Lambeth (giving order to my groome to lodge there with
my horsses till the morning), and betooke myselfe to a boate, landing
at Temple Staires; from whence I went into Holborne, to an old deare
freind's howse, where I found their hearts as well as their howse
(through the goodness of the Lord) ready open to receive me.

This was the sixth day of the weeke, Major Generall Lambert having bin brought prysoner by Hide Parke the beginning of the weeke,
beeing the tyme the randevouz of the cittizens of London was there;
which without doubt was the greater for the scattering of his party,
they with the auxiliary and some troops of horse amounting to about fowerteene
thousand, many corporations before being scrupulous of publishing the
proclamation sent them by the Councell of State, many troopes being
upon their march to have joyned with them, and the Irish brigade
generally enclyned so to doe. But I heard not of above three hundred
horse that were in a body with him. Colonell Richard Ingoldsby, one
of the King's judges, a kinsman and creature of Cromwell, was sent
to command the like body of horse, which was ordred to fight him.
And Stretor, who was lately made a colonell of a regiment of foote
by the Parlament (when they turned out so many of their freinds),
marched with a company of foote from Northampton to assist Ingoldsby; the Lord seeming heereby to point at our sin by our punishment, that as there had bin a consenting (instead of building the
howse, and doing the worke of God, when there was an opportunity)
to build a Babell, and to prosecute a personall interest before the
publique, therefore are they given up to confusion of language, and
to be divided one against another. Neither could I learne what Major
Generall Lambert intended, had he prevayled; but have heard that

he had two declarations prepared, no way consistent, and that a resolution was taken to publish that which might be most comprehensive of the greatest party, and because it could not **751** be agreed which of them was so, they thought fit [at present to publish?] neither.

The designe of Monke (whose orders ... [readily obeyed?] all who were touched with what concerned either the glory of God or the good of his people, yea or of mankinde .... [truth?] .... sensible of, it being so horrid a treachery and . . . impiety as no age could parallel. Yet the Lord [who had?] .... into the hands of the Parlament and army such a ... to promote his honnour, and the worke of their generation, (.... had bin afforded to the sons of men) seeing they would not heare his voyce, but either keepe up the [glory?] of Dan and Bethell, least the children of Israel, by going up to Jerusalem to worship, should translate the kingdome to the howse of David, or make them a captaine (some under one pretence, and some another) to conduct them to Egipt againe. The Lord's wrath seemed to be so kindled, that for the vindicating of his honour and great name, so much reproached, he was constreyned in mercey to his owne people, and in judgement to those who would be thought to be so, but were not, to stretch out upon them the lyne of confusion, and the stone of emptiness, as the prophet saith, Isaiah 34. 11. By the furnace of affliction he intends to purify and purdge the one, who as to sincere aymes had the roote of the matter in them, but to reject and cast off the other, who aymed rather at greatness then goodness, and at their owne more then the publique interest.

Major Generall Lambert had some foote, yet not many. Some of Ingoldsby's party, upon their march, met with Sir Arthur Haslerigg's son, and (as was sayd) with him a horse loaden with mony. He and his troope being knowne to have bin with Major Generall Lambert, those who seized him brought him to Ingoldsby; to whom he alleadged, that being unsatisfyed in the designe, he had quitted that party; to whom Ingoldsby replyed that that should be of no advantadge to him, unless he brought off his troope; which he thereupon promissed to endeavour, and accordingly did, when the two partyes were ready to engage; which had such an influence upon Major Generall Lambert's party, that by little and little they mouldred away, and those that went not over to the enemy thought it high tyme to shift for themselves. Major Generall Lambert, whether being at that tyme in parley with Ingoldsby (as hoping to take him off from engaging against him), or whether Ingoldsby were better horssed, I cannot say, but, upon the scattering of Lambert's party, Ingoldsby ridd up to him, and required him to yeild himselfe prysoner; unto whom he gave many faire words, desiring Ingoldsby's lordship to give him leave to escape; to whom he replyed that he knew not how to answer it to those who had imployed him. Thus low and successless was he, who had lately bin so successful and high, and it may be for that reason so abased. Colonell Cobbet, Major Creed and some other officers were taken prysoners, and with Major Generall Lambert were comitted to the Tower. Not many souldiers were taken, for that such as escaped not mingled themselves with the other souldiers, as also did Colonell Axtell and other officers. Neither doe I **752** thinke there was a desire in the troopers to seize more then they were con-streyned to doe. Some of those who escaped got to a castle in Wales, which as I remember was called Red Castle, held by some of their freinds. Against these, Colonell Pury, old Mr. Pury's son of Glocester (who with his father had bin alwayes with, I dare not say for, the Parlament), is ordred with his regiment (which the Parlament a little before bestowed on him) to march thither, which he accordingly did, and necessited them to surrender it. Thus our enemyes, even those of our owne howse (and none of Charles Steward's party), were instru-ments, yea rods in the Lord's hand, to scourge us, that so his dis-pleasure might the more appeare therein. And as we had the more cause heereby to bee humbled and abased, so the enemy had the less to be lifted up.

CHAPTER TWO

Untill this tyme, Monke continued his sollemne protestations that he would be true to the interest of the Comonwealth, against a King and Howse of Lords. Yet now finding the militia setled, and a Convention at Westminster (who called themselves a Parlament), and fit for his turne, he sends to those Lords who had continued with the Parlament till 1648, desiring them to take their places, that they might be a cheque to any exorbitancy that those who called themselves a Parlament might comit; which they doe, he engaging that no other should be permitted to sit with them; of which Mr. George Cooper, an honnest gentleman (though brother to Sir Anthony), had such an account given him that he looked upon them as the only ballance that the purchassers of publique lands had left them, and for the propounding of any tearmes to the King upon his coming in; for that seemed now to be concluded on. Yet to sweeten his returne of the King what might be, and to lull the Parlament party asleepe, most of the high cavaleers of the West signe a declaration, wherein they engage themselves to forget all that had bin done to them, and not to retaine any mallice against any who they conceived had injured them, and to endeavour that a generall act of indemnity should be passed, and that no blood should be shed for anythinge that was passed. And concurrent heereto, Charles Steward, being then at Breda, *having quitted the Spanish territory, according to the advise given him by Monke*, taking notice of that Convention at Westminster, sends a declaration; whereby, as he shewes his willingness to posess himselfe of England, Scotland and Ireland, so doth he promise his pardon to all those who should declare their acceptance thereof within forty dayes, except such as should be excepted by act of parliament, who he doubts not but will manifest their **753** sense of that crying sin, which had bin comitted . . . . the Protestant churches. *He promises therein liberty to tender consciences . . . . they trouble not the peace of the nation; and that hee shall bee ready to consent to any act that shall bee presented to him for that effect; and that all gifts and purchases of lands by souldiers, or others, shall bee determined as the Parliament shall thinke fit; and promiseth in conclusion to satisfy the arrears of the officers and souldiers of the army under Monke, and that hee will take them into his pay on the same tearmes as now they are. This declaration, which being dated the 14th of April was presented by Sir John Greenfell [to the?] two Howses on the 27th day of April; who had ben som time before incognito at London, and had consulted with Monke and others about the return of the King, and had brought to Monke a commission from the King to command* *all his forces in the 3 kingdoms, and as an earnest of his confidence delivered him one of his Privy Seales to dispose of as hee should thinke fit; by which hee gave him authority to constitute a Secretary of State, for which imployment hee designed his countryman Mr. Maurice; which being presented by* Sir John Greenvill to the pretended Howse of Comons, as also to that of the Howse of Lords, which was now full .... the Lords who were living that went to Oxford .... of .... those who were newly made, yea of [papists?] also .... Monke being so farr from hindring them, according to his promise, that (as I have heard) he invited them by letters to assemble in the usuall place at Westminster.

The nominall Howse of Commons, though called by a Comonwealth writ in the name of the Keepers of the Libertyes of England, so farr betray their trust and the publique cause that they vote the government of the nation shall be by a King, Lords and Commons, and that Charles Steward shall be proclaymed King of England, etc.; unto whom they retorne their humble thankes for his most gratious declaration, and give their thanks to Sir John Greenvill, and a considerable somme of mony to buy him a jewell, as a marque of their favour. The Lords, you may well suppose, were not wanting in their courtshipp. And *the proclamation being published at London and Westminster the 8th of May, Monke being present,* the citty of London and people of England, partely for feare and partely out of affection (as most agreable to their lust), seeme to express their joy, by making of bonfires, ringing of bells, and drinking etc.; of which I was an eare and eye witness, lying private till I could understand what the issue of these thinges would be; being informed that the Councell of State had issued out their orders, and sent them into the West for the seizing of me, that day I came to London; which probably I might have met with had I retorned by the usuall roade. But the Lord was pleased better to direct. *You may assure yourself Sir John Greenfall his negotiation was well approved of by the King, and the declaration signed and presented to Monke by the officers of his army, whereby they testify their resolution to become true and faithfull subjects of the King, and to accept of his grace and favour according to the tenour of his declaration; which Monke sends to the King by his brother-in-law Clerges, who for that, and the many other services hee did on this occasion, had a knighthood and many other favours conferred on him.* These Conventions, *which sate in the 2 Houses of Parliament,* that they might not be wanting in any point of flattery, resolve that comissioners be sent to Bredagh to complement Charles Steward *and to attend him into England.* Five were to be appointed by the Lords, and ten by the Comons. But every one of them expecting to have some marke of favour conferred on them for this service, great striving there was by most of the members to be of this number. Many also of the looser sorte of gentry, impatient of staying to present their service till his

comming over, repaire   **754**   to him at Bredagh; where it is said that
many of them being in the roome, and boasting much of their affections and services to him, Charles Steward called for some wyne, and
applying himselfe to his brother the Duke of Yorke, drinkes those
gentlemen's healths, and then told his brother that he was now even
with them, having done as much for them as they for him. Whether
this were soe or no I know not, but without wronging of them he
might have sayd so. For sure I am that this great chandge was brought
about by the imediate hand of God. And happy had he bin if he had
so seene it, as to have made good use of it.

I had not bin in London above a weeke, before I was informed
that those who sate in the Howse of Commons observing the forme
of appointing a Committee of Privilledges (as had bin accustomed),
the said committee (being appointed first to judge of the retornes and
then of the elections of their members) being sollicited by one Mr.
William Cole, an honest gentleman retorned for the borrough of
Downton in the county of Wiltshire, by the inhabitants whereof
another indenture was retorned for one who stood in competition with
him, upon the judging of his retorne to be good, myne also (being
of the same nature and in the same county), being retorned by the
bayliff of the borrough of Hinden and the sheriff for the county, was
declared by them to be reported to those in the Howse of Commons
as good, and that I ought to sit as a member thereof, and that upon
this reporte they had allowed of my retorne, and that I should sit as
a member. But withall, as appeared by the coppy of the order which
was brought me, I found an unusuall clause annexed, viz. that I
should attend my duty in the Howse and take my place by a day
prefixed, which was within ten dayes after the date of the said order.

Supposing that the ground of inserting thereof was from some information that was given them from the Councell of State that I had
withdrawne myselfe, I thought fit to make my application to Mr.
Ansloe (whom I knew was a leading man amongst them, and who
I had alwayes found civill and freindly to me), as well to give him
satisfaction as to the cause of my concealing myselfe, as to understand
from him what should be the reason of that addition to the sayd order.
Though, being   **755**   now declared a member of that which would
be thought a Howse of Commons, I knew no power without breach
of priviledge could seize on me, yet the same Councell of State sitting
that had procured from the secluded members a power to seize any
member that did not sit, and not knowing what a day might bring
forth when all thinges were carryed on by treachery and deceit, I
chose the covert of night to attend on the said Mr. Ansloe, first sending
my servant to acquaint him with my intentions of wayting on him;
who having conducted me into his gallery, I acknowledging his former

civillityes to me, acquainted him that the end of my wayting on him at this tyme was to assure him that the ground of my withdrawing of late was not that I had any designe to carry on against the present powers, but that (finding the wheele to goe round soe fast, and not knowing where it might rest) I, having bin engaged with the highest for a Commonwealth and against the King, was unwilling to be in prison at his entrance, and therefore desired him that he would please to favour me so farr as to satisfy those who were in power heerein; who as I was informed had issued out their warrant for the seizing of me, and upon which account I told him I supposed that the clause requiring my attendance at the Howse was added to the order for the allowance of my retorne for the burrough of Hynden.

His answer was that though I had bin zealous and earnest, yet both he and others were satisfyed that my intentions were for the good of the Comonwealth. And though he could not blame me for avoyding a restreint, yet he assured me that not an hayre of my head should suffer more then of his. But, sayd he, I cannot say so much for your freind Mr. Scot his hated head as he lately tearmed it; and then tooke an occation to relate to me the passadges that were in the Howse upon the reporte by Mr. Turner from the comittee about my retorne: that notwithstanding there was nothing to be sayd against it, yet because it concerned me (who as it was objected had bin in opposition to them, and withdrawne myselfe out of their protection), the vote of the Howse was like to pass against the agreeing with the report of the comittee, had not he (supposing upon the noyse of the yeas, when the question was put for the recomitting it, that they would have caryed it) stood up and desired the Howse that they would not, out of disrespect to any man's person (how obnoxious soever to their justice) doe an act, and make an order, which they would be asshamed of when they seriously considered; for that justice ought to be impartiall, and (in that nothing was alleadged against the report of the comittee touching the retorne) it ought to be taken for graunted to be good; if the person concerned had done anythinge amiss, he being a member ought to answer it in his place; which Judge Hales, then a member of that Howse, seconding, so wrought upon the Howse that they allowed of the report, with the addition before mentioned.

He **756** farther told me that there was a young heady party in the Howse who upon all occations flew high, but that as yet they had found out wayes to moderate and keepe them in order; and advised me by all meanes to take my place in the Howse as soone as might be; which counsell of his I thought fit to follow, not only to undeceive those who supposed I would continue to withdrawe myselfe, but also, by comming in before I was looked for, to surprise that party which watched for my ruyne, and which ... would have bin ready to have

effected it, had I forborne to have appeared till the day by them prefixed. I chose to come in at the first sitting of the Howse, and imediately turned up into the Speaker's chambers. It was a very great
mercey that Mr. Ansloe was not in the Howse at my entrance. For
had he bin so, and taken notice to the Howse of my coming in, as
one that was farr from concealing myselfe from them (which he proposed to me he would doe), the Howse had very probably entred into
a debate concerning me, and sent me to the Tower. I was no sooner
in the Speaker's chamber but Major Robert Harloe comes after me,
and desires me, if any objection should be made against me by any
member of the Howse (which he supposed might be), and that the
Howse should require me to answer thereto, that by all meanes I
would forbeare speaking anythinge in justifying the putting of the
King to death, for that it would not be borne; to whom I replyed
that unless I was constrayned to speake to it, I had noe reason to doe
it, but if my life lay upon it I could not disowne the justice of that act.

I had then the opportunity to observe the severall tempers of persons. Colonell Norton in some passion saith to me, You see into what
a condition you have brought us; whereunto I replyed, if he liked
it not, he might thanke himselfe and some others, for as for my parte
my conscience did not accuse me in having bin wanting in my duty
for the preventing thereof. He afterwards enquired of me whether I
had ever a horse I would parte with, intimating thereby that he
thought I was not like to be long in a condition to make use of any.
I told him I had, but not resolved to parte with it. Serjeant Maynard
was pleased to advise with me touching the act of indemnity, as to
the tyme to which all accounts should be discharged; that being
comitted to his care. But I had little desire to talke of those affaires.
Mr. Swinfen, one of that Councell of State the secluded members had
appointed, and which this Convention still permitted to sit and act
for the preparing of all thinges for the coming in of Charles Steward,
757 applyes himselfe to me, saying, I told you to what pass
thinges would be brought, in paring and streightning of your party
to a [very?] ...; to whom I replyed that he knew it was far from
my principle and practice, I having bin generally condemned for having bin too lardge therein. Some *of the Long Parliament*, as Mr. Gour-
don, Colonell Morley and others, though they durst not speake,
expressed their dislike of thinges by the shaking of their heads. Some,
who had joyned with the Comonwealth's party in Richard's Convention, now [appeare?] of another temper. And some, who then
opposed the honest party, now wisshed for some of them to ballance
the royall interest; as particcularly young Mr. Buller, a gentleman
of a considerable estate in Cornewall, who sitting by me in the gallery
bewayled the temper of the Howse, wisshing for Sir Henry Vane and

some others to be amongst them for the moderating of them. I could
not but express the joy I had to finde his spirit so sensible of the then
posture of affaires, and the hopes I conceived that the Lord might
yet make him and others serviceable for the releeving us from the
tyranny and oppression that was coming like a flood upon us. I discerned severall knots of cavalleers discoursing in the Howse, and as
I was perswaded of me, for their eyes were fixed upon me. But the
Howse being taken up about the appointing of commissioners which
were to attend on Charles Steward, they had not then the oppertunity
to move anythinge concerning me.

Much labouring there was by severall persons to get themselves
named for that imployment. And that the best care might be taken
for nominating of fit persons, the same method was proceeded in as
formerly was observed by the Parlament in those choyse of the Councell of State. Sir Richard Temple (who wayted with a trencher on
the late usurper Oliver Cromwell) and others sollicite me that I would
insert their names in my paper for them to be nominated for that
service. But whatever became of me (though I was got in amongst
this Convention, to play my game as well as I could for my owne
security), yet was I resolved to have no hand in the setting up of this
exploded idoll, so as to betray the cause of God and his people and
contract upon me the guilt of that blood which had bin shed in the
late warres, and therefore not to put in any paper as was ordered;
to which end, the Howse appointing their members to be counted,
that the number of the papers might agree with that of the persons,
I concealed myselfe in the Speaker's chamber. But the Serjeant, *one
Northcot*, attending the Howse, being commanded by the Speaker to
call in all the members of the Howse to be numbred, and having found
me out, he was very earnest with me to goe into the Howse. But I
telling him I would put in no paper, and therefore it was not convenient I should be numbred, he, being againe remynded by the
Howse to call   **758** [for?] the members, reitterated his importunity
so farr that nothing I could say would give him satisfaction; whereupon he threatned to informe the Speaker of me if I would not goe
into the Howse, which, had he done, without doubt had bin a rise
to have sent me to the Tower. But I desiring him, before he did so,
to enquire of some knowing Parlament man whether it was necessary
for one who would put in no paper to be numbred, I looking over
the gallary observed him to demaund the question of Mr. Pierpoint
and Serjant Glyn; who I observed to smyle thereat, but I suppose
satisfyed him that he neede not press me thereto; so I heard no more
of him about it. Mr. George Cooper upon the same account having
withdrawne himselfe, whilst hee and I were discoursing thereof, those
fower who were appointed to take an account of the papers (and to

reporte to the Howse who were first to be put to the question) being required to withdraw into the Speaker's chamber for the preparing of their report (that the Howse might goe on with some other affaires), finding us there, demaunded whether we had put in our papers; which question, unwilling to give a possitive answer to, we diverted by asking them some others, so that we were no further troubled therein.

During this while, the Howse were considering into what hands to put the Great Seale. Much objecting there was against the continuance of Mr. Fontaine, because having bin once for the King, he had bin since for a reformation of what was amiss in the law. Mr. Tyrill they were all well satisfyed with. And great pressing there was that the Earle of Manchester, being one of the Lords, might be added to the number (supposing that the Howse of Lords would not concurr for the other two, in case one of their Howse were not joyned with them). But it being objected that it would be a dishonour to the Earle of Manchester to be put into any place where he could not continue (which some undertooke to assure the Howse he could not doe in this, for that it was disposed of to another), it was not thought fit to be insisted on. The Howse also received a messadge from the Howse of Lords, desiring them to take off the sequestration of the Duke of Buckingham's estate; which Mr. Finch moved them to doe, from the consideration that none were concerned therein, except Mr. Henry Martin, whose name would be infamous to posterity; which discourse, together with the flattering of Charles Steward (wherein none exceeded Mr. William Pryn), made my eares to tingle, and my heart to ake, all thinges running counter to what the providencyes of the Lord had lead to for twenty yeares past.

At the rising of the Howse I observed Sir George Booth to bend his browes upon me, who had saluted me upon my entrance into the House very civilly, being it seemes at that tyme surprized, but having **759** now recollected himselfe, and having it may be conspired with his comrades to put in execution .... upon the dissolution of Richard's Convention. Mr. Pelham of Sussex, though he spake something against the excluding of the members in 1648, yet did it with civillity, telling me that he had sollicited his freinds of the Howse for the giving of their approval of my retorne (upon the reporte of the comittee), and had procured forty voyces for me. I acknowledged his civillity, but told him it was not now tyme to reply to what was said against their exclusion. In the afternoone, the Comittee for Elections sitting, knowing that without breach of privilledge none could seize me (being a member of parlament), I went to the said committee, which sate in the Howse, observing their debate, and watching an opportunity to move for a longer tyme for the hearing of what related

to my election; the other party having procured a tyme to be
appointed, within which it was not possible that those concerned
could have notice to attend. I found some of my owne countrymen
very shy of me; but Mr. Rolles, the son of the late Cheife Justice,
spake very freindly. Mr. Turner, the chaireman of that comittee,
made it appeare by his carriadge that the tables were turned upon
my application to him; which I did, that I might not be wanting
to assert the rights of the burrough, rather then out of any hopes I
had to advantadge myselfe thereby. For I observed the Howse, and
consequently that comittee, composed of such persons who would
make use of any pretext to give judgement on the behalfe of such as
were like to themselves, especially in a case wherein one of my principle and practice was concerned.

Therefore I had thoughts of going amongst them no more, being
sensible of the eminent hand of God in delivering me out of the
mouthes of those lyons that day; in which resolution I was the rather
confirmed by a messadge sent me on the day following (being the
Lord's day) by one of my brothers-in-law from a freind of myne, a
member of the Howse; who not daring to come himselfe, for feare
of being taken notice of, desired my brother to assure me that there
was a resolution taken by certeine members of the Howse, upon my
next coming amongst them, to accuse me of high treason and to send
me to the Tower, and therefore to desire me that as I tendred my
life I would forbeare coming into the Howse; which made me double
my watch, especially during their sitting, supposing that when they
found themselves disappointed of their prey in the Howse, they would
have made an order for the seizing of me where I should be found.
But presuming upon my privilledge as a member, when the Howse
was rissen (being first satisfied that the Howse had made no order
for the seizing of me) I tooke the liberty to shew myselfe in Westminster Hall, and sate amongst the members of parlament at the sermon in the Abby, desiring so to comporte myselfe as not to discover
any apprehension of feare, least thereby I should have encouraged
them to the more severity, to   **760**   which I knew the cavaleerish and
giddy-headed party were inclyned by principle; and .... had
appeared for the Parlament, in *carnall* prudence, hoping [by?] the
[sacrificing?] of some who had bin most faithfull to the publique, ...
[their owne?] peace, if not to gaine favour, and preferment; ....
engaged some members in the Howse, to give me [notice as soone
as?] anythinge was moved in the Howse concerning [me?], that [so?]
I might have withdrawne myselfe before they came to [a resolution?];
to which end I had many places in a readiness. I had taken I
could for the securing of my stocke in Ireland, which in sheepe, cattle,
horsses, corne, and howshold stuffe amounted to the vallue of fower-

teene or fifteene hundred pounds, giving particcular orders to my bail-iff for the disposing thereof, and for the gathering of my rents in the hands of my tennants. But little or nothing being done by him therein, I improved this tyme for the making over my stock to my brother Kempson (in satisfaction of my sister's portion), and earnestly pressed him to send over one forthwith for the taking posession thereof; which he not being expeditious in, Coote (without any order of Parlament) makes seysure of all, Colonell Theophilus Jones taking into his posses-sion fower stoned horsses that were in my stable, and Coote forcing my tennants to pay him fower or five hundred pounds due to me for rent, and commanding my servant that nothing of my stock should be disposed of without his order; those who had engaged with us outrunning others in rage and cruelty towards us.

Yet some of them (I have heard) were so honest as in their private debates to propose that a full indemnity should be graunted for what was past, without excepting of any person; and that the Earle of Northumberland did say that what was done upon the King, though he had no hand in it, he was against questioning those who had, sup-posing that example might be of use to affright other kinges from the like exorbitancyes; and that the Lord Fairfax upon that subject did say that if they would except any, he knew of one that was fit so to be, and that was himselfe, for that being then Generall he hindred it not when he might have done it. And when they were debating the conditions on which they should receive Charles Steward, I was informed that some were for a strict limitation, till at length finding Monke (who had the power in his hand) gave intelligence to Charles Steward of everythinge that was said, and by whom, they durst none of them further insist thereon, nor discover what was upon their hearts. Yet this wretched fellow, that he might complete his treachery (after Mr. Jacombs preached before him, and pressed it as a duty upon him to protect and secure all those who had acted under those by whom he was entrusted, affirming that, should any of them suffer for so doing in what kinde soever, it would be chardged upon his account, and would render his memory odious to posterity),   **761** he replyed to the Lord Say (when he proposed to him as his advice that, for the quieting of men's myndes, an act of indemnity should be passed, and some of those who had a hand in the King's death be excepted), in a great deale of seeming passion, Not a man, for should I suffer that, I should be the [greatest?] rogue that ever lived. And yet did this horrid creature [make?] pretence that the Howse might have better tearmes from Charles Steward by casting themselves upon his ingenuity [then by?] capitulating with him, especially at a dis-tance, when he could neither have such an understanding of thinges, nor with so much conveniency move that those commissioners might

be impowred to invite him over; which motion proceeding from
him, and concurring with the judgement of many, and those who
disapproved thereof not daring to say so (for feare of making themselves a prey), was resolved upon; the consequences whereof were
very obvious, everyone striving who should offer up the greatest
sacrifice to this rising sun.

And as Coote had seized Cheife Justice Cooke, a faithfull servant
of the Lord, in Ireland, so now (whether by order of any of the great
ones I cannot say) Major Generall Harrison is seized by some of
Colonell Bowyer's militia in the county of Stafford, with his horsses
and armes; which they easily did, he not being in a condition to make
resistance, and being so fully satisfyed in the justice of the cause which
the Lord had honoured him to be an instrument in, and of his duty
to seale the trueth thereof with his blood if the enemy durst power
it out upon that account, that he was not free to withdraw himselfe
out of his howse for the saving of his life, as apprehending his so doing
would be a turning of his back upon the cause of God; though I am
satisfyed, as well from the example as precept of Christ, that it is the
duty of the people of God when persecuted in one citty to flee to
another, Mat. 10. 23, and not to expose themselves to the mercyless
cruelty of their bloody enemyes when they can secure themselves without the use of sinfull meanes; it being properly a denying of the cause
when we shall disowne it to save our lives, not when in a warrantable
way we seeke to save our lives to promote God's cause; David flying
from the fury of Saul, and Christ himselfe (the greate and infallible
patterne) withdrawing himselfe from the people when they attempted
several tymes to kill him. Yet I dare not judge the Major Generall
for what he did, not knowing but that, for the greater justification
of the justice of the putting of the late King to death, he had a more
then ordinary impulse of spirit; who in respect of piety, zeale and
couradge, was every way so quallified as made him too stronge for
his adversaryes, according to the saying of Ciprian, Mori posse, vinci
non posse, a Christian may suffer death, but never conquest. Yet
though the Major Generall accounted the cause of God more deare
then his life, it's said he had some thoughts the Lord would not permit
it to be taken from him. But the Lord soone made it to appeare otherwise, that way of his **762** suffering being ordained, in the undaunted
carriadge of whom the Lord thought fit to be glorified, *and the more
in that it was under such a disappointment.*

Those who sate in the Howse of Commons, upon the encouradgement they had from Charles Steward, proceed in preparing an act
of indemnity, the benifit of which was generally agreed by them not
to extend to the King's judges, etc., that being an act which they
thought fit to disowne. All other acts, though necessarily conduceing

thereunto (yea those horrid crueltyes and treacheryes that some were guilty of, in contracting that blood upon their heads, by doing the same thinges for which he suffered), were thought fit to be passed over; *a certaine prediction to me what the issue of their counsells were like to bee. For that whereas the Lord sent them against an hypocriticall people in the 10th of Isa., to take the pay, and to treade them downe like the mire in the streets, howbeeit they meane not so, but it is in their hearts to destroy those who are faythfull to the cause, and worke of the Lord, who when hee hath don his whole worke upon Mount Syon, and upon Jerusalem, will punish the fruit of their stout heart. And though they will not see that God is abuseing the pride of man, yet they shall see and bee ashamed for their envy against his people. And though hee permits them to smite them with a rod, yet the staffe of destruction that they lift up against them shall be beaten backe on their owne heads, and that after the manner of Egypt. Yea, it will bee but a very little while before the indignation of the Lord shall cease, and his anger in the destruction of his enemyes.*

When the ambition of the court and clergy was growne to such a height in England, Scotland and Ireland that all was turned into will and pleasure, and religion into superstition and idolatry, the Lord in a wounderfull way raysed up for the Parlament, which began their sessions 3 November 1640. *How contrary to the will of the late King is notoriously known; as alsoe that what the King did in complyance with them, either in punishing of those who had beene offenders, or in makeing lawes for the prevention of the like mischiefes, were forced from him when all meanes contrived for the destroying of the Parliament itselfe failed him, and when hee found noe other way to secure himselfe from the storme that was falling on his owne head; hopeing (when he had got himselfe by this meanes rid of the Parliament) not only to renverse whatever hee had beene constrained to graunt, but to revenge himselfe on those who (out of their affection to the publique) had beene instrumentall therein;* which they foreseeing endeavoured to avoyd, as remembring how by his treachery and cruelty he had carryed it against those true and renowned patriots, Sir John Elliot and others, in the 3d yeare of his reigne; whose pockets and studyes he caused to be searched, and their persons to be imprisoned, as soone as the Parlament was dissolved, and that only for words spoken in Parlament, asserting the people's rights, for which by law they could not be questioned. Yea so cruelly were the said gentlemen used in the Tower that one of them dyed there, and others lost their healthes and estates; and this after he had protested at the dissolution of the Parlament that he would be as tender of their privilledges as of his owne children, and would redress greivances out of Parlament as well as in it. I say the Parlament remembring this, and considering that it was the King's necessity rather then his free will that occationed their summons (the King pressing for monyes to defray his expence, and to pay his army leavyed against the Scots), *and the Parliament (engaged*

alsoe to pay the Scots army) *lookeing upon it as their duty to prevent him from*
the executing of that power hee had assumed to himselfe of dissolveing parliaments
at his pleasure, take a rise from hence to prepare the draught of an act of parlia-
ment, which they present to the King for his consent, that they might not
be dissolved but by an act of parlament; *alleadging, which was a great*
truth, that without such an assurance they could have noe credit for the
procureing of him money. The King, as enforced, consented thereto.

The Parlament considering also, that when the tyme of their dissolution should come (which the King longed for, pressing them often
to present in a lump what they had to offer to him), the nation would
be little the better for what they had done or should doe, either as
to the propagating of the gospell or the instating of them in their civill
rights, unless the people had the sword to protect them,   **763** *and*
the power thereof put into such hands as were faythfull to what the Lord (by
his overruleing providence) had beene instrumentall in procureing the king to
consent unto, they therefore [desire?] him that the militia, the sword
or power of the nation, [might?] .... such hands; which the King
.... [and?] finding his plot discovered, resolves to [doe that?] ....
he could not effect by pollicy. *And having denyed them a guard for their*
security, though often petitioned by one for them, and .... *[three?]* hundred
ruffian-like fellows into Whitehall ... [pretence of?] a guard to his
person, he designed the seizing of some of the choycest of their
members; to which end he repaired to the Howse of Commons,
accompanyed with his servants and the aforesaid ruffians, armed with
swords and pistols, and entring into the Speaker's chaire demaunds
five of their members, as well knowing that if he could have seised
and beheaded them he should with ease have reduced the others. But
the said persons having notice of the King's intent, withdrew themselves into the Citty; and the birds being flowne (as the King tearmed
them), he also retires; who being thus disappointed, and finding he
had not only provoaked the Parlament, and Citty, but the whole
nation, thought it not fit to remaine any longer at Whitehall, but
repaires to Hampton Courte; where he began to raise an army, two
troopes of horse appearing in a warlike posture at Kingston-upon-
Thames, one of them being comanded by the Lord George Digby,
who was thereupon proclaymed traytor by the Parlament. The
Queene also was impeached of high treason, which impeachment was
carryed to the Howse of Lords by Mr. Denzil Hollis. The King sent
the Queene and Digby beyond sea, the latter advising by letters
(which the Parlament intercepted) that the King retire into some
stronge place, and declare, and then his freinds would come to him;
whose counsell the King followed, withdrawing from the Parliament
every day as well in affection as place.

The Parliament, haveing hitherto contented themselves with a

guard of the cittizens of London for their security, now seeing the
King's designes were carryed on by force as well as pollicy, and that
to that end he had withdrawne many of the Lords and Commons
from doing their duty at Westminster to attend him at Yorke (to
which place he retyred himself, and whither many papists and vitious
persons resorted, who affronted the comissioners of Parlament sent
to invite his retorne to them, Sir Francis Wortley waving his sword
over his head and declaring for the King, and the King himselfe (instead of harkning to the advice of the Parliament for his removing
of the mallignant councell that was about him, and retorning to his
Parlament) in his answer telling them he knew of no mallignant councell he had, except his two Howses of Parliament),   **764** the [dis-
pute?] as to the militia being growne to this height, the Parlament
send downe Sir John Hotham (one of their members) to take posession
of Hull, and to keepe it for the Parlament, it being a place of strength,
and therein a magazine of many thousand armes; which the King
marched to, supposing to be admitted or to enforce the surrender of
it; upon the consideration of which, the two Howses of Parlament
passed severall votes.

1. That the King seduced by evill councell endeavoured the leavying
of warr against the Parliament.

2. That his leavying of warr against the Parlament tended to the dissolution of the goverment.

3. That whosoever should assist the King in the sayd warr were traytors, and enemyes to the Parlament and Comonwealth, and should
be proceeded against accordingly.

The King sets up his standard at Nottingham, requiring all persons
by virtue of their tenures to attend him, and issues forth comissions
of array into the respective countyes for the raysing of forces; and
in short, notwithstanding all the meanes the Parlament could use to
disswade and hinder him, rayseth an army, endeavouring by open
force to render the endeavours of the Parlament, as to the promoting
of the spirituall and civill libertyes of the nation, useless; for the
defense whereof, the Parlament set forth severall declarations, first
to informe the people of the true state of thinges, and secondly asserting the justice and necessity of making their defence against the King;
and to that end invite all the well affected of the nation to assist them
with their persons and purses; *which by the Protestation* and by the Sollemne League and Covenant enjoyned themselves to doe, which was
taken by the Parlaments of England and Scotland, by which both
partyes stood engaged to roote out popery and prelacy, and to bring
delinquents and incendiaryes betweene the two nations to condigne
punishment. The King and Parlament both appeale to God to judge
betweene them in this controversy touching the power of the sword;

in which there was not so little as two hundred thousand men slayne, besides above *one hundred and fifty thousand* masacred in Ireland of the poore Protestants before the warr with England began (*not heere to insist on* the betraying and utter ruining of the distressed Rochelers and other Protestants in France, whom the said King encouraged (as being under great oppressions) to rise against the King, promissing them assistance both by sea and land, and yet afterwards tooke parte with the King of France, lending him twenty sayle of men of warr to destroy the Rochellers' **765** ships, yea and as farr as in him lay all the [Protestant?] .... France).

The Assembly of Ministers in Scotland, [having observed the King's?] carriadge towards the three nations of England, Scotland and Ireland, declared him to be guilty of the blood of [many thousands of?] his best subjects.

The Lord God also .... gives judgement against him, vanquisshing all his armyes in the feild, and causing all his strongholds to fall .... figgs into the mouth of the eater, Nahum 3. 12; yea, and [deliver?] him into the hands of the Parlament .... of ... not to be courted, but condemned; for, saith Solomon, It is not good to have respect of persons in judgement, Prov. 24. 23; and in Prov. 28. 17, A man that doth violence to the blood of any person shall flee to the pit, let no man stay him. And yet many of the Parlament (to promote their owne carnall ends, rather then the publique interest) make application to him for tearmes of accord; the conquering seeking to the conquered, without having reguard (as they ought) to the satisfaction the Lord required for the shedding of so much blood, which yet they had covenanted to make inquisition for. But the Lord having hardened his heart as Pharoah's, that he might make his power to be knowne upon him, he refuseth to consent to the Propositions that were sent to him by the Scotch, the army and the Parliament; the latter having applyed themselves to him to that end severall tymes, which yet prevayled not with him, but caused him to be more high and proud; the consequence of which was sad and dangerous, for it occationed a second warr; whereupon the Parlament (consisting then of two Howses), finding no meanes to bring him to an accomodation (and that when he pretended to be for peace, at the same tyme writ to his Queene in France that he would have none with them), voted they would make no more addresses to him, nor receive any from him. But not proceeding to doe justice upon him, or to settle the nation without him, the people (apprehending they should never have a settlement without his being reinthroned) make a generall combination (being influenced by him and his party) so as to force the Parlament to a closure with him upon his own tearmes. And at the same tyme Duke Hamilton invades England with above twenty thousand

Scots; which second warr (after much hazzard, and expense of much blood and treasure) being ended through the wounderfull blessing and mercey of God, those of the Parlament and army who minded the welfare of the publique interest, and had respected the blood that had bin shedd both of their freinds and enemies, looked upon it as their duty to hearken unto this and other loud voyces of the Lord's providences, so as to bring the authour of so much blood the King to justice, as a tyrant, traytor, murderer, and enemy to the Comonwealth of England; wherein the Lord was pleased to strengthen the hearts and hands of all that acted therein, who thought it best that as he sinned openly, so he should be tryed, sentenced and executed in the   **766** face of the world, and not secretly made away by poysinings and other private deaths (as in Scotland, and other partes of the world, other kings, farr less offenders, had bin treated).

1. That he was a traytor, it's evident, *at least as to those who ever owned the Parliament's cause*, in that, instead of making use of that power the nation intrusted him with for their preservation and protection, as to their liberties spirituall and civill, he endeavoured their ruyne and destruction in both, yea of the Parlament themselves; bidding them defyance by his leavying of armyes, and setting up his standerd against them before they made any preparations against him; intending heereby to put a period to that authority by force, whom he impoured by his owne act to continue till they should thinke fit to dissolve themselves; hereby rendring himselfe a traytor to the publique, and a falsefyer of his owne act.

2. That he was a tyrant, was no less evident, in that the whole course of his reigne was to trample upon the knowne lawes, wherein the liberty and propriety of the people were concerned, yea and upon parlaments also, that his lusts might have no controle, but will and prerogative rule. Yea he justified this horrid principle at the barr of the High Court of Justice (when it was chardged upon him that he had betrayed the trust the people had reposed in him), alleadgeing that he was entrusted only by God, and to render an account only to him, and that the kingdome was his by inheritance, to wit by conquest, that being the originall of his title.

3. His being guilty of murder, was most notorious, in that for the carrying on of this tyranicall principle, and treacherous and horrid designes, he issued out several comissions, by which severall of the good people of England were slayne, as at Keinton battle, at Brainford, Causham, Glocester, Newbery, Cornewall, Marston Moore, Naisby, and many other places in England and Wales, where many thousands were slayne by his express command.

4. That he was an enemy to the Comonwealth, appeares in that he was the supporter of all corrupt interests who united themselves

to extirpate what was most deare to the good people of the nation, either as men or Christians; and not only so, *but in appropriating to himselfe those powers and attribuits which are only due to the Lord, thereby doing what in him lay to make God their enemy; the people being oftentimes punished for the sins of the magestrate, 2 Kng. 23, 26, 1 King 18. 18, 15 Jer. 4. Those who were eminent for virtue amongst the heathen expressed the greatest hatred immaginable against such as deprived them of their liberty; insoemuch that M. T. Cicero, though hee had an esteeme for Caesar's person in his Phillipians, making mention of his death affirmes that al good men as much as in them lay killed Caesar: to some there waunted counsell, to others courage, to others opportunity, to none goodwill to have done it. And Seneca the tragedian, declareing that* **767** in the opinion of the Romans and Gretians, [there was no more?] acceptable sacrifice then the blood of a tyrant, ... useing to set up their portraiteurs in the [temples of their gods?] who had slayne a tyrant. And one of our.... of no meane account, declared in a very great .... assembly, That A Tyrant Ought To Be [Knocked On The Head?] As Foxes, Wolves, Lyons And Other Beasts Of Prey, Wherever They Are Mett. But because some of theise .... or not, according as they shall be judged prudent, [consideration being had?] to the circumstances of persons, tymes and thinges, I shall mention something, first in relation to that of murther, which the majestrate (who hath power in his hand) is possitively enjoyned to execute on the guilty, and hath no liberty given him to dispense therewith. And in the next place, I shall endeavour to prove that all these three circumstances abovesaid relating to those three particculars, and also in relation to this fourth (in case any prudentiall consideration might be had thereof), did at this tyme concurr for the justifying of the execution of the King.

The sin of murder and its punishment are written in the booke
1 of nature
2 of God's word. } That it is written in that of nature, appeares
in that Cain, after he had slaine his brother Abell, cryes out that everyone that mett him would slay him; and this before any written word was given by the Lord therein, and had bin without doubt put in execution upon Cain had not a marke bin set on him by God, lest any meeting him should kill him, as it's said in Gen. 4. 14, 15.

And that it's also written in the booke of God's word, there is no law therein more express. For the first law that God gave after the flood was against murder, as appeares in Gen. 9. 5, 6, And surely your blood of your lives will I require: at the hand of every beast will I require it, and at the hand of man; at the hand of every man's brother will I require the life of man. Whoso sheddeth man's blood, by man shall his blood be shed: for in the image of God made he man.

So in Exod. 21. 12, He that smites a man, so that he dyes, shall be surely put to death; and in vers. 14, If a man come presumptuously upon his neighbour to slay him with guile, thou shalt take him from mine altar, that he may dye; likewise in Levit. 24. 17, He that killeth any man shall surely be put to death. And it's expressly declared in Numbers 35. 31, Ye shall take no satisfaction for the life of a murderer, which is guilty of death, but he shall be surely put to death. In this sense only is the saying of Christ to be understood, who came not to destroy the world, but to fulfill it: Mat. 26, 52, *Hee that taketh the sword, shall perish with the sword; and those of the holy spirit in the 13th [Rev.?] 10, Hee that killeth with the sword, must be killed with the sword.* Yea, in case of fayler in duty in proceeding according to this most cleare and possitive rule, the magistrate (who hath power in his hand to execute the same) sinnes not only against his owne soule, but contracts a guilt upon the whole land wherein the blood unavenged is shed, as appeares in Deut. 19. 10: the children of Israel were required to doe as is there directed, concerning the cittyes of refuge, for such as slew their neighbour ignorantly, as by the slipping of the head of an hatchet from the helve etc., that innocent blood be not shed in thy land which the Lord thy God giveth thee for an inheritance, and so blood be upon thee; verse 11: But if any man hate his neighbour and lye in wayte for him, and rise up against him, **768** and smyte him mortally that he may dye, and flees into one of these cittyes; vers. 12: Then the elders of his citty shall send and fetch him thence and deliver him into the hand of the avenger of blood, that he may dye; vers. 13: Thine eye shall not pitty him, but thou shalt put away the guilt of innocent blood from Israel, that it may goe well with thee. This is also most clearely asserted in Numbers 35. 33, Ye shall not pollute the land wherein ye are, for blood it defiles the land; and the land cannot be cleansed of the blood that is shed therein, but by the blood of him that shed it.

Notwithstanding the possitiveness of all which lawes, some will object, yea even of those who were engaged in the Parliament's cause against the King (and therefore thought not themselves guilty of the blood shed, but that consequently he was, nothing being more cleare then that blood was shed, and that the guilt must be charged somewhere), that those lawes ought to be executed against particcular persons, but not against kinges. Marcus Tullius Cicero, in his Oration in the behalfe of *Rabinus*, saith, *If it were unlawfull to put Saturninus to death, it was unlawfull to make warre against him,* but that if it were lawfull to make warr against *Saturninus*, it was lawfull to put him to death. But to come to the infallible word of God, the rule of faith and manners, the severall texts that have bin quoted being generall, it belongs to those who will have any sort of men excepted, to prove that they ought so to be; to which end some have urged Prov. 8. 15, 16, By me kings reigne, and princes decree justice: by me princes rule, and nobles, even all the judges of the earth; *which though it bee only intended to bee by way of permission, when they are set up contrary to the Lord's institution* (as appeares in the witness God bore against the children of Israel's making choyce of a king, saying, that therein they had rejected him rather then Samuell), yet can it be supposed that because God permits kings, princes and judges to rule in the earth, that therefore they are to be exempted from punishment on the breach of God's lawes, whom they pretend to derive their authority from? No, in no wise. For as by God, kings, princes and judges of the earth rule, so it's said, and decree justice; intimating by this clause that whoever is a majestrate, that is his duty, namely, to decree justice, either as directed by the light of nature, or the word of God. Otherwise, if we thinke that God will support magistrates (who are his vicegerants) to commit murders, and therein destroy his owne image in man, as it's called in Gen. 9. 6, we in effect say that God can deny himselfe, which is blasphemy; for saith the Apostle, 2 Tim. 2. 13, God cannot deny himselfe. *Yea, by this text all the judges of the earth are exempt from punishment, as wel as kings.*

But the example of David in not slaying Saul is much insisted on, because it was in his power so to doe.

To which it's easily answered, that David was then only a private person, and no magistrate; *and David could have saved himselfe from Saul by flight, and therefore it was unlawfull for him to kill him. But it's ridiculous to imagine that David, who led an army for his defense, would have stood still, and suffered Saul to have murdered him. But if the law of God say the king is not enough, and David should say otherwise, we are to believe the law of God before him.* That also of David's murthering of Uriah, and yet confessing he had sinned against God only, is made use of to prove him unaccountable; whereas he expresseth himselfe in that nature rather to aggravate his sin against God, then to extenuate it in relation to man; having pronounced the sentence of death upon **769** himselfe, 2 Sam. 12. 5, 7; which for ought I know had bin put in .... [against him?], had he bin publiquely charged therewith, and had .... the Lord pronounced him pardoned, *2 Sam. 12. 13*, who could [have?] .... men for the doing of it; though otherwise, how [could?] it be [expected?], when in the case of Joab's murthering Abner ...., 2 Sam. 3. 39, That the sons of Zeruiah were too [strong for him?]. As they had not only the cheife comand in the army, but as men of admirable couradge and vallour, they were .... [in the hearts of the?] people, *that any should bee found to execute justice on David himselfe. It may bee alsoe heereunto further answered, that sin, as sin, is most properly against God; and therefore it's that God, against whom it is, can forgive it, 2 Marke 7, he only.*

Another scripture the King himselfe made use of, when speaking against the jurisdiction of the Court, and which by his direction was afterwards published; this beeing the only scripture he urged, viz. Ecclesiastes 8. 4, Where the word of a king is, there is power, and who may say unto him what doest thou. But how little to the poynt may easily be discerned. For the reason why none might say unto the King, What dost thou?, was because the King had power. But seeing the King had no power, it might be said unto him, What dost thou? or rather, What hast thou done? Yea, to me the argument seemes very strong against him; for if, where the word of a king is, there is power, where there is no power there is no king. But upon the appeale that was made to God, that he would judge the controversy betweene him and the Parlament; he being devested of power, and the Parlament cloathed therewith, he ought to have submitted himselfe unto those on whose side the Lord had judged the appeale, and not to have said unto them, What doe yea?

How many kinges did the children of Israel put to death before they posessed the land of Canaan, as may be seene by the execution which Joshua made upon five at one tyme, Joshua 10. 17, 18, 22, 23, 24? *Yea hee slew all their kings (whose heart the Lord had hardened) and tooke all their cittyes in battaile, ii Joshua 17, 18, 19, 20, save the Gibeonits, who were a Commonwealth . . . . , 10 Josh. 2, and had their lives given them for a prey, because they believed none of the Lord, and opposed not his worke, 9 Josh. 9, 24, 26 verse.* And did not Samuell the prophet of the Lord the like to Agag, the King of the Amalakites, commanding him to be brought forth, when Agag said, Surely the bitterness of death is past, 1 Sam. 15. 32, heweing him in peices before the Lord in Gilgal? And doth not the prophet sharpely reprove Ahab from God, because he had suffered Benhadad the King of Syria to escape, whom the Lord had delivered into his hands, to be slayne? Yea; for saith the prophet, 1 Kings 20. 42, Thus saith the Lord, because thou hast let goe out of thy hand a man whom I had appointed to utter destruction, therefore thy life shall goe for his life, and thy people for his people.

But some will say, these kinges were enemyes to the people of God, and therefore appointed to destruction, *and kings taken in battaile*. But was it ever heard that the people of God destroyed their owne kinges? Truly, it's in one sense acknowledged that though the people of God wound their king, they cannot destroy him, because as the prophet Jeremiah describes him *who is borne King of the Jewes, 2 Math. 2*, to be the true God and the living God, so is he said to be the everlasting King, Jer. 10. 10. Therefore said Gideon to the children of Israel (when they would have him and his sonnes to rule over them, Judges 8. 22), vers. 23, I will not rule over you, neither shall my son rule over you, the Lord shall rule over you. But suppose it lawfull for the people of God to cast off the goverment he had set over them, and to be like other nations, *[they?] adde unto all their wickednesse, not only of Samuell, but the Lord himself, in setting* up a king over them. Yet that kinges over such a people should not rule according to their lusts, the Lord appoints them a rule to walke by; as you may see in Deut. 17. 18, 19, And it shall   **770** .... upon the throne of his kingdome, that he shall .... a coppy of this law in a booke, out of that which is before [the priests?] and the Levits. And it shall be with him, and he shall .... all the dayes of his life, that he may learn to .... Lord his God, to keepe all the wordes of this law, and ... statutes to doe them; that his heart be not lifted up above ... brethren, and that he turne not aside from the comandement, to the right hand or to the left, to the end that he may prolonge his dayes in his kingdom, etc.; which otherwise might be shortened, especially if he should be found a murtherer, and so guilty of blood. For saith the Lord, in Gen. 9. 6, At the hand of man, at the hand of every man's brother, will I require the life of man. And in that same relation a king is said to be, in the above recited place, Deut. 17. 20.

And Solomon, the most absolute King that ever was over the people of Israel, layes it downe for a possitive rule without exception, Prov. 28. 17, A man that doth violence to the blood of any person shall flee to the pit, let no man stay him. And what is left on record, Prov. 24. 21, My son feare thou the Lord and the king, etc., doth wonderfully magnify the wisedome of God; who (foreseeing that these wordes, feare the Lord and the king etc., would in after ages be wretchedly misapplyed by such who (making their belly their God) would exalt man in the place and stead of God) doth pre-caution, as in vers. 23, that these thinges also belonge to the wise, etc., that is, to the spiritually wise, who acknowledge the Lord Christ to be their King, 1 Sam. 2. 10, Psal. 2. 6, Dan. 7. 14. And what thinges are those that belong to the wise? See the following words, in Prov. 24. 23, It is not good to have respect of persons in judgement; explaining it further, in vers. 24, 25, He that saith to the wicked thou art righteous, him shall the people curse, etc.; but to them that rebuke him, shall be a delight, and a good blessing shall come upon them. So that if no respect ought to be had to persons in judgement, then are not the greatest of men, not kings, to be excepted as above judicature, which some weakely pretend. Nor did Saul, who was a king, think so; for if he had, he would not have put himselfe and Jonathan in one lot, and the people in another, and afterwards himselfe in one lot and Jonathan in another, in a business that was made capitall, 1 Sam. 14. 40, 41, 42. Yea, did not the people, when the lot fell to Jonathan, refusing to let him dye according to the sentence and oath of the King,

vers. 44, 45, plainly demonstrate that their authority was still para-
mount to that of the kinges?

Likewise did not Jehu, by the comand of God himselfe, destroy
Joram the King of Israel, and Jesabell, and all the children of Ahab,
and though (because he did it to exalt himselfe) the Lord saith he
would avendge the blood of Jezreel upon the howse of Jehu? Yet
was not Jehu comended, yea rewarded for his worke, so that to the
fourth generation of his seede sate upon the throne? Yea, did he not
also put Ahaziah the King to death? And if it be said that Jehu had
no comission so to doe, I answer, he was not reproved for so doing.
Yea, he was comended tacitly for killing Ahaziah also, for it's said
that Jehu did well in executing that which was right in the Lord's
eyes, 2 Kings 10. 30. And Jehoiada the high priest, that good man,
made no scruple, **771** when he had a power in his hand, to put
Achaliah to death for . . . . and usurpation, notwithstanding her crying, Treason, treason; and no doubt had her party prevayled (though
the attempt of Jehoiada was just), they would have condemned him
for treason and murder. And though Joash (following the steps of his
mother) proved so ungratefull as to put Zacharias, the son of this good
Jehoiada, to death, for reproving him and his councellors for their
sin, and that for the blood of the son of Jehoiadah the priest the King's
owne servants conspired against him and slew him, and that Amaziah
his son (as soone as the kingdome was established to him) slew those
who had killed the King his father, yet if you consider the text, it
will appeare that though the act was a good act, it was not well done,
for those that did it were private persons, and his servants.

And some also observe that one of them was the son of an Ammone-
tess, and the other of a Moabetess, which nations the Lord had
ordered to be destroyed. But if you reade to the end of the same
chapter, 2 Chron. 25, you will finde that the same Amaziah, when
he turned from following the Lord, for his misgoverment the people
in Jerusalem made a conspiracy against him. And though he fled to
Lachish, they sent to Lachish and slew him there, and brought him
upon horsses, and buryed him with his fathers in the citty of Judah.
And all the people took Uzziah, his son of 16 yeares of age, and made
him King in his roome. But we read of no inquisition made by him,
or any other, after the death of his father; which together with the
sending after him to Lachish, to put their designe in execution, plainly
implyes that the princes and cheife of the people were engaged
therein. Yea, Uzziah himselfe was dethroned, and submitted to dwell
in a howse by himselfe as a lepper, being for his leprosy cut off from
the howse of the Lord *for violating a part of the ceremoniall law*. And shall
the law against the crying sin of murther have a more favourable *execution*? Shall a leaper be put from the throne, and not a murtherer?

Shall a leaper be shut up from the people, and shall not a murderer be cut off? Yea David the King, the man after God's owne heart, after he encouradges the people, in Psal. 149, to rejoyce in him that made them, and to be joyfull in their king, vers. 2, to wit Christ, he incites them, as to have the high prayses of God in their mouthes, so a two-edged sword in their hand, vers. 6, to execute vengeance upon the heathen, and punishments upon the people, to bind their kings with cheynes and their nobles with fetters of iron, vers. 7 & 8. And is this all? No, see vers. 9: To execute upon them the judgements written, to wit upon kings and nobles. For in vers. 7, he speakes of executing vengeance upon the heathen, and punishments upon the people; which had not David knowne to have bin agreeable to the mynde of God, he would never have incited any *soe* to doe, as their duty; and then concludes, This honour have all his Saints.

Now if this were the opinion of the King of Israel touching this particcular, and the kings of those people were thus treated in the case of justice (as you see, kings chosen by the free vote of the people), after they were acquainted by Samuell what kings would doe, which might imply they were chosen on those tearmes, and were annoynted by the appointment of God to the said office (wherein, as also in their persons, how farr they tipified the kingly office of Christ over his church, I shall not heere undertake to discuss), how much stronger is the case against **772** those .... refuse to owne his authourity from the choyce of the people, but claymed it by inheritance, viz. by conquest; a most unjust and tyranicall title, for the maintenance of which, [and exalting?] himselfe in the roome of God, he usurps the crowne .... [of Jesus?] Christ; trampling his people, and the law of the ...., and (that he might mainteyne his arbitrary and [tyranicall power?]) engages in a bloody warr against the people in .... title which was unjust in the beginning, beeing not made good .... of tyme. That the goverment by the sword is unlawfull, appeares in that it is against the end of goverment, which is the glory of God and the good of mankind; whereas that by the sword is to advance man in the roome of God, and to rule men not by reason but force, like beasts. Yea, it's against the whole series of God's word and promises, which declares that in the latter dayes vyolence shall be no more heard in the land, that there shall be no neede to learne warr any more, that the lamb shall lye downe by the lyon, and the leopard by the kid; with many places to the like effect.

And as the said King's title was ill founded *(and not much better in relation to his pretensions of succession, in that it offers violence to nature itself, which is often more liberall in bestowing magistratical endowments on many thousands then on the royall progeny, and on severall other accounts)*, so he (managing the power he had, not for the terrour of evill doers and encouradgement of those who did well, but to the contrary), had he had a good title to his power, he thereby deprived himselfe of it. And instead of the image of God upon him, such a magistrate as we are bound to obey for conscience sake, he had imprinted on him the image of the Devill. For as Christ told the Jewes, they were of their father the Devil, and the lusts of their father they would doe, John 8. 44. And the Apostle saith, Rom. 13. 3, that rulers are not a terrour to good workes, but to the evill, which implyes that when they cease to be so they cease to be magistrates, and (having only power on their side) prudence only obleidges them to give them obedience. Yea, the rules and directions given throughout the New Testament, touching majestrates, describe them only under the name of powers; which, as they stand related to particcular persons, I finde to be divided into these three sortes.

The one as to a higher power which is indisputably so: this though an unjust power, yet if we receive protection from it, we are bound to pay subjection to, either actively or passively; which obedience the good people of England gave to the King before the warr.

The second sort of rules relate to two powers that are in dispute, which of them is the higher; in which case we are directed to joyne with that which the Lord sets upon our heart to have most of his image on it, and to it to pay custome, feare and honour. This consideration lead most of the good people of England to owne the party of the Parlament against the King.

The third and last sort of rules relate to those who have a cleare call to their power, and desire to dischardge their duty therein; and that is, that they may be a terrour to evill doers, and a praise to them **773** that doe well. This consideration prevayled with . . . . an army, into whose hands the Lord had put a cleare and [indisputable?] power (least by suffering tyranny and murder to go unpunished they should encouradge evill doers, and discouradge the good people of England from ever appearing for the cause of God . . . . and so not only contract the guilt of innocent . . . . [their?] heads, but betray the cause of God), to proceed against . . . . as they did, and to execute the judgement that . . . .

Yea, so much are the contrary party to seeke of . . . . for the justifying of this unaccountableness of . . . . earthly power, that they (knowing the greatning of him is the most probable way to support them in their ambitious, avaritious and other corrupt interests) scruple not to wrest the scripture itselfe to a contrary sense to what the spirit of the Lord intended it; as in particcular those words of Psal. 105. 15, Touch not mine anoynted, and doe my prophets no harme, which (that they might the better apply to the kings of England) they

continue the anoynting of kings at their coronation, in allusion to the
anoynting of old the kings of Judah (who as was said before, being
types of Christ, were therefore anoynted); but though the king typi-
fied being come, the type ceaseth. These worldly polititians, having
the vayle upon their faces, and wilfully blynd, doe in this (as other
in their religious services) continue their ceremoniall worship, as if
Christ were not come in the flesh. But how this argument of theirs
reflects upon them will be easily discerned, if we consider that these
words, in Psal. 105. 15, were spoken of the children of Israel, as they
passed from Egipt, till possessed of Canaan; at which tyme they had
no king. And it will be more cleare, if we take notice of the precedent
words (in verse 14), that he reproved kings for their sakes, saying,
Touch not mine anoynted, etc., to wit the people of God; every one
of which, as sanctified, are said to be made by Christ, kings and priests
unto God and his Father, Rev. 1. 6. But the more ingenious of them,
being convinced of the thing itselfe, doe yet quarrell about the manner
of doing it, desiring that he should have bin tryed by twelve of his
peeres, a greater number then the scripture foretells the Roman
monarchy should be divided into; all which also will be found in the
same condemnation with him, and therefore not propper judges, having given up their power to the Beast.

But it's objected, that the oath of supreamacy and allegiance bound
those who tooke it from attempting anything against his person. The
oath of supreamacy was against the Pope's supreamacy in the church,
and not for his. And both that and the oath of allegiance bound us
to obey the King in his politique capacity, not in his personall; to
the King governing according to law, not contrary to it; to the King
of England that never dyes, not a mortall man like ourselves; *to the
King that cannot erre, not to him* that perverted the power he was
entrusted with, to destroy the lives, religion and libertyes of all the
good people of England, yea parlaments themselves, the vissible bul-
wark of all these. But   **774** [it's?] further objected, that the comission
of the Earle of Essex was to fight for King and Parlament. It's true,
and it had bin well if the Parlament had bin more cleare in their
declarations; for then the warr in all probabillity had come to a
speedier and better issue. But without doubt the King there meant
was the King in his pollitique capacity, not his personall; or otherwise
the Earle of Essex would not have judged himselfe at liberty to have
fyered the great gun that was on the left wing of his army against
the right of the King's, where it was thought the King in person then
was. However, to make this the more cleare, for the satisfying of those
who scrupled fighting against the King, in the comission which the
Lords and Comons gave to Sir Thomas Fairfax, those words, for the
King, were left out.

But it's objected, that by the Covenant we were obleiged to mainteyne the prerogative of the King, and the priviledge of Parlament;
both which were violated in putting the King to death, and the seclud-
ing of the major parte of the members of parlament for the making
way thereto.

To which it's answered, that it was not to be supposed one parte
of that Covenant was to be so intended as would clash with another;
as the swearing to defend the King's person (notwithstanding he
should be guilty of the blood of thousands) would with that of bringing
delinquents to their condigne punishment. Yea the additionall clause
to that of maintenyng the King's prerogative and the priviledge of
Parlament, viz. in the preservation of the lawes of the land and the
liberty of the subject, plainly holds forth what they intended thereby.
And if it consisted with the liberty of the subject for one who had
murdered many thousands of them to goe unpunished, then they violated the Covenant who brought the King to justice, otherwise not.
Besides, I have alwayes understood that a covenant must be recipro-
call betweene those who make it and those who expect any benifit
thereby. Now the King was so farr from giving those who tooke the
Covenant any benefit thereby, that he never tooke it, but opposed
the substance of it, and those who tooke it, to the very death. This
clause was interpreted publiquely in this sense in the Howse by Mr.
Henry Martin and myselfe, and some others, at the tyme of the taking
of this Covenant. And this was the ground of the addition of this clause
by Sir Henry Vane (comissioner on the behalfe of the Parlament of
England), when it was agreed upon by them and the Parlament of
Scotland to be taken. And in this sense we were obleiged to preserve the
priviledge of parlament; that which rendred them so acceptable to
the good people being their usefulness for the preserving of their libertyes from the encroachment of the prerogative of the King. But if they
joyne with the prerogative, not only to the destruction of their liberty
(and to render them in a farr worse condition, though conquerors,
then if conquered), but also to contract the guilt of blood upon their
head, the Covenant itselfe (preferring the liberty of the subject before
the maintenance of their priviledge, looking upon the welfare of the
people as the supreame law) obleidgeth them   **775** not any longer,
even to the observation of the .... That the King was guilty of
blood that the Lord [delivered?] .... did formerly Agag and Benhadad,
Joram and Amaziah, into the hands of [those?] .... to have done justice
upon him, hath bin sufficiently evidenced; as also that they instead
thereof, notwithstanding [the?] .... [they?] had made to bring delinquents to punishments, sue to .... for tearmes of peace, and though
severall .... [refused?] .... proceed not to doe justice upon him, [nor
to?] settle the nation without him; which occasioned a second

[bloody?] . . . . , which blood I cannot in some sense cleare the [Parliament?] of.

For had they done their duty at the end of the first warr, they had not probably had the second; for which the Lord might justly rent their authority from them, and cause the life thereof to goe for his whom the Lord had marked out for justice, *as Ahab's was to doe in the case of Benhadad, 1 King. 20. 24.* But so hardned were they in their apostacy, that they came to a conclusion with this man of blood; wherein they passed over the blood of the first and second warr, without any reall satisfaction, and give up the cause itselfe unto him; not taking care for the extirpating of episcopacy, which both nations had expressly covenanted to doe, and taking a lease of the militia of him for a few yeares, of which the people of right had the inheritance *and now the actuall possession*; which horrid vote of theirs some of us bore our witness against in the Howse, for that (according to the rules of law) they heereby forfeit their right, and acknowledge to have done the King wrong in contesting with him, even to blood, for that which is his right to give or not as he pleased. Therefore we desired our protestations might be entred to that purpose, telling them that wee now looked upon them as forsaken of God.

The army, now finding thinges brought to this pass, looke upon it as their duty rather to cut the roape, to violate the priviledge of parlament, then suffer the good man to be hanged, the cause of God through the treachery of men to be destroyed. And can they thinke hardly of this, who first invited others to the like attempt, as the cittizens of London, yea a rabble of vaine and idle weomen, to importune the Parlament and the members thereof to a closure with the King; and the reformado officers, in a tumultuary way, to force the Parlament to a complyance with them in their desires; and the apprentices and other loose persons of the citty of London, and the countyes of Surrey and Kent, to force the Parlament's guard, yea the Parlament itselfe, throwing stones in at the wyndows of the Howse of Lords, knocking at the doore of the Howse of Commons, and compelling the Speaker to retorne into the chaire after the Howse was adjourned and rissen, yea coming into the Howse 60 or a hundred of them, enjoyning the Howse to vote what they pleased touching the retorne of the King, and this to the apparent ruyne of the publique cause and all the faithfull assertours of it? Can these (I say) blame the army, and those of the Parlament who fled to them for protection, for releeving of them from this vyolence thus offred them, and for making use of that power the Lord had put into their hands, to rescue that cause from being betrayed, which cost so much blood and treasure, and **776** which the Lord in many wounderfull wayes had so emynently owned? Have they cause to complayne of the army's violating the priviledges of parlament, which had before (by their own inciting of others) so oft bin defloured upon base and unworthy accounts, and was so farr only to be reputed sacred and inviolable as it was made use of as a meanes tending to the advancement of the glory of God, and good of the nation? For my parte I must acknowledge I was so well satisfyed in the justice and necessity of this undertaking (looking upon a good cause and a good sword to be a good authority), that, as I had (long before it was put in execution) earnestly desired and prayed the Lord would open a way and fit instrument for it (not seeing any other way to appease the wrath of God towards the nation for the blood that had bin shedd during the warrs, nor to settle the peace of the nation for the future, but by bringing of the King to justice, and no other way to effect that in so regular a way as by excluding those members of parlament who, being by some temptation or other drawne off to the King, obstructed the same), so I did contribute my utmost endeavours, wheresoever I had to doe, to promote the putting of the same in execution.

But to speake something in justification of those whose principles lead them not to be active in the excluding of the said members, and yet were satisfyed they were bound in conscience to proceed juditially against the King, as farr as providence opened them a way. The members were excluded. A quorum notwithstanding, viz. forty members and more, were admitted. These upon complaint made to them, that some of their members were excluded, send the Serjeant with his mace for them, and (finding they were excluded by order of the Lord Fairfax their Generall) send also to him, they could not get them restored. What would you have had them to have done? Should they have quitted their stations, and left the goverment of affaires in the hand of the military sword? Was it not better to preserve the face of civill authority? Should they have bid defyance to the army, and so (by weaking of their hands) have given an opportunity to the comon enemy to have taken advantadge to have effected his mallice and revenge upon all the honest interest? Yea, should they neglect the calling of the King to account for the blood that had bin shed, being that which they were convinced was their duty to doe, as required of them from the Lord, and from the good people of the nation (by many of which they were petitioned to that end, as the only way to appease the justice of the Lord and to settle the publique peace)? I assure myselfe there is no conscientious unbyassed person would blame them for steering the course they did, yea that would not have condemned them as the betrayers of the cause of God and the country had they steered any other.

I make no mention of the Howse of Lords, because they withdrew themselves from the exercise of their dutyes without any force being put upon them. Besides, they were rather the councell of the King then of the people, **777** and therefore (being his shaddow) were unwilling to ... themselves unnaturall in destroying themselves, to wit their substance, the King. And of that Howse some of them were willing that .... be done, though not by their hands; which appeares in that they afterwards declyned their peerage, and accepting a call .... the people sat in the Parlament, as parte of their representative .... chosen ....

I presume enough hath bin said for the [justice?] of both Parlament and army, in what they did as to the King, [both as it related to the?] possitive and indispensible law of God, and to the meanes [that were made?] use of in order thereto. It remaines that something be said to the prudentiall parte of it, viz. as it related to the advancement of the gospell of Christ, and the setting up of his scepter and rule; and secondly, to the good of the publique.

As to the first, though Charles Steward was not the Anti-Christ spoken of by the Apostle, yet was he one of the kinges that gave his power to the Beast. Yea, albeit in appearance the nation had cast off that yoake, yet did he assume to himselfe the headship of, the church, and in effect (as farr as he could) obstruct the propagation of the gospell, no other doctrine being willingly permitted to be taught within his dominions but such as suited with and supported his corrupt interest of tyranny and domination; which being witnessed against by the spirit of the Lord, from the beginning of Genesis to the end of the Revelations, he therefore used his utmost endeavours for the hindring of the publication of that holy word; as resolving that Jesus Christ should not rule over him, nor to receive his crowne upon the tearmes of the gospell (which directs that the desciples of Christ should not exercise dominion over one another, as the kings of the Gentils doe, but those who would be great should be the servant of all), nor by the rules Moses gives touching kinges; which (amongst others) that they should walke amongst the people as brethren to them. But how unsuitable the principle and practice of the said King was to such express comands was apparent to all who were not wilfully blynd, he owning the people to be his by inheritance, to wit by conquest, and that he was accountable for his actions to none but God.

As to that consideration which related to the good of the publique, could there be a greater assertion of the King's pretension to an interpretation of the lawes, to the command of the militia, to a negative voyce (upon the resolution of the whole nation), to an unaccountableness, in effect to an absolute, arbitrary and tyrannicall power in church and state, then for a Parlament, whose sessions the Lord by his wounderfull providence had continued till they should thinke fit to dissolve themselves, and whose battles the Lord had fought and

owned (to a very myracle) to the delivering of his and their enemye
into their hands, to be still suing unto a man of so much guilt and
blood, as if he were the life and very being of the nation, and all its
prosperity and welfare were wrapped up in him? Needed hee any
other to destroy all that should oppose him, but his owne hands? May
he be allowed to murder as many as he please, and yet be not only
unaccountable but King still? Had the Parlament lost but one considerable battle, both they and all that adhered to them had bin dealt
with as traytours and murtherers. And now the   **778** [Lord was
pleased?] to render them absolute and entire conquerours, and put
[the?] power into their hands of doing whatever was in the hearts
of men .... for the good of the nation, shall they put them into a
farr worse condition then if they had bin wholy vanquished? Now
what more .... that it was so. For as one said well in the Howse of
Commons, [it would be farr?] more desirable the King should wade
to his [tyranicall?] throne through the blood of the Parlament and
[people?] then that he should be advanced thereto by their consent.
For upon the first account he could have but a title thereto by dis-
seisure, as his predecessor William the Bastard (commonly called the
Conqueror) had; which he could keepe no longer then whilest he was
the stronger, and which we might dispossess him of when we had power
so to doe. But what the nation, when the power was intirely in their
hands (as now it was), should freely give him, would be his upon the
strongest title imaginable, consent taking away all errour. And truly,
what people would ever be so mad as to appeare on the behalfe of
a parlament againe, when they see that the best issue they can expect,
after such vast expense of blood and treasure, is but to loade themselves with more fetters, and to render their posterity more slaves then
before? It was also most vissible, that the not executing of justice upon
him at the end of the first warr was the cause of the shedding of many
thousand men's lives in the second. And had it not bin done at the
end of the second, it would have occasioned a third, or worse, viz.
the giving up of the cause unto him; which was about to be done,
had it not bin obstructed upon the consideration aforementioned.

Neither hath it any weight in it, for such as endeavoured the betraying of the cause to say, in their excuse, that the King owned the justice
of the Parlament's cause; that he left the militia to the two Howses for
ten yeares; that he confirmed the sale of bishops' lands for a hundred
yeares; that he excepted some of the party out of the act of indemnity.
For though he owned it in words in the preamble, yet the Parliament
accepting of his graunt of the militia, and the confirmation of bishops'
lands upon those tearmes, plainly justified his cause. For though the
Lord, upon the appeale, had given the militia to the Parlament, yet
they thinke not their title good to it without his consent; and (instead

of the inheritance) now they accept of a lease of yeares (and that but
of tenn), by which they confess it to be of right in the King. And
what more cleare then that the Parlament, accepting of a lease of
a hundred yeares of bishops' lands, of which they had sold the inheritance, and taken mony for it, acknowledged thereby that they had
sold what was not theirs, and that the inheritance was still the
bishops', and so they not rooted out, though the two nations by a
Sollemne Covenant had in the face of the world sworne to doe it,
as was before hinted?

As to the exception of some of the King's party out of the act of
indemnity, it was but a mocking of justice, there being none of the
said persons   **779** in custody. And had they bin, how unreasonable
had it bin to have brought them to justice who were but accessoryes,
and to have [let?] the King not only goe free, but be King still? And
if any [thinge in these concessions?] were intrenching upon the
prerogative, and tending to publique good, how easy was it for him
to render it fruitless, by [pretending that when he?] consented thereto
he was not free, being then .... was not cause to thinke, considering
his [treachery and falsehood during?] the whole course of his life that
he wanted .... [that, so also?] they, who observed (even by those
who had bin ....) .... upon him, and flattering there was of him,
.... most worshipping him as the rising sun, and [endeavouring?]
to get places for themselves and relations, had little cause to doubt,
when he was on his throne (his guards of his own choosing), and when
he by his presence influenced the Parliament and citty of London,
that he would want power to put the same in execution.

Notwithstanding what hath bin sayd heerein, some who were concerned of their duty, considering the hazzard and difficultyes that
probably would accompany the execution thereof, might yet want
zeale to engage therein. As Major Generall Skippon once sayd to me
(who had *usually* resolution to prosecute what he undertooke), though
he waunted couradge to appeare in that affaire, yet professed he
highly honoured those who had. But for those who ever owned the
cause of the Parlament against the King, not only to disowne that
act, but to prosecute those to the death, yea to make use of treacherous
and underhand dealings (as they did in conspiring with Monke, that
monster of mankinde, for the butchering of those whom the Lord
honoured to be instrumentall in the dischardge of their duty therein),
could arise from nothing but the depth of mallice and revenge,
because an obstruction was put thereby to their ambitious designes
that they fancyed to themselves in the bargaine they had driven with
that man of blood; they having had all the tenderness and freindshipp
exercised towards them and their interest, during their exclusion from
the supreame authourity, that could consist with the safety of the

publique, nor any of those ministers (though continually bidding defyance in their pulpits to the authority that afforded them protection and countenance) being deprived of their advantadges, except Mr. Love, who, not contented with the liberty (or rather licentiousness) that was assumed by those of his party, contributed to and contrived the restoring of Charles Steward, the irreconcileable enemy of the Comonwealth (though he had formerly preached publiquely, before the comissioners at the treaty at Uxbridge, that no reconcilliation could be had with that familly untill they had made satisfaction for the blood that had bin shedd); for which, as he justly merited, he was deprived of his life.

Neither was any gentleman, or others, barely upon the account of their former carriadge, or present dissatisfaction, deprived of their estates. But suppose it possible that they could imagine themselves strong enough (after they had suppressed those of the Parlament and army who in their principles and interest were most engaged against Charles Steward and his familly) for the promoting of that goverment in the church which they looked upon themselves bound in duty viis et modis to advance, had it not bin prudence in them to have left that judgement and proceeding against the said King unwitnessed against, that by such an example the beasts of prey, the kings of the earth, might be kept more in awe, and so rendred fitter to be conversed with for the future?

But for those *who (as Salmasius observes) in their Declaration on the 26th of May 1642 affirme, they have the sole power to interpret the lawes; that this ought not to be contested by the King, nor any of his subjects, but that absolutely the welfare of the people, the safty of the kingdom and the conservation of the King, is in their hands, and depends on their will; that noe allegation or example ought to bee produced that may prejudice their deliberations, or present actions, because they themselves are the rule of what they doe; that the Parliament in consideration of the publiq good may dispose of all affaires, where the King or his subjects pretend to have any interest, because the Parliament may decide anything that concernes the good of the state, without the interposition of the King, and that it is not necessary to wayte his consent in such cases; that the Parliament hath full power to pronounce definitive arrests touching the lives and libertys of all the King's subjects, and of the lawes that are to bee made for their good and safety, haveing power at all times without reserve (provided that the greatest parte of the one, and the other House consent thereunto) to abolish them, and that the King may not couver them with his protection; that noe member of either House may either bee prosecuted, or accused of felony or any other crime, before the case be first presented to them; in [fine?], that the supreame power resides in the two Houses of Parliament, and that the King hath noe . . . . opposition or refuse, that is, noe negative voyce; and as the same Salmasius observes, that in their addresses to the King about the militia, etc., they tell him they [take it?] from him because it is not his; that the welfare of the kingdom depended not on him, or his race; that they were above his person, and might dispose .... pleasure; that without exceeding the bounds of modesty they might degrade him; I say for those who dealt thus clearely and freely with him, and ....* **780** rightly distinguished betweene his politique capacity and personall, and owned his politique capacity to be in the Parlament, and under that banner made warr against them in his personall capacity, and through the blessing of the Lord upon their councells and forces subdued and tooke him prysoner (yea though, as an irreconsileable to them, he made a second warr upon them whilest a prysoner), not only formerly to make tearmes with him (wherein they gave up their cause), but, for this and other reasons (which some thought very sollid and rationall) being excluded from Parlament by a vote of the Howse of Commons (who all acknowledge to be judge of their owne members), to make use of a force for their restoring into the Howse (having engaged before they came in to deliver up the cause), and being there (which they had no more right to bee as members, then those who never were chosen) for them to undertake to put a period to that Parlament without asking the Lords' or King's consent (which according to their principles were necessary to be had) for the avoyding of that which was continued by act of parliament, and for them (whilest they appoint the Covenant to be hung up in the churches and other publique places) to appoint a new Howse of Commons to be chosen in the name of the Keepers of the Libertyes of England, and that the party of the King themselves be electours of members to this representative, and that this representative, called by the Comonwealth writ, should take upon them not only to act as a Howse of Commons, and to conclude upon tearmes (or rather to call in the great enemy of the Comonwealth without tearmes), but to agree that those who appeared in that famous act of justice against the aforesaid King by virtue of the commission they received from the lawfull authority of the nation, the Parliament (which as hath bin made appeare is yet in beeing) should be left to be devoured by the son of him who was justly condemned as a tyrant, traytour and murtherer (divers also of those members, who had a hand in the warr against the King, being also members of this representative, and consenting to if not promoting of this horrid treachery and butchery), I leave it to Indians, Turkes and heathens to judge thereof; not doubting but those of posterity who have any sparke of love to morality and common honesty, much more to religion, will have it in horrour and detestation.

But I would not be thought to include all of that Convention, or of the secluded members, under the like guilt, and so under the same condemnation. Some I know who, though unfree to sit in Parliament

after the force was put upon them (as doubting least the goverment
of the army, being monarchycall, would therefore obstruct the interest
of a Comonwealth, and reduce the civill goverment into the like constitution with itselfe), were yet unfree to countenance the force that
tution with itselfe), were yet unfree to countenance the force that
Monke put upon the Howse for the betraying of the publique cause.
I knew divers also, though they thought the most probable way to
settle all thinges in church and state (and to free themselves from the
power of the military sword, by which they and the honest interest
had much cause to complaine that they had bin, since Cromwel's
usurpation, imposed upon) to be the bringing in of the King, yet
desired it might be upon strict tearmes, as the confirmation of all sales,
and a full indemnity for whatsoever had bin passed. Yea, I knew
others   **781** who were fully in their affections and principles against
his [coming?] ..., but, seeing the streame run so stronge for it, they
having done that ..., by the rigour of the law (when the interpretation
thereof should be [in?] the judges of the King's appointing, and the
juryes, who were to be judges in matter of fact, chosen by sherifs of
the King's making), they were lyable to be ruyned as well as others,
thought it prudence to swim with the streame, and to sacrifice some,
hoping thereby to secure themselves; which though it might extenuate, could not expiate their cryme. And others, by complying for the
present, judged it the most probable way to be serviceable to honest
men and their interest for the future.

But to forbeare speaking any further of instruments, or of causes
that moved them to what was done, I am assured it was done by the
wise disposing hand of God, without whose providence not a sparrow
falls to the ground, much less the blood of any of his pretious saints
and faithfull witnesses; whose dispensations heerein, as they have bin
righteous (in that the nation in generall seemed not to be fitted for
that glorious worke which hee seemed to bee doing for them by the meanes of
some of his poor people, and that they themselves, yea the best of them, were
to seeke of the way that lead thereto, a spirit of disunion and division being
got in amongst them), soe I am most confident these verry dispensations will
in the issue, and that in a short time, appeare to bee in mercy and peace to
his poore people, and to all who desire to live godly in the land, and that when
in the furnace they are melted into one lamp, they shall come forth as refined
gold. But it's the Lord's pleasure they should take this turne in the wildernesse,
and that man may not have whereof to boast. Hee seemes to take the rod into
his owne hand to correct them for their disobedience and unsuitable returns to
all those eminent appearances of his amongst them; Charles Steward and his
party not contributing the least to their restitution, but were altogether passive
therein, whilst those who were engaged against him, by clashing one with
another, give an advantage to him (their old and irreconcileable enemy) to breake

in upon them, I trust for the driveing of them together, and for the makeing them to prise the libertys and priviledges they did (or might have) enjoyed, had not their lusts interposed, that soe, beeing united to Jesus Christ their head, they may for time to come walke together in love as members of the same body, and may not bee confederating any more for the makeing them a captaine to lead them into Egypt. Yet soe it is, that the Lord is pleased for the present to make them the tayle, who before were the head, and that they should bow downe that their enemyes may goe over them.

And (as the prophet Isaiah saith, chapt. 59. 14) judgement being turned away backward, justice standing afarr off, trueth fallen in the street, and equity not able to enter, great endeavours there are to make voyd all that God had wrought for twenty yeares past, and to shew their hatred to the Lord's worke by their mallice to severall of his instruments. Care is taken how to sacrifice them to the lust and rage of the tyrannicall and popish interest; to which end, it's resolved by the junto who carryed on the counsels of the Convention (who called themselves a Howse of Commons) that on the   of May, all those who signed the warrant for the execution of the late King should be taken into custody; which was not carryed so secretly, neither was I so destitute of freinds, but that notice thereof was sent me by severall members of this Convention, as also to Mr. Scot and Mr. Phelps; the latter of which I found, upon conference with him, resolved to provide for his safety by going beyond sea. But Mr. Scot and myselfe were not yet fully resolved thereupon, but rather to conceale ourselves till we could more clearely see the issue of their councels. But being assured that the howse where I lived would be suddenly searched, I walked private wayes towards Marybone Parke, resolving to spend my tyme thereabouts till noone, and then to repaire to a kinswoman's howse of myne in Southampton **782** Buildings in Holborne, [whereto I had?] appointed some of my relations to repaire to me with an account of what had passed at Westminster. But my watch [deceiving me?], I mistooke two howres of the tyme appointed, and came not thither till after two of the clock; when passing through Baldwin's . . . . Gray's Inn, a gentleman of the King's party, knowing [what?] . . . . had done concerning the King's judges, and that I was [one of them?] . . . . he saw me, as he afterwards acquainted a . . . . was unfree to seize me; which I desire to owne as proceeding from the hand of the Lord.

When I came to the howse, I found my freinds had bin much in doubt of me, having fayled of my tyme. And upon the account I received of them as to the state of affayres, it was thought fit (seeing the entrance into that howse was very publique, and probably some-one or other might have seene me at my comming in) that I should remove to another freind's howse not farr from thence, the back doore

whereof being private, and leading into severall howses, might better
serve for the amusing of the enemy, should any happen to see me
enter; where I resolved to stay till night, and then to move to a private
howse in London that a friend of myne had provided for me a weeke
before. But when the night came, my deare freind (though sensible
of her danger in harbouring me, yet willing to hazard her all rather
then let me expose myselfe to danger by going abroad that night)
supposing the watch in London would be more strict then ordinary,
would therefore by no meanes let me goe; which, together with the
advise of some of my neere relations, made me looke upon it as a call
from the Lord to stay there; in which I was the more confirmed when
I was assured the next day that the watch looked into the coaches
as they passed through London that night, and as was supposed for
the discovery of such as were ordered by the Howse to be seized. I
heard not of any apprehended by this order for some dayes after its
issuing out, everyone concealing themselves with their friends, which
(as bad as the tymes were) they were not destitute of.

The Howse, finding themselves thus disappointed of their prey,
exercise their rage in ordering, in an extraordinary manner (upon
a supposition that they were fledd), the seizing of their reall and personall estates; it being contrary to law that the personall estate should
be confiscate till after conviction, and that whatever disposall thereof
is made before that tyme, by the person accused, should remaine good.
But these men, who are but the shaddow of a parlament, make use
of their arbitrary power that so they may trample the law of the land,
as well as conscience and reason, under foote. But that apostate
Coote, desyrous to outstripp all others in cruelty and wickedness, had
by his owne authourity made a seysure of my estate in Ireland before
the order came to him, taking from my tennants fower or five hundred
pounds that they had in their hands of rent due to me (*as before
mentioned*), and forceing my servant to engage not to dispose of any
of my stocke but by his order; I having at that   **783** tyme upon
my ground neere two thousand sheepe and [about?] .... mares, colts,
and horsses of all sortes, and as much corne and other [cattle?] as
was worth betweene three and fower hundred pounds .... an agent
of my brother Kempson's to take posession [of my?] stock; to whom
I had really, and bona fide, sold it for .... of mony which I owed
him, and whom he sent into Ireland for that end. But blessed be the
name of the Lord that [I had anythinge?] ... loose for him; for he
who lent them may call for [them, and it's not?] just that I should
willingly restore them.

I was no sooner thus driven out of the way, but my election for
the bourough of Hinden, to serve as a member of this Convention,
is brought upon the stage by the Comittee of Priviledges; wherein,

though I expected as in all other proceedings nothing but club law (and was put out of all hopes, had the election bin judged good, to have bin in a capacity of dischardging that trust), yet thought myselfe bound (as much as I was like to stand in neede of that little providence had left me) to mainteyne the right of the said election what lay in me, that so the towne, for their affection which they had manifested to me, might not suffer in their liberty. But the case in itselfe was so cleare that even the members themselves in private could not but confess that the right was on my side. Yet could my sollicitour scarse get any councell to appeare on the behalfe of those who had chosen me. And when it came before the comittee, though the chiefe witness of the other parte, one Cantlo, who (as Steward of the said place for the Bisshop) severall tymes before, in the elections for the said burrough, denyed not only those who payd not scot nor lot to have voyces, but having also much the lesser number of those 5 or six and twenty who ought to have voyces, returned Mr. Thomas Bennett to serve in Parliament (as by a letter under Mr. *Alisbury's* hand, who owned the other party, I had to make appeare), yet some of the comittee publiquely alleadging that, the case concerning a traytor, they needed not search any further thereinto, and so, stopping the mouth of councell and witnesses, proceeded to a resolution to the prejudice of the honest burghesses (if any president that such a corrupt comittee should make could be of weight).

Major Generall Harrison being brought to London, and the Howse acquainted therewith, they ordred him to be sent prysoner to the Tower, and directed that his horsses, which those who seized him had plundered him of, should be carryed to the Muse for Charles Steward's use. Justice Cooke also being sent by Coote to London, was by the like order comitted to the Tower; where those two faithfull witnesses, being much of the same spirit, enjoyed as much comunion the one with the other as the distance of the place would permit them to have.

The comissioners from the pretended Parliament attend Charles Steward at Bredagh; where the papists already were growne so high, that though those in the Howse of Commons had delivered the chardge to Mr. Denzill Holles of imparting their desires to the King, Mr. Henry Howard, brother to the Earle of Arundell, ruffles with **784** him, [on the behalfe?] of ..., one of the comissioners and a kinsman of [his?], alleadging that it had belonged to him to present the same, and that [it?] was a great insolence in Mr. Hollis to undertake it. But he affirming that he was entrusted therewith by the Howse, it being not yet tyme for Charles Steward to discover his inclynation to favour the popish party, he tooke up that difference. Fifty thousand pounds was sent over by them to Charles Steward, for the paying of his scores and the fitting him for his journey into England, and a considerable some to the Duke of Yorke and the Duke of Glocester. Many private persons also present Charles Steward with somes of money. Amongst others Mr. William Lenthall, Speaker of the Parliament, presented him with three thousand pounds. The person whom he made use of to that end, according to the comission he had received, moved Charles Steward, on the behalfe of Mr. Lenthall, that he might continue his imployment of being Master of the Rolles; but he replyed that it was already disposed of. It had bin happy for him, if he had dealt so cleerely in all other thinges; but the Lord had not that mercey in store for him.

Yet is he, who was lately excluded by articles from France and Holland, now courted by them. And being invited by the latter to honour them with his presence before his departure for England, he accepted of a treatment at the Hague (where they had shewed affection to his familly and interest), but refused to goe to Amsterdam (where they had bin at great chardge, in making ready some roomes in the State Howse and many other preparations for his enterteynement). And when the French Ambassadour came to attend him, he made him wayt long before he would admit him; and when brought in, he reflected upon the hard usuadges which he had from that nation, telling them he had bin so long thence that he had forgot the language. It's reported by some that the Spanyard, who had conferred most kindness on him during his banishment, would have deteyned him, to have forced him to have concluded on tearmes with them before he left them; and that he, having suspition thereof, went out of his teritoryes without taking any leave of the Governour of the place (to the dissatisfaction of the Governour), upon pretence that he would have done him this affront at his departure. Whether there were ground for this report, or whether Charles Steward had any for this his jealousy, I cannot say; but in case he had not, the Govenour in my opinion had for his dissatisfaction, for that his master and he were so ill requited for the kindness shewed him.

Those in the Howse of Comons in the interim labour hard for the preparing of the bill of indemnity, to be in a readyness against Charles Steward's comming over. It's resolved, without any contradiction, that some of the King's judges shall be excepted out of it as to life and estate, as a peace offring for themselves and the rest of the nation. The dispute amongst them is only touching the number to be **785** excepted. Some propose all, others twenty, others thirteene. But Monke, who had betrayed all, would be thought to be a mercyfull man, and to press for moderation; whereupon they are brought downe to nyne; which number Mr. Prin that beauteffeu, contrary to the order of the Howse, takes upon him to name. Yet I was so much beholden to him as that he named not me. Monke, speaking once more in this matter, prevayled with the Howse to bringe the number to seaven.

Of those who had withdrawne themselves, two, viz. Colonell Jones and Mr. Gregory Clement, were discovered. The first of them as I have heard, walking in Moore Feilds in the evening to take a little ayre (his lodging being neare that place), was seized on by some that knew him. And Mr. Gregory Clement lodging at a meane howse in Purple Lane neere Gray's Inn, better provissions being observed to be carryed in there then was usuall, upon suspition of some of the rabble and meaner sort (who generally, as of least understanding, were very zealous for his sacred Majestie) procured an officer to search the howse, and there found Mr. Clement; whom they concluding to be one of the King's judges, though they knew him not, carryed before the comissioners for the militia for that precinct to be examined; one of which, albeit he well knew who he was, after some slight examination of him, not willing to draw upon his head his innocent blood, was so farr from discovering him that he had prevayled with the rest of his company for the dismissing of him. But whilest he was withdrawing, it was the will of the Lord that a blynd man who was crowded into the roome, having some knowledge of Mr. Clement, and ghessing by his voyce (which was somewhat remarkable) that it was he, desired hee might bee called in and asked whether his name were not Mr. Gregory Clement; which the comissioners, not knowing how to refuse, did; and he, not daring to lye for the saving of his life, became thereby to be discovered. Both these also by order of the Howse were sent to the Tower.

Many of the King's judges got into Holland, and other partes beyond sea; of whom some escaped very narrowly, as Mr. Cornelius Holland, who had like to have bin seized at Colchester. The Maior being acquainted that a suspitious person was at the inn, who they supposed was Major Generall Lambert, sent thereupon and seized his horse and portmantle *at 4 of the clock in the morning*. But he by a good providence being abroad to receive money of his merchant (*who was to begin his journey early that morneing for London*), having notice of it, was by the favour of a freind conveyed out of the towne, *and (though examined by the watch) permitted to get off* on foote. I have heard also that Colonell Walton and Colonell Hewson both narrowly escaped, when Colonell Desbrow, **786** [who?] was not in that danger, was taken and persecuted by the boyes as he was carryed to the Councell of State. But they treated him [more?] civilly, [as one?] who by his carriadge in the army towards the [Parlament?] had much promoted their interest. For the [reception of?] and attendance on Charles Steward, most of those who had bin officers in his army, or were zealously affected to him, repayred to London, and at their great expense fitted themselves with horsses and cloaths (which most of them tooke upon credit), forming themselves into troopes, some under the Lord Lichfeild, others under the Lord Cleeveland, and others under that apostate Browne, and such like officers.

CHAPTER THREE

Newes being brought to Dover of Charles Steward's being put to sea, Monke with his garde *etc.* marcheth to Dover to meete him; where upon his landing *the 26th of May*, wayting on him, Charles Steward ownes Monke to be his father, *embraceing and kissing him.* And truly they were as brethren in iniquity, in treachery and falsehood neare allyed. The King bestowes on him the George *at Canterbury*, and the Duke of Yorke puts on him *the George, the Duke of Glocester* the Garter. Thus began the pageantry. And because the army who had fought against him were in their affections still the same, it was thought fit (besides the Declaration that was sent by Sir John Greenvill from Bredagh, wherein he oblieged himselfe to confirme all sales, and to give liberty of conscience, and to leave those thinges and the payment of the souldiers' arreares wholy to the Parlament), further to cajole the army, that Charles Steward's lodging, and his brother's the Duke of Yorke, be taken up at Colonell Gibbons his howse, a collonell of the army living at Rochester. Many knights were made as he came to London; and amongst others Mr. Robert Reynolds, for the good service he did in complying with Monke for the restoring of him; which some who were of the King's retinew observing, imediately told him that he had bestowed honour upon one of the veryest knaves of the Parliament party; which he seemed troubled that he had done, but sayd that Clergyes (whom he had before given a pattent to to be a baronet) had presented him to him as one that had done him very good service.

It was so ordred that he should make his entrance into London upon the day of his birth, which was the 29 May. As he came on the roade, the giddy multitude, promissing themselves all the felicity imaginable, make bonefires, burning the armes of the Comonwealth, the badges of their owne freedome. *Monke's army was drawen up on Blackheath, who merrited better the fool's coate then the souldier's cassaque.* The Lord Mayor, sheriffs and aldermen of the Citty *treated him under a tent in George's Field, with a collection;* and above five or sixe hundred cittizens were ordred by the Comon Councell, in black velvet coats and gold chaines, to attend him on horseback, which they did riding in their companyes, with trumpets, standards, and many footemen attending on them. *Browne the woodmonger with 300 horse had the van; Robinson followed .... 1200 in velvet cassaques and 12 ministers; the King's guard commanded by Gerrard; the Mareshal and officers of the Citty. Then the two sheriffs, and the aldermen, the heraulds and the serjeaunts, preceded the*

*Lord Mayor with his [naked sword?] ; and then the Duke of Buks. and Monke ;
and [then?] the King, with his two brothers on each hand ; the King's servants ;
a troop of horse ; Monk's guards commanded by Richard Howard ; five regiments
of horse of the army commanded by [Rupert?] ; and, after, 2 troopes of gentlemen
bringing up the reare.* Severall regiments of *the army foote, and the trayned
bands,* were ordred to make a guard for him as he was to ryde along;
in all which it is admirable that poore creatures should thus tamely
be brought to consent to their owne ruyne, many of them seeming
to rejoyce as if it had bin the day of their nuptials; Colonell Pride's
sonn, as he was in the head of his company,   **787** making up one
of that number.

And it is no less remarqueable that this cowardly enemy (whom
the Lord had so oft routed and witnessed against in the feild), having
not in the least contributed to his comming in, either by force or pollicy, should express such insolence and impudence (Monke and the
Duke of Yorke shewing them the way) as to ride with their drawne
swords through the citty of London to Whitehall; intimating thereby
their resolution to mainteyne that by force and vyolence which they
had gained the posession of by the height of treachery. And as Charles
Steward passed through the street, multitudes being gathered
together to see the sollemnity, though his lookes were very ghastly
at the best, yet was it observed that for the most parte they were full
of revendge, as if he would have the cittizens to see that he reteyned
in his memory the injuryes which his father and he had received from
them. Yet to some of his favourites he would looke with as pleasant
an aspect as he could; and particcularly on Mr. Mordant's lady, who
had ventured so much for him, and who, ravisshed with the honour
he did her, as she stood in her balcony at Carew Howse, and with
the joy of his arrivall, in a complement withdrawes into her chamber,
and beeing neere her tyme was presently delivered.

The Duke of Yorke, instead of thanking the people, who out of their
misguided affection press to see him and his brother, in a rage cuts
and slasshes them, against the rules of common prudence, yea
humanity. The Lords, and those who sate in the Howse of Commons,
attend at Whitehall to receive Charles Steward, and to give him his
welcomb thither; where you may presume the Speakers of both
Howses were not wanting in the flattering parte. His reply I heard
was very shorte, alleadging for his excuse his present indisposure,
by reason of the great acclamations as he passed alonge, which he
said were the more aggreable to him in that they expressed the affections of his people. All episcopall ceremonyes were prepared by Mr.
Busby and others of the Abby of Westminster, where it was expected
he would at his first coming have rendred himselfe to have retorned
thankes for his restitution. But he must yet carry it faire with the

presybterians; Mr. Calamy, Mr. Case, and severall others having gone to meete him, and promising themselves a great share in his favour. The only son of Sir Thomas Witherington, being sent by his father to pay his homadge to this idoll, in his journey was (by the just hand of the Lord) taken out of this life *by a violent feaver*.

Those who attended this sollemnity, after they had brought him to Whitehall (Fleete Street and the Strand being full of those who followed), retorned through Holborne to the citty of London; by which meanes I saw the army horse, and Browne and his troope, and severall others, riding with their swords drawne, and the cittizens of London with their pageantry; I lying concealed at a freind's howse in Holborne. That night the debauched party through London manifested great joy that now they were in a way of enjoying their lusts without controle. And I observed a vintner, who set out a hogshead of wyne, making those drinke the King's health who passed by, which they did upon their knees till they lost the use of their legges. The good gentlewoman with whom I was, to avoyd suspition of being disaffected (least by such a jealousy her howse should be searched, and I in danger of being seized on), causeth a fire to be made before her doore; this vice of drunkenness   **788** and debauchery being growne notorious.

Charles Steward, for the satisfying of the presbiterians, for whom he [had yet?] a job to doe, sets forth a proclamation forbidding the drinking of healths. But within a night or two, being privately invited to a supper in the citty of London, he was there till one or two of the clock in the morning, violating his owne law of drinking healths to excess (as he did also at the Mulbery Garden, and many other places whither he was invited). Those of the Howse of Commons make all the haste possible for the preparing of the act of indemnity (yet rather for their own personall security then for that of the publique), and proceede, in order thereto, to the nomination of those seaven of the King's judges whom they propose to be excepted, viz. Major Generall Harrison, John Lisle Esq., William Say Esq. And while they were in the nomination, it was so ordred (whether by Monke's contrivance or no I cannot say), out of a desire to have me one of the number, that a letter was to be sent unto him, informing him that I was got into one of the islands which are called the Holmes, with two or three hundred men, and that I there declared against the Parlament; with which the Howse being acquainted, and perswaded of the trueth thereof, they were ready to answer the end of those who raysed the report, and to have inserted me amongst those who were to be excepted. But the Howse for that tyme adjourning, one Captaine Dover (who had bin alwayes high for the King) having bin ingaged by a sister-in-law of his on my behalfe, and being apprehensive of

my having bin civill to him at the tyme of his composition, repaires
to her with an account of what was reported concerning me; telling
her that he had the assurance of many of the King's party in the Howse
that they would be for me, but that, if this were so, neither he nor
they could possibly serve me, and therefore desired her that, if she
knew where I was, she would give me notice, that I might take some
course to satisfy them therein.

This she promised to endeavour to doe, but withall assured him
that upon her reputation the reporte was false; of which passadge
betweene them it was not long before I had notice, and doe beleeve
that, upon the assurance she gave heerein, most of the Howse were
satisfyed in the falsehood of what was related concerning me. For
when they proceeded to compleate the number of seaven to be
excepted (Colonell John Jones, Mr. Cornelius Holland, and Mr.
Thomas Scot being also named and agreed on), one Colonell Skip-
worth proposed me to be the seaventh man, but was not seconded
by any; and another member proposing Colonell Berkstead as more
obnoxious then myselfe (none daring to speake anythinge either in
extenuation of the pretended cryme, or commendation of any of their
persons), he being so adjudged by them I came to be excused. Cheife
Justice Cooke, who was Sollicitour to the Courte, was also excepted
by them out of the act; and so was Mr. Broughton the Clerke of the
Court, and Mr. Edward Dendy Serjeant-at-Armes. And that they
might leave no meanes unatempted, either of fraud or vyolence, to
ruyne and destroy those whom the Lord had engaged in this worke
(having already, under pretence of some of the judges being fledd,
given order for the seising of their estates, reall and personall), it's
now contrived by Charles Steward's creatures that he shall be
petitioned to by both Howses to issue out a proclamation for the
requiring of all those of the King's judges, and others therein
named, **789** to render themselves as therein directed, within the
space of 14 dayes after the publication thereof, under the penalty of
being excepted out of the act of indemnity as to life and estate. And
least the act of indemnity should meete with some obstruction, the
Speaker's Clarke and the Maior of London's having all the mony they
could (for the attesting the submission of those who layd hold of the
proclamation sent out by Charles Steward at Bredagh), those in the
Howse of Commons, before the forty dayes mentioned in the sayd
proclamation were expired, attend Charles Steward at Whitehall,
and on the behalfe of all the Commons of England clayme the benifit
of the sayd proclamation, thereby performing the condition therein
mentioned.

It may be taken for graunted that the petition for the proclamation
from both Howses aforesaid would receive no denyall from Charles

Steward, it having had its rise from thence. The proclamation requiering the judges of the King to render themselves was published neere
the place where I lay, in my hearing. But what to resolve therein as
to my owne particcular, I was to seeke. For though Charles Steward
had, in his proclamation from Bredagh, declared his inclynation to
be satisfyed with having some of those only excepted who had an imediate hand in the death of his father, yet now (finding himselfe
posessed of his throne) he influenced those of the Howse of Commons
to greater severity, and (partly out of coveteousness, and partly
revendge) to except twenty more out of the act of indemnity as to
their estates, who had bin of the Parlament party; for the making
up of which number, though the mallice that the court had against
Sir Henry Vane, Sir Arthur Haslerigg and some others (together with
the sweet morsell of their estates) caused them to be made of that
number, yet the greatest parte was made up of such as had closed
with Cromwell's usurpation in opposition to the civill authority; a
demonstration of what was most offensive to the generallity of the
people. Mr. Robert Reynolds, though he had got a knighthood from
Charles Steward, scarsely escaped from being one of that number;
and so did Mr. Boulstred Whitlock. Mr. Prinne, desirous to ruyne
as many as possible of those who had bin faithfull to the publique,
bringes in a clause for the excepting of those who had taken the oath
at the Councell of State, for the abjuring of Charles Steward and his
familly. And Mr. Darnell, the second Clarke in the Howse of Commons, who had served in that imployment many yeares together in
the Parlament, and had other places of profit under them, officiously
presumes to reade the said clause; for which Clergyes, Monke's
brother-in-law, sharply reproved him, saying he had no order from
the Howse for his so doing; Vice Admirall Lawson, whom Monke
had engaged to preserve, being concerned therein.

Severall of the King's judges who had withdrawne render themselves into the hands of Sir Harbottle Grimstone according to the proclamation, as Mr. William Heveningham, Mr. Symon Maine, etc.;
who acquainting those in the Howse therewith, they ordred them to
be secured by their Serjeant attending on them. My deare wife
heereupon endeavours to informe herselfe, from knowing freinds,
what they would advise me to doe in this case. Some of them were
for my rendring of myselfe. Others were unfree to declare their judgements, being in a case of life, yet intimated that, if my case were theirs,
they would not put themselves into the hands of their enemyes. And
one who was a faithfull freind, and **790** ... in the secrets of the
enemy, advised that by no meanes I should [render?] myselfe; all
which my wife comunicated to me.

But my estate (by reason of the suddenness of the chandge) being

altogether unsetled, and those in the Howse of Comons having not
named me of the seaven to be excepted, I judged it might be a voyce
unto me to improve this opportunity, at least to settle as well as I
could my private affaires, [if I had not their?] favour in relation to
my estate, for the providing for my familly. And to that end I enclyned
to render myselfe within the tyme limitted by the proclamation. And
that I might deale as cautiously as I could (knowing those in the
Howse were influenced by the Court), my wife, endeavouring to feele
their pulses what she could, made application to the Earle of Ormond,
there being some relation betweene that familly and myselfe. Many
complements she received, and understood from her unkle Colonell
Thomas Stradling that, whilest he was attending the sayd Earle,
Colonell Theophilus Jones (who with Sir Charles Coote, two fawning
parasites, endeavoured to get an interest in the Courte by casting dirt
on me) informed him (the said Earle) that I was of such a disobleiging
nature, and so much an enemy to the gentry, that I had bosted to
him I never did a curtesy to any man, nor ever preferred a gentleman
to any imployment; whereunto my unkle replyed that it was very
unlikely to be truth, for that both he, and as many as ever he spoake
with of the King's party, had found me the most civill to them of
any of the contrary party; the Lord of Ormond also saying that he
had alwayes heard the same character given of me, and that severall
of his relations had received civillityes from me in Ireland. But whither
will not mallice carry men, and how doth the spider convert whole-
some food into poyson?

If he had any couller to fasten those words upon me, it was when
he, being a Major of that regiment of horse I comanded as Colonell,
came to me at Monketowne (my howse in Ireland), whither I retyred
myselfe after Cromwell had trampled the civill authority under foote,
not daring contrary to oaths and engagements betray my conscience
in joyning with him in that horrid impiety and treachery, who (having
done this act, and conscious to himselfe that the very stones of the
streete would rise up against him for betraying so excellent and righteous a cause which he once owned) endeavours to make sure of those
whom he doubted might oppose him therein, and gave order for that
end touching myselfe; of which (as I remember) discoursing in my
garden with the sayd Jones, I imparted unto him the reasons of my
declyning to act longer in the civill authority (it being only in answer
to the call I received from the Parliament that I had acted therein;
and that their authority being usurped, I durst not owne that usurpation by acting under the usurper; that as to my owne particcular,
I was very well pleased to be freed from that trouble, for though I
did my utmost to obleidge all persons what I could therein, yet, not
daring to act contrary to the dictates of my conscience, I found that

I disobleiged as many or more then I obleiged; for those who have
right on their side attribute their success thereto, and those who have
not   **791** esteeme you not a freind if you will not stand by them
[therein?]). And speaking to him of the groundlessness of the jealousy
that was conceived of my stirring in opposition to them, from severall
considerations, I remember I mentioned for one my cautiousness, for
feare of drawing a suspition of that nature upon me, of preferring
any to imployment in the army during that yeare I commanded in
cheife, putting in only some into places untill further order [where
necessity?] required, because the troopes and companyes, if destitute
of officers, could not well dischardge their dutyes (though I might
have done it if I had pleased, and would have done it had I designed
the making of any opposition).

But it was a great mercey to me that my enemyes were so put to
their shifts to finde wherewith to asperse me, and were constreyned
to put a false gloss on that which deserved a better construction, for
want of some reall cryme whereof to accuse me. But I bless the Lord
my care was not so much how my service was accepted of men, as
of the Lord. Neither had I an eye so much to the success of thinges,
as what the duty incumbent upon me was. This was my difficulty
in steering my present course. For though I was not convinced of my
duty to that abollished forme of goverment, as now restored by the
consent of the generallity of the nation (well knowing the fraudulent
meanes that were used to trappan them thereinto, contrary not only
to their interest but even their intention (at least upon the tearmes
it was brought in upon them), and that the Long Parlament was still
the *lawfull* authority of the nation, being never dissolved by its owne
consent, which is required by act of parlament it ought to be before
it could be dissolved), yet, having looked upon the welfare of the
people as the supreame law, and judging their liberty and good to
be preferred not only to the prerogative of the King but to the priviledge of parlament itselfe, and concluding that though there was no
legall foundation for this present goverment, yet having gotten into
posession of the power (which could not without great hazzard and
inconveniencyes be gott out of their hands), if they would make use
thereof (as indeed it was their interest) for the countenancing of the
good and discountenancing of the evill (that being a meanes to render
an authority lawfull which was not so in the originall of it), I thought
myselfe at liberty to promise my submission, and to that end drew
a petition; the substance whereof was, that whereas I had bin engaged
with the Parlament on the behalfe of the Comonwealth, and had discharged the trust that was reposed in me with faithfulness and as much
tenderness to those of the contrary party as consisted therewith, the
Lord by his providence having thought fit that the ancient goverment

should be established over these nations, of which being a member I thought it my duty to declare it my resolution to give submission thereto, might I with the rest of the good people of the nation enjoy the benefit of its protection.

This my wife acquainted Mr. Onsloe with, desiring his advise therein; he having expressed himselfe freindly   **792**   to me, as I have before recited. But being now sworne of his Majestie's Privy Councell, and with his condition changed his nature (or at least his civillity), after he had perused it, delivers it back to her, saying upbraidingly before many people then present that her husband was very good to draw letters of recomendation; to which she replyed, it was as much as he could say; whereunto he answered, he were better say nothing; which carryed a truth in it, for that some who petitioned those in the Howse, and not acknowledging a fault, were therefore excepted, which as was supposed they had not otherwise bin. She was informed also that Charles Steward refused to receive any application till the Parlament (as he called it) were come to a resolution, he having referred himselfe to them. However the Earle of Ormond, holding her in suspense, was very earnest to know of her whether I were in England or no; but she, being before cautioned concerning him, desired him to excuse her therein. And a very good freind contynued his advice (at first given) by no meanes to render myselfe, assuring her that to his knowledge the House of Lords would except more, and that some of them spake of excepting me. Though I had a very great inclynation, for the reasons aforementioned, to render myselfe, yet was I much startled at this, being unwilling to be in custody and to have my life depend upon the pleasure of such an uncerteine sorte of men. And therefore, the last day save one of the 14 dayes being expired, my wife repayred to Sir Harbottle Grimstone, who was Speaker in the Convention, and imparts to him the difficulty I was under; whereof he seemed very sensible, yet expressed it as his thoughts that the Lords would rest satisfyed with what was done, and, though they should not, yet that it would be the horridst thinge in the world should those in the Howse agree with them in the excepting of any of those who had rendred themselves; but withall told her, that the Howse was so composed that no man could undertake what they would not doe; and further said, that he was that day to dyne with Mr. Hollis, and some other considerable members of the Howse, and that he would informe himselfe from them in that particcular, and would then give her advise as to his owne child.

The tyme which he appointed her to attend being come, he acquainted her that he had comunicated it to them, and that they were of opinion that the Howse would never be so unworthy as to give way to it, and therefore persuaded her to advise me to render myselfe, promising to speake to the Serjeant-at-Armes attending him to deale freindly with me in my security; which he sayd was all the freindship he could shew me. And that I might not be seized upon as I came to render myselfe, he gave a pass under his hand for my coming to him in order to my **793** submission; under the protection of which I went to a place where .... severall of my freinds for the sealing of some writings for the setling of my estate; which, as I afore-mentioned, was that which much prevayled with me to render myselfe. It was neare sunset before I could dispatch that affaire, and so render myselfe to the Speaker; at which tyme I went to his chamber. But he not being there, I understanding that he had given order to the Serjeant concerning me, I repayred to his howse, having Mr. James Herbert a member of this Convention with me, who gave his word to the Serjeant for my appearance till I had given personall security so to doe; in which condition I contynued for two or three dayes, during which tyme I was in a great streight, being obleiged that he should not suffer for his freindship to me.

And therefore I pressed the Serjeant to take my security, which I had provided of such persons as would make a faire shew, and yet not be prejudiced by the favour they did me; which were, my unkle Colonell Thomas Stradling (who had bin constantly of the King's party, and who by reason of his kindness in being engaged for his brother Sir Edward Stradling had little left) and Colonell Edward Sutton (who was also of the King's party, and knighted by him since his coming in, having no estate but in the right of his lady). I had also got two others; the one whereof had bin a gentleman of a considerable estate, named Mr. Ethrinton, but for many yeares had not bin worth a groate, and one Thomas Ashton, who was a cittizen of London, who had bin my taylor, but now worth no more then Mr. Ethrinton. Colonell Sutton, comming to me, was arrested by the way, and so hindred. Mr. Ethrinton was furnished with a cleane band, hat and cloake, and passed without dispute. I would have had my unkle Stradling excused, and Thomas Ashton to have bin bound in his stead; but Colonell Stradling's security having bin proposed, it would have given cause of suspition, and therefore was it not declyned. The bond which they were bound with me in was for two thousand pounds. Mr. Etherinton I gave twenty shillings to, and to Thomas Ashton five shillings for his readyness; with which they were satisfyed, and I well pleased that this business was over. The Serjeant had twenty peeces of me for his fees, and his man a gratuity, for that I found him civill and freindly (being instrusted by the Serjeant for the taking of my security).

When Sir Harbottle Grimstone reported to the Howse that I had rendred myselfe, and desired to know their pleasure concerning me, some of them said, Send him to the Tower, to the Tower. But none of them publiquely moving it, and others desiring that I might be continued in the Serjeant's custody, he put that question, and it was ordred accordingly. Some of the members (supposing that the Howse would have proceeded against such of the King's judges as were not excepted, by imposing fines on them) desired of my relations before my submission that they would send them a particcular of my estate; which they promissed should not be made use of to my disadvantadge, they only desiring it that thereby they might the better know how to moderate my fine when it came to be debated; which I prepared as well as I could in the condition I was in, and **794** [sent?] two or three coppys thereof to my freinds who desired it; which was truly one reason that enclyned me to render myselfe, supposing they understood the resolution of the Howse to extend favour to us.

For from the King I expected little, my lady Vane having informed my wife that she was assured that Monke's wife had sayd she would seeke to the King, upon her knees, that Sir Henry Vane, Major Generall Lambert and myselfe should be hanged rather then we should escape. And a freind of myne informed me that whilst he was in the presence of the Kinge, Monke told him that there was not one in the three nations more vyolent against him, nor more dangerous to his interest, then I was; the King replying that he had bin otherwise informed concerning me, when he was beyond sea, by many of his party to whom I had done civillityes. Yea Mr. Maurice (whom Monke had preferred to be Secretary to the King) being spoken to by a freind of myne, who understood the correspondency that was betweene him and me during Mr. Richard Cromwel's Convention, advised him that wherever I was I should keepe close, for that if I should be taken I was a dead man, yet promissed to speake with Monke to take him off his vyolence against me. But though he and Captaine Gabriell Pile (who had bin formerly Cornet of my troope, and since engaged in the service of the King to the hazard of his life), who volontarily coming to see me, freely proffered to improve his interest with Mrs. Monke to that end (having had great intimacy with her as he said), yet, finding those who went to the Lyon's Den to have Vestigia Nulla Retrorsa, it made me conclude what success they had.

But my business being thus in a probable way in the Howse of Comons, my father Oldsworth endeavours to remove the rubb that was supposed I should meete withall amongst the Lords, and to that end sollicited many of them, both before and after my submission. And neere twenty of them which he spoake to he found wholy ignorant of any designe amongst them to make any alteration of what was resolved in the other Howse, and professing a readyness to doe me all the favour which lay in them; only the Earle of Northampton (a great favourite of Monke's) expressing his dissatisfaction with me, as one who had bin a great enemy to the King. But it seems that neither of these were acquainted with the secret counsels that were carrying on. However things would be, I resolved to improve my tyme for the setling of my private affaires, and to that end put the best countenance I could upon my condition, especially to those whom I imployed about my estate in Ireland, supposing that thereby they would be carefull of their deportement; which was not *altogether* without its effect, my brother Kempson prevayling with my Lord Broghill (by the meanes of the Lady Ranello his sister) to write to Sir Charles Coote, that he might have the posession and **795** managdement of my stock, giving security to be responsible for it to those to whom it should be adjudged to belong. But he was so farr from answering him therein, that doubting least I should get to be in a condition to call him to an account for the injustice he had done me, he writ a letter to the King, in which he enveighed against me as the bitterest enemy the King had; acquainting him that when he was with me at my howse at dynner, I had imparted to him that Cromwell had declyned prosecuting the King his father had not I pressed him thereto, and (for confirmation of the truth of what he writ) desired the Lord Broghill might be interrogated therein, he dyning the same day with me. But so ingenuous was he that when the King discourssed with him about it, he professed he could not chardge his memory therewith; and further said that if he could, he thought it not becoming him to remember anything to the prejudice of a gentleman that was spoken by him at his table. Of this I was informed by very credible persons.

I dare not say I spake nothing of that nature in their presence, but cannot tell whether it was a narrative of that passadge aforesaid betweene Leiftenant-Generall Cromwell and me, which related to the duty and adviseableness of bringing the King to an account, or to that betweene me and some of my Comonwealth freinds before his tryall, who were dissatisfyed to take him off before some other goverment were setled in the place thereof. But sure I am I could not so forget myselfe as to take upon me that what I sayd could divert Lieftenant-General Cromwell from what he before intended in that particcular; well knowing that, had that which I offred weight in it, he (being steered rather by interest then reason) was not to be swayed by me. But how little soever there was of trueth in such like artificiall fetches, they tooke such effect that my freinds at Court let me know my worst enemyes were those of Ireland.

Those in the Howse, besides those twenty they except from any benifit of the act of indemnity save as to life, add to that qualification Mr. Robert Wallop, Sir Henry Mildemay, Sir James Harrington, Mr.

James Challoner, the Lord Mounson (who, being commissioners for the tryall of the King, had sate in the Court, but not at that tyme when sentence was pronounced, neither set their hands to the proclamation for the holding of the Court, nor to the warrant for his execution), and Mr. John Phelpes, one of the Clarkes of the Court, to whom it was pretended that favour was extended in confidence that he would render himselfe thereupon; they intending to make use of him to informe them of many thinges relating to the provission that had bin made for ministers, which he was very well able to doe. For the presbyterian party were not yet altogether out of hopes of doing something on the behalfe of their interest, Charles Steward thinking it adviseable to give them faire wordes, and some casts of his favour, the army being not yet disbanded. And therefore Mr. Baxter and Mr. Calamy are appointed chaplins in ordinary; though Charles Steward and the Duke of Yorke were observed to spend most of the tyme, whilest **796** they were preaching, in looking upon the pictures that were in their bibles. Colonell Edward Harloe, one of the eleaven members who was accused of high treason by the army, was appointed Governour of Dunkirke, and his brother Major Robert Harloe is to have the command of the regiment of horse which belonged to that garrison.

Yet could they not forbeare, by their deportement, to express sometymes the enmity they had towards those of that perswasion. And in particcular I have bin credibly informed that Mr. Case, conceiving he had deserved very well of the King, pressing with the same confidence into his presence as he had formerly done unto the members of parlament, and being kept back by the doore-keeper, sends his name, desiring admittance; which though in answer to his importunity was graunted him, yet, by the carriadge of all towards him, he might well observe how unagreable his company was there; they deriding his habit, to wit his night cap, his round robbyn band (as they called it), his want of a canonicall coate and girdle, his approaching the King without the usuall sollemnity; who giving him an opportunity to discover what he had to say, he expressing himselfe (in his familliar way) that he had a word of advice humbly to offer to his Majestie, the King replyed that he did not remember he had made him of his Councell, but however for this tyme desired him to goe on; which he did, perswading him to a tenderness towards those of his party; whereunto the King gave an eare, but not without some impatience; and having dismissed him, instead of being wrought upon thereby, scoffed at him and what he sayd.

Yet were the Earle of Northumberland, the Earle of Manchester, the Lord Roberts, and Mr. Denzil Hollis sworne of his Privy Councell, and the Earle of Manchester made Chamberline of the Howsehold.

And Monke, as a reward for his treachery, besides the Garter *and the Captaine Generalship of all the forces, hath the parchment honours of Duke of Albemarle, Earle of Torrington, Barron of Potteridge, Beauchamp and Tees conferred on him, together with the being Gentleman of the Bedchamber, and one of the King's Privy Councell, and the Leiftenancy of the provinces of Devon and Middlesex, and of the bourrough of Southwarke. And besides all his pensions mentioned in his letters patents, hee hath settled of crowne lands about [Tibbots?] and elsewhere lands on him and his heires to the valew of 7000 per annum, and the* Mastership of the Horse *bestowed on him*; which place he and his wife (who *having ben* an exchandge woman, and one of the dirtiest and most vitious in the pack, knew how to drive her bargaine) by selling of all inferiour places to the pence, so as to make the utmost improvement of them. Yea so impudent was she growne that the secluded members (when they posessed themselves of the supreame authority) as a reward for her brother Clergyes's treachery having given him the Hamper Office (which as alleadged was by a precedent pattent given to another), the King, that he might make good his former graunt to Tom Killigrew, desiring Clergys to give way thereto, promising to gratify him with the better place, he, suspecting to be dealt with as he deserved, not only refused so to doe, but making his complaint to his sister, she thereupon runnes to the King, and scolds at him like a Billingsgate oyster-wench; of which her husband being informed by the King, it was reported that he cudgelled his brother Clergyes, and that   **797** his wife the dirty Dutchess hardly escaped the like treatment. However, Clergyes would not let goe the hold he had of his office, nor the posession of some lodgings he had in the Mews that belonged to some of the servants of the Howshold; which rugged carriadge very much displeased the courtiers.

But it was not yet a tyme fully to discover their anger; but without doubt treachery and treason will have its reward. Monke, though he had received the pattents for those honours, falsely so called (having probably contracted for them when he first agreed to sell the cause of God and his country, and to betray the trust reposed in him), yet tooke not his place in the Lords Howse till the act of indemnity was ready to be sent up thither, pretending an endeavour to have it as lardge and comprehensive as he could, yet intending only the preservation of those who had joyned with him in his treachery (some whereof were apparent enough). Others also were by some supposed so to have done, whom I am unwilling to beleeve any such thinge of; yet if it be so, the day, as the Apostle saith, shall declare it, when every man's worke shall be manifest, 1 Cor. 3. 13. In the meanetyme their owne consciences, if enlightened, will accuse, pursue, and torment them, for the butcheryes of many of the eminent servants of God, the oppressions of the people, the promoting of superstition and idolatry, prophaness, etc., yea the suppressing of the preaching and preachers of the gospell, that hath and will ensue as the necessary consequences thereof.

For my parte I looked upon it as without dispute to be much better to suffer from them then to reigne with them. Yet that I might not be guilty of my owne sufferings, but by improving the opportunityes put into my hands I might preserve myselfe at liberty what I could for the being yet further instrumentall in the worke of my generation, if the Lord should thinke fit to call me thereto (having imparted to my security, at the tyme of their engaging for me, my intention to withdraw myselfe in case I found my life in danger), I tooke care whilest those of the Howse were sitting (least I should be surprized and seized on by an order from them) to have timely notice of it by some of their members. And least I should fail of that, I gave order that the gates of the howse wherein I lived, which were many, should be straitly guarded. And for the most parte I retired to some other howse during that tyme, where they would not probably looke for me. And when the Howse was rissen I was more confident, having daily assurance by some or other of the members that they had made no order concerning me before they rose, and knowing that it was against the priviledge of parlament for any other to seize on me whilest I was prissoner to the Serjeant attending the Howse of Commons; wherein I was confirmed, in that I understood that the Howse of Lords ordering their officer (called the Master of the Black Rodd) to take into his custody the body of Colonell Tichborne (he being before a prysoner to the Serjeant attending the Howse), they ordered him to be retorned to him, which was done accordingly.

Yet durst I not altogether neglect my watch, knowing that if Charles Steward should streyne a point of the law I was like to get no remedy as thinges stood. And, as I was informed by my best freinds, there was no cause I should be confident of him though as he had before expressed himselfe to Monke, when he was **798** rayling against me to him. So a kinswoman of my wive's was sent to by my lady Wynter, to acquaint my wife that her husband Sir John Wynter (Secretary to the Queene Mother) having had discourse with the King concerning me, and informed him of the civillityes performed to him and others by me, that the King replyed he was resolved to shew me as much favour as to any of that party. And my wife (desiring to be informed more particcularly heerein), attending on the Lady Wynter, was assured by her of the trueth thereof; which lady being a person of honour, though a great votary to the popish religion, tooke notice of the *just* hand of God in making better provissions for those who acted zealously, according to their light, then such as *steered* more slowely, according to their corrupt interest. This lady, meaning well herselfe, supposed others to doe so. But she will finde in the issue that, as the designe of that party is in the generall for the exalting of the wisedome, power and corrupt interest of man, and destroying the holy law and will of the Lord, so, that they will not stick to make any use of any treacherous and bloody meanes that conduce to that end.

In the Howse of Lords, much striving there is of severall partyes to encrease the number of the excepted. Mrs. Penruddock, Dr. Hewit's widdow and severall others sollicite for particcular satisfaction for the death of their relations, and a Comittee of the Howse is appointed to examine their desires. And much adoe they make, by their inspection into severall men's carriadges, in the proceedings that had bin against them. Mr. Hugh Wyndham, who was one of the Justices of the Comon Pleaes, was amongst others much pressed upon. And the Lords were enclyned to make some examples for those of their number that had bin put to death by the High Court of Justice, and not by the judgement of their peeres, by whom they conceived they ought to have bin tryed. And it was proposed that one of the judges should be excepted for each Lord that was so put to death, and that the next of kin (that was of the Howse of Lords) to him that was put to death should name the person to be excepted. Colonell Croxton, as I have bin informed, was proposed by him nearest related to the Earle of Derby; Major Waring by the nearest of kin to another of them; Colonell Tichborne by another, and was thereupon ordred to be taken into custody by the Master of the Black Rodd, as hath bin before recited. Sir John Thorowgood was also taken into custody on the same account, but he endeavoured to make it out that his sitting in those Courtes was only for the service of those who were tryed. The Earle of Denbigh, whose sister Duke Hamilton had marryed, was called upon to name one, to make satisfaction for the death of the Duke his brother-in-law. He named one who was dead; which being taken notice of by some of the Howse, he was desyred to name some other. He refused so to doe, alleadgeing that seeing providence had so directed it, he desired to be excused from naming any other (and very probable that what he did was of set purpose, being very much a gentleman in his spirit and deportement, and a lover of his country).

As it was thought necessary, upon the restitution of this abollished goverment, for the quieting of the myndes of the generallity of the people, **799** that the act called an act of indemnity and oblivion should pass, so likewise that mony should be raysed for the disbanding of the army, as was judged necessary to be done before they went too farr in [discovering?] what they intended. And those in the Howse of Commons (having ordred the oaths of allegiance and supreamacy to be taken by all their members), to shew their great zeale to the idoll that was set up, and their mallice to those that scrupled an oath or made a conscience of running to the same excess of wickedness with themselves, insert a clause in the act of assesment, requyring those who refused the taking of the said oathes to pay double. But for the sake of the papists, who owne the Pope's supreamacy but not the King's, it was omitted. And when the sayd oathes were taking by the Lords, those who were popish withdrew, and came not into the Howse againe till that affaire was past; which the Earle of Oxford (who was zealous for Charles Steward's service, though unacquainted with the depth of the designe) observing, moved the Howse that the popish Lords might be required to take the said oathes, but was not seconded by any. And when the Howse was rissen, the Duke of Yorke asked him what he meant by his motion. He answered he had no other intention therein but the promotion of his Majestie's service. The Duke replyed to him that if he knew all he would be of another opinion, and therefore desired him for the future not to appeare in any such matter. This I had from a very sure hand.

Some heates now begin to breake out betweene the episcopall and presbyterian party in the Howse of Commons. Mr. Prinne, at a comittee, expresseth much dissatisfaction with an order that was brought to them, that had bin issued out by some of the Bishop's substitutes about Redding in Berkshire; the presbyterians hoping, if they could not sway all, at least to share with the bisshops. But the episcopall party begin to discover, upon debates in the Howse, they were the greater interest. However, the army not being disbanded, it's not thought fit as yet to come to any determination, but to adjourne that debate till Michaelmass Tearme, untill which tyme also the Howse itselfe was to be adjourned, and before that time to reduce the souldiery, and other thinges, into a more suitable posture. And to that end they had carryed a vote in the Howse, which they adjudged to their purpose; at which the presbyterians, much enraged, refused to have candles brought into the Howse, for the entring of the said order; which though carryed that they should be, Mr. Hollis and others of the presbyterian party put them out with their hatts; Dr. Cleyton, who served for Oxford, being as vyolent on the other hand. The newes of this heate being carryed to Charles Steward, the next tyme Mr. Hollis came into his presence he drolled with him about it, as he yet thought fit to doe with all that party; Mr. Calamy and Mr. Baxter being permitted to preach in their turnes before him, though the latter of them refused to give way for the playing of the organs before he had pronounced the benediction, and, when mynded so to doe by some who pulled him by the gowne, he refused to take notice thereof.

Amongst those who sate in the Howse of Commons, many of the cavalier party thought fit to appeare zealously to witness against any that reflected upon the presbyters, and in particcular against Mr.

John Lenthall (a better oratour then his father that had bin Speaker
of the Howse), for asserting in the Howse that those who made warr
against the King, and deteyned him prysoner, and treated him as
they had done, were as much guilty of his death as they who were
his immediate judges, yea   **800** as he who executed him; for which
wordes he was questioned and called to the barr by the royall party;
the presbyterian perswading themselves that this was done in favour
of them, *which was only* to sylence them for the present; the mallice
of the royall party sufficiently appearing against them in pamphlets
published by them, which were sold without controle; the scope of
the title of one of them being The Discovery of Mr. Baxter's Enmity
to Monarchy. The words themselves I remember not. But in the body
of it, it was made appeare how inconsistent what he had said and
writ was to the interest of the King; as also the proceedings of Mr.
Denzill Hollis towards those of the Howse of Lords, when sent by the
Howse of Comons to them with a messadge about the militia, where
after the Lords had severall tymes refused to joyne with the Commons
in setling that affaire without the King, he desired to have the names
of those Lords who denyed to joyne therein, and that the rest would
come to the Howse of Commons and sitt with them; an evident argument, saith the pamphletter, that they were resolved to receive no
denyall. He also recites the words of Mr. Love (who afterwards was
put to death for appearing for Charles Steward) which he had in his
sermon preached before the Parlament comissioners at the treaty at
Uxbridge (viz. that the King was a man of blood, and that no peace
could be made with him or his till satisfaction were made for the blood
that had bin shed), and possitively declared that those who made a
warr with him in his personall capacity, dividing that from his pollitique, had bin more guilty of the King's death then those who were
his imediate judges; for that they (to wit the Parlament) had unkingd
him, and put him into a private capacity, whereas the other had but
cut off the head of Charles Steward, when declared to be but a private
person *and conceived to be guilty of blood.* Thus the presbyterians having
shaved the halfe of the beard, the cavaliers begin now to shave the
other halfe.

The royall party in the Howse of Lords begin now to discover the
trueth of what I formerly heard, as to their intentions to except all
the King's judges out of the act of indemnity; the newes whereof put
my wife upon seeking to Sir John Wynter, who had sent the messadge
aforementioned, for his advise heerein. But she not finding him at
his howse, he the next day in the evening was pleased to come to
my howse; by whom I understood that Sir Henry Vane, Sir Arthur
Haslrerigg and the Marquess of Argile were seized and carryed to the
Tower by order of the King. He confirmed what I had formerly heard

of the discourse betweene the King and him concerning me, adding that he had proposed to the Lord German (with whom and others he was in comission for the disposing of the Queene's revenue) that it would be very adviseable to take in some of the contrary party, and that, as he judged, I might be as propper to receive an engagement of that kind as any; which he sayd was acknowledged, but that German replyed, Hee is so fixed and resolved in his course that there is no possibillity of bending him; which words I conceived he let fall to observe how they would **801** worke with me.

But I being at a point as to the justice of the cause wherein I had bin engaged, and of my duty, having put my hand to the plowe, not to looke back, I answered that I had acted according to my light, for the glory of God and the good of mankind, and without having mallice to anyone's person; yet seeing the pleasure of God was to retorne the ancient goverment, might I enjoy the benifit of its protection, with the rest of the good people of the nation, I thought myselfe bound to pay it subjection; and further said, that the King coming in without blood, should he looke only forward, and give to all their fitting liberty, and content himselfe with so much power as the people in Parliament would give him, the nation might be happy in him, and he in them. He replyed, that he knew the King a while since would have bin satisfyed with the exception of one or two (nay, now Cromwell and Bradshaw were dead, without excepting of any), but now he thought some (it may be, sayd he, one or two) will be made examples. I tould him, as I judged the fewer the better, and they would in the issue finde it so. He advised me to make mine application to the Duke of Yorke, as one in whom I perceived the papists had most confidence, and that therein I would use Sir John Barkeley. In the conclusion he said that I must alter my discourse, for that he would have me to be imployed; but however intimated that he should be sorry to have me taken into custody, which was a freindly caution to me.

Speaking upon this same subject to a very good freind of myne, who had no less interest with the King, but no papist, I propounded to him, as a motive to moderation, that other manner of proceedings would tend to the irritation of a considerable party, and would not at all keepe them from doing the like when there should be an opportunity. For if the execution of highwaymen would not terrify others from doing the like, though convinced of the evill of it, much less would severity terrify those from appearing in that (when they had an opportunity) which they conceived themselves bound in duty to owne. This gentleman conceived that it was not the intent to imploy the clergy in civill affaires as formerly, and that they would be contented with a kind of superintendency in ecclesiasticall affaires. But the issue hath made it appeare that he was not acquainted with the councels of the caball, or at least that he would not have me to be so. Yet was he so faithfull and affectionate to me as to advise me rather to withdraw myselfe out of the hands of my enemyes, then to submit to their mercey; acquainting me that, whilest Charles Steward was agitating with Monke about his reestablishment, he apprehended not any difficulty so much as how to keepe me from obstructing his designe (having then the command of the forces of the Parliament in Ireland), but that he was resolved to have given me whatsoever conditions I would demaund, which he supposed I would not have bin so desperate as not to have accepted of, *and hath since acquainted my wife that the King had comissionated him to offer me the Earledome of Essex.*

He also assured me that the King was for some yeares before his retorne so abandoned by his owne party, that he had not a thousand pounds per annum contribution from them, till some monyes were sent unto him for the holding of intelligencyes and other necessary expences relating to Sir George Booth's rising; and that for necessity, oft tymes when the steward of his howshold brought him word that he had no mony to buy meete for dinner, he went to dyne with some gentleman or other, that so he might avoyd the coming of company; **802** [making?] an emynent demonstration of the nation's having layd aside all thoughts of monarchy, and of their inclynations at least to submit to the goverment of a Comonwealth, had they not bin abused and betrayed by Cromwell, whom they entrusted, and by Monke (a fit servant for such a master), into that which they had prayed against and bled in opposition to.

Although my condition was as you have seene, yet a kinsman of myne preferred a bill in Chancery against me (rather out of hopes I durst not give in my answer), that so he might gaine an advantadge against one Mrs. Goodman, who had preferred a bill against him for a debt due unto her chardged upon lands that he had sold, and disposed of the mony that was given for the same. But I being fully satisfyed in the justice of Mrs. Goodman's case, though she were a papist, aventured into Chancery Lane. And as I was going over against Whitehall, Charles Steward being there, a kinsman of myne takes notice of me; but finding me unwilling to be seene, as he afterwards let me know, he forbore to speake of it. One of the Masters of the Chancery refused to give me my oath unless I would lay my hand upon the booke; but another who was in his office, close by, gave it me without that ceremony. But whether my kinsman informed Chancellor Hide, I know not; but he having notice of my being so farr abroade, checqued the Serjeant for letting me have so much liberty, who thereupon threatned to restreyne me; which enforced me to sweeten him with a present of five pounds more, being willing to attend a while

longer, till I could see what the result of the Lords would be concerning those in my condition.

Colonell Ingoldsby was not excepted out of the act of indemnity,
because of the service he did in the suppressing of Major Generall
Lambert's party, and seizing of him after he had made his escape
out of the Tower. Colonell Hutchinson had the same favour extended
to him, because he had gotten the King's pardon before his coming
over, and had joyned with Monke in his treachery, pressing the Howse
to execute their sentence against that emynent patriot Sir Henry
Vane, and improving all opportunityes against the honest party, of
which he formerly professed to be a zealous wel-wisher. Colonell
Scroop, upon the interest of his brother-in-law Mr. Waller, was proposed by those in the Howse to have the benefit of the act of indemnity,
paying one yeare's vallue of his estate. And so was Colonell Lassells
(though as farr engaged in the death of the King as others), because
his son had married a popish lady, sister to Sir Robert Talbot, an
Irish papist in armes. Major Lister was left out of the exception, as
is presumed upon the account of Mr. William Peirpoint. Colonell
Thomlinson was excused, upon the information (given to the Howse
by Mr. Seymore a member thereof) that the late King, when he
wayted on him a day or two before he suffred, signified to him his
desire that he should receive favour, because he had deported   **803**
himselfe civilly towards him. But as I heard from a private hand,
Charles Steward thought not that ground enough for his exemption,
but professed his desire to have him suffer as well (or rather then)
any other, because he had an opportunity and a faire offer to let him
escape, and would not; of which the Lords being acquainted by the
Earle of Lichfeild, since Duke of Richmond, who moved that he might
be excepted out of the act of indemnity, it was like to give an occation
of quarrell betweene him and the Earle of Bristoll; who being
engaged on the behalfe of Thomlinson, and presuming upon his interest and his knowledge of Charles Steward's desire therein, tooke upon
him to reprove Lichfeild for his contesting with him therein. These
and other conflicts about the act of indemnity caused so much delay,
that the people began to doubt they should have nothing of that
nature pass for their security.

CHAPTER FOUR

The Court party finding it not a tyme to disobleige, by reason the army was not disbanded, press for the hastning of the act. The Earle of Bristoll, a Jesuited papist, though engaged for a particcular person, yet manifested his bloody intention in a speech he made, which according to his usuall vaine way of ostentation he caused to be printed; wherein taking occation to vaunt of his imployments he had whilest beyond sea, desires, for the expediting of the act, that they would pass it with the only exception of those who had a hand in the death of the late King, who he moved might be more particcularly described in an act that should be afterwards passed to that purpose; wherein for ought I knew he might intend to include not only the judges, and the members of parlament who sate after 1648, with those who petitioned for justice to be done upon him, but all those who made warr against him. The Earle of Lincolne, who had sate in the Howse of Lords during all the tyme of the warr against the King, was as vyolent against us as any, blaming some of the popish Lords for not expressing so much zeale therein as he would have had them done. Neither was the Lord Seymour, who once passed for a patriot, much behinde him.

Endeavours were used by the freinds of the twenty, who were proposed by those in the Howse of Commons to be excepted, to get them omitted by the Howse of Lords. And the Earl of Litchfeild sollicting the Lord Sturton for his favour on the behalfe of Leiftenant Generall Fleetwood, he promised it him so as he might have his on my behalfe, whom he tearmed his freind (as he informed me when he and his lady were pleased to give me a vissit; his lady telling me that I needed not have bin in this condition if I would have bin ruled by her; to whom I answered that I did what my conscience lead me to). Observing which way the Lords enclyned, I drew up the state of the case of those who had rendred themselves upon the proclamation, with such reasons as I could thinke of why those in the Howse of Commons should not give way to any enlardgements of the exception. This I thought to have had printed, and delivered to the members. But sending it to Mr. Henry Martyn, he judging it would be taken for a libell if no name were to it, advised   **804**   that it should be presented by way of petition; but none would undertake the presenting of it.

Notwithstanding all the messages Charles Steward sent to the Howse of Lords by Hide and others, the act of indemnity upon severall accounts receiving obstruction, he resolves personally to press them to the passing thereof. And in a great blacke plume of feathers, an unheard-of ornament for a member of those councels, he stammered out a speech that was prepared for him; which being published in prynt, I came to have the vieu of, and therein found his thanking the Howse of Lords for excepting the King his father's judges, whom he expressed to be guilty of such a cryme for which they could not pardon themselves, much less desire it of others; in which he not only manifested his owne bloody and revendgefull temper, but his perfidiousness in falsifying his word (which he passed in his proclamation before his coming from Bredagh, engaging to referr himselfe to the Parlament as to the pardoning what had bin done against him during these late troubles), and his imprudence in violating, in the open veiu of the whole nation, the privilledge of the Parliament, not only in taking notice what was depending before the two Howses before it came to be judicially presented to him, but in fomenting a divission betweene them, and that in a business of his owne concernement.

He also presseth them in his speech to omit all other thinges for the expediting of that bill, telling them that other wayes might be contrived for the meeting with those who were of turbulent and factious spirits; wherein he made appeare that his intentions were not to conteyne himselfe within the bounds of the law, but had secret reserves for the rendring of the act of indemnity insignificant. He concludes with his requests to them that they would be carefull to make provission for his Irish subjects, for that they had manifested great affection to him during his exile; expressing the like zeale in the latter parte of his speech for the countenance of the Irish popish rebells, as he had done in the former for the destruction and butchery of the faithfull witnesses of Jesus Christ. Yea so confident were the rebells growne, upon the assurance they had of his favour and their interest in him, that one Fitzharris in Westminster Hall publiquely affirmed to Captaine Walcot, a faithfull servant of the Comonwealth, that the Irish were the King's best subjects, and that they would have their lands againe; of which the Howse being informed, the said Fitzharris was by them comitted to the Gatehowse, but by the interest of the Court was within two dayes discharged from thence.

Some difficulty ariseth at the Court how to juggle with the officers of Ireland for the present, Charles Steward being engaged by his articles that Ormond had made with the Irish on his behalfe to give them their lands, the English souldiery being in posession thereof. It was sayd **805** that Monke, whose interest was linked with the [souldiers when he contracted?] with Charles Steward to betray the nation into his hands, had made it [his?] bargaine that he should be Leiftenant of Ireland. But it being insisted on that if he had that imployment he must goe [upon the place to?] execute it, he was unwilling to accept it on those tearmes, knowing how easy it would be to destroy him when at a distance, his owne conscience telling him that an opportunity was [waited?] for to that end. And the Earle of Ormond would not accept of the civill goverment, and be subordinate to Monke in the military parte, who was then owned Generall of the forces in the three nations. Therefore as an expedient, the Lord Roberts is proposed to goe as Deputy to Monke. But though he had the name of Deputy, and was applyed to under that notion, yet finding he was made use of but as a stale, and for the serving of the present turne, he desired to be excused from that imployment, which I presume was much to the trouble of the presbyterian party; one of whom, viz. Colonell Audley Mervin, coming to vissit me, expressed himselfe much dissatisfied that Charles Steward was preferring Bramwell (the late Bisshop of London Derry) to the Archbishoprick of Armagh, saying he would ruyne himselfe if he preferred such men. But whatever he thought, the popish and prophane must be advanced.

He acquainted me alsoe that he did, as he had opportunity, instill good apprehensions of me into those he had to doe with, his company being acceptable to the greatest of them, and said that he had taken some off in the Howse of Lords from particcularly reflecting on me. Colonell Harvy Baggot (a civill gentleman, who had bin unhappily engaged in the service of the King), having bin faithfull in what he undertooke, being invited to a place at Courte, hearing I was at my howse, thought fit in this my persecuted condition to give me a vissit, and to assure me of his readiness to doe me all the good offices he could; which I tooke kindly of him, not having seene him in twenty yeares before. I had the like expressions from Captaine Dover, whom I formerly made mention of; notwithstanding which, I found the clowde gathering so thick that I thought fit to double my care as to my preservation, and in order thereto not to continue at my owne howse, nor to come thither but by stealth; which withdrawing of mine caused Cheife Justice Cooke to suspect his life to be in more danger then before, he supposing that whilest I continued at my howse I had some ground so to doe, which might have an influence upon his security. The good gentlewoman his wife lodging in the howse with us, I had opportunity to heare often from him. He rejoyced much in that the Lord thought fit to honour him to be in bonds for him. And in the letter I received from him, I observed in him a most Christian frame of spirit, willingly resigned up to the wise disposing hand of his heavenly Father, not much sollicitous as to his owne particcular what the issue of his sufferings were, so as the Lord might be glorifyed thereby. And so highly was I obleiged to him, that he sollemnely professed he could freely lay downe his life for the saving of myne.

The Earle of Antrim, though an Irish papist, was seized the same tyme **806** that Argyle was, and sent to the Tower; but on different grounds, the one for the service he had done against popery and prelacy, and the other for having sayd that the Irish had authority from the late King for what they did. They both came to London, the one from Scotland, the other from Ireland, to congratulate the establishment of the King. The Earle of Argyle was seized by the Leiftenant of the Tower, by order of Charles Steward, as he was attending to present himselfe to him. The Laird Swinton, a discreet and honest gentleman of the Scotch nation, was at that tyme seized by Charles Steward's order, and sent to the Gatehowse. The generall reporte upon his first seysure was that he would have stabd the King as he was making the people beleeve his touch healed them of the disease called the king's evill. But it was afterwards said that it was for his having deserted the Scots after the fight at Dunbar, and rendred himselfe unto Cromwell. It was pretended also for the seizing of Sir Henry Vane and Sir Arthur Haslerigg that they had bin in councell with some of the officers of the army, for the drawing them together in opposition to the present authority. But it soone appeared that this was but a fiction, and the designe was to take away their lives; Charles Steward being heard to say, when newes was brought of their being in custody, he would lay a groate they should not soone come out againe. And Colonell Axtell, an honest and faithfull servant of the Commonwealth, whose blood the Court party thirsted after, being trappaned into their hands by a cavaleere who pretended to buy of him some lands, and coming to treate about the same, was seized and sent to the Tower; Charles Steward saying that he looked upon him as one of his greatest enemyes.

The Lords being pressed, as you have heard, for the expediting of the act of indemnity, come at length to this result, as to the twenty proposed in the act of indemnity (sent up by those of the Howse of Commons) to be excepted as to the benifit of the act of indemnity save as to life, viz. that Sir Henry Vane, Sir Arthur Haslerigg, Major Generall Lambert, and Colonell Daniell Axtell, fower of the said twenty, should stand excepted out of the said act as to life and estate, and the other sixteene should be made uncapable of bearing any office in church or state. This newes was carryed by the Duke of Yorke, the Duke of Buckingham and Monke to Charles Steward, who rejoyced greatly, as I understood from one that was then present; who imediately gave me an account thereof, and that they told him Cheife Justice St. Johns narrowly escaped being put into the same condition with the fower, which Charles Steward expressed he desired to have had done also.

That which remained now to be resolved on was touching those of the King's judges that had rendred themselves upon the proclamation; which held not much dispute with the Lords, those of that **807** Howse who had any sense of honour being by farr the lesser number. Yet some there were who bore their testimony against so horrid a treachery. And in particcular, as I have heard, the Earle of Southampton moved that, if it were not thought fit to secure the lives of those who had rendred themselves, they ought at least to have the like fowerteene dayes allowed for the saving of themselves as they had for their rendring. But Finch, that grey-headed traytour and inveterate enemy to the good of the publique, opposed that motion, alleaging that so they might come againe to doe more mischeife (as he had found he had done). Mr. Thomas Challoner was, with those who had rendred themselves, put in the exception for life and estate. And (as I have heard) Sir Henry Mildmay narrowly escaped being put into the like qualification. But he, Mr. Wallop, the Lord Mounson, Sir James Harrington, Mr. James Challenor and Mr. John Phelps were excepted from having any benifit of their estates, and left to such further punishments as should be thought fit, their lives only to be preserved. And the two persons who were upon the stage when the late King was beheaded, in the frocks and vizards, were excepted as to life and estate. And so was Colonell Francis Hacker, to whom the execution of the warrant signed by those of the Court was directed with others, and Mr. Hugh Peters the minister.

This act, with these alterations, was sent to those in the Howse of Commons for their approbation; who, being not yet altogether so depraved as the Lords, could not satisfy themselves to betray those who had (upon their invitation and promise of favour) cast themselves upon them; neither would consent to the exception of Sir Arthur Haslerigg, Sir Henry Vane or Major Generall Lambert out of the act as to life, alleadging that they having not had any imediate hand in the death of the King, that they might as well except most of themselves. But they agree to except Mr. Hugh Peters, Colonell Daniell Axtell, and the others as desired. Yea, to shew their desire to gratify the lusts of Charles Steward with the blood of as many of the faithfull witnesses to the justice of the Lord executed on the late King as they could have the least shaddow for, they sacrifice to him Mr. John Carew, under pretence that he rendred not himselfe; he being first seized by a warrant from a Justice of Peace in the country, where he had passed up and downe about his occations, not at all concealing himselfe. But his name being mistaken in the warrant, he acquainted the officer therewith, and told him that he might doe therein as he pleased; whereupon the person sent to execute the warrant thought not fit to deteyne him. Yet Mr. Carew told him he conceived he was the person intended to be seized upon, and that if they had a minde to have him, he intended to goe to a place neereby, and to stay there this night, where, saith he, you may finde me if you thinke fit; whereupon the officer got his warrant as to his name amended, and then came and seized him; which by the major parte of the Howse of Comons was adjudged not to be a rendition of himselfe (though it was within the fowerteene dayes limitted by the proclamation, and he in his way to London, the place where they were directed to render themselves); whereupon he was excepted out of the act as to **808** life and estate.

Mr. Gregory Clement, being also a prysoner in the Tower before the proclamation, was put into the like condition. And Colonell Adrian Scroope (whom those in the Howse of Commons had resolved should be admitted to a composition for a yeare's vallue of his estate, and who, in prosecution of the proclamation, rendred himselfe into the hands of the Serjeant of the Howse), upon information given to the Howse, by that apostate Browne the woodmonger, that he accidentally meeting with the said Colonell Scroope at Sir Harbottle Grimston's chamber, and having had some discourse with him about the death of the late Kinge, he was so farr from expressing himselfe sorry for the same that he justified what was done therein, those in the Howse were so farr from proceeding according to rule of justice, that as they had already excused severall who had as much hand in that affaire as others (for that they acted therein without any conscience, for carnall and corrupt ends), so now, without hearing of this person (who had rendred himselfe into their hands upon assurance of favour), it being informed that what he did therein was according to the light God had given him, he was excepted out of the act from having any benefit of it as to life and estate. The man of blood Charles Steward, not satisfied with these sacrifices, but as the horseleach (crying, Give, give, presseth by his creatures in the Howse of Lords to insist upon the excepting of his father's judges, and the other persons aforementioned. Those in the Howse of Commons being not satisfied in honour and conscience to agree thereto, for that some of them rendred themselves upon assurance of favour, and others on reasons above mentioned, a conference was appointed; wherein Hide, their Chancellour, asserts that the proclamation was but in the nature of a subpeena; which yet did not satisfy those in the Howse of Commons.

A lady dining at Colonell Alexander Popham's, hearing one of the members of the Howse speake of that affaire, and taking notice how he inveighed against those in the Howse for making choyce of those seaven persons they had done to be excepted out of the act (alleadging that they had left out those who were much more obnoxious, particcularly naming me), she was pleased to acquaint me therewith, but withall that he sayd, seeing it was done, they were bound in honour not to deliver up those that upon their encouradgement to render had cast themselves upon them. But I could not put much confidence in the wordes of such men who, being governed by their lust, were ready to be disposed by them who could nourish them therein; as Charles Steward then was, and yet is, subservient to the lusts of others; as appeared by what the same lady informed me touching a passadge relating to her husband Dr. Wilkinson; on whose behalfe the Countess of Derby solliciting Charles Steward that he might be contynued in his enjoyment of the Canon's place of Christ Church in Oxford, and having obteyned a warrant to Secretary Maurice for the doing of it accordingly, he being pressed by the lady for her dispatch, and refusing to doe it, in conclusion told her that he durst not, having received an order to the contrary. Nor could any other answer be drawne from him, though told that, having the King's order therein, it was apprehended none had power to supercede the same. And upon a second application of the **809** Countesse of Derby, Charles Steward replyed that he desired to be excused in that thinge, but that he would consider him in some other way; to whom she replyed, that if the Doctor might not have justice from him, he would not flatter himselfe with the hopes of favour. But it is the misery of a poore wretch governed by lust not only to be a slave to his owne, but to the lusts of others.

But seeing it was the will of the Lord we should be under such governours, I thought it my duty to use all the prudence I could for the keeping myselfe out of their hands, and therefore withdrew myselfe, not appearing any more in publique. However, in the night I sometymes went to see my relations, and to conferr with them about what was necessary. And having heard that the Serjeant-at-Armes had bin at the out-doore of my howse, and had sent in one of his servants to finde whether I were in my howse or no, that so he might seize me, I tooke an occation, when my wife had appointed one of his servants (no ill-wissher to the publique interest) to come to her, to be there at that tyme to speake with him, and to deale freely with him touching my intention to render myselfe, in case I could have the conditions made good to me that were promised by the proclamation, but otherwise not; who told me, though he had bin full of hopes that the Howse would make good their word unto those who had rendred themselves, yet now he began to doubt thereof; the poore man expressing himselfe thereupon very honestly. Robinson also, the Leiftenant of the Tower, had let fall words intimating his desire to have those of the judges who were in the Serjeant's hands to be comitted to the Tower, as being the pryson of the Parlament, and his resolution to move the Howse to that end; which made me jealous what the designe of the Court party was concerning me, being perswaded that this proposition of his had its rise from thence; which made me the more cautious.

And being willing to enjoy the benefit of the ayre during this debate
betweene the two Howses, I had to that end two freinds' howses in
my thoughts, the one belonging to a kinsman of myne, the other a
faythfull well-wissher to the publique cause. Finding, upon a discourse
with the latter, a great freedome in him to enterteyne me, I made
choyce of his howse, whither my wife and I repaired by water, and
where we resided with much secresy, comfort and satisfaction. And
having sometymes an opportunity to walke in the great parke at Richmond, and calling at the inn by the parke gate, I understood they
provided every day ten douzen of bread for Charles Steward's doggs,
which he made his almes people, contrary to Bisshop Whitguift's
judgement (formerly Archbisshop of Canterbury) who, having built
an hospitall at Croyden which he filled with poore people, and being
asked by the French Embassadour why he kept not hounds, as their
bisshops and cardinalls did, he carrying him to the hospitall, and
shewing him the poore people, said, These were the doggs with which
I hunted the kingdome of heaven. But Charles Steward not only gave
the children's bread to dogges, but with his bloodhounds hunted
after the lives of the pretious servants of God. Another thinge I
observed in my retirement, as I walked on the outside of Major
Generall Lambert's howse at Wymbleton, that was on the banqueting
howse words written to this effect, The way to ruyne your enemyes,
is to divide their councells; which lesson had he well learned, and
bin cautioned by, the confusion we   **810** [were?] brought to might
have bin probably avoyded. But the Lord knowes what is best for
us, and how to advance his owne glory.

During this debate, Sir John Bouchier, one of the King's judges,
who had rendred himselfe upon the proclamation, being aged and
sick, was permitted to lodge at one of his daughters' in London. And
the symptoms of death appearing on him, his sonne, and some other
of his relations, conceiving that his acknowledging himselfe mistaken
in having bin instrumentall in the late King's death would tend to
the procuring of them favour from the present powers, pressed him
earnestly thereto. But he sitting in his chaire, though not able to stand
without helpe, receiving new life and strength from the satisfaction
he had in his appearing therein, forceth himselfe upon his leggs, saying, I tell you it was a just act, and God and good men will owne
it. In a short tyme after he had borne this faithfull testimony, he departed this life. Those in the Howse of Comons, to shew their readyness to stretch their consciences to the utmost for the satisfying of the
lusts of Charles Steward, consent to sacrifice Sir Arthur Haslerigg's
estate and liberty to him, but reserve to him by the act of indemnity
his life, and that Sir Henry Vane and Major Generall Lambert shall
stand excepted out of the act of indemnity as to life and estate, on

this condition, that the two Howses shall joyne in their petition to the King to pardon them as to their lives, in case upon their tryall they should be found guilty. This petition of theirs being ordered by the two Howses to be presented to Charles Steward by his Chancellor Hyde, hee makes report to the Howse that the King had graunted their desire, as may appeare more fully in the records of Parlament of the

And seeing the royall party in the Howse of Lords cannot prevayle with those in the Howse of Commons to consent fully with them, in delivering up those to the slaughter whom they had invited to render themselves upon promise of favour, they propose an expedient; wherein the Chancellour, at a conference betweene the two Howses, is made use of as their mouth, declaring that they consent in substance with what the Comons desire, only differing from them in the manner of putting it in execution. The expedient is, that they shall stand excepted out of the act of indemnity as to life and estate, but the sentence that shall be pronounced against them upon their inditement shall not be executed but by act of parliament; which he assured himselfe the Comons would be satisfyed withall, yet expressed his hopes to them that they will not extend this favour to any of the King's judges who had since their surrender withdrawne themselves out of their protection; wherein I have grounds to beleeve he cheifly aymed at me, for that the serjeant his deputy with a guard of souldiers had bin to search my howse for me upon supposition that I was withdrawne. Those of the Howse of Commons, partely out of principle, and partely to secure themselves and the rest of the nation by the passing of the act of indemnity, consent to the passing of these alterations as they were made by the Lords, or rather the King; though had there bin any weight to be layd on Charles Steward's word (they having in the name of the people claymed the benifit of the proclamation published by him within the tyme limmitted, **811** the proclamation giving a pardon to all who did so, save such as should be excepted by the Parlament), the nation in generall, and they in particcular, had bin sufficiently secured thereby, or at least as well secured as they were like to be by this act. For though they now call themselves a Parlament, and are owned by the King for his present turne to be so, yet as summoned by the Commonwealth's writ, and not in the name of the King.

It's already publiquely avowed by some of his party that they were not [to be?] looked upon as such, but made use of for the quieting of thinges till the sectarian army were disbanded, and that their turne should come next to be suppressed; of which some of that party growing sensible, one of those who was most active in preferring the chardge of high treason against me to the Parlament put forth a state of the present posture of affaires by way of Queries; wherein he demaunds, Whether the late King had not a hand, or gave not too much countenance in the massacre of the Protestants in Ireland, by the Irish papists? Whether the Parlament when called together for the releeving of the people from the encroachments that were upon them, by the Court, in their libertyes, propertyes and religion, could avoyd engaging against the King in a warr, without betraying the trust reposed in them by the people? Whether the late King, having left the manadgement of the warr against the Irish rebells to the Parlament, did not violate his owne act, in not only treating with the Irish rebells without the consent of the Parliament, and in making a truce with them, but in concluding with them a peace in opposition to the Parlament? Whether those who made a warr against the late king were not as much guilty in contriving his death as those who sate as his judges? Whether the blood shed in the warr must not be chardged somewhere, and if not upon the Parlament, whether then not upon the King? Whether the Long Parlament were not still the lawfull authority of the nation, it having bin contynued by act of parlament, and never legally dissolved, and whether it might not be brought to the exercise of its authority againe? Whether it may not be supposed that the King having bin educated amongst the papists, and favouring principally those of that religion, yea, of the Irish rebells themselves, that he is of that religion, etc.? Many other Queryes there were to the like effect, of which some related to those lands purchased from the Parlament; which said Queryes went so to the quick, that (as I have heard) five hundred pounds was offred to discover the authour of them. They were very hard to be gott at the first publication, but an Answer to them being printed with them, they were commonly sold; which Answer some supposed was put out by one of the same mynd with him who writ the said Queryes, in most of the particculars leaving those who read them more unsatisfyed then before, as, to instance in one for all, viz. Whether the Long Parlament may not againe retorne to the exercise of their authority, etc.; whereunto is answered, Yes, if the oppinion of those be true who hold that a revolution of all thinges will be once in ten thousand yeares, but seeing that Parliament hath no power to support its authority, and this Parlament hath, this is the authority, and not the other; whereby **812** he layes the foundation of their pretended authority upon force, and not upon right, and yet will presume to question those who went before them for what they did under a lawfull authority, that had the vissible power of the nation at their comand.

But where lust and revendge beare sway, it may not be expected that a measure of proceedings can be taken from the rules of reason, much less of piety and Christianity. Therefore the Howse of Comons agreeing with the proposition that was made by the Howse of Lords, according to what was moved by Hide at the conference, order the Serjeant attending them to deliver those of the King's judges who were in his custody into the hands of the Leiftenant of the Tower of London; which was done accordingly of as many of them as would come in upon the summons of the Serjeant to whom they had given security, to the number of nineteene, viz. Colonell Adrian Scroope, Mr. William Heveningham, Mr. George Fleetwood, Colonell James Temple, Mr. Peter Temple, Mr. Henry Smyth, Mr. Symon Maine, Colonell Thomas Wayte, Colonell John Downes, Colonell Vincent Potter, Colonell Henry Martyn, Colonell Edmund Harvey, Alderman Isaac Penington, Mr. Gilbert Millington, Colonell Robert Lilborne, Mr. Augustine Garland; Colonell Owen Row withdrew himselfe for a while, but afterwards upon the perswasion of his freinds rendred himselfe; Sir Hardres Waller had ben in France, but rendred himselfe upon the proclamation upon his retorne into England, and finding the issue of his rendition not like to answer his expectation, concealed himselfe; and so did Alderman Tichborne; whereof the Serjeant acquaints those in the Howse, as also that I was not to be found, being called upon to give an account of his prysoners. But the next day those two render themselves, so that none being now withdrawne but myselfe, those in the Howse, as they were filling up the act of indemnity, are moved to put my name amongst those who were to be excepted for life and estate. But as some of my countrymen had before sent to me for a particcular of my estate, intending to make use thereof in the lessening of my fine, which they supposed would have bin put upon me, so now Mr. Swanton, my countryman and Clarke of the Assize for the Westerne Circuite, being a member of this Howse, moves that before they did that, they would take a veiu of the bond I had given for my appearance, that so they might be satisfyed I had broken the condition before they put me into that quallification, or gave order for the suing of the bond, which was also moved. Hereupon the Howse deferred doing anythinge, it may be hoping that by their forbearing thereof I might be perswaded to come in and submit myselfe.

Of this passadge, and how the whole affaire stood, the said Mr. Swanton and Colonell Henley (my fellow prysoner at Oxford and now a member of this Howse) came **813** to my father and mother Oldsworth to informe them, upon the comon rumour, of what was agreed. My wife went to London for better information; but the allarum growing hotter, I thought fit to hasten after her, that so we might consider upon the place what course to steere. I repayred to a private howse in Westminster that was alwayes ready to receive me, and from thence made a stepp to my owne howse; where I had an opportunity to see and take my last leave of my deare mother, who kept her bedd, having her usuall distemper much encreased by the apprehensions that were upon her on my behalfe. My wife I found gone to the howse from whence I came in the country, spending the greatest parte of the night in going thither and retorning; which she imediately did, understanding of my remove. This was the night of the seaventh day. The next day we spent in seeking the Lord, and advising what to doe. On the day following, in the morning, the tyme being very short, my freinds divided themselves. My deare wife repaired to Sir Harbottle Grimstone, who was Speaker, to consult with him at his howse what was adviseable for me to doe. And my deare mother Oldsworth, whose heart the Lord had enclyned towards me, as if I had bin her owne sonne, from the tyme I had the happyness to be knowne to her, made her application to a freind *and kinsman* of myne, who was very able to advise her. Sir Harbottle Grimstone was very full in his advice for my rendring myselfe. My wife objected to him the danger my life was in if I should so doe, in that no assurance could be had that they who, to gratify the King, had receded so much from themselves as to give way that those who had rendred themselves should be excepted out of the act as to life and estate (with the limitation therein expressed) would not goe farther, and consent that, when they were declared guilty, an act should pass for the putting the sentence in execution, and, in case they should not be brought to so horrid a peece of treachery and cruelty, they might be dissolved, and the excepted persons kept in prisson till such could be gott to meete in that Howse as would be prevayled with so to doe; to which he answered, You will be wiser then the Parlament; she having observed unto him that the proviso agreed upon to be inserted in the act concerning them, that the sentence (as it related to their lives) was not limitted to be put in execution only by act of this Parlament, but not by act of parlament in generall. And when she was going downestairs and parting from him, hee followes her, saying he would wash his hands of the blood of her husband before she went, in letting her know that if he rendred himselfe his life would be as secure as his, but if he did not she would be left the poorest widdow in England, and if he were taken he would be the first that would bee executed.

But the freind whom my mother Oldsworth applyed to was of a contrary oppinion touching **814** my rendring of myselfe, whether as better acquainted with the treacherous and bloody intentions of Charles Steward, or because he was more affectionate and tender of me, I cannot say. But as before, so now, he advised me to withdraw out of England; assuring that if I stayd I was a dead man, and so would Major Generall Lambert and Sir Henry Vane be (notwithstanding the engagement given to the contrary) as certeine as he was living; adding I might possibly escape away, and whilst there was life there was hope, and that applications might be made by my wife for a subsistence the better for my being abroad. And when it was urged that the Parlament was engaged to doe somewhat for those who rendred themselves, he replyed, What will you say when the Parlament is adjourned *or dissolved*, if you never see a Parlament meete more; and further assured her that there was an intent to seize the estates of all who were outlawed in the late King's tyme; amongst which number my father having bin one, he sayd that were I free upon my owne account, I would be ruyned upon his. The cleareness and heartyness of this freind's advise much wrought with me to resolve upon my flight, having had full experience of his affection to me, and being confident of his knowing of the secretest cabals of the enemy; in which resolution I was confirmed from the like freindly councell I had from the Lord of Ossery, eldest sonne to the Marquess of Ormond, and likewise from Mr Cardinall, who, being admitted at the Lord of Elgin's howse at Clarkenwell into the company of many of the Lords who there often met and debated of publique affaires, and finding, though they had as little against me personally as any other, yet that thinking I might be dangerous to them for the future, my stay might therefore be hazardous to me, he found out a way by a second hand to acquaint me heerewith, and that he supposed within three or fower monthes the heate and rage would be over, when I might have an opportunity to retorne againe. The fickelness, instabillity and injustice of those in the Howse of Comons, in having so unworthily sacrificed Mr. Carew and Colonell Scroope to the lust of Nero, made me unwilling to put my life upon a moote point before such partiall persons, especially seeing Hide had in his speech, wherein he proposed the expedient for the reconciling of those in the Howse of Commons and those of the Howse of Lords touching this particcular, expressed his hopes that this favour (as he called it) should not be extended to those who had since withdrawne themselves out of their protection, poynting therein as **815** I apprehended at me principally; whereby my life after I had bin in hold would have lyen at the mercey of any member of the Howse that would have moved I should have bin excepted upon that account, I not being like as thinges stood to have many advocates.

Severall lodgings I had proposed for my retreate. But an old and faithfull freind was pitched upon, who, though she had appointed to goe the next day into the country, undertooke to secure me in her howse, and comitted me to the care of a gentlewoman, with whom she left in the chardge her whole familly which was great. The evening being very darke, I had the opportunity to pass through James's Feilds, and so through Holborne Feilds to the place where I was expected. But as I came to the doore, a coach with three or fower lackeys (who carryed each of them a torch) came hurrying upon me; which to avoyd, lest some in the coach might discover me, I went forward. But the place having no passadge through, had there not bin some boards behind which I concealed myselfe, if I had not bin discovered who I had bin, yet might I have bin looked upon in the posture I was as a suspitious person. But the lights being entred with the person whom they attended into the howse, I retorned to my freind's, where I found the doores readily opened for me; the Lord haveing enclyned the gentlewoman's heart to receive me with much kindness and affection, and to avoyd suspition of the rest of the familly lodged me in the chamber of that gentlewoman with whom she left me in chardge. The next morning the mistress of the howse takes her journey. The gentlewoman with whom I was left was not acquainted with my particcular condition, and was supposed not to have knowne my person, especially being disguised by the growth of my beard. But the lady, having seene me formerly in that howse, knew me well enough, and what my condition was, and accordingly told me, saying she woundred that either the gentlewoman of the howse or myselfe would intrust her in that affaire, seeing that both her relations and herselfe were knowne to be well-wisshers to the King, but yet professed she would dye before she would betray the trust reposed in her. And truly she was as carefull of me as if she had bin my sister, bringing me provissions with her owne hand, and watching that none of the familly should come neare her chamber for feare of making a discovery; in all which I desired to see and be sensible of the overruling hand of the Lord.

My wife came daily to me, acquainting me how things stood, and in particcular, that my father Oldsworth meeting accidentally with Mr. Denzill Hollis, and speaking with him about me, and being encouraged by him to perswade me to come in, my mother Oldsworth (who never neglected any oppertunity that was to be improved for my advantadge) repaires to him for her further information and advice; who declares to her as he had formerly done to her husband, assuring her that if I rendred myselfe, my life would be as sure as his. It may be so, replyed my mother, for I beleeve you cannot long promise yourselfe security; and then acquainted him **816** with what she had heard from my freind touching the intentions of the caball, concerning the person from whom she had it; whereto he made no other answer, but that he hoped it would not be so. My wife also, upon conference with a very knowing and faithfull freind, being informed of a designe carrying on by so considerable an interest that the Court party could not make any opposition to, did propose unto me whether I would not forbeare going away for a forthnight, till the issue thereof might be seene; which I suppose might be something relating to the restoring of the Long Parliament, I having seene a manuscript asserting that the Long Parlament was still virtually in being. But not beleeving that it was yet a tyme to expect deliverance, I resolved to hasten my departure.

The manner of my getting away I proposed to be in a sayler's habit. But some of my freinds, to whom I referred myselfe therein, contrived it in another way; wherein the Lord's assistance was more emynently seene. The fifth day in the evening, being the tyme agree on for my journey, my wife and some other of my deare relations coming to the howse where I was an hower or two before night, after I setled with them the best I could the affaires of my estate, in the duske of the evening I went with them into their coach, and passed through London, and so over the bridge to George his church in Southwarke; where an horse which a freind had hyred as for himselfe was ready for me, together with a guyde on horseback, who knew every creeke of the way we were to pass. There was also a portmantle of cloathes to carry with me. All thinges being thus in a readyness, together with letters and instructions that my guyde had to a merchant at Lewis to provide a vessell for my transportation, and with those I had to a merchant at Deepe to receive and enterteyne me when I came into France, I tooke my leave of my deare relations, my poore wife and another freind accompanying me to my horse. My guide brought me such back wayes that I avoyded all the townes where any souldiers might be lodged, and by daybreake came into the howse appointed for my stay till my shipp was provided; for which end my guide departed to the next sea-port. And in the meanetyme, having put my horse to grass, I lay as privately as I could from the sixth day in the morning, till the second day of the next weeke; at which tyme about an hower before night he came to me, with an account that a vessell was in a readyness for me. The woman of the howse where I lay was earnest with me to acquaint her with my name. I told her it was not convenient at this tyme, but if ever the Lord retorned me by that way, I should make myselfe knowne to her.

The guide conducted me very private wayes over the Downes, to the mouth of the harbour where the shallop lay. **817** It was neare midnight before I got thither. The wynd was very high, and shallop without any deck to shift the wasshing or breaking in of any water; and a vessell lay at the mouth of the harbour cast away. I therefore desired a lardger vessell if it were to be had, there having bin a [one ... for?] me, that had transported some weekes before Mr. Richard Cromwell, and was stuck upon the sands as it was falling downe the river to receive me. I was carryed into that vessell to stay in her till it should be convenient to put to sea; which [proved?] a providence as to my preservation. For the next morning, one of the searchers, coming to search the vessell that was going out, satisfyed himselfe with searching the shallop, and not that wherein I was, as not suspecting anybody to be in her, because she was stuck upon the sands. The storme contynuing, the maryners not thinking it safe to put to sea, I lay in the harbour that day. The master of the ship inquiring of me touching Leiftenant Generall Ludlow, whom whilest he was in Ireland he heard spoaken of, desiring to know if he were in hold, I replyed I thought not.

The next morning, though the wynde contynued boysterous, we resolved to put to sea. And so having shipped myselfe in the shallop about seaven of the clock in the morning, these seamen (which were French), setting sayle, covered me with their coates as we passed in the veiu of those who were unlading the shipp that was cast away in the mouth of the harbour. The sea went not so high as we expected it would have done. The Lord blessed us with so favourable a wynd, that we recovered into the harbour at Deepe before the gates of the towne were shut. And by reason it was in the duske of the evening, I got on shoare from one vessell to another, they lying very close, without being taken notice of by any of the officers of the Custome howse, the marryners being carefull to conceale me; who having conducted me to Madam de Caux, a gentlewoman's of that towne, who though she was herselfe at her country howse, upon the delivery of my letters of recomendation of her factor, I was kindly received. And being destitute of the language, providence so ordered it that a young apprentice of Madam de Caux, speaking English, was my interpreter upon all occations. The gentlewoman, being informed of my being at her howse, hastned her retorne, and was exceeding courteous and civill to me, putting it to my choyce either to stay with her in the towne, or to goe to her familly in the country. I chose the latter, as supposing I should have more liberty of walking abroad there; that towne being full of Irish, who might probably have seene me in Ireland.

I had not bin there many dayes before I received letters from my relations, with a printed proclamation of Charles Steward, taking notice of my having withdrawne myselfe and escaped out of custody, forbidding any to enterteyne or **818** [receive?] me under penalty of high displeasure, and requiring all officers and others to seize and secure me. This proclamation was published in the Pallace Yarde at Westminster, and other places, the seaventh day of the weeke, the same tyme I lay at a private howse in Sussex in expectation of a vessell for my transportation. And my lettres imparted that, whereas at such publications the people used to express much joy, it was observed they did not so now, but rather the contrary. It may be this was only the apprehension of some who, wisshing me well, were apt to beleeve

others did so to. By these and other letters I perceived the clowdes
to thicken. Yet I was willing to have continued in some private place
thereabouts, till I could have seene more danger, or more hopes. But
the freind whose heart the Lord moved to recomend me thither
(whose face I remember not that I ever saw, nor of 3 or 4 more whom
he made very instrumentall in the conveying me away), fearing lest
my being so neare I might be seized on, and so bring him into trouble,
prest by his letters my removall further off; which finding to have
an operation amongst those with whom I was, I resolved to remove
whatever inconveniencyes I underwent. A sonne-in-lawe of the lady's,
having a vessell bound for Holland, perswaded me to take the advantadge thereof for my going thither. But I liked not putting to sea
againe; neither did I approve of being in a country which depended
so much on England as I knew they did upon the account of trade.
And therefore looking into the mapp for some inland Commonwealth,
judging such an ayre most suitable to my constitution, the Lord was
pleased to direct me to the consideration of Geneve, a citty very
renowned for liberty and religion; and on further enquiry thereof,
I was encouraged to make thitherward by Dr. Hughs, sonne-in-law
to Madam de Caux.

And now the greatest difficulty was how to get thither. A merchant
of the towne, being obstructed in his trade by reason of many losses,
was proposed to accompany me; but by reason of some affaires he
attended to dispatch, he could not yet goe. Dr. Hughs having a
brother to be imployed by the merchants of Diepe to sollicite on their
behalves at Paris, he was pleased to offer me the favour of his company
to Paris, and from thence, after he had dispatched his affaires (which
he hoped to doe in a few dayes), to Geneve, and to stay with me the
wynter following. Being not willing to neglect any   **819**   opportunity,
rather then to stay where I perceaved a desire I should goe, I resolved
to lay hold on this, and wanted only a horse for my journey. I enclyned
to one which belonged to the sonne-in-law that was the merchant,
as judging him fittest for my occation. And he being one who
expressed much affection to the Reformed Religion, and pitty to those
in my condition, was pleased to offer him to me. But the docter alledging that his horse was much more fit, and he being the person that
with the broaken Latin I had I could converse with, and so consequently rely upon, I resolved to cast myselfe upon him, and according to his demaund gave him twenty five pistolls for his horse, saddle
and pistolls; looking more (as my concerne) to be furnished with a
horse that might doe my business, then at the prise I gave. The lady
and all the familly I found much civilillity from. Neither could I fasten
anythinge upon her for my dyet, though I earnestly endeavoured,
and had no way more then by wordes to testify my acknowledgement

thereof, save by some small present from Paris which I resolved upon. It was noone before we could set forward for Rouen, so that we were necessited to ride much beyond the rate of the country to recover our journey's end that night; which might be the cause that my horse went stiff the next morning, being of an heavyer make then our English horse.

The third day after our setting out from Diepe, we arrived through mercey at Paris, where I attended eight dayes in expectation of the dispatch of Mr. Hughes his affaires; and in the meanetyme got a bill of exchandge from Mr. *Margas* (to whom I was consigned by Madam de Caux) for the paying of monyes to me at Geneve; and got acquaintance with Mr. Copley, an English merchant in Paris, from whom I received much civillity and freindship; he helping me to buy those toyes I sent to Madam de Caux's daughters, and the rest of her familly, and shewing me those thinges in the towne that were esteemed worth seeing. And being in the Pallace Royall at the tyme of the elevation of the Host, we were both much put to it to avoyd the idolizing thereof; and so I was at another tyme in the streete as it was carryed by, some of the baser sorte revyling me for that they observed me to turne my back upon it. He accompanyed me also to the Lovuer, which seemed to me more like a garrison then a courte, being full of *souldiers and* dirt, as was also the whole towne. Beeing weary of this place, and loathing to see so many idle droanes running up and down in anticque habits (wherein they place their religion), who eate the bread of the poore, yea of the plowmen themselves, leaving them to be distinguished from those of other nations by their thinne cheekes, wooden **820** shooes and [canvass breaches?], and observing Mr. Hughes his affaires in no probabillity of coming to an issue, I enclyned to set forward for Geneve. And to that end, being informed of the tyme of the messenger's departure to Lyons, Mr. Copley having a freind that went thither, I resolved to accompany him. But in the evening, before the messenger was to departe, I understood this gentleman could not be furnished with a horse (and therefore resolved to goe by water), and that the messenger was so full loaden that he could not carry my portmantle.

However, I resolved to put it to the hazzard, and the next morning sent my horse and portmantle to the inn where the messenger lay; and having the favour of Mr. Copley, Mr. Hughes, and another gentleman's company of Deepe, they prevayled with the messenger to undertake the carriadge of my portmantle for what they agreed with him, as they did also for myselfe and horse to Lyons, which I looked upon as a mercy to me in many respects. As soone as I came to the end of the towne, a gentleman with his servant who was to goe with the messenger overtooke me, with whom entring into dis-

course I found him bound for Geneve; of which I was very glad, and
the more for that I ghessed, by some expressions which fell of his dislike
of fasting days, that he was no Roman Catholique. Three or fower
Almaines, knowing the roade, were gone before to the inn, so that
when we came to supper our company consisted of 9 or 10; all of
them, as farr as I could ghess by their discourse, of the popish religion,
at least not of the Reformed, and pressing me very earnestly to discover of what judgement I was, and finding I was not of theirs were
no less desirous to know whether I were a Lutheran or Calvinist; I
telling them I was for both as farr as they agreed with the word of
God, and for neither any further. This gentleman, whom I tooke to
be a Frenchman, and myself to be so happy in his company, proved
an Almaine, but infected with the levity of the French as well in religion as garb and humour, presently cryed out, He is a Quaker, a
Quaker; to whom I replyed, I was one who desired to tremble at
God's word; wherein it's said by the apostle Paul, he feared that
he had bestowed his labour in vane, upon those who sayd they were
of Paul, of Apollo or Caephas, seeing Christ who dyed for them was
not divided. This gentleman, and another of the company whom I
tooke to be a young Jesuite, finding my horse like to fayle, exercised
the little wit they had in deriding and scoffing at me on that account,
till, notwithstanding the condition I was in, I was constreyned to tell
them I had heard the French were civill to strandgers, but found it
otherwise, but did acknowledge the Almaines were such of whom it
was otherwise reported (being mistaken as I afterwards perceived not
only of the country to which that gentleman, but others also of them,
related), adding withall that I chose rather to receive injuryes then
offer any, but loved neither; which, with what else I then sayd, had
such an   **821** operation that from thenceforward in my journey with
them I was treated very civilly, that gentleman whom I tooke for a
Frenchman (being a German lord) desiring me to lodge in the
chamber with him.

Three days' journey short of Lyons, my horse fayled me, so that
I was forced to hire one for two dayes, which for his hyer, meats and
carrying back cost me a pistoll. And glad I was to have him so, for
otherwise I could not have kept company with the messenger, which
would have bin very inconvenient, and it may be dangerous, to me.
The last day from *Tarrara*, I lighted upon an empty horse that was
going to Lyons. My great difficulty was now how to get into the towne
without giving in my name at the gate, I being assured some constantly attended there to take notice of all strangers that came into
the garrison, which was every night presented to the Governour for
his veiu and consideration; who for ought I knew might have beene
desired by Charles Steward to make stay of such as had escaped out

of England and fledd that way. And though he might not be advertised of my name, yet, upon the account of my being an Englishman,
I supposed he might make enquiry after me, and so come to the knowledge of me. And therefore, willing to shun it what I could, when
the Almaines of our company had given an account of themselves,
they being knowne to some there present, I passed away with them.
And though those who attended called after me, I pretending not
to heare, at least not to understand, got into the towne without being
any more questioned; where I was no sooner come into my inne, but
severall of the popish Orders came to demaund, or rather command
something; one whereof deported himselfe in so lascivious a manner
towards a youth who came in our company from Paris, that it made
me blush to see.

Understanding that the messenger of Geneve departed the next
day, with the helpe of Mr. Francis Richy (a merchant of that towne,
to whom I was recomended by Mr. Coply from Paris) I made an
agreement with the messenger for the conveying of me to Geneve,
leaving my horse at Lyons to the care of Mr. Richy, who promissed
to send him after me as soone as he was able to travayle. In my journey
from Lyons I found a very great alteration in my company, having
two of the Reformed Religion with me to ballance that young man
whom I tooke for a Jesuite, being the only person from Paris who
continued the journey; in which we came through a streight passadge
called the Recluse, within 5 or 6 leagues of Geneve, where the King
of France hath a garrison, towards the confines of his teritoryes. And
being in the night, and not understanding their languadge, I thought
they would have examined me, and constreyned me to render my
armes; but being informed by the messenger they only desired money
to drinke, I freely gave it, and was glad I was so ridd of them. When
I had passed the River of Roane, I understood I was within the teritoryes of Geneve, which I was much rejoyced at, not only as supposing
myselfe in more surety, and in that I had a great love and inclynation
to the ayre of a Commonwealth, but for that I hoped to enjoy the
society   **822** of mankind, and above all the servants, and ordinances,
of Christ.

I had now tyme to ruminate of the great mercey and overruling
hand of God in bringing me safe through the country, where those
currupt interests prevayle and beare sway, which the Lord and all
his faithfull servants abominate; to any of whom, had my condition
bin discovered, I had in all probabillity become a prey. But the Lord
hid me in the hollow of his hand. O that I might be so affected therewith as to sacrifice the remainder of my life entirely to his praise and
service. I supposed I might have heere heard of Mr. William Cawley,
an antient member of parlament, and a faithfull and zealous patriot,

having bin assured he escaped out of England into France. And by one Mr. *Moneery*, who lodged with me in the same howse at Roan, I was enformed that an English gentleman (who by the description he gave of him, I knew to be the same) was passed by that way. But by Mr. Charles Perrot of Geneve (who spake English, and had bin engaged for the Parlament, and marryed an English woman), coming to vissit me, I was enformed that there was no English in the towne, except one Mr. Felton, and another who belonged to him; he thereupon inviting me to lodge at his howse, he enterteyning pensioners. I was glad to lay hold of the opportunity, as well in respect of the society of some of my owne country, and of conversing with those whose languadge I understood, as in that this gentleman's howse was the only one that was furnished with beere in these partes; which I looked upon as a mercyfull providence so hapyly to meete with, my body being very much disordered by rheumes in the constant drinking of wyne, and in a short tyme having the benefit of my accustomed drinke, was brought to its usuall temper. The next day after my arrivall I received a bill of exchandge, by direction of my dearest relation, from Monsieur *Margas* of Paris, for six hundred crownes, chargeable upon a merchant of Geneve. But having betweene fifty and threescore pounds of the stock I brought out of England with me yet left, and not having any letters of advice touching this mony, I writ to Mr. Margas, desiring him to deteyne the money in his hand till I should heare from my wife concerning it.

The first Gazet I saw, I found, on supposition that Colonell Whalley and Colonell Gough were retorned into England, an hundred pounds promissed to him or them who should seize upon either of them, and three hundred pounds to any that should seize and secure me; which caused me the more to prize the mercey of the Lord's delivering me out of their hands, whose mallice seemed so great towards me. Severall reportes I heard were raysed concerning me in England, as that I was taken endeavouring to get away in a disguise, having wasshed my hands and face in the liquor of walnut leaves, and put a black patch upon one of my eyes; which was commonly beleeved for some dayes. But my relations were assured of the contrary, being advertized of my safe landing in France. Others also reported that, being in the howse of a countryman which some had notice of, they endeavoured to have seized me,   **823** and had done it, but that the man in whose howse I [was?] .... [more affection?] to me then to the mony proferred for me, let me out of his back doore. My enemyes, being thus amused, were the more earnest to be rid of me, suspecting me to be still in England, and doubting [least?] the army (not yet disbanded) should make head against them, and I be made use of to that end.

And for the better disguising themselves till this were done, the Convention (which called itselfe a Parlament) having, before their adjournement (which was to Michelmas Tearme following), referred the composing of the differencyes betweene the episcopall party and the presbytery to the King, he in prosecution thereof requires each party to consider how farr they could be satisfyed to condescend for mutuall accommodation, and for keeping peace in the church. The presbiterians meete at Zion Colledge, and agree to the bisshops in many particculars, reserving for themselves only to be dispensed with-all in some small circumstances, as the wearing of the surplice, the reading of the litturgy, and the using of some ceremonyes; on which conditions they promise to subject themselves to the bisshops as superintendents, some of the ministers being joyned with them in poynt of ordination. The propositions and condescentions were ordred by Charles Steward to be comunicated to the bisshops, and the bisshops to them. And upon the perusall of that from the bisshops, it was found that they consented not to the abatement of any of their grandure, except that in the tyme of ordination some presbyters might have the liberty to stand in the presence of the bisshops with their hats on; notwithstanding which mockery, and that it was publiquely knowne that Shelton the Bisshop of London (the great steeresman of ecclesiasticall affaires) had discovered his oppinion to be that the cause of their former miscarriadge was their too much moderation, and their taking of middle wayes, and that they ought therefore to offend no more on that hand, the presbyterians feede themselves with hopes. And the army being not disbanded, nor the blood of those poore innocent lambes of Christ yet powred forth who had bin betrayed into their hands, it was thought fit that both partyes should have a conference at Hide's lodgings, where Charles Steward was present.

And though the bisshops, as more confident of their power in the militia then in the strength of their arguments, were as inflexible as before, Charles Steward for the reasons aforementioned puts forth a declaration, wherein he asserts the episcopall interest, but with the like quallifications as were desired by the presbyterians, forbidding that the litturgy, surplice etc. should be imposed upon those who were unfree to use them; which seeming moderation tooke so much with the presbyterians (who would have gone to the utmost of their teddar to have kept themselves in play) that they present their thankes to Charles Steward for the same. The same method was observed for the quieting of the purchassers, who had a promise made them of satisfaction in the proclamation Charles Steward set out from Bre-dagh; the Convention aforementioned having before their adjourne-ment referred it to the King to put into a way the giving them satisfac-tion, who appointed comissioners under the Seale to that end; who

after they had **824** sate [once or?] twice, some of the bisshops
enveighing against the sale of those lands as sacralegious, the comissioners for the most parte being [persons?] of the same interest with
them, that affaire became so blasted that the purchassers were discouraged any further to sollicite the same. It was not yet thought
adviseable to bring the King's judges upon their tryall, thinges and
persons being not fully pact to their purpose, Sheriff Love being too
honest to be made use of in that horrid and bloody tragedy. And therefore it's deferred till the new election of sheriffs. In the meanetyme,
that active instrument on the behalfe of the publique cause Mr. Hugh
Peeters, being excepted upon that account out of the act of indemnity,
and discovered to be hid in a Quaker's howse in Southwarke, was
by virtue of a warrant signed by Secretary Nicholas seized, and sent
to the Tower.

The great worke of the gentlemen in the country that are members
of the Convention, during this tyme of their adjournement, is to be
assistant in the raysing of those great sommes of money which they
had layd upon the people; for the payment whereof their argument
is, that it is for the disbanding of the army, that the lawes might runn
in their propper channell without controule; *whereas the true reason of
hastening it is, that those in power may free themselves of such who have imployed
their sword for the reduceing of gouverment into its proper channell (to wit for
the advancement of God's glory, and the good of mankind), and that the sword
and word of their King, with the assistance of such fooles and knaves as are
in confederacy with him, may passe for a law without controule; which being
now effected in a great measure, they looke on themselves as in a capacity to
put their bloody designe in execution.*

CHAPTER FIVE

Within fowerteene dayes after my coming to Geneve, I finde in the Gazet the execution of Major Generall Harrison, Mr. John Carew, Cheife Justice Cooke and Mr. Hugh Peters; the first upon the 13 October, the second upon the 15th, and the two last upon the 16th, at the place where Charing Cross stood (as well to revenge the wrong done to that sacred relique, as to gratify Nero with the sight of that tragedy, the shedding the blood of those eminent servants of the Lord). The next weeke's Gazet gave an account of the execution of Mr. Thomas Scot, Mr. Gregory Clement, Colonell Adrian Scroope and Colonell John Jones, on the 17th of October, at the same place with the former; and of Colonell Francis Hacker and Colonell Daniell Axtell at Tybourne, the comon place of execution, upon October the 19th.

Major Generall Harrison was in his younger yeares trained up to the law. He remembered his Creatour in the dayes of his youth, imploying much of his tyme in prayer, and studying the scriptures. In the begining of the warr betweene the Parlament and the King, he being then about the age of 24 yeares, the Lord enclyned his heart to take armes on the behalfe of the Parlament, and to list himselfe in the Lifeguard of the Earle of Essex, then Generall, which consisted of one hundred gentlemen, each one having his servant; in which capacity, after serveing at the Battle of Keinton Feild, at the taking in of Redding, and elsewhere, with very good reputation, he was made Captaine of a troope of horse, and then Major to Colonell Charles Fleetwood's regiment; in which quallity, after he had bin very service-able to the publique, he was made a Colonell of a regiment of horse, and was chosen a member of parliament; wherein he made appeare that he was a lover of justice, a great favourer of good people, and a discountenancer of vice and wickedness, carrying himselfe with much constancy and resolution. He was oft tyme chosen **825** by the Parlament a member of the Councell of State, and appointed Major Generall of their forces in South Wales; and for some tyme comanded their forces at London, together with five thousand volontiers of that citty, who enlisted themselves under him for the service of the Parla-ment. He [wayted for the?] accomplishment of those promises that relate to the setting up of the scepter of Jesus Christ, neglecting no meanes [that?] he judged conducing to that great end. He was one of those who, being unsatisfied with the course the Parliament tooke in treating with the King at the Isle of Weight, and in voting as they

did the 5th of December 1648 that the King's answer to their propositions were a ground for the Howse to proceed upon for setling the
peace of the kingdome, joyned with Comissary Generall Ireton and
others of the army for the purdging of the Parliament, in order to
the preserving of the publique cause from being betrayed, and for
the bringing of the King to justice; looking upon him as a man of
blood, and the Achan that troubled our Israel.

He was imployed by the army for the seizing of him in the Isle
of Weight, and the bringing of him to London, and as a member of
parlament was active in the constituting of an High Court of Justice
for the tryall of him; and being appointed one of the said Court, was
no less active, in putting what he was entrusted with in execution;
in which he received so much satisfaction that, when the publique
cause was betrayed by the meanes and stepps before mentioned into
the hands of their common and irreconcileable enemy, he rejoyced
to have an opportunity to seale the justice of what he had done, in
executing the judgement written against the blood-guilty with his
owne blood; which though God had so clearly witnessed unto, not
only in his word, but by a series of providencyes writing his approbation thereof, as it were with the beames of the sun, yet this generation
of bloody men, who had not contributed in the least to their owne
restitution, made such use of this extraordinary providence (which
spoake the chastising of us for not improving the merceys of the Lord
as we ought, and not the approving of them or their courses) to rebuild
that with hewen stone, which being of brick was throwne downe, and
to lay the foundation thereof in the blood of these faithfull witnesses
and lambes of Christ. Neither shall there be wanting instruments, nor
a forme of law, to couller these their horrid butcheryes. For sheriffs
being chosen as aforesaid for their turne, it's very well knowne how
easy it is to pack a grand jury and a petty jury, that shall doe whatever
is desired of them, especially at such a tyme and in such a business
as this is. The comission for the hearing and determining of this matter
is directed to thirty fower persons; most if not all of which (excepting
the Lord Mayor) were since Charles Steward's retturne put into
places of trust and proffit; fifteene of which had engaged in the warr
with the Parlament against the King, some as members of the said
Parlament, others as judges under them, many of them as officers in
their army.

Whether they all sate, I know not. But Monke did, that monster
of mankind the devill's great **826** instrument in this chandge (who
had so oft declared himself against the shedding of any blood, especially to Mr. Scot); as also did the Earle of Manchester and Mr. Denzill
Hollis, two of the six members that the King pitched upon to destroy
for their seeming zeale to the publique interest, for the defence of

whom, next to that of the comon cause, the warr against the King
was entred into; wherein they shewed themselves as forward as any,
till after they had engaged many of those gentlemen, on whom they
sate now as judges (having made their owne tearmes), not only leave
them in the lurch, but condemne them to death for being faithfull
to that cause which they had betrayed; the latter of them, to wit Mr.
Hollis (as it is expressed in a booke intituled An Exact and most Impartiall Acount of the Inditement, Arreignement, Tryall and Judgement
of Twenty Regicides (as he calls them) etc., begun at Hicks Hall on
Tewsday the ninth of October 1660 and continued at the sessions in
the Old Baily, untill Friday the nineteenth of the same month,
published by the permission of John Birkenhead their overseer of the
press), venting himselfe in much passion against Major Generall Harrison and Colonell Axtell when upon their tryall at the barr. And
so did Mr. Arthur Ansley, who had bin also a member of parlament
whilest they were engaged in the warr against the King. Those of
the grand jury of which I had a veiu in the booke above mentioned
were many of them such as had bin engaged in armes on behalfe of
the King against the Parlament, and so not like to be competent
judges of what had bin done by virtue of their authority, and for their
service.

   That anti-dated traytor Finch, old in wickedness as well as yeares,
instead of being arreigned for the treason whereof he was accused by
a full parlament neere twenty yeares before, and for which he had
no doubt bin condemned had he not saved himselfe by flight, now
retornes to judge severall of his judges. And Sir Orlando Bridgeman,
who being a member of the Parlament, and finding his endeavours
in the said Parlament not effectuall for the betraying of the libertyes
of the people, who had intrusted him, quits his said trust and repaires
to the King to Oxford, attemting to doe that by open force which
he could not by treachery; but the Lord blasting that, and bringing
him with the rest of that party upon their knees, he was permitted
by Cromwell (who had sacrificed the publique cause to his lust) to
enjoy his chamber practice, under pretence whereof he had opportunity to be both spy and agent for his master; whom the Lord permitting (for the punishment of his owne people, who were growne
wanton in their outward enjoyments, had almost lost the savour of
religion) to be restored, this serpentine creature, that he might shew
the venome that was in him against the righteous seede, is chosen
out of those *who were appointed commissioners for the tryall of the King's
judges to have the cheife* manadgement of that bloody tragedy.   **827** And
in his speech to those who were pickd out by Charles Steward to be
of the Grand Inquest for this affaire, he discovers not only the rotten-
ness of his principle, but the mallice of his heart against the Lord and

his people; giving those powers and attributes to a poore worme that are only due to God himselfe, publiquely declaring the King to be the head of the Comonwealth, and that it was an inanimate lump without him; as if he were so the life thereof that they received their beeing from him, and not from the fountaine of all beeings, who declared to his people Israell, when they chose a king, they had rejected him.

Yea so bold was this worme growne as to deliver it in his chardge to the grand jury as law, that no authority, no single person, nor comunity of men, not the people collectively, nor representatively, had any coercive power over the King of England; and for proofe thereof, urgeth Spencer's case in Edward the Second's tyme, in Calvine's case, second Report: as strong an argument as the present proceedings (when judges, juryes and witnesses are packt, according to the pleasure of a tyrant) will be to after tymes, should the Lord permit this corrupt constitution to continue. But I desire to know of this person (that makes it his worke to comply with the lusts of Charles Steward, rather then with the will and word of God), who made the King thus absolute? Doth the word of God make any King so? If not, how had he this power? By conquest, or by consent? If by conquest, it's an unjust title, and not to be justified before God, or good men. And if the people were conquered, upon the appeale made to God by him and the people in Parliament touching that point, they releeved themselves from that vassalage, the Lord having given judgement on their side against the King. And if he derives his authority from consent, a people can never be supposed so much their owne enemy as to set one over them that should not be accountable to them. But could that be, and should that binde their posterity (which is denyed by all) then could it no longer last then they please to continue it; it being a principle granted by all, that the power which makes a thinge is greater then that which is made, and may also unmake it.

But saith he, law bookes are the ground from whence we must draw all our conclusions for matter of goverment. Whatever the word of God saith, it matters not in the oppinnion of this and such sorte of men. And because these law bookes (which have bin composed by such as have bin the absolute creatures of kings) call them God's Leiftenants, and say that he is imedeate from God, and **828** hath no superiour, and that the statutes say, the Crowne of England is imediately subject to God, and to none other, and that the King is not only the head of the people but the head of the Comonwealth, the three states, though the word of the Lord, and man's right reason, speakes other languadge, yet notwithstanding the lawyers will have it so, because by this craft and cheate they gaine their living, and many others enjoy their lustes. And from some words that some flattering parasites have foysted into acts of parlament, viz. We your Lords and Comons, your faithfull subjects etc.; and, That this Realme is an Empire, as in the 24 Henry 8th Cap. 12; and, That they doe recognize no superiour under God, but only the King's grace, as in the 25 Hen. 8. 21; to gratify the lust of that horrid tyrant, it must be concluded that it is just and reasonable, yea the will of God it should be so; whereas the very urdging of these statutes, for the quallifying of them such, implyes that they had power so to doe. And their recognizing the King under God to be their superiour, as it makes him so, it doth not exclude them from having a power above him who made him to be so. But this gentleman now findes out a distinction without a difference. For he will have the King of England to have an imperiall crowne, and yet not to governe absolutely, to have an absolute monarchy and yet not a goverment absolutely without lawes; and that though the King be supreame, and the only supreame, imediately subject to God, and not punishable by any person, yet for all this he cannot rule but by his lawes; and that the King his person and the people's rights are preserved.

It's an easy matter for one in a scarlet gowne, attended with a sufficient number of souldiers and court parasites, to perswade those who are before resolved to be satisfied with anythinge that is suitable to their owne lustes. But first, where is the liberty and rights of the people, if the lawes by which they are defended are the King's lawes, such only as he (who it's not to be supposed will willingly consent to any that shall intrench upon his person and boundless prerogative) will graunt? And what execution can we expect of those lawes, whilest the great executours of them, both judges and sheriffs, are of the Kinge's owne appointing? And of what use are those lawes, if good and rightly executed, if the King may in his owne person robb me not onely of my propperty and liberty, but of my life itselfe, and it shall not be in the power of any man, nay not in the **829** whole body of the people either collectively or [representatively?], to doe me right, or to call him to an account for the same? There are none, who are not wilfully blynd, but must see through [this cobwebb?] covering, and that the crying up this absoluteness and unaccountableness of the King's person is but (in order to the advancing of their corrupt ends) to betray all that is deare unto the people into the disposall of him and his accurssed instruments, and to put them also, as well as him, into a condition of being unaccountable for these horrid villanyes they shall perpetrate. For who shall ever dare to question them for whatever they shall be guilty of, when it lyes in the power of him who set them on worke to revendge himselfe with his owne hands upon them who doe so, even to the powring out of their blood? Yea, according to this doctryne, parlaments are as farr from giving remedy as private persons, they being used to be called at the pleasure of the King, and dissolved upon the same account. And if they are not murthered and ruyned whilest sitting, how easy a thinge is it to doe it when thrust out, daily experience acquaints us.

But to trace him a little in his arguments, for the proof of his assertion, The King Can Doe No Wronge (a rule he saith in law, and therefore not to be punished for any wronge), if this rule were as authenticque as gospell (the best exposition of difficult texts therein, being the comparing of them with others), this king heere meant will appear to be the King in his *politique* capacity, or rather goverment and law, if compared with another maxime in law, as well knowne as the former, to wit, the King Never Dyes; seeing experience tells us he is mortall, and subject to death, even by the hand of an executioner, and that kingship may dye, and the people be happy, yea much more happy under a Comonwealth goverment (and might have soe continued, had not the lust of som persons or partys interposed). But that you may see he can wrest scripture contrary to its genuine sense, as well as law, he urgeth that portion in Psal. 105. 15, Touch not mine annoynted, etc., for the unaccountableness of the King; where these words were spoken of the chosen ones of the Lord when they had no king, yea when kinges (as in the wordes imediately preceding that text) were reproved for their sakes. And therefore this wretch, if he had not bin very ignorant, or withheld this trueth in unrighteousness, might have applied these wordes to those Saintes then at the barr, whose blood he was about to wash his hands in. But what will such a fellow as this stick at, who dares assert that the people of England have no right to libertyes but as they derive them from the concessions of their princes, as if the people were made to serve the lusts of tyrants? Surely if the great God of heaven and earth were not infinite in patience, **830** he would send fyer to consume such who, in thus idolizing of a worme, robb him of his glory and his people of their right.

And now having endeavoured to make out the unaccountableness of the King's person (as if he were a distinct substance from other men, nay the cheife good, and so he for whom all the nations were created), he descends more particcularly to discuss that point for which they were met, to make inquisition. And he by implication affirmed that the highest authority of the nation, the Lords and Commons joyning unanimously, could not justify the calling of the King to account, though never so guilty and deserving of death; whereas Mathew Paris, making mention of the sword of St. Edward that the Comes Palatii did carry before him at his coronation, saith it was in token that if the King himselfe did transgress, he had of right a power to restraine him; which law with others William the Conquerour confirmed. And Bracton that antient and emynent lawyer, Lib. 2 cap. 8, affirmes, that Non est Rex ubi dominatur voluntas, et non Lex; and Lib. 3 cap. 9, Rex est dum bene regit; tyrannus, dum populum sibi creditam violenta opprimit dominatione. And ibidem, exercere debet rex potestatem juris, ut vicarius et minister Dei: potestas autem injuriae Diaboli, est non Dei: cum declinat ad injuriam Rex, Diaboli minister est; and Bracton, Lib. 1 cap. 8, and Fleta Lib. 1 Cap. 17, Non debet esse Rege major quisquam in exhibitione juris; minimus autem esse debet in judicio suscipiendo, si peccat: some reade si petat; and Bracton, Lib. 2 Cap. 16, and Fleta Lib. 1 Cap. 17, In populo regendo rex habet superiores, legem, perquam factus rex, et curiam suam videlicet, comites et barones: comites dicuntur quasi socii regis; et qui habet socium, habet magistrum; et ideo si rex fuerit sine freno, id est sine lege, debent ei frenum imponere. But as the law of God must now be sylent (which saith, he that sheddeth man's blood, by man shall his blood be shed, and the land cannot be cleansed from blood, but by the blood of him that shed it, as hath bin before mentioned), so must all those of the land too, that suite not with the present designe.

But he would make the fouleness of the fault to appeare, in that the execution of the King was by order from a few members of the Howse of Commons, who had taken the oath of supreamacy and allegiance, and yet take upon them to make a law **831** for the erecting of an High Court of Justice to sentence the life of their soveraigne, who had reduced all greivances at the beginning of the Parlaiment, and had granted what could be desired of him at the Isle of Weight, and in that they put the soveraigne to death as King (having excluded the rest of the Commons, and rejected the Lords that then sate) at his owne doore, and that at nooneday. Thus doth he, with a multiplicity of wordes, endeavour to darken (yea blacken) justice, by words without knowledge, as in another case the Lord reproved, Job. chapt. 38. 2 and 42. 3. And though he will not allow a quorum (which the number of forty is) of the representative of the people to judge of what is their duty to doe in relation to the will of the Lord, and the dischardge of that trust which God and good men had reposed in them, yet he, a private person, takes upon him to censure the proceedings of this authority, yea this authority itselfe; which he cannot but acknowledge is the only lawfull authority at this tyme, that Parlament being contynued by act of parlament not to be dissolved but by its own consent, which not one of the three estates (supposing they had bin all in being) ever consented to. But the Lord having, upon the appeale made by the Parlament and King touching his clayme, given judgement against the King, and delivered him into their hands, those of the Comons who judged their cause just thought it their duty to deale with him as guilty of the blood which had bin shedd, both in the first and second warr; the Lords refusing to joyne with them heerein withdrawing themselves, and those of the Commons who could not give satisfaction touching their having quitted the interest of the Commonwealth, and espoused the King's, being excluded by a vote of the Comons; which consisted of two hundred and threescore that sate after the death of the King upon the Commonwealth account, as may appeare by their subscription to the engagement lying amongst their records; and some of the Lords themselves sitting with them upon the election of the people, not ten of which were present at the tyme of the putting of the question by the members legally secluded who were brought in by Monke for the dissolution of the Parlament; the Lords not then sitting, nor having their consent ever since desired in that particcular; so that this authority de jure being yet in being, this gentleman that calls himselfe Cheife Barron, and Charles Steward that pretends to make him so, yea those of that Convention who take upon them the title of Parlament, are to be looked upon but as private persons. But having gained power by treachery, they resolve to keepe it by the effusion of innocent blood. And the vilest of men being exalted by swearing and lying, they will take upon them, contrary to the opinion of the Lords and Commons in Parlament assembled, to interpret the oathes of supreamacy and allegiance to binde those who tooke them, not only against the Pope's supreamacy and his sentence, but against all *endeavours for the promotion of the gospell*; nor to the King only in his polliticque capacity, but in his personall,   **832** and that absolutely against all attempts by any power or authority whatsoever.

And for the casting of dirt upon this eminent act of justice (wherein the Lord was highly glorified, in that he who made himselfe as it were his rivall, who had the blood of thousands lying at his doore, and the judgement written in the booke of God, yea in the booke of nature, executed upon him), his good deeds which he did in redressing of greivances at the beginning of the Parlament, and his concessions at the Isle of Wieght, must be reckoned up; whereas his owne conscience tells him that those were wrested from him by that publique spirit which now arreigns and judges, and that it was his resolution to have avoyded what was thus extorted from him as soone as he had an opportunity so to doe; his treachery as well as blood-guiltyness having bin sufficiently evident in that of Rochell, the massacre and rebellion of Ireland, and with his dealing with the Parlaments of England and the Kingdome of Scotland throughout his whole reigne. But he would have it a cryme that this act of justice was publiquely owned, and that it was not done in hugger-mugger, as this generation of men hate the light, because their deeds are evill. But this act will endure the

light when the mouth of all wickedness shall be stopt, and those who
have appeared in opposition to it, without serious and timely repentance, be cast into outer darkness. As to what he saith touching the
Court of Common Pleaes not having power to proceed in those cases
that are determinable at the Upper Bench, it hath not the least weight
in the ballance of right reason, as to what he applyes it; those being
subordinate courts, and regulated according to law; the Parlament
having in them the legislative authority, and (as hath bin made out)
those of the Parlament who gave comission for this act having, by
a series of providence, all the authority and power of the nation in
their hands; to which as all are required, Romans 13. 1, to subject
themselves, so they judged it their duty not to beare the sword in
vaine, but to imploy it for the terrour of evill doers, and for the praise
of them that doe well, as the Lord commands, 1 Pet. 2. 14.

And as this private person takes upon him to be an oracle in the
law, as opposing the judgement passed and executed on the late King,
so likewise doth he in levying of warr against the King, which he declares to be treason by the 25 Edward 3; that being only declarative
of the comon law. But how this man in his next words contradicts
himselfe as to what he would be at, viz. that to levy warre against
the King's authority is treason, is most cleare, in that thereby he makes
all those traytours who assisted the King (who in his personall
capacity is not to be looked upon in law to doe any act against the
Parlament, the King acting there in his highest authority). And all
those cases which he produceth, of taking up armes under pretence
of expelling aliens, of pulling out Privy Councellours, against particcular lawes, to reforme religion, to pull downe enclosures, to be judged
high treason, within that branch of the statute, and these instances he
produceth for proofe of those **833** in Henry 8th, Queene Elizabeth,
and King James his tyme, if judges and juryes were as just as they
ought to be therein, yet doth it not in the least justify that the levying
of warr by authority of the people in Parlament assembled against
the King (their servant who set up his standard in defyance of them)
is treason; those cases he instances in concerning only private persons.

But heere is the height of the aggravation of this fact, to wit that
there is not only a making warr against the King and his authority,
but against the lawes, and setting up of new lawes, and modells of
their owne; and hinc illae lachrymae. For great is Diana of the
Ephesians; for by this the lawyers not only flea the skin, but as the
prophet speakes of those who governed in Israell of old, Zephany 3.
3, Her princes within her are roaring lyons: her judges are evening
wolves; they know not the bones till the morrow. Even so are the
men of this wicked generation in respect of their injustice and cruelty:
they robb the people of their fleece, they flea their skinne, knaw their

bones, and feede upon the entrailes of the people's lives, libertyes, estates, and whatever is deare to them. And therefore it's no marveyle that they cry out upon others' doing of justice, and releeving of the oppressed in breaking their bonds and yoakes, as a most horrid thinge. Yet a righteous spirit judges otherwise, as thinking it most just and equall that the people (on whose side the Lord had judged upon the appeale made) should, after the expense of so much pretious blood and treasure, choose what lawes and goverment they will live under, and not still submit themselves to the lawes of the Norman Yoake their Conquerour, or rather of his successour now conquered; which, according as they are now executed, are so partiall and unjust, especially wherein the King is concerned (judge, jury and sheriff being in effect of his owne appointing, as likewise his counsell the bloodhounds, who are to hunt the lives and seize the estates of these poore innocent lambes), that it were much more ingenuous to knock the poore prysoners in the head, or to cut their throats before they are brought to their tryall, then to murther them with so much formallity and ceremony. But as in their religious worship, so in their civill administration, the power and substance being wanting, yea the whole substance of righteousness and holyness being endeavoured to be perverted, they will make it up with formallity and shew.

But God will not be mocked. For though as David prophecied, Psal. 2. 2, 3, The kings of the earth sett themselves, and the rulers take counsell together against the Lord, and against his annoynted, saying, Let us breake their bands assunder, and cast away their cordes from us, Yet saith the prophet, vers. 4, 5, 6, He that sits in the heavens shall laugh, the Lord shall have them in derission. Then shall he speake unto them in his wrath, and vexe them in his sore displeasure. Yet have I set my king upon my holy hill of Zion. Yea when the great legislatour shall come to throw downe all principallityes and powers, and set up his owne, and when he shall come to judge the quick and **834** the dead, as the Apostle saith he will at his appearing, and kingdome [2 Tim 4?], then the treading under foote of the holy and righteous law of God, and the powring of the Saints' blood for contending for it and witnessing to it, will not be counted a small matter, but will certeinly then (if not sooner) bring downe vengeance upon their heads without their repentance, and weeping over Christ whom they have peirced, and crucifyed in his members, the wrath of God impending not to be appeased (to use his owne words) without a bloody sacrifice. And it is my desire (if the Lord see good) that the blood of the Lord Christ may be this sacrifice in being powred on their hearts and not on their heads, that by a timely humilliation and confession they may give glory to him, who is King of Kinges, and Lord of Hostes.

All thinges being prepared as hath bin mentioned for this bloody tragedy, and those who called themselves a Court sate at the Sessions Howse in the Old Baily, Sir Hardress Waller, Major Generall Harrison and Mr. Heveningham are comanded to be brought to the barr; to whom the inditement being read, chardging them with many black and ugly expressions, Sir Hardress Waller being knowne to be one who would say anythinge to save his life, and being prepared to that purpose, is first demaunded whether guilty or not guilty; whereunto with some circumlocution he pleades guilty, and thereby takes the blood upon his owne head; which was so contrived, hoping that as one sheepe having leapt and lead the way, the rest would follow though into the sea. But as this great champion, who was called upon in the next place to give his answer, had the glory of God and the fulfilling of his word in his eye in what he did, and not his owne carnall and selfe ends, so had the presence of the Lord assisting and directing him what to answer; who though [*seemingly?*] reproved, yet laboured what he could in justification of the fact itselfe, and of the authority that comissionated him thereto; but was knockt downe by clubb law, and threatned to be proceeded against as a mute if he answered not, Guilty or not guilty; to which, that he might have an opportunity to speake what the Lord should set upon his heart, rather then on any other consideration, he submitted to, and pleaded not guilty. And being then asked by whom he would be tryed, he answering, By the lawes of the Lord, to which it being replyed that if he sayd not, By God and the country, it would be all one as if he pleaded not at all, upon the consideration aforesayd, after he had told them he would be tryed as they would have him (and that the forme of words which they used were vaine words), if they would not admit him to pleade otherwise, he would be tryed in their owne way, By God and his country.

This faithfull servant of the Lord being brought the next day to the barr, and made choyce, or rather admitted, of twelve of those forty seaven which Charles Steward had pickt to judge, or rather condemne him, the bloodhounds the councell are now to act their part. What Keeling sayd to enforce the **835** chardge, it seemes was not thought worth prynting; neither had [what Finch?] sayd to the same purpose, who had got many thousand pounds under that authority he now trampled upon. But to shew as well the atheisme and blasphemy of this generation of men *as their ingratitude*, he affirmed that on the life of the King depends the lawes, libertyes, estates, propertyes, wealth, peace, religion, and in summe the glory of the nation, intitling him the light of Isráel, and in a religious sense the breath of their nostrills. And though the Parlament that commissionated the High Court for the tryall of the King would not be owned by him to be an authority for the justifying of this act, he concluded his harrangue that he had records of that Parlament which he judged authenticque evidence for the condemning of those who acted by their authority.

When Turner came to act his parte, his memory served him to recite what Amaziah did when he was established in his throne, in calling to an account his father's servants who had murthered him; but takes no notice of the men of Jerusalem sending after the same Amaziah (as in the latter end of that chapter) to Laish, and slaying of him there, and bringing him upon a horse to Jerusalem, and burying him there, and setting up Uzziah his son to reigne in his stead; who we never reade did question any who slew his father, because it was done by the people. But it's the enemy's worke to asperse and not to justify, to darken truth rather then cleare it. And therefore he as well as Bridgeman wrested the scripture, in applying what was spoaken touching the Lord's annoynted, to wit his people, to the person of the King, so as to serve their present purpose; but how improperly hath bin already made appeare. Many witnesses were produced to prove the Major Generall's being in the Court at the tyme of the King's tryall and sentence, as also of his signing the warrant, for executing the sentence; whereupon he told them that he came not thither to deny anythinge that in his judgement or conscience he had comitted, but rather to bring it forth to the light, that he beleeved his name subscribed to the two warrants were his owne handwriting. And when they had concluded their evidence, and aggravated it what they could, he, being permitted to speake for himselfe, bore an eminent witness to that act of justice which the Lord called forth him and others to appeare in in those dayes; affirming that as it was not done in a corner, so the presence of God accompanyed those who were imployed therein, to the dread and terrour of their enemyes, and all such guilty ones. However, for ends best knowne to the Lord, he suffred this chandge to pass upon them; and that though he had sought with many teares to God, that he might be convinced if he had done amiss in that act for which he was accused, he had rather received assurance of the justice thereof; expressing his confidence that the thinge which had bin done would be owned from heaven, and that there was more of the power of God in bringing that person to justice then many men were aware of; professing that, of himselfe, he would not offer the least injury to the poorest man or woman that went upon the earth; alleadging the contests that had bin in the nation for many yeares, and chardging divers of those who sate upon the bench as his judges to have bin formerly as active therein as himselfe or any other.

But being heere interrupted and reproved by the Court for his reflecting on them, in speaking the trueth, he proceeded to affirme that what he did was done by him out of conscience to God, who put him upon bearing his testimony against those who **836** afterwards turned aside, and having put their hands to the plow looked back; and that he chose rather to suffer imprysonement many yeares, and to be seperated from his wife and familly, then to comply with them, though it was said to him, Sit at my right hand; making thereby appeare he had not bin acted by, or for, himselfe; professing that though he might be somewhat mistaken in the way he tooke, yet he did all to the best of his understanding, desirous to make the rule of God's word his guyde; insisting further, that what was done by him was in the name and by the power of the Parlament, and that it was not in the power of this, or any other inferiour court below the High Court of Parlament, to question him for what he had done; being done by the authority of the Parliament, the supreame authority. And for making of this out the more clearly, he desired counsell might be assigned him; and then justifying the authority which had comissioned him to doe that action, as he had before done the action itselfe, affirmeth, whereas it had bin said they did assume and usurpe an authority, that it was done rather in the feare of the Lord. The Court againe interrupt him, crying, Away with him, and wisshing him to consider where he was; endeavouring to make him beleeve that he was in an assembly of Christians, who could not heare God made the authour of treason and murther; refusing to permit him to say anythinge in his owne defence that was essentiall thereto. And Finch, that should have bin hanged for his treacherous and treasonous practices against the Comonwealth, amongst other of his rhetoricall flourishes with which he was used to abound, agreed with the rest of the Court that it was not to be suffered that he should run out into those damnable excursions, so as to make God the author of this damnable treason. But it was never the more so because one who stood accused of high treason before the Lords and Comons of England tearmed it so.

The Major Generall insisted upon the having of councell assigned him; whereunto the Court replyed, If you appeale to your countrymen, they will crye out and shame you; to whom he replyed, My lords it may be some will, but I am sure others will not. But both judges and jury being a packt party, as you have heard, his plea was overruled; Bridgeman boldly againe affirming that neither both Howses of Parlament if they had bin there, nor any single person, community, nor the people either collectively, or representatively, had any collour to have any coercive power over the King; which Mr. Ansloe and Mr. Hollis, two members of this Court, who had bin members of the Howse of Commons when they joyned with the Howse of Lords in imprysoning the King, were so farr from speaking against that they aggravated with a great deale of bitterness the chardge against the Major Generall, and so consented to the overruling of his plea; as if it had not bin enough to contract the guilt of the blood of the faithfull assertors of the publique interest that had bin shed in a way of judgement, by endeavouring to betray **837** the cause of God and his people, as also of the nation, to the King, but [that?] now they might wash their hands in the blood of Saints, in a way of seeming justice.

Yet the Major Generall, as encouraged from on high, affirmed that notwithstanding the judgement of so many learned ones that the Kinges of England are no wayes accountable to the Parlament, the Lords and Commons in the beginning of the warr declared the King beginning a warr upon them, etc.; and going on to say, The God of Gods, was interrupted by the Court, and demaunded whether he would render himselfe so desperate, as not to care what language he let fall; to which the Major Generall replyed that he would not will-ingly speake to offend anyone, but God is no respecter of persons; his setting up his standard against the people, etc.; whereupon the Court interrupted him, and told him that he must not be suffred, and that that did not at all belong to him; whereupon he went on, and told the Court that under favour it did belong to him; for saith he, I would have abhorred to have brought him to an account, if the blood of Englishmen had not bin shed. But the counsell with fowle language endeavoured to sylence him, moving that he might be sent to Bedlam till he came to the gallows to render a further account of this, it being in a manner a new impeachement of this King to justify a treason against the last. Another moves that the jury might goe together upon the evidence; a third, that seeing he had the plague, none should stand neere him for feare of infection, etc. But Bridgeman (after he had intituled those knowne truthes, which he would have asserted blasphemy) permits him to goe on to extenuate his crimes (as he called them), but not justify them; whereunto he replyed, I must not speake so as to the pleasing of men, but if I nay not have liberty as an Englishman, etc. But the Court againe interrupted him, and after permitting him to proceed, he denyed what was objected against him as to his moving to blacken the King, declaring his abhorring of any such thinge; and likewise denyed any hard usuage of him in bringing of him to London, affirming that what he did therein was by command of the Generall. The Court taking notice to him, that the end of his speech was only to infect the people, the Major Generall replyed, You are uncharitable in that; and then after some inter-ruption by one in the Court, he told them that the thinges that had bin done, had bin done in the sight of the sun.

But the Court continuing to interrupt him, not daring to let the

rayes of truth breake forth (lest it should discover their workes of darkness), declare that this is a continuance of the justifying of the fact,
and that therefore there needed no further evidence; and so told him
that they must give direction to the jury, if he would not goe on to
speake touching the fact; whereunto he replyed that what he did,
it was by the supreame authority, and therefore he appealed to their
owne consciences that that Courte could not call him to an account;
and then declared that by reason of his having bin kept six monthes
a prysoner, he had no tyme to prepare himselfe for his tryall by councell; and then produced **838** severall acts of parlament of the Howse
of Commons, shewing the proceedings of that Howse. But he was told
by Bridgeman that if he shewed never so many of that nature, they
would not helpe him. The Court concurring with him, he gave directions to the jury; who upon the same carnall, selfish and devillish principle by which they were acted, would have given their vote to have
crucifyed the Lord Christ *in person had hee ben before them*, as well as
condemne this emynent servant of his for what he did in obedience
to his comand, will, and word.

But the prophecyes must be accomplished, and the witnesses must
be slayne, in order to their standing on their feete again. And therefore
are these instruments of an Anti-Christian magistracy and ministery
permitted to have the power of this pretious Saint's life, and to declare
him guilty of high treason; as they did, Sir Thomas Allen, their foreman, giving in their verdict for them; which was no sooner done, but
by the confederacy of this bloody crew, judgement being demaunded
to pass upon the verdict, the Court asked the Major Generall what
he had to say why judgement should not pass; to which he replyed,
he had nothing further to say, because the Court thought not meete
to heare what was meete for him to speake in his deffence; upon which
Bridgeman gave judgement in these wordes. You that are a prissoner
at the barr, you are to pass the sentence of death, which sentence
is this. The judgement of this Court and the Court doth award, that
you be lead back to the place from whence you came, and from thence
to be drawne upon a hurdle to the place of execution, and there you
shall be hanged by the neck, and being alive shall be cutt downe,
and your privy members to be cut off, your entrailes to be taken out
of your body, and you living, the same to be burnt before your eyes,
and your head to be cut off, your body to be divided into fower
quarters, and your head and quarters to be disposed of, at the pleasure
of the King's majesty. And the Lord have mercey on your soule.

Thus do these miscreants not only as canibals content themselves
to devoure the flesh and bones of the faithfull servants of the Lord,
but like the Devill their master, whose worke they were imployed in,
satiate themselves with venting their malice and hatred against the

righteous secd, in their barbarous and inhumane butcheryes; the hangman in his ugly dress, with a halter in his hand, being placed before the Major Generall all the tyme of his tryall to terrify and aston-ish him. But blessed be the Lord his soule was above their reache, being carryed above the feare of death, as it is recorded of the martyrs of old, Heb. 11. 34, who through faith quenched the violence of fire, and escaped the edge of the sword, etc., though burnt by the one, and cut off by the other, because the Lord tooke away the feare of death, and carryed their spirits above it. **839** And so was this emynent servant and martyr of Christ borne up also, conquering in his spirit whilest his flesh was conquered. For when malitious [. . .?] devils and death looked him in the face, he undantedly outfaced them all, and after sentence pronounced sayd, Whom men have judged, God doth not condemne; blessed be the name of the Lord. And as he was carryed away from the Court through the crowde, the people shouting, he sayd, Good is the Lord for all this, I have no reason to be asshamed of the cause I have bin engaged in. Some freinds asking him how he did, he answered, Very well, and cannot be better if I had the desires of my heart; we must be willing to receive hard thinges from the hands of our father, as well as easy.

And when he came to Newgate, chaines being put about his feete, he said, Welcomb, welcomb O this is nothing to what Christ hath undergone for me; this is out of his great loving kindness and faithful-ness, and my God is all-sufficient in all conditions. What occational speeches and memorable passages fell from him after his comming to Newgate, may be seene more at lardge in a booke set forth by a lover of trueth shortly after his execution, together with his speech upon the ladder; wherein it's mentioned he sayd that this dispensation was an answer of his prayer, having many a time begd of the Lord that if he had any hard thinge, any reproachfull worke to be done by his people, he might be imployed in it; and then blessed the name of the Lord, who had put him upon this hard service for his Lord Christ, acknowledging it to be nothing to what Christ had suffered for him; expressing with much confidence to his wife, that though he had nothing to leave her but his bible, he was assured the Lord would make up all her losses in due tyme; recommending her to the care of those who loved him.

And as he was comming forth of the dungeon to suffer, he spake, saying, I bless the Lord who hath called me forth, and enabled me in the power of his strength to offer my life with satisfaction and cheerefulness, in obedience to the will of God; praysed be the Lord I am full of the manifestation of his love, in the Lord Jesus. It's a day of joy to my soule, I say God hath enabled me, to whom all the nations of the earth are but as a drop of the buckett. And said he,

I doe finde so much of the power of the Lord comming in, that I am carryed farr above the feare of death, being going to receive that glorious and incorruptible crowne that fades not away, which Christ hath prepared for me. He assisted the Sergeant to tye the rope about his shoulders and back, desiring his freinds to take notice that God had given him power to receive it with thankesgiving. And to a freind, who came weeping to take his leave of him, he sayd, Hynder me not, for I am going about a worke for my master; and looking about him sayd, Sirs, it is easy to follow God when he makes a hedge about us, and liberall provission for us, but it's hard for most to follow him in such a dispensation as this; yet my master and Lord is as sweete **840** and glorious to me now, as he was in the tyme of my greatest prosperity. He also said, that according to the light God had given him, he had served him and his country with integrity and uprightness of heart, not willingly nor wittingly wronging any. He professed that death was not terrible to him, having learned to dye long agoe; and was often heard to say, Shall not the Lord doe with his own as he pleaseth? And as he was drawne on the sledge, he was often heard to say with a loud voyce, Next to the sufferings of Christ, I goe to suffer in the most glorious cause that ever was in the world. And one, as he passed by, asking him in derission where the goood old cause was, he with a cheerefull smile clapt his hands on his brest and sayd, Heere It Is, And I Goe To Seale It With My Blood.

In his speech on the ladder, he highly justifyed the cause wherein he was engaged, and the action for which he suffred; blessing the Lord from his heart that he had accounted him worthy to be instrumentall in so glorious a worke; professing that his ayme in all his proceedings was the glory of God, the good of the people, and the welfare of the Comonwealth; and would have suffered more then this, rather then have fallen in with those who, having bin emynent in the worke, did wickedly turne aside themselves, and (to set up their nest on high) caused great dishonour to the name of God, and profession they had made; and then desired all to take notice, that for being instrumentall in the cause and interest of the Son of God, which hath bin pleaded amongst us, and which God had witnessed to, by appeales and wounderfull victoryes, he was brought to that place to suffer death that day; and if he had ten thousand lives, he could freely and cheerefully lay them downe all, to witness to this cause; professing that though he had gone joyfully and willingly many a tyme to lay downe his life upon the account of Christ, yet never with so much joy and freedome as at this tyme, not laying it downe by constraint but willingly. For if he had bin mynded to have run away, he might have had many opportunityes; but being so cleare in the thinge, he sayd he durst not turne his back, nor stepp a foote out of the way, having bin engaged in the service of so glorious and great a God. However men call it by hard names, yet he beleeved ere long the Lord would make it knowne from heaven that there was more of God in it then men yet understood. All the nations of the earth, sayd he, are but as the drop of a bucket to him, to whose glory I **841** shall surely goe, and shall sit on the right hand of Christ in heaven, it may be to judge those who have unjustly judged me.

Being then remynded by the Sheriff of the shortness of his tyme, he expressed his great desire that all there might feare the Lord, and consider their latter end, that so it might be well with them; and for the worst of those who had bin most malitious against him, he said that from his soule he forgave them all, so farr as anythinge concerned him; and so farr as it concerned the cause and glory of God, he left it to him to pleade. And as for the cause of God, he professed himselfe willing to justify it by his sufferings, according to the good pleasure of his will; praising the Lord that he had a life to loose upon so glorious and honourable an account.

And then, having prayed to himselfe with teares, he desired the people of God not to have hard thoughts of the good wayes of the Lord for all this, for that he, having bin for severall yeares in a suffering state, had found the way of God to be a perfect way, his word a perfect word, and he a buckler to those that trust in him; assuring them, that though the people of God might suffer hard thinges, yet the end would be for his glory, and his people's good; and therefore encouraged them to be cheerefull in the Lord, and to hold fast that which they had, and not to be affrayd of sufferings, for God would make bitter thinges sweete, and hard thinges easy, to those that trusted in him; and that notwithstanding the clowd that was now upon them, the sun would shine, and God would give a testimony to what he had bin doing in a short tyme. And then comitting his concernements into the hands of the Lord, and his saviour Jesus Christ, he breathed forth his soule into his bosome, where it rests, singing perpetuall Hallelujahs, whilest his blood, and the rest of those who have bin slayne for the word of God, and the testimony which they held, cryes with a lowd voyce from under the altar, How long O Lord, holy and true, dost thou not judge and avendge our blood on them that dwell on the earth. The bloody and barbarous sentence against him was as inhumanely executed, it being credibly reported that he had so much life in him as to behold his privy members after they were cut off, and his entrailes after they were plucked out. But the God of patience is pleased to permit these crueltyes for a little season, till their fellow servants also, and their bretheren that should be killed as they are, should be fulfilled, Rev. 6. 11.

Mr. John Carew is the next whom the Lord, having eminently

quallified, suffers to be brought upon this bloody stage, and so to the shambles. He was a gentleman of an ancient **842** familly, of the county of Cornewell; trained up at the Universsty and Inns of Court; having a plentifull estate left him by his parents; was chosen by his country to serve as a member of the Great Parlament; and of them chosen of the Councell of State; and being imployed in business of great importance, made it appeare he was highly quallified for the same. His company was always acceptable to the civillest sorte of gentry. But in the last ten or twelve yeares of his tyme, he made it his great business to be fitting himselfe for his great change, and neglected no opportunity of encouraging others to doe the like; looking upon it as his great concernement to be found upon his watch, and working in the Lord's vyneyard. He and Major Generall Harrison, as they were neare of an age, so of the same spirit and principle, much in prayer and searching of the scriptures together, as well as aparte; and in their deaths they were not divided, refusing to save their lives by retiring from or running out of the hands of those who sought to slay them, though they had many opportunityes so to have done; Mr. Carew expressing himselfe, the night before he suffered, that the sealing the cause wherein they were engaged with their blood would be of much advantadge to the churches of Christ in forreigne partes, as well as in England, in that the blood which was now to be powred forth would warme the blood that had bin shed, and cause notable execution to come downe upon the head of the enemy.

He was treated both by judges, councell and jury at the same rate as Major Generall Harrison was. The cryme which he was indited for and accused of was, that he not having the feare of God before his eyes, but seduced by the instigation of the Devill, did imagine and compass the death of his late Majesty. He declared himselfe resolved ingenuously to acknowledge the whole truth as to matter of fact, but possitively denyed that what he did was not having the feare of God before his eyes, or that he was moved thereto by the Devill, or that what he did therein was with a trayterous and malitious heart; professing in the presence of the Lord, the searcher of all hearts, that what he did therein was in his feare and in obedience to his holy and righteous lawes; for demonstration whereof, he informed them that he russhed not into that undertaking, but with due consideration of the weight thereof engaged therein, having struck his name out of the act when it was before the comittee to whom it was referred, as thinking there were enough who had more experience then himselfe for so great a worke. But when the bill was brought into the Howse, his name being put in, he durst not but appeare therein, first in obedience to God, which was the cheifest thinge, secondly in obedience to that authority which was due to the *supreme* authority of this nation.

And because the Lord had given an answer upon the sollemne appeales, on that which was   **843** now in dispute, he declared that he would mention it very [breifly?]. Then going on to lay before them what passed in the [declarations and?] remonstrances betweene the King and Parlament [concerning the?] .... of the warr, Bridgeman interrupted him, refusing to [give?] him [the?] liberty to speake anythinge in justification of that which he called a horrid and notorious treason. He might speake anythinge to condemne himselfe, but nothing to justify the righteous and holy law of God, his cause, and so himselfe. But the tyme is comming when judgement shall be given without respect of persons, and the mouth of all wickedness shall be stopt.

Mr. Carew, finding himselfe thus streightned, and the truth with himselfe thus oppressed, told them they said they sate there by the lawes of the land, and were sworne to mainteine the said lawes, by the which he was obleiged not to pleade to this inditement, seeing what he did was by an act of parliament; to which the Court in passion replyed that this must not be let fall without reproofe, or rather punishment; to which he answered, he beleeved there was no presi-dent for it. But the Court telling him that there was no such act of the supreame authority as he pretended to, he went on desiring to have tyme to speake how it was begun and carryed on, for that otherwise he could not be able to make his defense, or lay before them the par-ticculars he would insist upon. Being about to shew the grounds upon which the Parlament did proceed, Bridgeman interrupts him saying, If that be your ground, I have something to offer to the then Howse of Commons; to which Mr. Carew sayes (for the mainteyning of this), It was in my humble oppinion by authority, the supreame authority by which this was done; often pressing to be heard in point of law, before he spake to matter of fact, but being perremptorily refused so to doe, and earnestly pressed by the Court to confess matter of fact before he could be permitted to shew the reasons why he did it. In confidence of that liberty he said, I doe acknowledge I was at the Courte, and did signe the warrant for summoning of the Court for tryall of the King, and also that for executing of the King.

The Councell and Court (presuming now they had him fast enough as the jury was packed) sayd to him, Goe on, and say what you will; which he laying hold on, alleadged: That in the yeare 1640 there was a Parlament called according to the lawes and constitution of the nation. And after that there was some difference between the King and Parlament, the two Howses of Parlament, Lords and Commons. The Kinge thereupon withdrew from the two Howses of Parlament, as appeares in their owne declaration, the great remonstrance in 1644; and thereupon the Lords and Commons did declare—But though the

Court, to ensnare him, promised him liberty to speake, yet knowing
that their covering of cobwebs were not thick enough to keepe out
the light of the trueth he was produceing, they stopp his **844** mouth,
telling him that what he was about to say tended not only to justify
his act, but to cast bones of dissention amongst them. But he going
on to say, The Lords and Commons by their declaration—Foster, a
popish judge, tells him he went about to rayse those differences which
he hoped were asleepe, and therefore he did ill to blow the trumpet
of sedition; demaunding of him, if ever he heard, or could produce,
an act of parlament made by the Howse of Comons alone; to which
Mr. Carew replyed, Neither was there ever such a warr, or such a
president; and insisted upon the legallity of that authority by which
he acted. Mr. Ansloe, one of the secluded members, being one of this
Courte, aggravated the proceedings of the army against the Parlament, chardging it upon the prysoner, and concluded that his plea
was overruled, as it had bin the day before; to which Mr. Carew
answered, I am a stranger to many of those thinges that are offered,
but it's very strandge that you who sit as a judge should give evidence.

But the Courte, not daring to withstand the force of truth, tell him
that if he had nothing but such kinde of discourse, they would give
direction to the jury; to which Mr. Carew answered, that he was willing to leave their undue proceedings against him with the Lord, if
they would not permit him to open the true grounds of those thinges
which were a satisfaction to his conscience that what he did was not
by the instigation of the Devill as he stood accused, but from the Lord.
And therefore said he, Gentlemen of the jury, I shall leave it with
you; the authority I speake of is right, which was the supreame; it
was well knowne what they were. The Court interpreting this sort
of language to be blasphemy against God and the King, or rather
against their King their God, and tending like poyson to infect the
people, doe therefore resolve to sylence it, and to give direction to
the jury; who being of the same confederacy with those men of blood
upon the Bench, soone declare him guilty; which when pronounced,
he was demaunded what he could say for himselfe, why judgement
should not pass according to law. He answered that he comitted his
cause to the Lord, who would assuredly avendge the blood of his
Saintes.

Colonell Adrian Scroope was arraigned the same day with Mr.
Carew, for that he sate as judge on the late King, signed the warrant
for the summoning of the Court, and for his execution; all which he
denyed not, pleading that what he did was by authority of Parlament.
But the Court over-ruled him therein, knocking him downe by club
law, as they had done others. He denyed that he had any mallice
in what he did, having done it according to his knowledge and

conscience. That apostate Browne (who formerly betrayed him, and got him to be excepted out of the act of indemnity, by informing those of the Howse of Commons of the private discourse betweene them two, touching the putting of the King to death, after he rendred him-selfe **845** into the hands of the Serjeant, not only upon the publique proclamation, but upon an order that was made by the said Howse for the admitting him to compound for a yeare's vallue of his estate), nowe comes into the Court as an evidence against him, and, to let the Court party know that he was one for their turne, and would not sticke at anythinge wherein he might gratify their lustes and his owne, desires throughly to embrew his hands in the innocent blood of those who as of the Parlament party he had formerly owned. And as he had before got him to be excepted, so now will assist in the butchery of him. He sweares, that Colonell Scroope making himselfe knowne to him at the Speaker's chamber, and he the said Colonell Browne speaking of the sad condition the kingdome was brought into since the murther of the King, Colonell Scroope replyed, Some are of one oppinion and some are of another; and that he the said Colonell Browne demaunding him, whether it were well done of those to murther the King, Colonell Scroope replyed, Sir I will not make you my confessour. Colonell Scroope denyed not but that a discourse to this purpose passed betweene them, yet possitively affirmed that he was not the beginner of it; which shewed the horridness and baseness of this trappanner's temper, to designe the way of his preferment by laying his foundation in the blood of the Saints. The jury was no sooner directed by Bridgeman, who acted the parte of President of the Court in this tragicall scene, but as thirsting after, and drinking this pretious blood with delight, without stirring from their places, declared him guilty. But blessed be the Lord, there lyes an appeale to him at the great tribunall.

Mr. Thomas Scot was brought the same day to his tryall, or rather to receive his sentence of condemnation; it being resolved on before he came there. His chardge was, that he sate as one of the late Kinge's judges, signed the warrant for summoning the Court, and for execution of the King, and that he did boast of what he had done. One Biddolph, a member of Richard's Convention, testifyed that he said in that Convention he desired when he dyed that a tombestone might be layd over him with this inscription, Heere lyes Thomas Scot, who adjudged the late King to death. Colonell Copley also, one of the secluded members, testifyed that Mr. Scot, speaking of the death of the late King, sayd he hoped he should never repent of it, and desired that when he dyed, it might be written on his tombestone, Heere lyes Thomas Scot, who adjudged to death the late King. And that apostate Browne, one of the said secluded members, testified that

at the same tyme Copley mentioned, being the last day of the Parlament, Mr. Scot did say, I had an hand in the putting of the King
to death, and I desire that the world may take notice of it, and that
when I dye it may be written upon my tombe, I doe not repent of
anythinge I have done, and if it were to doe, I would do it againe.
And Mr. William Lenthall, Speaker of the Parlament (who when the
late King entred the Howse of Commons, and demaunded of him
the five members, told the King that he had neither eares to heare,
nor eyes to see, nor mouth to speake, but what that Howse gave him),
is now so farr degenerated as to appeare on this bloody stage a witness
against Mr. Scot, a member of that Parliament, for words spoken
in the Howse; which **846** his [owne?] conscience told him was a
high breach of privilledge. And though forsooth his memory would
not serve him as to many of those particculars which others testified,
yet he remembred that Mr. Scot did much justify that act of the death
of the King, and that himselfe was much offended thereat. When it
came to Mr. Scot to answer, he said, I have no certeinty from the
witnesses that I was there, but in a wandring way. They know not
where I sate, nor my posture. As to the warrant you speake of, I know
not what it signifyes. I desire to know what the nature of it is, for
they may very much mistake my hand. You speake of words that I
should utter in the Parlament. I doe humbly insist upon it, that they
are not to alleadge, nor I to answer to anythinge of that nature, it
being a high breach of privilledge; to which the counsell answered,
there was no priviledge of parlament for treason; to which he replyed,
I humbly conceive it was a testimony ought not to be given to you;
whatever I say in parlament, the privilledge extends to no more then
this, that I may be lawfully secured till the Parlament hath bin
acquainted therewith, but not finally concluded till the Parlament
hath heard it.

But Bridgeman objecting that the Howse of Commons did not try
treasons, Mr. Scot answers, I humbly conceive there is such a privilledge, that no man shall ever be called to an account for anything
spoaken in parlament, if he be not called to an account by the Howse
before any other member be suffered to speake. But I have a great
deale of hard measure in being chardged, that I should say, I hope
I shall never repent. For I take God to witness I have often (because
it was well spoaken of by some, and ill by others) by prayer and teares
sought the Lord, that if there were iniquity in it, he would shew it
me. But the Court telling him that he was not heere charged crimin-
ally for speaking of those words that had bin testifyed against him,
and being pressed by them to answer to the fact, whether he did it
or not, he said, Whatever I did, be it more or less, I did it by the
comand and authority of a parlamentary power, and that doth justify

me, whatever the nature of the fact was. But being overruled therein
by the Court, and told that the assuming to doe what they did by
that authority was an aggravation of the fact, and not an extenuation,
he replyed, My Lords, I humbly pray leave to say, without offence
to the Court, this Courte hath not cognizence to declare whether it
were a parlament or no. But being demaunded by the Court to produce one instance that ever the Howse of Commons did assume the
King's authority, Mr. Scot said, I can many, when there was no more
but a Howse of Comons, in the Saxons' tyme. But the Court answering
that he spake of tymes wherein thinges were obscure, he (going on
in his defence) said he knew not but that it might be as lawfull for
them to make lawes as this present Parlament, being called by the
Keepers of the Liberty of England. My Lords I have no seditious
designe, but to submit to the providence of God.

But they continuing to overrule his plea, he presseth the allowance **847** thereof in these wordes. The parlament in former tymes
consisted not so much of King, Lords and Comons, as of King and
Parlament. In 1641 the bisshops were one of the three estates; and if
two estates may take away the third, if the second doe not continue to
execute their trust, he that is in occupancy may have a title to the
whole. I doe affirme I have a parlamentary authority, a legislative
power, to justify me; which he pressed so strongly that Finch the old
fornicator, and state pander, not being able to answer with reason,
breakes forth into these passionate expressions, Sir if you speake to
this purpose againe, for my parte I will professe myselfe, I dare not
heare further of it. It is so poysonous, blasphemous a doctrine, contrary to the laws, if you goe on upon this poynt I shall, and I hope
my Lords will be of that opinion too, desire the jury may be directed.
Whereunto Mr. Scot replyed, I thought my Lord you would rather
be my councell. It's not my single opinion, I am not alone in the case,
therefore I thinke I may justify myselfe in it. It was the judgement
of many of the secluded members to owne us to be a parlament; to
which Mr. Ansloe answered with a great deale of bitterness, expressing much of mallice and revenge, and concluded that the secluded
members could not have discharged their duty to God and the
kingdome if they had not appeared in parliament to have dissolved
that Parlament, and so by their joynt consent put an end to all pretences; which if they had not done, they had not so soone arrived
at their happiness, nor others at their missery.

Whereupon, the Court telling Mr. Scot that the justification com-
prehends treason, and that by law they ought not to heare it, therefore
if he had nothing to say for himselfe they must give direction to the
jury, he craves leave to move the jury that they bethinke themselves,
and consider of it rather as a speciall verdict then as a difinitive one,

for that he was of opinion there was cause for their so doing. But the Court going on, in their old peremtory manner, to shut their eyes and eares to all reason, Mr. Scot desires to know what particcular law he had transgressed in this thinge. The Courte answered, The law of God, and man, 25 Edw. 3; to which Mr. Scot replyed, that he humbly conceived that that statute reached not this case: you will not say the King shall be a traytour if he shall compass the death of the Queene. The Court sayd that the Queene was a subject. Mr. Scot answered, I am not yet convinced (and might have said, the King ought to be subject to the law of God, which saith the murtherer shall be put to death, etc.). But Bridgeman going on to direct the jury, Mr. Scot pleades and claimes that he was within the compass of severall pardons, and desired councell in that particcular, alledging that he was within the compass of the King's pardon. But though he was trappand to rendition of himselfe **848** upon that proclamation (he being invited thereto by name in the said proclamation upon promise of favour, when he was before particcularly excepted by the vote of the said Convention), now he is told it's impropper to pleade a pardon which implyes a confession of guilt, after a justification, but withall is made beleeve that the King's proclamation should inviolably be made good; they knowing he was not within the letter, though within the equity of it, and that it was in their bloody intent to execute upon him what was agreeable to their lustes and corrupt interest, and not what was suitable to law or equity. Mr. Scot desires counsell touching the 25 Edward 3. And that you may see the contradiction of this diabolicall assembly, though when Mr. Carew desired liberty to proceed to matter of fact or law, as he judged most advantagious to his plea, the Court answers, No, no, you must first speake to the fact, you may be after heard as to matter of law, for that matter of law in this case must arise from matter of fact, that they might ensnare him by drawing him to confess the fact, now the case is altred, and that in the same day, and Mr. Scot is told by the same Court that he should have demaunded councell before he had confessed the fact; but he replyed that he might doe it in arrest of judgement. But that the jury must be directed is answer to all objections, be they of never so great weight. The jury, being already bloodied, without any dispute swallow downe the blood of this faithfull assertor of the cause of God and the publique liberty. But both they and their posterity, as they will have cause, so time enough to repent them of this their horrid confederacy. I wish with all my soule, if it be the will of God, they may be sensible thereof ere it be too late.

Colonell John Jones and Mr. Gregory Clement are set next to the barr. Mr. Clement preferrs his petition to the Court; and the inditement being read against them both, the Court told Mr. Clement that, if he confessed his offense, his petition would be read. He finding that whatever was pleaded in vindication would nothing prevayle with these men (resolved on what they would doe), and being perswaded by some of his relations that the only way to save his life or his estate (which was very considerable) was to confess himselfe guilty, he consented to them, and did so. And Colonell Jones, finding that if an angell from heaven were brought before this Court and jury they would declare him culpable, having confessed he sate, and that the names subscribed to both the warrants were like his handwriting, and being demanded what he had to say for himselfe before chardge were given to the jury, he told them that he had little to say for himselfe, seeing the Court had already heard what was to be said in the case, and therefore said he was not able to pleade   **849** anything especially in matter of law, but did wholy referr himselfe to the Lord, the Court and jury; from whom he could expect no more favour then those who went before him. These men of blood being resolved to doe their master's worke throughly, with as little consultation or rather consideration as before, declare him guilty; so that now, according to the formallity of their proceedings (nothing of substance being to be expected from them), there remaines nothing but the demaunding them severally what they had to say, why judgement should not pass according to law, before sentence be pronounced; whereunto Mr. Carew (as aforementioned) sayd that he committed his cause to the Lord. The other five submitted to the mercey of the King, whose mercey they found to be cruelty.

The bloody sentence you heard recited before, in the case of Major Generall Harrison. The harrangue usshering of it in, spoken by Bridgeman, was stuffed with such frothy contradictory expressions that I judge them not worthy to be taken notice of; only to shew how grossly hee misapplyed Eccles. 8. 4, Where the word of a King is, there is power, and who may say unto him what dost thou? And yet he would question and condemne those who had authourity and power for doing that which the word of God comands them to doe, Rom. 13. 4, against one who was therefore no King because he had no power, seeing by that text itselfe it appeares, that King and power are termini convertibiles; and how he misinterprets that saying of David in Psal. 51. 4, Against thee, thee only have I sinned; as if he had not offended man or could not, and therefore was not to be punished by man, whereas *hee had sinned against himselfe in some sense, Cor. 6. 18, and against Uriah whome he murdered, and Barshebah whome he had defiled, and ought to have dyed for his sin had not the Lord sent a prophet to signify his pleasure that hee should not die.* And David's worke was not at that tyme to exalt a boundless prerogative over the people, but to lay himselfe low in the sight of God; and to that end acknowledgeth that his sin was cheifely and principally against the Lord, and that though men should pardon him, yet he should be still guilty before the Lord.

I shall not heere insist upon it, how farr all sin as sin is most properly against the Lord, and punishable only by him, though that is implyed by our Saviour. As hath bin before said, none can forgive sins but God. But taking sin against our brother as an offense against him, doth not the law without exception of persons say, an eye for an eye, and a tooth for a tooth? Doth not the rule given to the children of Israell touching their choyce of a king, Deut. 17. 15, (when they would set one over them) direct, that he should be chosen from among his bretheren? And in verse 18, 19 is it not said, that he should write him a coppy of the law in a booke, out of that which is before the preists, the Levits? And it shall be with him, and he shall reade therein all the dayes of his life, that he may learne to feare the Lord his God, to keepe all the words of this law, and these statutes to doe them? That his heart be not lifted up above his brethren, vers. 20? And doth not the Lord say in Gen. 9. 5, At the hand of every man's brother will I require the life of man, he that sheddeth man's blood by man shall his blood be shedd? And *did not* David passe judgement against the fact, when it was stated to him by the prophet as a case of robbery? And much *more* against himselfe who was guilty of murther; which had it *not ben pardoned by the Lord, as is before mentioned, but* bin brought publiquely **850** upon the stage, before those who had power to execute the sayd sentence, without doubt it had bin duty to have ordred it to have [bin?] *put in execution*. But if the sonnes of Zeruiah were too stronge for David, as he alleadged in the case of Joab's murthering Abner, being generall of his army, *soe as* he knew not how to bring him to justice, may it not very well be supposed that David was too stronge for the Sanhedrim, which had he not bin, and the people as zealous for executing the Law of God as they were for the avenging of themselves upon Azaraiah for his misgoverment, he had without doubt bin dealt withall as Azaraiah was?

And if these words of David must be taken strictly in the letter, the rule of our Saviour, touching his being in danger of the judgement who shall be angry with his brother without a cause, and of his leaving his guift before the alter, *till* first reconciled to his brother, if he remember he hath ought against him, before he offer his guift, as is enjoyned Mat. 5. 23, 24, *are either in vaine*, or David, and so other kings, must not be looked upon as Isralites, to wit as members of the church of God, or bound by his law. But should any yet be so blynd as to lay any weight on these words in the sense they are urged, how can they be applyed to our King, who layes the foundation of his authority upon force and conquest, whereas the other was chosen by the free

vote of the people? And as David was annoynted by command of
the Lord, so made he use of his power for fighting the battels of the
Lord; whereas this man, as he denyed to derive his power from the
people, but claymed them to be his inheritance, so made he use of
his power to roote out the holy and righteous seede out of the land.

But I spend too much tyme in this, having already treated on this
point. But this much I thought fit to say for satisfaction of those who
are swayed by reason, and not by lust and passion, as those are who
are the principall mannagers of these unjust, cruell and savage proceedings against the faithfull witnesses of the Lord, and would be as
zealous for a crowne upon a hedge stake, or a king of cloutes, as they
are for this or would be for any other, because by this meanes their
corrupt interests are supported, and their confederacyes strengthned,
for the obstructing of the people in the enjoyment of their just libertyes, and the setting up of the righteous scepter of Jesus Christ.

The 13 of November 1660, Major Generall Harrison had the sentence aforementioned executed upon him at the place **851** where
Charing Cross formerly stood; Charles Steward beholding that object
with much delight. The 15th of the same Mr. John Carew was ordered
to be executed there also, *as is before hinted. And it was then* thought
fit to stopp his mouth as soone as possible, they not being able to withstand the spirit by which he spake. But his blood, like that of Abel's,
though he be dead yet speaketh. Whilest he was in prison, when many
came drooping in spirit to him, by reason of the darkeness of this dispensation, they went away refreshed and comforted by the many gra-
cious expressions which fell from him. Some of his freinds shedding
teares the night before he suffred, he perceiving it said to them, O
my freinds, if you did know and feele what joy I have, and what a
glorious crowne I shall receive from the hand of Christ for this worke,
you would not mourne, but rejoyce that I am counted worthy to be
a witness to this cause; and said further, The Lord preserve you all
from the portion of this generation, for assuredly there is great wrath
from the Lord, that will reach them to their destruction. He had much
assurance of his interest in Christ. And being asked if he had anything
of conviction upon him, as to that for which he was to suffer, he
answered, No, not in the least. For saith he, though men have condemned, yet the Lord hath and doth justify; and added, that the Lord
had justified it in the feild once already, and he will doe it againe
with a witness. He dyed in full assurance of the resurrection of this
cause, and said, what he had done, if it were to be done againe he
would doe it, and that the way they tooke to suppress and destroy
those who did not think the King's person sacred, their blood would
make many hundreds more perswaded of the truth of it. He sayd that
the gospell was going from London, and that popery was coming in,

and that it would be a rare thinge to finde a professour in London shortley; and encouraged those about him to keepe close to the Lord in this evill day. He declared himselfe of opinion that this was the last Beast, and that his rage was therefore greater because his tyme was shorte. In all his words and manner of speaking, he manifested the highest Christian magnanimity and holy greatness of mynde. And such a spirit of joy and glory rested upon him as was to astonishment.

It greives me, saith he, to thinke how popery is comming in upon these nations like a flood, and of the great judgements that will follow. But, saith he, the Lord will be a hiding place for his people untill the indignation be over past, and God will poure out of his spirit seven fold on those who are left. Let not therefore the enemy thinke to extinguish the spirit by putting us to death. And as for the enemy, the Lord hath set their feete in slippery places, so that when they have filled up their measure they must be cast downe. He rejoyced that he was thought worthy to weare a cheyne for Christ, and that the Lord was pleased to honour him above many of **852** his brethren to seale to the Lord's worke with his blood. And as for death [or?] the fear of it, he said he was *got* above it, through the beholding of the glory of the Lord, and rejoyced that he dyed not only in, but for the Lord. And, said he, thinke not that this blessed cause shall be lost, for it shall reach to the ends of the earth. And thinke not that your prayers are lost; for your prayers and teares, with our blood, shall shortly fall downe upon Babylon (although they thinke to heale her), and shall give her a greater blowe then we could have done in our persons. When he was going to the sledge, with a smyling countenance he uttered these wordes: My Lord Jesus, for the joy that was set before him, endured the cross and escaped the shame, and is now sate downe at the right hand of God, whose steps I desire to follow. It was observed that the cheerefulness of his countenance remayned all the way as he went to the gibbet, to the encouradgement of the faithfull and admiration of the enemy; he uttering many cheerefull expressions setting forth his joy in the Lord. Before he went up the ladder, he exhorted severall freinds standing by to be faithfull unto the death, and not to be ashamed of the cause for which they suffred, and they should receive a crowne of life; and further sayd, that he hoped the truthes of the kingdome, which he had preached, would not be the less esteemed for that he came now to seale them with his blood.

In his speech upon the ladder, he comunicated his experience of the working of the spirit of God upon his heart; and in short unfolded the mistery of the gospell so clearely, that those words of Elihu, Job 32. 8, There is a spirit in man, and the inspiration of the Almighty gives them understanding, and those in Job 36. 4, Truly my words

shall not be false, he that is perfect in knowledge is with thee, may
be very propperly applyed to him; the great scope thereof, as was
the latter parte of his life, being the setting forth the riches of the grace
of God (to lost man) in Jesus Christ, and to himselfe in particcular;
he owning all his life, joy and strength to be in Christ and in him
alone, and his righteousness to be of his working according to his owne
grace and mighty power; by which he had bin kept, in a very wicked
and evill day, in a desire to serve the Lord in the integrity of his soule,
without prejudice against any creature, and to approve himselfe faithfull to God and man; having done what he did in obedience to the
Lord, that being the thinge which was in his eye and heart. He bore
his witness to such a magistracy as is according to the word of the
Lord, and such a ministry as is from the annoynting, and beares witness to the Lord Jesus, and hath his holy spirit. That testimony he
desired to stand faithfull in, with integrity to the Lord Jesus, as King
of Saints, and King of nations; esteeming this to be the accomplishment **853** of the promises: magistrates as at the first, and
councellours as at the beginning, men fearing God and hating
covetousness; and of ministry, that preach the everlasting gospell.

But this testimony of his being directly opposite to the designe carrying on by those in power, the Court parasites present put the Sheriff
upon interrupting him; who thereupon said to him, it was desired
he would spend the rest of his tyme in preparing of himselfe. Another
sayd, You spend yourself sir in this discourse; another said it rayned.
Then said Mr. Carew, I will pray; wherein he cast himselfe upon
the free grace of God in Christ, desiring that through him his person
and services might be accepted. He recomended with much earnestness to the holy Lord the cause and interest of his people, desiring
that he would revive it in his owne appointed tyme, and that in the
meanewhile he would support and strengthen his servants; the spirit
of the Lord assisting him to expatiate on the behalfe of himselfe and
the Saints, yea his enemyes, with many savoury and significant expressions; concluding with thankes to the Lord that he had brought him
to suffer in his cause; desiring that his spirit might be poured forth
upon the nations, till the whole earth were filled with the knowledge
of the glory of the Lord, that Christ Jesus might have all the honour,
praise and glory, and dominion for ever; and desiring that his soule
might be breathed forth into the armes of God, and bosome of Jesus
Christ through the annoynting of the spirit. And with a sollemne and
audible voyce saying, Lord Jesus receive my spirit, Lord Jesus into
thine armes I commend my spirit, he fell asleepe. Thus doth the Lord
thinke fit to suffer his lambes to be slayne, that the measure of the
sinns of this generation of evill men (as of the Amorites of old) may
be filled up, in order to the pouring out of his fiery indignation upon

such especially as are implacable, and the wyping away of all teares from the eyes of his owne people.

Although Colonell Scroope, Colonell Jones, Mr. Scott, and Mr. Clement are under a sentence of death, yet Cheife Justice Cooke and Mr. Peters being butchered before them, I thinke fit to make mention of the proceedings that were against them, and of the barbarous usuadge they met with, before I receite the execution of the aforesaid fower gentlemen.

This person, Cheife Justice Cooke, in his younger dayes travayled through France and Italy; and being at Rome, spake freely *on the behalfe* of the Reformed Religion, and so farr discovered his zeale and abillityes therein that no endeavours were wanting for the drawing him to owne the popish interest. But he, as enlightned from above, was not the least shaken by their tentations. Residing for some monthes at Geneve, at the howse of Mr. Deodat, he was observed to live a very strict and pious life, and to be a constant frequenter of publique ordinances. He was appointed Sollicitour by and to the High Court of Justice for tryall of the King, without any knowledge or seeking of his; and was taken by Leiftenant Generall Cromwell **854** with him into Ireland, and by him appointed Cheife Justice of Mounster; in which capacity, and those other places of judicature wherein he was imployed, he deported himselfe with much integrity and abillity for many yeares, to the satisfaction of his very enemyes. And it may be said of him, without flattery, that he was of a most upright and conscientious spirit, one who did justice, yet loved mercey; an affectionate and tender husband, a loving and carefull father, a true and faithfull freind; a lamb in prosperity, a lyon in adversity; of a meeke and lowly spirit in the thinges of his owne concerne, couragious and bold in what concerned the glory of God and the good of his country. It hath bin already mentioned how he was seized by that apostate Coote, who, joyning with Monke in betraying the publique cause, sacrificed this person to Charles Steward, in satisfaction of the blood which he shedd of his party. For a man, as in the case of Jehu, may be guilty of the blood even of the enemyes of God, when it's shed for carnall and base ends.

The chardge exhibited against him was, for preferring an impeachment of high treason against the late King to the High Court of Justice, in the name of all the good people of England, for leavying warr against the Parlament, etc.; and for signing the said impeachment; and for that when the King demurred to the jurisdiction of the Court, he pressed that the chardge might be taken as if he had confessed it; and that he demaunded the judgement of the Court against the King, etc. He well knowing the corrupt constitution of the lawes as now practiced, and how all thinges are prepared for

the destroying of those whom they designed for the slaughter, and
that to this end the jury-men were packed, makes no objection against
any of them; only desired, that seeing his life depended upon the indifferency of these persons, the Sheriff might be demaunded whether
he had not heard them, or any of them, say that they were pre-in-
gaged, and that he might give an account whether there were not
some butchers amongst them. The mallice towards this gentleman
was very great from those of his owne robe, not only because he was
Sollicitour to the Court, who tooke off the head of their Diana (by
whom they got their unjust gaine), but for that he constantly pressed
for a reformation of what was amiss in the lawes. And therefore such
as were concerned in them appeare as witnesses against him; in which
testimony of theirs, though some of them express much venome and
rancor, yet one of them acknowledgeth he owed all his knowledge
in the lawes to him; and another, that he had a very great respect
to him for his profession sake, being learned therein. And none of them
charged him with any morall evill, *yea, for nothing* but desiring the
judgement of the Court touching the King (or, if they would search
into the bottome of his intentions, *and give impartiall judgement*, for moving that one who was guilty of the blood of many thousands of the
good people of England should be brought to an account for the
same).

When he came to answer his chardge, he divides it into three
heades: first, that he with others propounded, counselled, contrived,
and imagined the death of the late King; secondly, that to the perfect-
ing and bringing **855** about this horrid and wicked conspiracy, he
with others did assume [an?] authority and power, then to accuse,
kill and murder the King; thirdly, that there was a person unknowne
that did cut off the King's head, and that he was abetting, ayding,
assisting, countenancing, and [procuring?] of the said person so to
doe, contrary to the forme of the statute, etc. To the first he answers,
that he could not be said to plot, contrive or councell the death of
the King, because their owne witness made it evident that the proclamation for the tryall of the King was before he was appointed Sollicitour to the Courte before whom he was tryed, the proclamation
being made the 9th of January, and he not appointed Sollicitour till
the 10th; which the Court admitting of, and that he was so assigned,
he proceeded to observe that that cannot be sayd to be done mallitiously, or with a wicked intention, which he was comanded to doe,
acting within his sphere and ellement as a councellour and not otherwise. Againe he alleadgeth, that words will not amount to treason, and
that there was no cleare proofe that it is his hand to the chardge;
that words put in writing, though in themselves treasonable, yet if
but writ according as directed by another, he conceived did not render

him guilty of treason who writ them, because he discovered not a trayterous heart in so doing; that the praying and demaunding of justice,
though injustice be done upon it, cannot be treason within the statute;
that if the Court will not admit that to be an act *of parliament* which
authorized him to doe what he did, yet they will allow it to be an
order, which would be enough to justify him; that he was neither
accuser, or witness, jury, judge, or executioner, and therefore could
not be said to be guilty of treason; that if it shall be conceived to
be treason for a counsellour to pleade against his Majestie, then it
will be fellony to pleade against any man who is unjustly condemned
for fellony, the councellour being to make the best of his clyent's cause,
and then to leave it to the Court; that when he demaunded justice,
it might be of acquittall as well as of condemnation; that sometymes
the councell hath bin sorry that the verdict hath gone for their clyents,
when they have seene the right on the other side, and so might he
in this; that the King was then a prysoner, but not to him, and when
a man knowes himselfe innocent, what doth such a prysoner desire
more then a speedy tryall; so that making the tryall more speedy
cannot be said to be done trayterously; a tryall naturally follows
imprysonement as the shaddow doth the body.

He pleaded also the act of indemnity, in that he neither councelled,
comanded, acted or did anythinge in that for which he is charged,
as is mentioned in the preamble to the act of indemnity; that he
neither sentenced him, nor signed the warrant for the execution of
him; and therefore, that no word might be insignificant, this word
instrumentall must be applyed to sentencing or signing, or otherwise
sentencing and signing were insignificant, because comprehended in
the word instrumentall; seeing, if it have a retro-spect, none knowes
where it will rest; and therefore there was no neede of putting a comprehensive sense upon that word, but that the sense should be this:
that those who did sentence and signe, and those that were instrumentall in taking away his life after the sentence, and not before. He
observed that it was sayd further in the act, that it was done by force
and armes, whereby   **856**   he urgeth he could not be meant, because
no souldier, and that it's not said instrumentall in order to the taking
away of his life, or advising, etc., but instrumentall in the taking away
of his life. He urgeth that he did it not, and therefore false as it's
charged upon him, he not inventing nor contriving anythinge, not
malitiose, he doing it for his fee; that he was not magisteriall in the
case, but minesteriall; that he had no power to give an oath, and
therefore the witness was mistaken in his evidence against him touching his examining of him. To that of the King's declaration from Bredagh: being then in Ireland, he put in a petition to the Comissioners of
Ireland, that he might have the benefit thereof, before any exception

was made of him or any other; that in this declaration it's sayd, that for the restoring of the Kinge, peeres and people of the kingdome to their just rights and libertyes, he will graunt a free and generall pardon to all, excepting such as shall be by parlament excepted, and within 3 or 4 lynes after it is said, a free parlament; and therefore that this parlament as to this particcular purpose ought to be a parlament to be called by his Majestie's writ, according to the lawes of the kingdome; and that though his Majestie is pleased to confirme this, yet is it not such a parlament that was to except by the declaration.

He alleadgeth, it was adjudged treason in the 44 Eliz. 3 instit. in the Earles of Essex and Southampton, in conspiring to take the Queene prysoner and to remove her councellours, because (if it had taken effect) it had bin the dispoyling of her Majestie of her regall goverment. And the case is instant in Phillip, who was a nominative King, and therefore not treason to have attempted anythinge against him. The reason holds, that it was not therefore treason to doe what he did against the King, when not in a capacity to exercise the regall office; he being a prysoner, and not by his meanes. The learned judges have bin of opinion from tyme to tyme, that no semblable treasons, made by presumption, or straines of wit, should be judged to be within this statute, except specified therein; as if a child should kill his father, etc. The act of this Parlament calls this Court tyranicall, and unlawfull; yet a tyranicall and unlawfull Court is a Court de facto, though not de jure. This was a Court, had officers attending them, some say they had authority. And therefore for one to come and act within his sphere, they being an authority de facto, and no other in being but themselves, must needs be justifiable. Otherwise it were not lawfull for any man to exercise his profession during such a power; but counsellours might, and did, then exercise their functions, as well as others.

And to the jury he said, An evidence as to matter of life must be so cleare that everyone that heares it may understand it. It's called an evidence, because it's evident by its owne reason. The prysoner is not allowed councell for matter of fact. And it's a propper word to say, the prysoner is convicted, that is, as much as may bee his mouth is stopped. And therefore, said he, I hope I may speake it to you without offence, as Jeremy in another case, when the people would have had him put to death, As for me, behold I am in your hand, doe with me as seemes good and meete to you; but know ye for certeine, if ye put me to death,   **857** ye shall surely bring innocent blood upon yourselves, etc., Jer. 26. 14, 15. If the Lord had permitted me to kill a man, when I had bin drunke, for which I ought to have dyed, I would, instead of speaking for myselfe, have rather intreated the jury to have found me guilty. My name was in the proclamation for rendition, which certeinly was with an intention to have extended favour to me, though (by reason of my being a prysoner some monthes before) I could not performe the condition theirin requyred. Punishment is not so much for expiation, as for prevention. Therefore if a man kill another, saith Grotius, Aquinus, and Amesius, though he repent never so much, that others may be deterred from committing such acts, the majestrate is bound to put him to death. But heere all thinges are setled, there is no danger that ever such a case can come againe. I acted as a councellour, I had no malitious intention, I only prayed the doing of justice.

But sayd he what he would, or was possible to be said in equity or reason, it was resolved by this caball he must dye for it, not being of opinion thinges were so setled but that it might concerne them to endeavour the prevention of the like justice being done. And therefore doe they thinke fit, that those who were willing and able to manadge such an affaire should be terrified from so doing; one of them saying, that it was an aggravation of his cryme that he who knew the law so well should so much transgress it; and afterwards said that a lawyer, as he was, of much understanding and good partes knew well there were no accessaryes in treason; another acknowledging he had made his defense with much skill and cunning, etc. And Bridgeman, the mouth of the Court, did acknowledge him to be a man of great partes in his profession. And it was worth taking notice how he scoffed at the expression of Wayting on God, saying that it was used nowadayes when some horrid impiety followed, and that it was but a canting language. So was it what he said touching subjects not using to make kings prysoners, but death followes; he thereby evidencing that the High Court of Justice did no more but put in execution what was begun by the Lords and Comons assembled in Parlament; and then afterwards acknowledged that he had said as much as any man could in such a case, and that it was pitty he had not a better to mannadge. To that which Cheife Justice Cooke had urged touching his desire of having the benefit of the 11 of Henry 7, which tooke care for the security of those who followed the King de facto though he was not soe de jure, extended to him for obeying an authority de facto (it being much more strong in this case then the other), it was answered that this law was made for the maintenance of monarchs and monarchy, not for majestracy and authority; as if the latter were but subordinate to the former, and that authority, yea mankind itselfe, were made but to serve the lusts of a monarch and his creatures. Had the King made this law without the people, some coullor might have bin for *putting such an interpretation on it. But seeing it was cheifely made by the people, can it bee immagined they would not have a regard principally to their owne security and indemnity? It's easily to be descerned by the reasoning of*

these men, expressely against the word of God and the interest of the publique,
what their designe is; they beeing more zealous for their law then the law of
God, and more enraged that monarchy should be put to death then the monarch.
858 Therefore is it that the good man (for saying that the monarch
must dye and monarchy with him, and for the demaunding the doing
of justice, and saying that the innocent blood that had bin shed, rather
then he, called for it) must be offered up. And the whole Commonwealth, if it lay in their power, they would sacrifice with him. But
though the Lord thinkes fit to permit this confederacy of wicked men
to prevayle against the life of this his pretious Saint, and to declare
him guilty of what he is accused, yet will he restreyne their rage, and
cause the remaynder thereof to worke out his prayse.

Seeing Mr. Hugh Peters and Cheife Justice Cooke were executed
together, I shall write in shorte what I finde remarqueable in the proceedings against him; the substance of whose chardge was, the compassing and imagining the death of the King, and to that end that
he conspyred with Cromwell at severall places and tymes, and
procured the souldiers severall tymes to cry, Justice, Justice; that he
preached many sermons to the souldiery in direct tearmes for taking
away the King, comparing him to Barrabas, and applying that portion of scripture, Psal. 149. 8, To binde their kinges with chaines and
their nobles with fetters of iron, to the present proceedings against
the King, observing that in the next Psalme, which is the last, there
were twelve Hallelujahs, Praise the Lord, Praise God in his sanctuary,
etc., and desiring them to turne to their bibles, assuring them they
should finde there, That whosoever sheddeth man's blood, by man
should his blood be shedd, and that neither the King nor any other
are excepted out of this generall rule; and that he applyed that text,
concerning the two-edged sword being in the hands of the Saints to
execute the judgement written, to the executing of justice upon the
King; that he in the midst of his sermon tooke an occation to produce
a text, Isaiah 14. 18, 19, 20, the latter words of which are, Thou shalt
not be joyned with them in buriall, because thou hast destroyed thy
land, and slayne thy people: the seede of evill doers shall never be
renowned; which he applyed also to the King; that the Lord's day
before the King was brought to his tryall, he in his prayer before the
sermon had this expression, I have prayed and preached these twenty
yeares, and now may be said with old Simeon, Lord, now lettest thou
thy servant depart in peace according to thy word, for mine eyes have
seene thy salvation; that he did say to Dr. Young, he came out of
Holland that he might bring on the kingdome to be a Commonwealth,
and that in order thereto the Levits, the Lords and the lawyers must
be taken away; and that he did say, it was an unjust law that the
King as to his person should be exempt from the lawes, that the King

was a tyrant and not fit for that office, that the office was chardgeable, useless and dangerous; that he comended Bradshaw and Cooke for their carriadge at the tryall of the King; and that he did say, I cannot but reverence the High Court of Justice, for it resembles the judging of the world at the last day by the Saints.   **859** These were the principall points of the chardge of high treason against Mr. Peters, and the particculars of the proofes; which, had not the tymes bin as the prophet complaines, Isaiah 59. 14, that judgement was turned away backward, and justice stands afarr off, for truth is fallen in the street, and equity cannot enter, would have tended to Mr. Peters's great praise and comendation, and no doubt as a faithfull testimony will to his comfort in the day of the great tribunall.

The great thinge Mr. Peters laboured to cleare himselfe of, was the mallice and evill intention with which it's said he did what he did; and to this end sayd, that the warrs were begun before he came into England; and that, since his coming, he had laboured to promote three thinges, first, that there might be sound religion, secondly, that learning and the lawes might be reformed, thirdly, that the poore might be cared for; and for the effecting of these, that the Lord had set it upon his heart, as also upon many other ministers, to promote the interest of the Parlament and army; and that however prejudice and revenge might posess men's hearts, yet (said he) there is a God who knowes all thinges, that hath a reguard to the people of England, which is as the cabinet of the world; who beareth witness with my conscience, that though I was active for the promoting of these ends, yet in a way that was honourable, without mallice, avarice or ambition. But these carnall wretches notwithstanding condemned him, for having preached and practiced (so farr as in him lay) according to the true and everlasting gospell of our Lord and Saviour Jesus Christ.

Nothing having bin sayd, previous to the black and ugly sentence pronounced against Cheife Justice Cooke and Mr. Peters by the Court, but those bald and thredbare thinges formerly mentioned to be spoken upon the like occation, I thinke not worth the repeating; these two emynent servants of the Lord being ordred to be butchered upon the 16 October. Having spoaken a little of the past life of Cheife Justice Cooke, I shall doe the like as to that of Mr. Peters, who was a minister of the gospell; in the dischardge of which function, having laboured with much success for many yeares in England, he was at length forced thence by the tiranny and persecution of the bisshops, not daring to submit to their humane inventions which they would set up with the worship of God. He spent some tyme in Holland; and also in New England, labouring in the word and doctrine there, till the Lord put into the hands of the Parlament an opportunity to releeve the people of God from the yokes under which they lay; at which tyme he retorned into his native country, very much encouradging the people to appeare on the Parlament's behalfe; going personally into Ireland, as a chapline to a brigade **860** sent against the bloody rebels; where observing the necessityes and misseryes of the poore plundred Protestants to be very great, he, having a good interest in Holland, went thither, and improved it to soe good success that he obteyned to be sent them from thence to the vallue of thirty thousand pounds. He was reputed to have bin very instrumentall with those majestrats for the reforming of many thinges relating to the Sabbath. He was eminently active for the releefe of the poore distressed Protestants in Piedmont, and was very dilligent and industrious to compose the difference betweene England and Holland in their late warr. He was sollicitous in setting the poore on worke, and that provission might be made for such as were past their labour. But those who promoted the popish religion, and wisht well to the Irish rebellion, and are so far from Agur's prayer (to be fedd with food convenient) that (for the advancing of their Diana their idoll) would have the people impoverished and enslaved, judged him unworthy to live, for theise his honest and pious endeavours. But it matters not whom or what man condemnes, so as the Lord justifyes.

Whilest Mr. Cooke was in the Tower, his deare wife then residing with my neere relations, and being denyed admittance to him, he sayed rejoycingly out of the wyndow, Goe home to thy freinds my deare lamb; I am well, blessed be God; they cannot keepe the Comforter from me. And being threatned by the jaylor to be sent to Newgate, he said, If the way to the New Jerusalem be through Newgate, blessed be God for Newgate. He blessed God that he never acted mallitiously or covetously, but in a spirit of simplicity and integrity. However, said he, the good will of the Lord be done. He commended his deare, loving and faithfull wife, and childe, to their blessed husband and father Jesus Christ, with three scriptures especially for their portion: the widdow's cruse, and barrell of meale, 1 Kings 17; Isaiah 54. 5 to 11 verse; Jer. 49. 11; earnestly desiring that his child might be religiously educated in the nurture and admonition of the Lord; and said, he blessed God he durst not wrong any man; for, said he, I know that I shall meete them at the last day, before the barr of Christ's judgement seate; and rejoyced that he was going to heaven, where the Saints are all of one mynde, which his soule had long desired to see; adding that it rejoyced his heart to thinke what a perfect happiness he should have there, the best condition heere being but mixed, whereas in heaven there was no sorrow or trouble. Neither have I, said he, one dramme of trouble upon my spirit at this tyme; blessed be God, he hath wiped away all teares, and I could with Paul and Sylas singe in prison for joy; blessed be the Comforter. Oh what a blessed thinge is it, said he, to have an helper when one comes about that sollemne worke to dye; the Lord will be our everlasting light, and our God will be our glory. Welcomb everythinge that gives notice the howre is at hand; welcomb **861** sweete death, my good freind that will bring me so neare eternity. O this Christ is a blessed Christ, he answers all thinges, and within [few?] howres we shall be cloathed with glory and victory.

At midnight he prayed so fervently that the common prysoners heard him, and seemed very sorrowfull by their expressions, saying, Sir the Lord be with you, O that our soules might goe where your soule goes. In the morning, speaking to his deare wife as she was weeping by him, said he, Deare lamb, doe not dishonour my last wedding day by any trouble for me, for if my judges did but know what joyes and glory I shall be in before twelve of the clock, they would desire to be with me. And let the executioner make what hast he can, I shall be beforehand with [him?]. Before he can say, Heere is the heart of a traytour, I shall be in [heaven?]. This day I shall enter into the joy of my Lord. Lying downe upon his bedd, he said, It's no more to dye tomorrow, then it is to sleepe tonight; I bless the Lord I am free from trouble, and my poore heart is as full of spirituall comfort as ever it can hold, and this joy none can take from me.

The doores of the pryson being opened in the morning, he spent the little tyme he had in prayer and heavenly discourses, preparing himselfe for his suffering with such cheerefulness as was an astonishment to the spectatours; and speaking to his wife sayd, Farewell my deare lamb, I am now going to the soules under the altar, that cry, How long O lord holy and true, doest thou not avendge our blood on those who dwell on the earth. And when I am gone, my blood will crye and doe them more hurt then if I had lived. But I am going to eternity, blessed be God. Be not troubled for me, because I goe to my father and your father, to my God and your God; and after some tyme spent in prayer, desyred his wife not to withold him by an unwillingness to parte from him, when God called him to be offered up a sacrifice for his name and cause. But she weeping, he said, Let those weepe, who parte and shall never meete againe; I am confident we shall have a glorious meeting in heaven; heere our comforts have bin mixed with checquer worke, but in heaven all teares shall be wiped from our eyes. On the sledge with him was carryed, with the face bare towards him, the head of Major Generall Harrison; notwithstanding which dismall sight, and barbarous usuadge, he passed rejoycingly through the streetes, as one borne up by that spirit which man could not cast downe. Being come to the place of execution, when he was taken out of the sledge, he said it was the easyest charriot that ever he ridd in in all his life. Being come to the ladder, and the rope put about his neck, he rejoycingly said, Blessed be the name of God that I am bound for the sake of Christ.

When he was upon the ladder, after he had sought the Lord for a blessing upon what he had to speake, he began thus. The Most Glorious Sight That Ever Was Seene In The World Was Our Lord Jesus Christ Upon The Cross; and next to that it's *the most* glorious sight to see any poore creature suffer in his cause. He blessed the Lord for the peace he found in his soule, through the application of the blood of Christ, for sanctification; professing himselfe ready to beare a testimony unto God, and to Jesus Christ, for justice, and truth, and righteousness, and holyness. He cleared himselfe from having any mallice, against jury, Court, or King, or any man living. But, said he, poore we have bin bought and sold by our brethren as Joseph was. Brother hath betrayed brother to **862** death, and that scripture is in a great measure fulfilled, Mat. 10. 2. However (saith he), I desire to kiss the rodd. He professed that his faith was founded on the Rock Christ, and that he expected not salvation for anythinge that ever he did, but that he layd hold on Christ as a naked Christ, and there bottomed his soule. He professed further, that he had through grace endeavoured to doe that which might be to God's glory, according to the best of his understanding; that he had stood for a gospell majestracy, and ministery, and that many delayes in the law's practice might be removed, and that publique justice might be cheapely and speedily administred; which thinge he declared he had much suffred for. He professed himselfe to be (as to fellowshipp in the gospell) of the congregationall way, and for liberty of conscience to all who walke humbly and holily before the Lord; that he was not convinced of anythinge he had done amiss, as to that whereof he was chardged; that he understood not the plea of the Court, that if the Lords and Comons had brought the King to the barr it had bin treason in them; saying he desired never to repent of anythinge he had done therein, but desired to owne the cause of God and Christ, being ready to beare witness to it.

Heere the Sheriff interrupted him, and desired him to forbeare such expressions; unto whom Cheife Justice Cooke replyed that it had not bin the manner of Englishmen to insult over a dying man, nor in other countryes, amongst Turkes or the most barbarous heathens. The Lord helpe every one of us, that we may looke more to the honour and glory of God then the concernements of our owne lives. For alass, what is a poore misserable life to us, unless therein we give honour and glory to the God of all our merceyes? He recomended, to the congregation of which he was a member, two texts of scriptures, Phil. 2. 7, 18; and prayed that the Lord would keepe England from popery, superstition and prophaneness. And seeing the Lord had forgiven him

many talents, he said he might well forgive those few which were
owing to him; and then affirmed he had endeavoured not to doe
anythinge but with a good conscience, and through the integrity of
his heart, though accompanyed with many frailtyes. The Sheriff
againe interrupting him, he replyed, Sir I pray take notice of it, I
think I am the first man that ever was hanged for demaunding of
justice, therefore I hope you will not interrupt me. If you will beleeve
the words of a dying man, I say, as I must give an account, I have
nothing lying upon my conscience. Wee must all meete together at
the great day of the Lord, to give an account of all our actions, and
then it will appeare; the Lord graunt wee may meete with joy and
comfort. He recomended to his wife and child Isaiah 54. 4, 5, 10 versses,
and desired in the feare of the Lord to yeild up himselfe a living sacrifice. And then powring out his soule by faith and prayer unto God,
on the behalfe of himselfe and those he was bound to pray for, being
eminently assisted by the spirit of the Lord, intermixing his prayers
with such heavenly praises as if already at the gate of heaven, expressing it as his perswasion that if the angels were capable of suffering
they would willingly come from heaven to suffer in such a cause as
this for which he now suffered, he resigned up himselfe into the
bosome of the Father's love, and so entred through Christ into that
glory which is endless and boundless.

863 An enemy brimfull with envy and mallice, writing observations upon the speeches and prayers that were published of this blessed
martyr, acknowledgeth his partes, yea his virtue, in these words. If
treason ever wore a cloake, you may see it heere now palliated to
the life: a quaint oratour strugling for life, under the sad pressures
of a heavy chardge; a man bred up where law was more in force,
at least more in practice then the gospell. I am sorry pearles for elo-
quence, and the very marrow of the law, should prove destructive
to the owners. Sum up all his virtues in a schedule and at the end
write, etc. I mention this the rather to take notice of the subtilty and
success of our common enemy in corrupting so much [sonne?], and
blynding others of our party, that this choyce man, when propounded
to the Parliament for imployment, was represented a light person,
and incapable thereof; which kinde of treatment most who were of
publique principles and sincere spirits met with, so that we seemed
full ripe for this reproofe, that we might have a right apprehension
of God, his worke, his people, and ourselves; which I trust will be
the happy issue of this bitter dispensation.

Mr. Peeters was thought fit to be brought next to this slaughterhowse. He was exercised under great conflicts in his owne spirit during the tyme of his imprysonement, fearing (as he would oft say) he
should not goe through his sufferings with couradge and comfort; and

said to his freinds that he was somewhat unprepared for death, and
therefore unwilling to dye. Something he said he had comitted, and
other thinges he had omitted, which troubled him; but though it
was a clowdy and darke day with him for a season, yet hoped the
light of God's grace would breake forth at last. And so the favour
of God did at last appeare. For a little before he went forth to execution (as many can testify), he was well composed in his spirit; and
cheerefully said, I thanke God, now I can dye, I can looke death in
the face and not be affrayd. As for that slaunderous reporte (which
was too much enterteyned by good people as well as bad), to wit that
he was guilty of uncleaneness, a freind coming to him in prison put
that question seriously and soberly to his soule; to whom he replyed,
that blessed be the Lord he was wholy cleare in the matter, and that
he never knew any woman but his owne wife. To some of the episcopall clergy, who tooke hold of the present temptation wherewith he
was assaulted (perswading him to repent of his former activity in the
Parlament cause, promissing him his life if he would doe so), though
he was much afflicted in spirit at that tyme, he answered that he had
no cause in the least to repent of his adhearing to that interest, but
rather that in the prosecution thereof he had done no more for God
and his people in these nations.

When Cheife Justice Cooke was cut downe, and brought to be
quartered, one Colonell Turner called to the Sheriff's men to bring
Mr. Peters neere, that he might see it. And by and by the hangman
came to him all besmeared with blood, and rubbing his bloody hands
together tauntingly said, Come Mr. Peeters how doe you like this
worke? To whom he replyed, I am not I thank God terrifyed at it,
you may doe your worst. When he was going to execution, he looked
about, and espyed a man to whom   **864** he gave a peece of gold
which he had bowed; and prayed him to goe to the place where his
daughter lodged, and to give that to her as a token from him, and
to let her know that his heart was as full of comfort as ever it could
hold, and that before that peece could come to her hands, he should
be with God in glory. Being upon the ladder, he spake to the Sheriffe,
saying, Sir you have slayne heere one of the servants of the Lord before
myne eyes, and have made me behold it on purpose to terrify and
discouradge me, but God hath made it an ordinance to me for my
strengthning and encouradgement. When he was going to dye, he
said, What, flesh! Art thou unwilling to goe to God through the fire
and jawes of death? O said he, this is a good day, he is come that
I have long looked for, and I shall be with him in glory; and so smyled
when he went away. Thus this bloody crew went on to fill up the
measure of their iniquity with both hands earnestly. In the meanetyme it's the howre of the Saints' patience.

On the 16th of the same month of October, Mr. Thomas Scot and Mr. Gregory Clement were drawne upon one sledge from Newgate to Charring Cross, there to have the bloody sentence executed upon them; and Colonell Adrian Scroope and Colonell John Jones upon another, from and to the same place and purpose. Mr. Scot was a gentleman bred at the University of Cambridge, till he atteyned the degree of Master of Arts; being left by his parents, and having in mar-riadge with his wife, a plentifull estate; on which he lived in the country, till the Parlament made their appeale to the Lord touching the justice of their cause; about which tyme he was moved to cast in his lot into their scale, and upon a recruit of the Parlament was chosen a member thereof, laying out his talent in their service with much zeale and constancy on the behalfe of the Commonwealth, and for the promoting of a faithfull and gospell ministry; insomuch that, during the interruption of the Parlament by the military power, his service had such an impression on the county where he lived that they expressed their esteeme of him in their choyce to serve for them, as oft as there was occation.

He held a constant correspondency with Monke for the restitution of the Parlament, when they were the second tyme interrupted by the army; wherein he was very instrumentall, causing those lettres which were sent by Monke, declaring his resolution to live and dye with the Parlament, to be prynted and published. After the Parlament was againe restored, he was appointed by them Secretary of their Councell of State, having severall tymes before beene chosen a member of that Councell. He was one of the two comissioners the Parlament sent to attend Monke on his march to London, and he to whome Monke at St. Albans sollemnely swore upon his salvation that he would be faithfull to the Parlament; in confidence whereof, when Mr. Scot retorned to his place in Parlament, he undertooke very farr for the integrity of the said Monke;   **865** whose treachery when *it was* made manifest *and even accomplished*, he endeavoured to save himselfe beyond the seaes; but was taken in his passadge by pyrats, stript, and set on shore in Hampshire; but by helpe of some freinds, got himselfe againe shipt for Flaunders; where he was no sooner arrived at Bruxels, but he was seized by   of Charles Steward's party; from whom he got himselfe free by Don Allonso Car-denas, whom he had obleiged when Embassadour in England on the behalfe of the King of Spaine. And finding afterwards his name inserted amongst other of the King's judges who were required to render themselves, as they expected any benefit by the act of in-demnity, assuring himselfe at least of his life, he delivered himselfe into the hands of the King's agent within the tyme limited by the proclamation. Being thus trappand, he was free to seale with his blood what he had done, which he did with much cheerefulness and satisfaction.

How he was borne downe at his tryall, you have heard. After his condemnation, his wife with other relations and freinds came to him, and demaunded how it was with him. Why, said he, blessed, O blessed chaines, I would not be without these chaines. Indeed it was a very darke, dismall and clowdy morning. I was brought to be content to perish, truly I thought I could not pleade at all, my soule was so sad because God hid his face. But I was resolved, said he, if I could have said no more, to tell the Court that the cause was the Lord's; and that the fault was not in the Lord, but my great personall unworthyness that I could not assert it; and that though I did sinke into the bottomless pit imediately, I durst not, no not for a world, but owne that cause which God had often honoured. But the Lord did helpe me for your sakes to say somethinge. And now said he, as darke as it was in the morning, 'tis so bright, so quiet, so calme, that truly I thinke if I were to be executed tomorrow, I could sleepe all night, as well as ever. But said he, I would not be too confident, O Lord pardon thy servant.

He was willing to have had a repreive for some tyme, that he might have his wedding garment in greater readyness. And Sir Orlando Bridgeman desiring to speake with him, and some telling him it may be that would prove an hower of temptation, Truly, said he, I bless God I am at a point, I cannot, no, I cannot desert the cause. And to his wife he said afterward, I could engage to live quietly, but for owning of guilt, that I cannot doe; for to this day I am not convinced of any as to the death of the King. I went too farr in asking the benefit of the proclamation, and I cannot goe any farther, no not to save a thousand lives. He answered to two ministers (who pressed him to acknowledge his guilt, judging it a meanes to save his life) that although he had often, and that with many teares, and as he thought with some brokenness of heart, sought the Lord to be convinced of it if **866** he had any guilt on him as to that particcular action for which he was in chaines and under condemnation (for, said he, I would not for a world dye with one sin unrepented of), but, said he, really to this day I have no such conviction. But, said the ministers, if any such thinge come in, will you tell it us? Yes, said he, I profess I will; if it come in at the last moment, even at the gibbet, I will tell the world of it. And it's considerable that some of his last wordes were, that God had engaged him in a cause not to be repented of, I Say Not To Be Repented Of.

The night before his execution he was somewhat sadder then at other tymes, the Lord suspending his comforting presence. But, said he, with an humble boldness I would speake it, the Lord shall not put me off with anythinge besides himselfe. After having spent some howers in prayer, his wife, children, and many other freinds coming to see him the morning before his execution, after Colonell Scroope had prayd, he embracing his wife and one of his daughters said, Ah my deare ones, God is good, he is come, he is come, I am full, I am full, O bless the Lord for me, and with me; O my soule, and all that is within me, magnify the Lord. And then prayeing himselfe, one would have thought he had bin as it were in heaven, his soule was so enlardged in blessing, praysing, and magnifying the God of his salvation; saying to his wife, I would not chandge this darke roome, meaning the dungeon wherein he was, for all the Starr Chambers under heaven. He desired his freinds that they would not be sollicitous for his body, but let them doe what they pleased with it, and exercise upon it what cruelty they pleased; saying it was meete it should be so, the dead bodyes of the witnesses must lye unburyed that the scriptures might be fulfilled.

When upon the ladder, he spake thus. Gentlemen, I stand heere a spectacle to God, angels, and men: to God and angels, to whom I hope I shall speedily goe, and now to you. I owe it to God, the nation, and myselfe, to say something concerning each. For myselfe, I thinke it may become me to tell you how and why I came hither, and something in generall concerning my capacity. In the beginning of these troubles I was, as many others were, unsatisfied. I saw libertyes and religion in the nation in great danger. To my best apprehension, I saw the approaching of popery in a great measure comming in upon us. I saw— Upon which the Sheriff interrupted him in these words, If you will betake yourselfe to prayer, you may. Mr. Scot replyed, I shall not speak to reproach any. The Sheriff interrupted him againe saying, Sir you have but a **867** little tyme, therefore spend that little tyme in prayer. Mr. Scot replyed, I shall speake— The Sheriff interrupted him againe saying, I beseech you to betake yourselfe to prayer. Mr. Scot said, It may become me to give an account of myselfe, because— The Sheriff interrupted him againe, saying, It doth not become you to speake any such thinge heere, therefore I beseech you betake your selfe to prayer; it's but a little tyme you have to live, you know that is the most needfull thinge. Mr. Scot replyed, It is so. The Sheriff interrupted him againe, saying, Sir, but when you came upon the stage you deprived yourselfe very much. Then said Mr. Scot, I thought to tell you how I came hither. Heere the Sheriff interrupted him againe, or else some besides the Sheriff, and spake to this effect, Everybody knows that. Mr. Scot said, It's hard an Englishman may not have liberty to speake. The Sheriffe interrupted, saying, I cannot suffer you to speake any such thinge. Mr. Scot said, I shall say no more but this, that it is a very meane and

bad cause that cannot beare the wordes of a dying man; nor hath
it bin ordinarily denyed to persons in my condition. The Sheriff interrupted him againe, Sir, you had a faire tryall, and were found guilty.
Mr. Scot replyed, 'Tis according to my mynde to speake what may
be said. Heere the under-Sheriff interrupted him saying, It hath bin
denyed to your predecessour, and will be denyed you.

He then prayed, laying himselfe in the dust before the Lord; acknowledging the riches of God's love to fallen man in Jesus Christ, and
cheifly to himselfe the greatest of synners; blessing his name for the
assurance he had given him, that he should be magnifying and
honouring him amongst the company of saints and angels, and the
spirits of just men made perfect, and that he had called him forth
as a witness for him, and enabled him to serve the Lord with faithfulness in his publique capacity and imployment. He acknowledged the
condition to which he was now brought to be the answer of his prayer
before his going out of England; having many tymes sought the Lord
with prayers and teares for advise, whether it were his duty to stay
and suffer, or to shelter himselfe abroade, and if it were his will to
take more honour to himselfe by his suffering then by his living, that
he would be pleased to remaund him back, and bring him hither.
He bewayled his want of a heart, tyme and convenience, by reason
of his being constantly in publique imployment, to looke after his
owne vyneyard as he ought to have done; and blessed the Lord for
the opportunityes he had to that end, whilest beyond the seaes and
since. He owned the free grace of God to him, in giving him much
comfort and satisfaction from the consideration of that cause wherein
he was engaged, and for which he suffered, A Cause Not To Be
Repented Of, I Say Not To Be Repented Of.

Heere the Sheriff interrupted, saying, Is this your prayer Mr. Scot;
desiring him to forbeare   **868** those kind of expressions. Others sayd
he contradicted himselfe and spake blasphemy; but this was only the
opinion of those atheists who would have Charles Steward owned as
a God, because his corrupt interest and principles tended to the promoting of their lusts. But Mr. Scot, going on to bless the Lord for
his comforting and assisting presence, prayes for the settlement of the
nation in peace, and in the power and purity of religion, and that
the kingdoms of the world might become the kingdoms of the Lord,
and of his Christ; desiring the Lord to owne his cause, and to remember the price of blood that had bin shed for the purchasing of civill
and Christian libertyes, to remember his enemyes that are not incorrigible to his truth and holyness, that they might see their errour, and
turne to the Lord with humilliation and heart-brokenness. He
remynded the Lord of Zion, desiring that no weapon formed against
his church might prosper, but that the walles of Jerusalem might be

repayred; affirming that the cause of the Lord lay neare the hearts
of his people; bearing witness that he had this income and assistance
from the Lord as a retorne of their prayers, and that he was supported
to beare this witness cheerefully and with satisfaction; desirous to be
found in Jesus Christ, abhorring all his sinnes, and renouncing his
services and sufferings as dounge, but as they were the fruits of his
grace; professing his desire to live was to serve the Lord better, and
love him more, but esteeming it infinitely best to confirme that testimony which is according to his blessed will; in this heavenly frame
of spirit desiring that the Lord's will might be done on earth as it
is in heaven, by himselfe and all the Lord's people, from henceforth
and evermore. He went to the full enjoyment of that, leaving a sweet
savour behind him amonge such as *truly* feare the Lord.

Mr. Gregory Clement, who was next butchered by this barbarous
crew, was a cittizen of London and Spanish merchant, possessed of
a very considerable estate, supposed to the vallue of forty thousand
pounds sterling; and being chosen a member of the Great Parlament
about the yeare 1646, did there dischardge the trust reposed in him
with much sincerity, closing alwayes with that party who were most
hearty to the interest of the Comonwealth. Being appointed by them
one of their Commissioners for the tryall of the King, hee durst not
withdraw his hand from that worke. He never had any place of proffit
under them. He had no good elocution, yet was of a good apprehension and judgement. He was troubled at nothing so much, as that
(to satisfy the importunity of his relations) he pleaded guilty at the
tyme of his tryall, and that he was unworthy to beare witness to so
glorious a cause, and suffer with so good company. And though he
was very sylent before and at the tyme of his execution, yet, so farr
as some discerning Christians could judge, he departed this life in
peace.

What Colonell Adrian Scroope was (who with Colonell John Jones
was **869** drawne upon one sledge to the same place of execution
with the former), as to his birth, education, and quallification, you
shall have out of the mouth of that enemy, who wrote observations
upon his prayers and speeches, as he did upon the rest of those in
his condition; whose words are these. If birth or education can render
a man accomplished, Mr. Scroope deserves a favourable censure; but
as the smallest spot is soonest discovered in a white garment, so treason
dishonours the highest extraction, and leaves a blot in the scutchion
of nobillity. A candid nature obleidgeth me to love the man; yet my
owne conscience, and that sollemne commandement, Feare God, and
honour the King, makes me pitty that which I cannot justify, and
condemne the treason as a person who once loved the traytour. Thus
farr his enemy. And the truth is, as he was of an antient familly, and

candid disposition, borne to a plentyfull estate, of an amiable countenance, and blessed with a hopefull posterity, so with the guifts, and
as farr as could be judged with the graces, of the spirit of the Lord.
He not accounting his life deare to him, in respect of the publique
cause, appeared in the army raysed by the Parlament at the battle
of Edgehill, in the head of a troope of horse; was preferred to the
command of a regiment as Major, and soone after a Colonell to a
regiment of horse; and for severall yeares was Governour of the castle
and garrison of Bristoll, the third cheife citty of England; upon the
sleighting of which garrison he was, with the Lord Broghill, Monke
and others, appointed one of the Commissioners for the goverment
of the civill affaires of Scotland; in all which imployments he acquitted
himselfe with much integrity and abillity. Being appointed by the
Parlament a Comissioner for the tryall of the late King, and looking
on him as a man of blood, he durst not beare that sword in vaine
which the Lord by his providence had put into his hand, but according to his duty made use thereof for the executing of the judgement
written, of shedding that man's blood who had shedd the blood of
man, yea of many thousands of men, that so it might not be chardged
upon him, nor the land polluted therewith.

After his condemnation, one of his children hanging upon him, he
said, Peace childe, peace, be still, not a word, thou hast a blessed portion. Who would be troubled thus to dye, for can anyone have greater
honour then to have his soule carryed to heaven upon the winges of
the prayers of so many Saints? As he sate at dynner, he spake to a
minister that was with him, and others, saying, I would speake it to
the glory of God's free grace, and the comfort of you all, that my
sinnes are all pardoned, not one unpardoned, not one unpardoned;
and God hath loved me with an everlasting love, and in the strength
of this will I goe to heaven. Speaking to some freinds that came to
vissit him, he said, I desire all the people of God to looke at the Lord's
hand in this dispensation, and to owne his soveraignty; to speake well
of him, and whatever he doth, to be at his foote with their mouthes
in the dust, and to live more in love and unity one with another. A
gentleman, coming into the dungeon to see him the night before he
dyed, sayd to him, Unkle, I am sorry to see you in this condition,
and would desire you to repent of **870** the fact for which you are
brought hither, and stand to the King's mercy; with other words
to the same effect; whereupon Colonell Scroope put forth his hand
and thrust him from him, using these words, Avoyd Sathan. Whilest
Mr. Scot and Mr. Clement were executing (the same sledd which
carryed them being appointed to be brought back for him and
Colonell John Jones), he lay downe, and slept so soundly that he
snoared very lowd, and so continued untill the sledd came for him;

whereupon being awakened, he rising up, and a freind, taking him in his armes, asking him how he did, he answered, Very well, I thanke God never better in all my life. And now, saith he, I will wash my hands in innocency, and so will I compass thine altar O Lord; and so with great cheerefulness went to execution.

Colonell Adrian Scroope and Colonell John Jones, two comely ancient gentlemen, being both drawne on the sledd, and being come to Charing Cross, the place of execution, Colonell Scroop was first brought to the ladder, where he spake as followeth. You see an object that hath bin in a better place, but howsoever, the Lord hath sent me hither that I should dye. I have no mallice, nor never had against any, nor any ill will to those who brought me hither, nor to the jury that found me guilty, nor judges who passed sentence, nor to him through whose meanes I was brought hither to suffer. I say once more, the Lord forgive him; I shall not name him, for I came not heere to reflect on any man's person. I shall not boast of my birth and education, or my deportement. Some that looke on, I am perswaded, know what it hath bin. Howsoever the Lord knowes all, and the Lord God is judge of all, and he will judge. I submit myselfe to his judgement, which is a righteous judgement. The judgement of men may goe wrong, but the Lord's judgement is right. I submit to his way. The Lord is the rock of ages, and my support under this great weight that is now upon me. I looke up to him alone. The Lord Jesus Christ is my saviour and redeemer, I am going into his armes, blessed be his name. I follow him, he is gone before me the same way, therefore it's no reproach or shame to follow him, to dye in his cause; for that is it which I judge I am now going to doe. That which I desire of you heere present is, that this day may represent to you the generall day of the judgement of Christ, where you must appeare, and when every man shall receive according to his workes. And at that tyme it will be knowne, I say at that tyme it will be knowne and seene whose workes are righteous, and whose are not. Therefore I would wish you to judge charitably of me.

Having thus with an humble and composed frame of spirit spoake unto the people, he recomended himselfe in prayer unto the Lord; casting himselfe wholy upon his fatherly love in Jesus Christ, for assistance in this his needfull hower; rejoycing that he was following Jesus Christ to his Father and his God; acknowledging his owne vileness and unworthyness as in himselfe; begging of the Lord that it might appeare that there was not a heart in him to doe anythinge with mallice or revendge; and **871** desiring that if there were anything of that nature on the other side, they might repent them of it, that so it might not be layd to their chardge. Thus contynuing to pray for the worst of his enemyes, begging of the Lord to looke upon him as

a tender-hearted father, and to be with him in this hower of temptation, and to carry him through it, he breathed his spirit into the hands
of him who had redeemed him, and who was and would be his portion
for ever; his blood now crying with the rest of the martyrs under the
altar, How long Lord holy and true will it be ere thou avendge our
blood on those who dwell on the earth.

Colonell John Jones, who next appeared on this bloody theatre,
was a gentleman of North Wales; of a competent estate and good
interest in his country, which he improved on behalfe of the publique
during the late troubles; being very instrumentall in many considerable services, especially in reducing the Isle of Anglesey to the obedience of the Parlament; of which he was soone after chosen a member,
serving in that capacity for many yeares with much integrity. He was
chosen by them a member of their Councell of State, and in the yeare
1650 was appointed and constituted one of the Comissioners of Parlament for manadgement of the civill affaires in Ireland; which trust
he discharged for many years with much dilligence, abillity and
fidellity; manifesting much tenderness and care of all such as feared
the Lord, and much zeale in making provission for a godly minestery,
and of bringing those to justice who had bin instrumentall in the
murthering of the poore Protestants there. Notwithstanding some
temptations which he lay under, he reteyned his affection to the interest of the Comonwealth. And when the Great Parlament was restored
to the exercise of their authority, after their long interruption, he was
chosen by them one of the eight to whom they comitted the care of
their safety, and entrusted with many other considerable powers till
they could establish a Councell of State; of which he was also chosen
a member, and soone after was sent by the Parlament to his former
trust in Ireland; where he continued till the Lord was pleased to
permit this great chandge in England, when his people were full ripe
for chastisement, in that they had not wisedome nor will to improve
those opportunityes he had put into their hands. He endeavoured to
conceale himselfe in the citty of London, but being discovered, was
seized and dealt with as in the precedent narrative.

What the frame of his spirit was after his imprysonement, you may
perceive by this following letter to a neere relation of his. I am very
much greived to finde (by the note I received from you) such darke
and sad apprehensions upon your spirit concerning me. We are in
the hands of the Lord, and what he hath appointed for us shall be
our portion, and none can frustrate his holy purposes concerning us;
which I question not but will be found to be in love, whatever appearance it may have to men. My advise to you and to all that love me
is, that in case I be removed from you, you doe not in reallity or outward garbe mourne for me, but rather rejoyce that my portion is in

heaven, and that my removall out of this earthly tabernacle is but in order to my cloathing with imortallity, and posessing of my eternall mansion, and to my being forever with Christ to behold his glory; and therefore that you do not behave yourselves as those that have no hopes but of this life. Secondly, that you take off your mynde from me, and fixe it immoveably upon **872** your eternall relation the Lord Jesus Christ, in whose glorious and blessed presence we shall meete ere long to our eternall rejoycing. It's the goodness of the Lord to remove all creature comforts from us, that our soules might have no resting place to delight in, or to promise themselves safety from, untill we come to the arke of his testimony, the bosome of his love manifested and exhibited for us in our blessed Lord Jesus Christ; reco-mending to their consideration the first and last verses of Psal. 27.

After the sentence of death was passed upon him, and he in his chaine in Newgate, observing one of Colonell Scroop's children weep-ing, he takes her by the hand, saying, You are weeping for your father, but suppose your father were tomorrow to be King of France, and you to tarry a little while behind, would you weepe? Why, he is going to reigne with the King of Kinges in eternall glory. And to a freind that accompanyed him into Ireland, Ah deare heart saith he, you and I were in that storme together, wherein he, Colonell Axtell and myselfe were going for Ireland; and if we had gone this journey of death then, we had bin in heaven to have welcomed honest Harrison and Carew. But we will be contented to goe after them, we will goe after. And speaking of those who were gone beyond the seaes, O deare hearts, said he, in what a sad condition are all our deare freinds beyond sea, where they may be hunted from place to place, and never be in safety, nor heare the voyce of the turtle. How much have we got the start of them, for we are at a point, and are now going to heaven. And speaking of the sled in which he was to be carryed to execution, It is, said he, like Eliah's fiery charriot, only it goes through Fleet Streete.

The tyme of his departure being come, this aged gentleman being drawne on the same sledd with his aged companion Colonell Scroope, their grave and gracefull countenance, accompanyed with courradge and cheerefulness, caused great admiration and compassion in the spectatours, as they passed alonge the streets to Charring Cross, the place of their execution; where after the executioner had done his parte upon three others that day, he was so drunke with blood, that like one surfeyted he grew sick at stomach, and not being able him-selfe, he set his boy to finish the tragedy on Colonell Jones; who, coming to the ladder with the like cheerefulness that his brethren had done before him, and being placed for the execution, he spake to this effect.

Two thinges are necessary now I am going through this narrow passadge to the eternall majesty, first peace with God, secondly peace with man. I shall speake something in the first place as to the Court where I received the sentence. It hath bin reported, as I am told, that I confessed I was guilty of murther under these severall qualifications in the inditement. I desire to cleare myselfe before the Lord and before the world in this particcular. For should I graunt that I was guilty in reallity and trueth of murther, and mallice, I should belye my owne conscience, and draw upon me a greater weight then I can beare. I confess I was willing to make the worke as short as I could, and therefore tooke the first jury, and confessed so much as I was convinced of as to matter of fact. I desire you will judge charitably of **873** this I speake, as in the presence of the Lord. It is not so really, viz. that I acknowledged myselfe guilty of murther, for I had no such thinge in my heart. I freely acquit the Court. Though there was not enough sayd to satisfy such a poore creature as I am, in so great and deepe a point as that was, I know not any man on the earth to whom I beare any mallice. I am in perfect charity with all men, and I hope the Lord is in charity with me. And as I desire to have forgiveness from all whom I have offended, so doe I truly forgive those who have in any measure offended me. As to that which concernes my peace with God, it's that which should be last upon my heart. It's not expected that I should give an account heere of my state and condition, for that is betwixt God and my owne soule. And I doe through the grace and goodness of God firmly beleeve that my redemption is wrought, and my pardon sealed, and that I shall be imediately in my Father's armes, and that I shall be translated and brought to behold the Lord Jesus Christ in glory; which comfort and fulness of joy he then in prayer begd of the Lord to open to him, and now to make good to him all the promises he had beleeved all the dayes of his life, and to give him the full enjoyment of himselfe; blessing the Lord for the opportunity he had given him to suffer for his name; praying for a blessing upon all present, and that the Lord would sanctify to them what they saw and heard; and for England, that it might be a land of trueth and happiness, that God would direct his people so to turne to him, as to divert the judgements that threaten these nations, because they have sinned against the Lord; that he would appeare to sanctify his name that it might not be reproached. Blessing the Lord for that his spirit is full of joy, he commits his soule into the hands of his Father, and so departed.

Thus did these servants of the Lord offer upp themselves a willing sacrifice to the Lord; this gentleman the night before telling a freind he had no other temptation upon him but this, lest he should be transported and carried out to slight his life, so greatly was he satisfyed to dye in this cause.

Colonell Danyel Axtell was the next whom the Lord called forth
to witness to this cause with his blood. The inditement against him
was that he did imagine and compass the death of the late King. The
particculars of his chardge were, that he commanded the guards at
the tryall and execution of the King; that he commanded his souldiers
to crye out, Justice, Justice, at the tryall, and afterwards, Execution,
Execution; that he threatned to shoote a lady (who out of a gallery
neere the Court (when President Bradshaw told the King, that the
chardge exhibited against him was in the name of the Commons
assembled in Parlament, and the good people of England) said
alowde, It's false, not halfe the people, Cromwell is a traytor) if she
held not her peace; and that he sent for the executioner, and
upbraided one with cowardice, to whom the warrant was directed
for the seeing of the sentence put in execution, for refusing to signe
the same. Colonell Hercules Huncks, one of those three to whom the
warrant for execution of the King was directed, and one of the forty
halberdeers, *and one who* did oppose *with more then ordinary violence* every
person then for the King, was one principall witness against him; and
another was Leiftenant Colonell Nelson, one of the same vissible
church society with himselfe. The evidence given in by both of these
Colonel Axtell sollemnely   **874** protested against as untrue; wherein
the scriptures were fulfilled, not only in that brother betrayes brother
to death, but that the Saints shall be accused falseley for the name
of Jesus.

Colonell Axtell in his defence, having in the first place acknowledged his owne ignorance of the lawes (the inditement itselfe being
matter of law), seeing they refused to allow him councell, desired that
for want of knowledge in the formalty, punctillios and nicetyes of the
law, he might not be ensnared; minding the judge by the oath he
had taken that he is to be a mediatour betwene the King and the
prissoner, and is to advise both in matters of law; resembling this day
to the judgement of the great day, when Christ will be judge; and
therefore desired that there might be nothing of mallice in the prosecution of him, hoping there would be none in prejudging or in pre-
cluding him to be so black a person as one of the councell would have
him to be thought. He proceeds to justify that authority under which
he acted; saying that the warr was first stated by the Lords and
Comons of the Parliament of England, and by their authority were
forces raysed, they pretending that by law the right of the militia was
in them, as appeares in the severall declarations and acts that were
set forth by them. This authority of Lords and Commons in Parlament
assembled raysed an army, made the Earle of Essex Generall, and
after him the Earle of Manchester of the forces in the Easterne Association, and after that Sir Thomas Fairfax Lord Generall of the forces.

By this authority, saith hee, I acted; and this authority I conceive to be legall, because this Parlament was called by the King's writ, chosen by the people, and a bill past that they should not be dissolved but by their owne consent, and was in being (to wit when the tryall was, and a great question *it is* whether *it bee* yet legally dissolved). And therefore having done what I did by virtue of an authority so legall and justifiable, I cannot be within that statute of the 25 Edward 3; for that (questionless) must intend private persons counselling, compassing or imagining the death of the King, this authority under which I acted being not only owned and obeyed at home but abroade as the cheife authority of the nation; states and kingdoms sending embassadors to them to that purpose, the judges of the land, who ought to be the the eye and guide of the nation, acting under them, and some of them, as Judge Thorpe, Nicholas and Jermain, having publiquely declared that it was a lawfull justifiable thinge to obey the Parlament.

But if their acts will not be allowed to be acts (though they entitled them so, and they were obeyed as such by the judges, ministers and officers of state, and all other persons in the nation), yet I hope they cannot be denyed to be orders of Parlament; and were they no more, yet were they sufficient to beare out those that acted thereby. This Parlament thus constituted having made their Generall, he by their authority did constitute me an officer of the army; and what I have done, I have done only as a souldier; and if I was at Westminster Hall at the tyme of the tryall of the King, it was by comand from the Generall. If it be so great a cryme to have bin an officer in that army, the Earle of Essex, the Earle of Manchester, **875** the Lord Generall Fairfaxe, Generall Monke, who acted by the same authority, were as guilty as myselfe. He pleaded also that the Lords and Commons, the propper judges and expounders of the law, had declared, upon severall statutes of Henry the 7th, for the justifying of all those who should take up armes under them, and in particcular as to the statute of the 11th of Henry the Seaventh, in these words, It is not, say they, aggreable to reason or conscience that anyone's duty should be knowne, if the duty of the High Court of Parlament be not a rule and guide to them. In the same Declaration the King quits that statute of 25 Edward 3. And the Lords and Comons doe possitively say, in their Declaration publisshed 1643, folio 27, That the persons who did act under their authority ought not to be questioned as persons guilty. And shall inferiour judges expound the law contrary to what the High Court of Parlament have declared? And if an Howse of Commons assembled in Parliament may be guilty of treason (for the truth is, if I acted treason, who acted under the authority of the Lords and Comons in Parlament, or of the Comons, then doubtless they must begin the treason), and if the Howse of Commons, who are the collective body of the nation, be guilty, all the people of England who chose them are guilty too, and then where will be a jury to try this?

Both Court and councell had nothing to reply to this his most sollid and rationall answer. Mr. Ansley (making it appeare, by his sitting as a judge of the Parlament's best freinds, that his exclusion out of the Howse of Commons in 1648, as one of those who had betrayed his trust, and complyed with the King's interest, was upon good grounds) chardges Colonell Axtell with being one of the greatest violaters of that authority under which he would now shelter himselfe; whereunto Colonell Axtell replyed, I never had any hand in that matter, this is all as to that parte. Next, heere I must ground my plea, and if I perish, I perish by a judgement in Parliament. My commission that was given me to obey my Generall beares date the 27 March 1648, ten monthes before the King's death. The commission by which Generall Fairfax was authourized to give me this commission, he received from the Lords and Commons assembled in Parlament. I did but my duty in going to my regiment. The Generall saith, Goe to such a place and stay there. If I refuse, by the law of warr I dye; if I obey, I am in danger likewise. The question therefore in poynt of law I humbly conceive will be this (and I humbly desire it may be truly and fairly stated by your Lordships and these honourable judges), that whether a man, being guided by the judgement of the Lords and Comons assembled in parlament, and acting only by that judgement of parlament and under their authourity, can be questioned for treason. Whereunto the councell answering that he was not charged for leavying   **876** of warr, but for assisting at the tryall and execution of the King, and for encouradging the souldiers to crye, Justice, Justice, Execution, Execution, he answered, I am no more guilty then the Generall. My being in Westminster Hall was not a voluntary act in me, I was there by comand.

This he pressed so hard upon the Court, appealing to them for their judgement therein, that they were necessited to fly to their old reffuge of questioning the authority itselfe, and that he ought to take notice of the action itselfe as well as of the authority; repeating againe the purdging of the Howse, which they supposed he could not but take notice of. But Colonell Axtell insisting on it, that he must serve and obey all his superiour officers by virtue of his comission, and if he doth not he must dye for it, Mr. Hollis (chardged with high treason by the King, and afterwards one of the eleaven members chardged with high treason by the army) vents his mallice against him as formerly Mr. Ansly did, chardging him to be one of those who came to the barr and chardged the eleaven members, and so proceeds against him in the accustomed streyne, saying in passion that he followed his lusts, and not any authority; to which Colonell Axtell answered, I desire to have no more interruption then is meete, in making my defence. My Lords, here are many thinges urged by way of motive to the chardge, I desire I may have that faire play, that nothing may be urged but what is in the chardge; Mr. Hollis replying unto him according to his passionate manner. Colonell Daniell Axtell denyes that ever he was at the barr, but upon presenting one petition to the Parlament from the army.

Having spoken to the authority by which he was sent to Westminster Hall, he proceeds to the particculars of the evidence; and first, to that touching a lady who spake something there: If there was any lady that did speake, who she was I knew no more then the least childe then. But to sylence a lady I suppose is no treason; if a lady will talke impertinently, it's no treason to bidd her hold her tongue. That of striking sayle, and casting anchor when coming into the mouth of the harbour, if that were said, it's no treason; no person, nor fact, nor designe being named. And if I smyled, as Colonell Temple affirmed, that is no treason if I did so. I beleeve I had as great a sense that day as many other persons there. As to that of beating the souldiers till they cryed Justice, Justice, it may be some of them crying so, with others I might **877** command them to hold their tongues, and to say, I will teach you to crye, Justice, Justice, and so the gentleman standing by might beleeve that I was the person that bid them doe it. Neither, saith he, that it was against any person. And Sir Edward Cooke holds, that in matters of treason, wherein a man is the most highly concerned in his life and posterity, there ought not to be construed against him inferences, presumptions or streines of wit. I hope it's no treason to desire justice. It's God's great attribute, it's God's ordinance, and that can be no treason. He that sweares I sent Elisha Axtell for the executioner is a person who confesseth himselfe provoaked by me, and (having bin in chaines in pryson) might be under the temptation to say anythinge to get his liberty. If there had bin any trueth in what he saith, which he absolutely denyeth, Elisha Axtell might have bin sent for out of Ireland, being the principall witness to have testified the same, as well as this person. If I spake to any person, sayd he, which I doe not remember I did, to let Mr. Temple have a sight of the King's body, this I hope will not amount to treason. If I said anythinge to Leiftenant Colonell Nelson touching the person who cut off the King's head, who it was I must invent it, for that I know not myselfe who it was.

He alleadgeth he was not put into the black catalogue of excepted persons till, by a servant of the King's who had promised to doe him a courtesy contrary thereto, he was seized by a warrant from the King and carryed to the Tower; that all that was alleaged against him was but wordes, and wordes not put in writing. He urgeth that he is not excepted by a free parlament, to whom the King by his proclamation from Bredagh (which in due tyme he claymed the benefit of) referred the power of excepting. But he received the same sleight answer that Cheif Justice Cooke had. And after many interruptions which he had from the Court, he concluded thus, I leave the matter to the jury, I leave my case, my life, and all in your hands. In answer to all that this gentleman urged, though Bridgeman (the President of this bloody conspiracy) undertakes to repeate all thinges that were said by him and against him, yet (relying more upon the assurance he had of the fidellity of the jury to his devillish worke they were about, then upon the weight of what he had to say in the case) satisfied himselfe for delivering for positive law that Unchristian, irrationall and detestable position, viz. That no person whatsoever, nor community, not the people either collectively, or representatively, have any coercive power of the King; and then quoting a president or two, as horrid and not at all to the purpose, concluded the case so cleare that the jury needed not goe from the barr. And they, packed for his purpose, having all or most of them already imbrued their hands in the blood of the Saints, neither mynding their ancestours, their posterityes, nor the eternall states of their soules, chose to obey man rather then God, and declared him guilty (according as **878** they were directed by Bridgeman) of the high treason whereof he stood indited. Thus doe they eate up the people of the Lord, as they would eate bread. But were their consciences in the least measure awakened, how might they justly feare, whilst it is in their mouthes, the heavy wrath of God would fall on them?

The inditement against Colonell Francis Hacker is for compassing and imagining the death of the King. The particculars of the evidence were, that he was one of the persons that were upon the guard, and kept the King prysoner; that the warrant for causing the sentence given by the High Court against the King to be put into execution was directed to him and two others; that in prosecution thereof he signed a warrant for the execution of the King; that he tooke the King, by virtue of the warrant directed to him, out of the hands of Colonell Tomlinson, and conducted the said King to the scaffold, where his head was severed from his body. Colonell Hunckes (one of those to whom the warrant was directed by the High Court) and Colonell Thomlinson (one of the High Court of Justice, and who had the imediate custody of the King's person during the tyme of his tryall) were the two principall witnesses against him. Colonell Hacker excepted against none of the jury, finding all those retorned by the Sheriff to be of the same mynde. Neither did he say much more in his justification, then that he did what he did in obedience to the commands of those who were over him, and that he had bin ever for the welfare of his country, and that civill power might stand. The jury, upon the like direction received from Bridgeman in this case as they had done in the former, make no scruple to draw his blood on their heades also as they had done the former, thus thirsting to fill up their measure.

Colonell Axtell, being asked by some freinds how he found himselfe fitted to encounter death, answered, I can say nothing till I come to dye, I dare not boast till I put off my armour, but desire your prayers till there be no more neede of them. To his wife, crying after his condemnation, he sayd, Not a teare wife, what hurte have they done me to send me sooner to heaven? I bless the Lord I could have freely gone from the barr to the gibbet. They had nothing against me, neither by God's law nor their owne, to condemne me. Was it ever knowne that a man should dye for such wordes? And further said, Though man hath judged, God hath not condemned. Some taking notice of his course lodging, he said, What matter is it to have a little dirty way? We have a faire howse to come unto; and then looking upon freinds about him sayd, If the sight of a few of God's people be soe comfortable, what will it be to enjoy all the Saints in heaven together? Towards evening he prayed (divers being then present, admiring the frame of spirit he was in), praysing God for all his appearances for his poore people; laying all his comfort in the blood of a crucifyed Christ, and upon the Covenant of free grace; heartily desiring pardon for all his judges, jury, and those witnesses who had sworne falsely against him. And having the bible in his hand after his condemnation,   **879** he said, I shall have the use of this booke for two dayes more, and then enjoy the fulness of the gospell to all eternity.

His daughter comming to him, he sayd, Where hast thou bin all this while? I thought thou hadst bin asshamed of my chaines. Those who will not beare the cross shall not weare the crowne. A gentleman coming to vissit him asked, Shall I petition for your life? Colonell Axtell replyed, Sir you offer me to my loss. The gentleman telling him he was going for Ireland, he sayd, Pray remember me to all Christian freinds there, and tell them (shaking his chaines rejoycingly) that you saw me in my chaines, and that I reckon all these linkes as so many pearles to adorne me, and I am sure they are so in Christ's esteeme. And tell them, that for that good old cause that we were engaged in under the Parlament, I am going now to be their martir. But they have meerely murthered me, and might as well have done it in the Tower as have brought me hither to make this bussle. I wish my blood doe not cry to the 3d and 4th generation. But I shall doe them more hurt in my death then I could have done them in my life. I wish I may see them all in heaven. A freind going into Glocestershire, Colonell Axtell desired him to remember him to all the good people there, and to tell them that their prayers were answered, and to bid them keepe close to Christ, and not touch with the surplice or Common Prayer Booke, and, whatever they did, to love the imadge of Christ whereever they saw it, in Presbiterian, Independent, Baptized or others, and to take heede of closing with anythinge that attempts the making voyd any of the offices of Jesus Christ.

Fower of his fellow prysoners passing by his chamber doore as they were going forth to execution, and being denyed a sight of them, he called them by their names, and with a mighty fervent spirit sayd, The Lord goe with you, the angel of his presence stand by you; and then turning to his freinds said, O they are gone to heaven before me, but we will give them up to the Lord; and so went to prayer. And presently after, he prayed againe, saying, God hath said he will make us joyfull in the howse of prayer. He performed the duty of prayer five tymes that day himselfe, laying himselfe very low before the Lord, acknowledging himselfe the worst of all the prysoners, and that he should have the least to say for God, desiring his freinds to say nothing of him till he was upon the uppermost round of the ladder. His daughter comming to him, he told her he had left Jesus Christ an executour in trust for her. He gave an account to some persons for their satisfaction about his proceedings against the rebels in Ireland, saying, I can say with all humillity that God did use me as an instrument in my place for the suppressing of the bloody enemy. And when I considered their cruelty in murthering so many thousand Protestants and innocent soules, that word was much upon my heart, Give her blood to drinke for she is worthy. And sometymes we neither gave nor tooke quarter, though selfe-preservation might have said, Give that which ye may expect to have. One telling him that his fellow prysoners dyed cheerefully, he said, How did they stand? Answer being made, upon a ladder, Blessed be God, said he, it's a Jacob's ladder. To Colonell Hacker he said, Come brother be not so sad, by this tyme tomorrow we shall be with our Father in glory, and what hurte will they doe us to bringe us through the cross to the crowne? Well, our God **880** is [the God?] of Newgate.

Taking leave of his freinds upon his going into the dungeon, he said, Love the Lord Jesus, love the Lord, and weepe not for me, for God hath wiped away all teares. To an emynent godly minister of the Presbyterian way, Colonell Axtell taking him by the hand sayd, I have one word to speake to you. It's much upon my heart, that one great cause why God contends so with his people, is for want of love towards those who were not of their mynds; to which the minister replyed, Truly sir, I thinke so too, the Lord helpe us that wherein we have done amisse we may doe so no more. Then sayd Colonell

Axtell, I bless the Lord I have not much to chardge myselfe with in this matter. Colonell Hacker then sayd, But I have much to complaine of in that matter. Colonell Axtell afterwards sitting on his bedside, clapping his hands, sayd, If I had a thousand lives, I could lay them downe all for the cause; whereupon another godly minister asking him what he meant by the cause, he answered, That cause which we were encouradged and engaged in under the Parlament, that was for common right and freedome as men and Christians, and against the surplice and Common Prayer Booke; and said further, the surplis and Comon Prayer Booke shall not stand longe in England, for it is not of God.

As he was at supper with severall of his freinds, the night before his execution, he sayd, Take heede of temporizing, etc., for that had bin the occation of great evill. Then speaking to an officer there present, that continued till of late in the army, he said, Brother thou hast beene greatly guilty heerein, the Lord forgive thee; to which the person replyed, I confess I have bin too much. Colonell Axtell answered, There is yet mercey for thee, if the Lord give thee repent-ance. Moreover, said he, the Lord forgive that poore wretch Leiften-ant Colonell Nelson, for he hath sworne falseley in his evidence; but now is that word made good, Brother shall betray brother to death. And speaking of Colonell Thomlinson, sayd he, Ah he hath appeared five pounds in twenty lighter then I thought him to be; and for Colonell Hunkes, he was the uncivillest of all about the late King, and yet comes in as a witness against Hacker and me. Praying with his freinds that evening, the Lord emynently assisting him in that duty, and bewayling much the devissions of God's people, he said, Lord if they will not live together in love, thou wilt make them lye together in sufferings. And minding his present condition, he sayd, Lord, death is the king of terrours to nature, but it is a beleever's choyce freind, it is thy high way to leade us unto glory. After prayer, he sayd to his daughter, Get an interest in Christ and keepe close to him, for he will be infinitely a better father then I; and so tooke his leave of her.

The day of his execution being come, severall godly ministers spent some tyme with them in prayer, viz. with Colonell Axtell and Colonell Hacker. And many freinds comming in to pay their last respects, Colonell Axtell, seeing one of his familliar freinds and companions, sayd, My deare brother, thou art better then I, yet I must goe to heaven before thee for all that. He very cheerefully sayd to divers **881** then present, Deare freinds rejoyce, I am going where you shall be also, yea where we shall be ever with the Lord, and never parte, and be without any more chandge. I beseech you, follow the Lamb wherever he goeth, for though he may leade you in a harsh, dismall, and difficult way, yet at last he will bringe you to a pleasant path, and cause you to lye downe in greene pastures in the land of rest. O be faithfull unto the death, and he will give you a crowne of life, as he hath given to your suffering brethren. Oh, all that we have, or doe suffer, is but to make Christ and heaven more sweete and glorious to us; and all the sad steps we shall tread on this ladder are but to mount us to heaven, for at the topp are angels ready to receive us. All thinges I meete with move me not, I bless my God, for I am sure to fight a good fight, and finish my course with joy. And then, taking leave of his sonne, embracing him sayd, My deare son fare thee well, I must leave thee, get an interest in Christ, and love him, nothing else will stand there instead. Then calling for his bible, he hugged it saying, This hath the whole cause in it, and I may carry this without offence. And calling to a freind, he desired him to remember his love to the congregation whereof he was a member; and after, tooke leave of all his freinds, exhorting them with much cheerefulness to love the Lord Jesus Christ, and keepe close to him; and so with great joy addressed himselfe to his next worke.

Colonell Francis Hacker was a man of few wordes, and had not the guift of oratory to express himselfe as others could; yet was sweetly borne up under his sufferings, and had a very comfortable assurance that God had pardoned and accepted him in the blood of Christ. He had bin a professour of religion many yeares in the presbyterian way, and a great lover of godly ministers; a man of just and honest conversation amongst men, and one who desired to walke blameless in the sight of God. His fellow prysoner, Colonell Axtell, said he beleeved Colonell Hacker had an interest in Jesus Christ. The said Colonell Hacker declared to severall of his freinds, a little before he suffered, that the greatest trouble he had upon his spirit was, that he had formerly borne too great a prejudice in his heart towards the good people of God who differed from him in judgement; and then brake forth into this admiration, O what am I a poore vile worme, that God should count me worthy to suffer with such precious soules as these are, against whom I have bin formerly so much prejudiced. And thus these two gratious persons having finished their course, and the tyme of their departure being at hand, were both brought forth of prison. And the sledd being ready for them, they tooke their leave of some freinds who stood at the doore, Colonell Axtell desiring them that they would be at the place of execution. And both, entring on the sledd, cast up their eyes towards heaven whither they were going; and then, with a cheerefull countenance setting themselves downe, were drawne to Tyburne, the place of execution, where a cart was set; into which they both ascended, their **882** countenances not at all changed (though now the king of terrours stared them in the face), the ropes being then put about their neckes and a burning fire kindled before their faces, and being ready to receive that sentence which nature would have sunke under, if grace had not supported.

First Colonell Axtell applyed himselfe to the Sheriff in these following wordes. Mr. Sheriffe, I am now as you see come to the place of execution, according to my sentence. I desire your leave that I may speake freely and without intteruption, first to this people, and then to God; for it's the last I shall speake in this world, and I hope it will redound to your account. The Sheriff having cautioned him not to speake anythinge that was prohibited by the Court, he then sayd, that the very cause for which he engaged was conteined in this booke (having the bible in his hand), both in the civill and religious rights of it, which I leave to you (giving the booke to Mr. Knowles). You see a dead man living, and yet I hope I shall live to all eternity, through the mediation of Jesus Christ, the mediatour of the Covenant of free grace. I must truly tell you, that before the late warrs it pleased the Lord to call me by his grace through the worke of the minestry. And after keeping a day of humilliation in fasting and prayer with Mr. Woodcock, Mr. Simeon Ash, Mr. Love, and other ministers in Lawrence Lane, they did so clearely state the cause of the Parlament, that I was fully convinced in my conscience of the justness of the warr, and thereupon engaged in the Parlament service, which as I did and doe beleeve was the cause of the Lord. And I adventured my life for it, and now dye for it.

Then Mr. Sheriff said, Sir remember yourselfe. Colonell Axtell proceeds, And after the worke of the Lord was done in England, my lot cast me upon the service of Ireland. And I thanke the Lord I was serviceable to the English nation in the country, and discharged my duty fully according to the trust reposed in me there. As for the fact for which I suffer, it's for wordes, and but for wordes, and the sentence is already reverssed in my owne conscience, and will be reversed by Jesus Christ by and by. I pray God, from the bottome of my heart, to forgive all who had a hand in my death, both witnesses and the jury and Court that passed sentence. For considering the doctrine of our Lord Jesus Christ as he hath layd it downe, Mat. 5. 44, It hath bin sayd of old tyme, love your neighbour and hate your enemy, but I say unto you love your enemyes, etc., I desire according to this doctrine from my very soule that God would give them true repentance, and not lay their sin to their chardge, nor my blood, which by God's law and man's I thinke could not justly have bin brought hither to suffer. But I bless the Lord I have some comfortable assurance that I shall be embraced in the armes of Jesus Christ, and have cause to hope that his spirit shall carry my soule into the Father's hands. And if the glory of this sunshine be so great (the sun then shyning bright), how much more is the glory of the son of God, who is the sonne of righteousness.

I think it convenient heere to give some account of my faith. I beleeve all thinges written in the Old and New Testament, as the principles **883** and doctrine of a beleever's faith. I beleeve the blessed ordinances of Christ, that it is our duty to heare the word of God preached, to seeke unto God in prayer, to performe familly dutyes, and to walke in the comunion of Saints. And for my owne parte, I am a member of a congregation which I judge to be the way of Christ (and were it for that only I were to dye, I could witness to it), which is a company of men borne againe by his grace, that walke in the way of Christ blameless and harmeless. I beleeve Jesus Christ dyed for poore synners, of whom I am cheife, as the Apostle saith. This is a faithfull saying, and worthy of all acceptation, that Jesus Christ came into the world to save synners, whereof I am cheife. And if the Apostle said so, much more may I. Freinds and country-men, I have reason to bewayle my owne unproffitable life, having bin very unfruitfull unto the people of the Lord. The Lord knowes I have much filth upon my heart, were it not for the blood of Christ that cleanseth and wassheth me, according to his promise, saying, I have loved you, and wasshed your sinnes with my owne blood. I desire you all to loath and cast off sin. For it's better to suffer then sin, yea, it's better to dye then sin. Nothing could greive our Saviour but the sense of our sin.

And therefore take heede of every sin. For you and I must meete one day at the barr of God, when Christ the son of God shall be our judge. For God hath committed all judgement to the Sonn, that all men should honour the Son as they honour the Father. This day is a resemblance of that day, therefore be serious. I begge as much good to your immortall soules as I expect to enjoy by and by. I beseech you, begg of God that he would save your soules, and omit no oppor-tunity through the strength of the Lord to beleeve. Labour for an interest in Christ, or else of all men ye will be most misserable; for I of all men should be so, did I not beleeve to see the goodness of the Lord in the land of the living. Blessed be the Lord who bringes me into this estate. Let the way or meanes be what it will, it's God's soveraignty, who made his creatures, to dispose of them as he pleaseth; and he hath ordeyned this death for me from all eternity. The Lord Christ oft prayed, Thy will be done. This is the Lord's will, he hath numbred my dayes, and my tymes are in his hands. Many seeke the ruler's favour, but everyone's judgement is from the Lord. When Pylate sayd to Christ, Knowest thou not that I have power to crucify thee, Christ answered, Thou couldest have no power to crucify me were it not given thee from above. Therefore I acknowledge the righteous hand of God. He is righteous, but I am sinfull. Therefore will I beare the indignation of the Lord, because I have sinned against him. It's sayd of Jesus Christ, that for the joy that was set before him he endured the cross and despised the shame, and is sate downe at the right hand of God; where I hope by and by to see him in glory and **884** majesty, and to see his angels and beleevers worshipping him. And therefore I despise the shame. Our Saviour dyed upon the cross without sin. I am a most sinfull creature, a wretched synner. And shall I expect better then he that was my master, he that was holy and harmeless, who never had a sinful thought in all his life, and dyed not for himselfe but us, that we might live through his death, and by poverty be made rich? And Christ having done this for his people, it should not be in your thoughts a despicable thinge that we should suffer for him, having bin engaged in the worke of God. But Christ must prevayle in righteousness, and will prevayle. After this, having thanked the Sheriff for his civillity, Colonell Hacker speaking something privately to him, he asked the Sheriff whether they were to dye both together. The Sheriff answering, Yes, Colonell Hacker then read a paper, conteyning these words following.

Freinds and Countrymen, all that have knowne me in my best estate have not knowne me to be a man of oratory, and that God hath not given to me the guift of utterance as to others. Therefore I have only this breifly to say to you that are spectatours. As the Parlament stated the case, I did in judgement and conscience joyne with them in the comon cause, and have through grace bin faithfull to it according to my measure. And as for that for which I am condemned, I doe freely forgive both judges, jury and witnesses, yea all others. And I thanke the Lord to whom I am now going, at whose tribunall I must render an account, I have nothing lyes upon my conscience as guilt, as to that for which I am condemned, and doe not doubt but to have the sentence reverst. I doe now apply myselfe unto my God by prayer, and desire the hearty prayers of all that feare the Lord, that I may have a sweete passadge from this mortall life to that which is immortall, which God hath prepared for all that are in Christ Jesus. Subscribed,

Francis Hacker.

After the reading of this, he desired that Colonell Axtell would be both their mouthes to God in prayer. Then Colonell Axtell sayd, I desire all who feare the Lord to heare me with patience, and to lift up their hearts to seeke the Lord with me, that we may have his strength, and the presence of his spirit from this world to everlasting life. **885** And with a wounderfull composed frame of spirit, and with

an audible voyce, he entred upon the following duty, wherein the
Lord healped him with excellent expressions suitable to both their
conditions, laying them low before the Lord in the acknowledgement
of their originall and actuall sins, and casting themselves wholy upon
the free grace of God in Jesus Christ for the pardon of and purdging
them from all sinnes, and justifying of their persons through his blood.
And seeing that it was the will of the Lord that the Passeover should
be eaten with soure hearbes, they declared themselves content therewith, blessing the Lord for providing not only sweete wyne for them,
but for keeping the best of it, the choycest of his divine comforts, untill
now; owning it best to have the cross with the crowne, our Lord having sayd that they that suffer with him shall also reigne with him.
He begd that they might have their faith strengthned, to lay hold
of a naked Christ, that his blood might be unto them for justification,
sanctification, and acceptation with the Father; that if any present
did not belong to Christ, and were not freinds to him, that the Lord
would convert them, and show them their undone and miserable
estate, and give them the pardon of a dying Saviour (saying, Thy
poore servants would not parte with a Christ for ten thousand lives).
He mynded also the condition of London, desiring the Lord to be
mercyfull to them, for that he hoped there were many tens of righteous
ones therein, for that it had bin a place where the Lord had bin glorifyed, and many godly ministers had bin encouraged; particcularly
desiring on its behalfe, that the gospell might have a free passadge
in the publique worship.

He prayed that the Lord would have mercey upon the goverment
and governours, and upon the Sheriff, who was come by comand to
see the sentence executed upon them; that the Lord would have mercey upon his soule, and that they might meete in heaven together
to be embraced in the armes of Christ; and for the executioner, who
was to wash his hands in their blood, that the Lord would wash his
soule in the bloode of Christ, that the Lord would remember him
in his low estate; then blessing the Lord for that he had pulled out
the stinge of death through Jesus Christ, in whom they had obteyned
victory, expressing much assurance that the angels were ready to
receive their soules, and to carry them into the bosome of the Lord,
and into the company of Abraham, Isaac and Jacob, and by the
blessed apostles, martyrs and witnesses of Jesus Christ, and of just men
made perfect. And for the King, he prayed that the Lord would make
him a freind to Christ and to the people of Christ, and to reigne in
righteousness and rule for God, before whom he   **886** and all others
must render an account in the day of judgement. The like he prayed
for all who had any uncharitableness towards them, that they might
see their sin, receive their pardon, and that their soules might live

in the Lord's presence; and that themselves and their enemyes might embrace one another, through the grace of God in Jesus Christ, one day in heaven, expressing their joy that this their death should put an end to sin, and to their greiving of the spirit of Christ and dishonouring God, and their prayers dissolved into prayses. He willingly offered up his body and soule unto the Lord, declaring it to be but a reasonable sacrifice, in that they were bought with a price, not with silver and gold, but with the pretious blood of Jesus Christ, and seeing the earth was the Lord's, and the fulness thereof, and by his soveraignty might command whatever he pleaseth. Into his hands as his Father he recomended his spirit, begging all this for the sake of Jesus Christ the mediatour of the new Covenant, and desiring that to him, with the Father and blessed spirit, all power, honour and praise might be given for evermore.

After he had ended his prayer, he gave the Sheriff thankes for his civillity; and then turning to Colonell Hacker, they salluted and embraced each other, and sayd, The Lord sweeten our passadge, and give us a happy meeting with himselfe in glory. Then pulling his capp over his eyes, expecting as was supposed the carte should be drawne away, with his hands lifted up he uttered these wordes with a lowd and audible voyce, Lord Jesus receive my spirit. But the cart staying a little longer, he lifted up his hands the second tyme, and with the like audible voyce sayd, Into thy hands O Father I comend my spirit. And yet, in reguard there was no man found to put forward the horse to draw away the cart, untill the common hangman came downe out of the cart himselfe to doe it (the carman, as many witnesses affirme, saying he would loose his cart and horse before he would have a hand in hanging such a man), by this meanes he had the opportunity to lift up his hands and to utter the like words a third tyme.

One thinge more is very remarkeable, that when Colonell Axtell and Colonell Hacker were taken out of the sledge into the cart, the spectatours, being in great numbers, behaved themselves very civilly; only two persons among them, as soone as the ropes were about their neckes, **887** cryed out very earnestly, Hang them, hang them, rogues, trayters, murtherers, Hangman draw away the cart. Whereupon a man that stood by desired them to be civill, saying, Gentlemen, this is not civill, the Sheriff knowes what he hath to doe. And thereupon they were sylent, and gave attention to Colonell Axtell's speech and prayer. But before he had done, those very persons were so affected that they could not refrayne from pouring out many teares upon the place, and went aside to a place more retyred to weepe. And that man who before desired them to be civill went after them, and beheld them to his great admiration, as himselfe related.

How Colonell Axtell came to be satisfied to engage in the warr raysed by the Parlament, ye have heard; in which service for his merit he was soone preferred to a foote company, and then to the command of the regiment as Major, and soone after as Leiftenant Colonell, in which capacity he acted at the tryall and execution of the late King. And when Leiftenant Generall Cromwell was sent by the Parliament with an army into Ireland for the reducing of the rebells, it falling to that regiment's lot, of which he was, to make one for that service, he cheerefully offered himselfe to that imployment; and for his fidelity, couradge and good conduct was imediately preferred to the command of a regiment, and not long after to the command of the garrison of Kilkenny, and of the precinct thereto belonging, which was very considerable; which trust he discharged with industry and success, expressing great zeale in the prosecution of the rebells for the innocent and pretious blood they were guilty of; for which Charles Steward (as well as for what he did in bringing his father to justice), being full of mallice towards him, one of his servants (whether by order or no I cannot say) pretending to buy some of Colonell Axtell's land, having appointed a meeting with him for that purpose, seizeth the sayd Colonell by his order; who being thus betrayed into the hands of this bloody enemy, who had creatures enough in both Howses to gratify his lust, he procured them to except him out of the act of indemnity; by which meanes, and those other contrivances before mentioned, he came to be thus inhumanely and cruelly treated.

Colonell Francis Hacker was a gentleman of a considerable estate in the county of Leycester, left him by his parents, which he imployed for the promoting of the publique service, engaging in the service of the Parlament in severall commands. And when the Parlament were constreyned to send an army into Scotland for their owne defense, he raysed a regiment of horse for the defence of his country, with which in his owne person he did signall service at the Battle of Worcester. And when Mr. Richard Cromwell, harkening to his young and giddy counsellours, was opposed by the more sound (or rather less corrupted) parte of the officers of the army, endeavouring to engage him on his side, had the night before his fall forced a knighthood (as **888** they called it) upon him, and given him two swords (he having at that tyme the command of the Horse Guard in the citty of London), he notwithstanding (judging that Mr. Richard Cromwell owned an interest most opposite to the publique) refused to obey his orders (though brought unto him by Mr. Waterhowse, a confiding servant of Cromwell's), and espoused the undertaking of the contrary party. He contynued the command of his regiment till the tyme of his being seized upon, which was some weekes after Charles Steward came into England. For Monke having assured him of a full indemnity for whatsoever he had done, he lived securely at his owne howse. And upon advertisement that he should come to London, he forthwith repayred thither; and coming to Monke, who could not be ignorant of the designe that was against him, yet received him with as much shew of affection as ever, enquiring of him with much kindness where he lodged. But the next day after he was thus carressed, he was seized, examined, sent to the Tower of London, and dealt withall as you have heard; all the favour that was extended to him more then to others being the not quartering of him, which was as much as nothing. The heads of Major Generall Harrison and Cheife Justice Cooke were set on Westminster Hall, Colonell Danyell Axtell's on the Parlament Howse. Mr. Cary's body was graunted to his freinds. The rest of those heads and lymbs were set upon the bridge and gates of London.

Thus did these blood-leeches drinke the blood of the precious Saints of the Lord, shedding it like water upon the ground. But the Lord, who bottles up their teares, will also manifest that their blood is pretious in his sight. And though he suffers his people to drinke of the cupp of his wrath, the dreggs thereof are reserved for his and their implacable enemyes; and the shamefull spewing shall be upon all their glory.

Captaine William Howlet being accused and prosecuted for having cut off the King's head, or at least for having bin one of those who were upon the scaffold, disguised, at the tyme that the execution was done, though severall witnesses testifyed that Gregory Brandon the Common Hangman had confessed he executed the sentence that passed upon the King, yet the jury, of which Sir Thomas Allen was foreman, declared him guilty. But the Court, sensible of the wronge done him, got his reprieve.

CHAPTER SIX

Before this Courte also were tryed those eighteene who had rendred themselves upon the proclamation published by the advice of the two Howses. And though they were excepted out of the act of indemnity as to life and estate, yet was provission made by the said act that, if found guilty, the sentence should not be executed against them as to life, save as should be declared by an act of Parlament; the names of whom were, Sir Hardress Waller, Mr. William Heviningham, Alderman Isaac Pennington, Colonell Henry Martyn, Mr. Gilbert Millington, Colonell Robert Tichborne, Colonell Owen Rowe, Colonell George Fleetwood, Colonell Robert Lilborne, Mr. Henry Smyth, Colonell Edmund Harvey, **889** Colonell John Downes, Colonell Vincent Potter, Mr. Augustine Garland, Mr. Symon Mayne, Colonell James Temple, Mr. Temple and Colonell Thomas Wayte. Sir Hardress Waller, as you heard before, confessed the inditement. So did Colonell Fleetwood. The rest at first pleaded not guilty. But when they came particcularly to plead for themselves, Colonell Tichbourne, Colonell Downes, Colonell Harvey and severall others (whether out of feare of death, love of life, hopes of favour, or being under a temptation by reason of old age, I cannot say) pleaded ignorance, and acknowledged the guilt, but denied the mallice. Some others, as Colonell James Temple, Mr. Peter Temple and Colonell Vincent Potter, confessed matter of fact, but denied the guilt; amongst which last number was Colonell Henry Martyn, who in shorte spake as much as could be said in that case, considering what before the Courte had overruled. He being charged with signing and sealing the praecept for summoning the Courte, and the warrant for execution, and for sitting almost every day, and particcularly the day of sentence, answered that he declyned not a confession as to matter of fact, the mallice set aside. But being told by the Courte that mallice is implyed by the law in the act itselfe, and it being observed by the droling councell that he was of oppinion a man might sit upon the death of the King, sentence him to death, signe a warrant for his execution, meekely, innocently, charitably and honestly, he replyed, I shall not presume to compare my knowledge in the law with that of the learned gentleman, but according to that poore understanding of the law of England that I was capable of, there is no fact that he can name that is a cryme in itselfe but as it is circumstantiated. Of killing a watchman, which had bin instanced, a watchman may be killed in not doing his office, and yet no murder.

But the councell, to prove that he did it mallitiously, produceth one to testify he did it merrily, sporting with Leiftenant Generall Cromwell at the tyme of signing the warrant; to which Colonell Martin replyed, That doth not imply mallice. And being charged that he advised that if the King demaunded by what authority he was brought to tryall, it should be answered, In the name of the Commons and Parlament of England, he answering that the comission by which they sate ran in that style and in that name, and therefore that it could be no great matter to move it might be so sayd, the councell (finding their aggravations so lightly blowne off) made up with passion what they wanted in the weight of reason; one of them, to wit the Sollicitour Generall, saying that all good people doe abhorr that action, and that he was sorry to see so little repentance; whereunto Mr. Martyn, with much temper and judgement, replyed, I hope that which is urged by the learned councell will not have that impression upon the Courte and jury that it seemes to have, as if I were obstinate in a thinge apparently ill. If it were possible for that blood to be in the body againe, and every dropp that was shedd in the late warres, I could wish it with all my heart. But I **890** hope it's lawfull to offer, in my owne deffence, that when I did it, I thought I might doe it. There was the Howse of Commons as I understood it. Perhaps your Lordships thinke it was not a Howse of Commons, but it was then the supreame authority of England. It was so reputed at home and abroade. My Lord, I suppose he that gives obedience to the authority in being de facto, whether de jure or no, I thinke is of a peaceable disposition, and farr from a traytour. There was a statue made in Henry the 7th's tyme, wherein it is provided that whosoever was in armes for the King de facto, he should be indemnifyed, though that King de facto was not so de jure. And if the supreame officer de facto can justify a warr (the most pernitious remedy that was ever adjudged by mankind, be the cause what it will), I presume the supreame authority of England may justify a judicature, though it be but an authority de facto. If it be sayd that it is but a third estate, or a small parcell of that, it was all that was extant. And I have heard lawyers say, that if there be comons appartenant to a tennant, and that the tenement be all burnt downe, except a small stick, the comons belonge to that one small peece, as it did to the tenement when all standing.

I shall humbly offer to consideration, whether the King were King indeed, such a one whose peace, crowne and dignityes were concerned in publique matters. He was not in execution of his office, he was a prysoner. I desire further that the jury would take notice, that though I am accused in the name of the King, yet if I be acquitted the King is not cast. It concernes not the King that the prysoner bee condemned, it concernes him that the prysoner be tryed. It is as much to his interest, crowne and dignity that the innocent be acquitted, as that the nocent be condemned. But notwithstanding this, those bloody conspyratours, having not the feare of God, remembrance of their ancestors, nor love unto their owne, their posterity, and country's libertyes before their eyes, but sacrificing their consciences to serve the lusts of a tyrant, that with and under him they may wallow in the myre of their owne corruption and enjoy their carnall and deveillish interests, and to that end crush what in them lyes the faith-full witness on the behalfe of the seede of the woman (which is to breake the serpent's head, and destroy all his spawne), declare them guilty of treason, and pronounce sentence of death accordingly.

But blessed be the Lord, he who is the infallible judge, in his holy law to which none may add, and from which none may diminish, doth not condemne those whom man hath judged, and that he hath enabled such of those, whom he hath called forth to seale the justice of this act with their blood, to doe it with much cheerefulness and satisfaction. But though the word of God be most cleare in this case, and his providence no less, and the King's party already in prynt affirmed that Mr. Hollis and his party had murthered the King (to wit in making warr upon him, and in dividing him in his pollitique capacity from his naturall), and in that Mr. Love, a leading minis-ter **891** amongst them, had at Uxbridge preached in his sermon that no peace could be made with that party till satisfaction were made for the blood that had bin shed (rather then those who sentenced him to death, and ordered his execution, yea then he who cut off his head, the former making of him no king, and the latter *makeing of him only noe* man, as they were bound to doe in case guilty of blood), yet some of these are not only satisfyed that these poore lambs should be slaughtered, but assist, *as in the condemning of them, soe in conducting of them to* the butchery.

Yea, such effect had the Declaration which Charles Steward lately published, for the composing of the differences betweene the episco-pall and presbyterian party, upon the ministers of the Reformed Churches in France, that two of the cheife of them (viz. Mr. Drelin-quort, and Mr. Langley of Canne in Normandy), by letters pretended to be sent to some of their relations, and published in prynt, express their great joy for the restitution of Charles Steward to his throne, the great hopes they have of his zeale for the Protestant religion, and great satisfaction they have in his declaration for the accomodating of the difference between episcopacy and presbytery (who, as one of them affirmes, agree in their fidelity to monarchy, and to him the monarch), and their great joy for the suppression of the sectarian party, and their desire that if ever they stirred againe they might be dissipated and confounded. Thus doth desire of domination blynd the eyes, and corrupt the heart. And for atteyning and preserving this sweete morsell, one man becomes a wolfe to another, one Christian to another, yea to themselves. And for to ryde in the chariot with the tyrants of the earth, yea though it be but behynde the chariot, they will stretch their charity upon the tenterhookes towards some, whilest in the meanetyme they scruple not to teare in peeces and devoure those who (their owne consciences tells them) have more of the spirit of God in them, and are more righteous, then themselves.

But a little to take a veiu of the ground of theise great hopes, Mr. Robert Long (one of his party) saith, The King is a good Protestant. The like doth Dr. Coussins, who himselfe was accused above twenty yeares since, before the Parliament, for his inclynation to superstition and popery. But the Lady Isabella Thin presents the King's remembrance to Mr. Langley, and his desires to him that he would pray for him; having bin once incognito to heare him, which many professed papists declyne not to doe, coming more for curiosity then for conscience sake. And if that commission were really given to the lady, in such a day as this, when religion by too many great professours was made a stalking-horse, it's no infallible marke of saintshipp underhand to send a complement of that nature to a leading man of a party, who as thinges stood might be instrumentall to helpe to set a crowne upon the head of him who sent it (especially when the same person bid open and constant defyance to those churches whose prayers he is sayd to have desired, by refusing ever to come amongst them, though earnestly pressed by some of his owne party to dissemble himselfe so farr as to doe it).

Yea so wilfully blynd are these men, that the preists and Jesuits acknowledging Charles Steward to be of the popish religion is made use of by them to prove the contrary. For, say they, if it were so, theise sophisters would not owne it. And they therefore give it forth to cast a prejudice upon him, and so obstruct his retorne, knowing how much that will turne to their ruine. But **892** a little time and patience will pluck off this vizard, and make these men sensible of their errour and folly, to give their credulity no worse name. But the Lady Turene desires this comendation to be given of him. And it serves the present turne. For if he be not of our party, it's hoped this may enclyne him to be, and therefore it's thought fit thus to represent him and others. But the tyme is approaching wherein all flesh shall appeare to be as grass, and the Lord alone shall be glorifyed, when all idols shall be discovered to be vaine, and those who trust in them to be like unto them.

This same spirit and principle yet prevayling in the secluded members, who presumed of their power to sway this Convention as they had formerly done the Parliament, propose their thankes to be

presented to their King for the accomodation proposed in the said
Declaration, and a comittee to be named for the preparing of an act
for the consideration of the Howse to the like effect, that so it might
be put into a law. For the bisshops and Charles Steward being agreed
in this juggle, the latter was permitted (for the quieting of tumultuous
spirits) to publish this Declaration for the present. And the other was
to be winked at in proceeding directly contrary thereto, for that the
King's Declaration could not supercede a law, which they affirmed
to justify them in what they did; for the prevention of which, the committee was called upon to make their reporte, which they were ready
to doe, and a day was appointed for the same. But the tyme being
come for the taking off the vizard, the King and episcopall party,
strongly uniting themselves against it, by proposing some other thinge
of a contrary nature, gave such a checque to that reporte that it was
not thought fit to press it any more, and so all that hopes vanished,
and the mountaine brought forth its mouse.

So high were the episcopall party growne (most of the army being
now disbanded (*notwithstanding the faire promises they had both from Monke
and the Kinge*), *all but Monke's one regiment of foote, having noe other reward
for their treachery but the payment of their arreares, and liberty to trade as
freemen in any corporation; which is also accompanyed with a [branch?] of
their trechery in their being owned to have bin instruments of the King and establishment, who (by the absolution that there is mentioned from their former rebellion) owne themselves to have ben traytors against the King, as they have ben
since to the Parliament; which the King's party observeing, thought not fit to
trust them, but being constrained to keepe on foote Monke's regiment, hee rayseth
a new one, with a guard of horse for the ballanceing of them; by which meanes
they looking on themselves surely settled, Colonell [Russh?] commanding the
regiment of foote, and the Lord Oxford that of horse, [and?] both of them being
highly engaged to their interest, they act for other ..., and haveing a guard
of horse for the King comanded by Gerard*), that Prinne, who was a great
instrument in disbanding the army, beginning to discover himselfe
fooled in his hopes, for desiring (upon the making of his report of the
numbers of regiments that were disbanded) that the Howse would
be carefull of doing those thinges which might draw them together
againe, was called upon with much earnestness to explaine and give
satisfaction; and it's thought had bin called to the barr, had not the
Howse rissen in some disorder.

Notwithstanding which, such an infatuation was upon this Convention, though called by a Commonwealth writ, that they continue,
as they began, to act diametrically opposite to the interest of those
by whom they were intrusted. And as if they had a minde to put the
people out of any hopes of remedy (parlaments being their usuall
refuge), besides the extraordinary sommes of money which they

charged the people with for the disbanding of the army and paying the navy, they present to the King the customs and excise during his life; which they would never have done, had they had the least sense of their owne or posterity's welfare. Yea though, before the passing of the act of indemnity, they seemed somewhat sensible of their being in honour engaged to make provission for the security of the lives of those of the King's judges who had rendred themselves into their hands (upon the proclamation which they had advised their King to publish), now, having slubbered over that business and **893** put it off their hands, though these poore trappand gentlemen lye under a sentence of condemnation, wayting for their resolution which they implicitely promised in their favour, they make not the least provission for them; and in the meanetyme execute the height of rage against those whose integrity to the publique cause doth and will rise up in judgement against them, and pass a pretended act of parlament for the atteinting of those of the King's judges, and some others, who were excepted out of their act, and had fled and escaped out of their hands, that they may dip their hands imediately in this innocent blood; wherein were many unusuall and unheard of clauses, amongst others that all trusts for their use should be forfeited. But the Duke of Yorke, upon whom all those confiscated estates were bestowed, must be supplyed, it matters not how, for the maintenance of himselfe and whores.

Yea so barbarous were these men growne that they tryumph over the bones of those whom they durst not looke in the face whilest living, some whereof had bin interred above ten yeares. They order the bodyes of Serjeant Bradshaw, President of the High Court of Justice, of Deputy Ireton, that emynent, faithfull, zealous, able, valliant and industrious servant of the Lord, to be taken up, dragd to Tyburne, and there to be hanged; which was accordingly as inhumanely executed so farr as they could. But the wise providence of God so ordred it that his body being interred in Ireland, that of Mrs. Claypoole's, a great freind of Charles Steward, was treated as his should have bin. The like execution had their order as to the corps of Generall Cromwell, not for having contracted the guilt of that, and the blood of thousands more, by betraying the cause and trust reposed in him, and sacrificing it to his own lustes, but for doing that which the law of God commanded to be done; which three heads are set upon poles on Westminster Hall, President Bradshaw's in the midst, the other two on each side. Colonell Pride's body was ordered to be so treated, but this order was not executed.

But as the Lord is pleased to permit his owne worke at present to be borne downe by a forme of justice, so doth he not suffer his bloody enemyes to escape the stroake of his imediate judgements. For as he had avenged himselfe on the Duke of Gloucester for the bloody motions he had made against his servants, marquing him at the tyme of his death with a bloody spot in his brest, so doth he vissit the Princess of Orrange (who had lately betrayed the little strength the Protestants had in France, by ordering the forte and towne of Orrange to be delivered into that King's hand), and with her life, which he takes away by the same disease that her brother dyed of. He suffered her to goe out in a snuffe; divers of the King's owne party confidently affirming that, though not marryed, yet she was great with childe when she dyed. And the French Gazet, which useth not to speake the worst of that tribe, expresseth more joy then sorrow for her death, alleadging that it was better she should dye then live to marry young Germin, which she was resolved to have done, her familly being too much addicted to that race.

The Duke of York also, **894** though he lives to doe more mischeife, yet by reason of the vitiousness, falsehood, giddy-headedness, and the disobleidging courses he takes, stinks in the nostrills of his owne party. You may judge of the rest by this one passadge, viz. the disposall of himselfe in marriadge, the sollemnest action of a man's life (to mention nothing of the familly of which his wife is, though of one of no great eminence amongst the gentry, and by whom he can have no hopes to gaine an interest, a daughter to one whom his mother hates and scornes, nor of his making her a whore before he marryed her). But that he should suffer her to pass for a whore till after she was brought to bedd; that he should suffer one Mr. Bartley, and as some say encouradge him, being a servant of his, to give forth publiquely that it might be his child, as well as the Duke's, for that himselfe and many more had layen with her, as well as his master; and after all this, that he had sent some to be present at Worcester Howse at her delivery, to observe whether it were not a fictitious childe, he should make her his wife, and continue the said Barteley his servant, I am perswaded the next age will not credit. And that it may appeare they are all birds of the same nest (participating in all these princely virtues), as he who is by them styled their King had fower or five bastards whilst he was abroad, which he publiquely ownes, so now doth he corrupt as many as he can, both of marryed and unmarryed weomen, being past all shame or sense of honour, not mynding his word of oath *to God or man*. I shall not mention heer anythinge of the falsehood and bloodyness of his disposition and practice, nor of the like quallifications of his ancestors, they being all well knowne to those amongst whom they lived in England and Scotland. And so are the judgements of the Lord which followed them where ever they went, a great plague succeeding the comming in of King James, and the like that of King Charles.

And it's observable that when hee, very desirous to have his statue cut in stone by that famous ingraver *Barnardino* at Rome, had sent severall pieces drawne by choyce hands, as Vandike and others, for his better direction therein, the said *Barnardino* delayd the dispatch thereof till, upon letters from England complayning thereof, he was pressed thereunto by the Pope and Cardinall Barbarino, who was entituled the Protector of the English. And when, upon much importunity, he gave an account to those who had set him on worke that he had finished it, hee said, There are so many cross-angles in the physiognomy of him for whom it's cut, that he would come to some ill end. And when the same statue was brought into England, being at the tyme when the Queene was going beyond sea to assist the King with forces and armes against the Parlament (and to that end carryed with her the crowne jewels), he, having given order to have it set up in his howse at Greenewich, after he had accompanyed the **895** Queene to Dover, came thither to see it. And whilest he was looking [on?] it, a bird (the wyndow of the chamber being open) flew against it, and imediately blood ran downe the face of the statue. But that which was the most remarkable was, that after the blood was wiped off by the Earle of Arrundell, which he did with his hand-chercher, that it should run downe afresh; which Mr. Babington, the Keeper of the Howse at Greenewich, assured Mr. Love, a member of parlaiment and my very good freind, it did. But why doe I mention these darke prognostications, when his bloody reigne was so legible, in his betraying the Protestants in France, and therein contracting the guilt of their blood; also in his countenancing and favouring the massacring of so many hundred thousands in Ireland, and in the unnaturall and cruell warr that he mainteyned for many yeares together against the Parlament and people of England and Scotland?

And now, by reason of our unworthy retorne for all our deliverancyes and merceys the Lord voutsafed us, he is pleased (after his people whom he had imployed in his worke were delivered to the slaughter), that they might seale the righteousness and justice of his cause with their dearest blood, yet further to suffer that the Queene, the relict as well as the counsellour and encourager of her husband the King in those treacherous and bloody enterprizes, should come into England to tryumph over the dead bodyes of the Lord's faithfull witnesses; whose conscience telling her that vengeance would pursue her, useth her black art for the prevention or at least delaying thereof. And to that end it's given out upon her landing that the Quakers had a designe of seizing her, that so a couler may be had for the securing of them; under which pretext many honest men were clapt up. Those in the Howse of Commons, many whereof were members of the Parlament who accused her of high treason, now congratulate her retorne, and present her mayden daughter with ten thousand pounds. But notwithstanding their flattery, and that they had espoused this interest by sacrificing to it the blood of the innocent, yet not being fully principled for episcopacy (which is to act its next parte upon this Anti-Christian stage), it's thought fit they should receive their dischardge, which is beforehand declared unto them to be intended on the 24th December; against which tyme it's desired that all bills under consideration may be in a readyness for the royall assent.

And lest the people should take occasion, upon the dissolution of this assembly, to get into a body for the asserting of their old principles and interest, which they were daily more and more convinced it was their duty and wisedome to owne and promote (it now being vissible they were dispoyled not only of the publique exercise of their religion, and of the enjoyment of their civill libertyes, but of the estates which they had purchased, many of them, being hitherto fedd with hopes, but now were plainly told that the King had his owne **896** freinds to gratify, and not those who had bin his enemyes), a great plot againe was pretended to be carrying on. And this must be for seizing of the King and the Tower of London, putting of the Queene and all the French to the sword, and for the restoring of the Great Parlament. Upon this pretence many are secured about London and throughout all England, principally those who might be likely to be usefull in the heading of the souldiery; something being contrived to be evidenced against one of Colonell Rossiter's troope, as if he should hint at some designe for the drawing of the army together, upon dissatisfaction of the present posture of affaires. Major Generall Overton, Colonell Desbrow, Colonell Salmon, Leiftenant Colonell Farley, Major Whitby and severall others are clapt up in London. Colonell Duckenfeild, Major Anthony Morgan and severall others were imprysoned in the country. Colonell Kempson and many others were imprysoned, because unfree to take the oaths of allegiance and supremacy.

The Queene, more out of discontent (she not being as yet able to worke her son to follow her counsells, and to declyne those of Hide's) then out of feare of any designe that was carryed on against her (it being knowne to her and everyone else that this plot was a meere fiction), retornes with her daughter and Germaine to France. As she lay at Portsmouth for a passadge, her daughter was vissited with the smallpoxe, of which as soone as she was recovered the Queene held on her journey. The difference betweene her and Hyde was so high and vissible, that though (by the great importunity of her son Charles) she permitted the Duke of Yorke's wife to come into her presence, which till then she refused to doe, it was observed she never spake to her to sit downe, but that, applying herselfe to other company there

present, soone after went out of the roome, without any respect shewed
to her, not thinking her worthy to be treated as a daughter.

At the dissolution of this mock monstrous Parlament, Sir Harbottle
Grimstone, who had acted the parte of Speaker of the Howse of Commons, vents himselfe to their King in high flattering expressions, as
if he were the life of the nation, the breath of their nostrills. And Hide,
called the Chancellor and Speaker of the Howse of Lords, is not ungratefull in his retorne, speaking on the behalfe of their King;
applauding their prudence and wisedome in his Restauration, and
their dilligent endeavours to give his Majesty satisfaction in setling
thinges so as might prevent the breaking forth of new disturbances
and troubles; yet not without   **897** some reflection upon them, for
their not having invested the King with the militia, nor having declared anythinge therein, but leaving it as uncerteine as they found
it, and so consequently a foundation of new difference, it having bin
the great bone of contention during the late warrs; telling them that
for want thereof, the King for the preserving of the peace of the nation
would be constrayned to establish it for the present, as formerly his
praedecessour had done, but that he was resolved to exercise all
moderation therein.

And for the convincing them of the necessity of this arbitrary procedure, according to the old court pollicy, he layes before them the
late plot which they themselves had framed. And then (as Cromwell,
when he spoake upon the like occation of the dissatisfaction of some
with his usurpation, sayd they were as inconsiderable to give it any
disturbance as the motes in the sunbeames were to hynder it from
shyning), so now Hide observes they were only the lees of the people
who were engaged in this conspiracy *to disturb the peace of the nation,
and to settle the governement in the way* of a Comonwealth; but that seeing
it was not wisedome to neglect small beginnings, and that for the
carrying on of this designe all thinges were brought even to an head
(I having bin nominated by them to have bin designed to have commanded two thousand five hundred men, that were even ready to
have drawne together to have seized the Tower of London, *as he
affirmed*, and had as many enlisted under my command for the carrying
on of this worke in the westerne partes of England, and another, whom
he named not, having the like number enlisted under him in the North
for the same purpose), he thought it prudent to put the nation into
a posture for the prevention of those inconveniencyes.

For the better collouring of these falsehoods, all places where it
might be suspected I lay concealed were searched for me. My poore
wife was severall tymes plundered of her waring clothes. My brother
Kempson his lodgings were ransacked, and he robd of above twenty
pounds worth of goods. All my writings which lay at a freind's howse,

by reason of the great rewards that were promissed to any who should discover me, were seised by the treachery of a servant in that howse, together with fowerscore pounds worth of goods apperteyning to the said freind; the most parte of which were restored. My servant who wayted upon me in my chamber was plundered and imprysoned in the Gatehowse, and lay there ten weekes because he told them not where I was. But though the Lord was pleased to permit this wicked crew to lay their hands upon my estate and relations, yet as in mercey he suffered them not to touch my person, so did he support my deare wife, and all others related to me, so gratiously, that none of them that ever I heard of murmured under his hand. And some of them, I mention it to his prayse, rejoyced that they were thought worthy to suffer for his name. And for my parte, to be judged **898** worthy to be one of the number of the suffering people of God, who desire to releeve themselves and others from the yoakes under which they are, as soone as the Lord opens a way, though they are termed the lees of the people by those in power, I esteeme it more to my reputation and honour then for having contracted the guilt of the blood of thousands and betrayed the cause of the Lord; yea, upon any tearmes whatsoever to have had the greatest title that the usurper takes upon him to bestow upon his flatterers, and those who are partakers with him in his treachery and oppression.

This mock Parlament being thus put an end to, and Charles Steward gone to Portsmouth to accompany his mother so farr on the way to France, Mr. Venner a wyne-cooper in London, and about the number of fifty others, being satisfyed in their spirits that the tyme of the Lord was come for the giving of the kingdoms of the earth to the Saints of the most high, and that the Lord had promissed not to doe his worke by might or power but by his spirit, and that the little stone hewed out of the mountaine without hands should breake in peeces the mountaines of the earth, they though a small number should be assisted by the Lord to be instrumentall in this great worke, as they haveing attempted to get into a body for that end in the tyme of Cromwell, as hath bin formerly mentioned, and now finding whoredome, idolatry, treachery, blood-guiltyness and all manner of iniquity abound, resolved to draw together, at a tyme prefixed, in the citty of London; which nine and twenty of them did, with musquets, pikes, and such other instruments as they thought most convenient; with which small number, that being the most I ever heard were together of them, they march up and downe in the night through the Citty, and come to one of the gates; where being examined by the guard, who they were and for whome, they sayd, For King Jesus. And being further asked what they would have, they said they would have the limbes and members of the Saints taken downe. But the guard refusing to give way thereto, saying it should not be done till the morning, they retired into the Citty, and keeping in a body dispersed those who were got together to oppose them, marching up and downe the streetes till towards the morning; at which tyme they marched to a wood neare   about five myles distant from London, where next day they were begirt by a party of Charles Steward's souldiers comanded by Sir Thomas Sands.

But the Lord suffered none of them at that tyme to be seized; which, together with the success they had the former night in the Citty, encouraged   **899** them to put their designe on foote the second tyme. And to that end they march into the Citty two nights after. And being assaulted by Charles Steward's guard of horse, they put the guard to a shamefull flight, and gave such an allarum to the Court that the two infamous Dukes, Yorke and Aubermale, and all the force they could make, were drawne forth to suppress this dangerous conspiracy. In the meanewhile they, marching through the Citty, declare for the Lord Jesus, and against Charles Steward, and the apostate Browne (then executing the power of the Mayor of London). They were met neare Leadenhall by two of the trayned bands of the Citty; who being chardged and fyred upon by the nine and twenty were put to a disorderly retreate, even as farr as Wood Streete; this small number pursuing their advantadge and killing some of them, one of the captaines of the said two companyes being (for his security) with some others got into a belcony to observe the event. But these poore well-meaning men being overpowred and encompassed by great multitudes of men, after they had done more then could be expected from so small a number, Mr. Venner, who was their Captaine (and had at the beginning of their attempt encouraged them in their undertaking with a speech in the streete after they were gathered together, and recomended them and their affaire to the blessing of God by prayer), being rendred unserviceable by reason of the many wounds he had received, and in consequence being taken prysoner, and some others being slayne, the rest were necessited to make their retreate; in which severall of them were taken prysoners. Five or six of them, being got into a howse and pursued, made the best defense they could, refusing to take quarter till all of them were slaine, except two; who having nothing left to deffend themselves, were seized. But one of them, taking the advantadge of his guard's weapon, had like to have slayne him, but being prevented was secured. In the whole, about fifteene were taken prysoners and sent to Newgate; amongst which Captaine Venner was desperately wounded, as also were some of the others. About 4 or 5 of them were slayne.

Upon their examination, they justifyed that not above fifty had knowledge of the designe, and that, as they judged, they had a call

from God to doe what they had done. At their pleadings for their
lives, they alleadged they had not comitted by the law of the land
any treason against Charles Steward, because he was not crowned,
and untill then no King. But judge and jury being packt by those
whose enemyes they had declared themselves to be, they had little
hopes, by anythinge could be said, to move them from the resolution
they had of taking away their lives. Thirteene of them were executed,
to wit Mr. Venner, John Cullin, Stephen Hall, William Asham,
John Tod, John *Elson*, William Corbet, Thomas Harris, John
Gardner,   **900** and John Gaoler, etc.; all dying in full assurance of
the Lord's sudden appearance for the reviving of his cause, and the
advancing of the scepter of his deare son. Captaine Venner and
another of them, after they were hanged, were quartered according
to the bloody and tyrannicall custome. The other eleaven, by the
peculiar order of Charles Steward, had their heads cut off, which with
the other two were set upon London Bridge. It's necessary that the
word of the Lord, which saith, *20 Rev. 4*, that the witnesses *that* shall
be put to death *are to be beheaded*, and their bodyes to be exposed to
the veiu of all nations, be accomplished, 11 Re. 9. One of those who
was condemned, when asked what he had to say why sentence should
not be pronounced against him, sayd he hoped the Lord would put
it into the King's heart to shew mercy. The Lord was pleased so
to overrule the heart of that man of blood, that this, and another man's
life who was condemned, were spared.

I dare not say but that these good men might have satisfaction in
what they did, being perswaded in their consciences that they had
a call from the Lord thereto, they making his glory their principall
end therein. Yet I judge it very adviseable in matters of so great weight
(wherein not only our lives and libertyes are concerned, but those
in some degree of all the Lord's people) to be carefull wee make not
haste, in the procuring of what is in its own nature lawfull (yea most
desirable), but, as we have his glory as our cheife ayme, so that we
make use of such meanes as he approves of, and directs unto, for the
accomplishment thereof. But though the Lord was not pleased fully
to owne the endeavours of those good men at this tyme, yet did it
much dampe the spirit of the prophane Court party to observe such
high courradge and resolution amongst those they thought wholy
subdued and trodden under foote, and such an indifferency in those
of the citty of London towards the suppressing of them; whereby they
visibly discovered they apprehended not their interest so much concerned in that of the Court, as of late they had done. However, that
it may be thought an acceptable service in the Citty, as the Duke
of Yorke acknowledged Brown the Mayor's forwardness therein, so
did those of the militia that of Captaine Henshaw's, who comanded

one of the trained bands, ordering their sayd acknowledgement to be entred for his honour upon their bookes. But let him and them know, that the account of this blood is entred in a booke which they must be tryed by at the last day, when all other records shall be burnt with fire, and the judgement which these martyrs have contended for shall be given to the Saints of the most high. In the meanetyme the measure of the Amorites is filling up, whereunto without doubt this pretious blood doth much contribute.

In Ireland the Convention, which acted in most thinges as a parlament, deported itselfe much after the same rate with that of England, flattering and fawning upon Charles Steward, who they could not but see watched for an opportunity to dispossess them of **901** their estates (the proprietours invested by authority of Parlament making up the greatest parte of that assembly, and he being engaged, by the articles which the Earle of Ormond made on his behalfe with the Irish rebells, to restore them to their lands). But the tyme was not come to pull of his masque, Monke and Coote having yet too great an interest in the sayd lands, and in the army, to be disobleiged. And therefore, till the Earl of Ormond can be sent over his Leiftenant, this intention must be dissembled. And the Lord Roberts having refused to goe as Deputy, the Lord Broghill, Sir Maurice Eustace who acts the parte of Chancellour, and Sir Charles Coote, or any two of them, are entrusted with that power as Justices. This Convention, notwithstanding the experience they had of the villany of the King in countenancing (if not encouradging) the rebellion, and that he had acted by his owne power in opposition to the authority of Parlament, and preferred his owne personall and arbitrary power before the peace, happyness and welfare of the whole Protestant and English interest, now thinke fit to order the taking of the fyle of all those proceedings, since the yeare 1641, against the Earle of Strafford, the Bisshop of Derry, now called Archbisshop of Armagh, and others; thereby disowning those necessary proceedings that then the three nations thought fit to take for the vindication of their libertyes. And that they may in some thinges outvye that of Westminster, they, in an act which they agree to pass against the late King's judges, provide that none of their sonnes shall be capable of bearing any office in the Commonwealth, excepting notwithstanding out of the same proviso the son of Mr. Thomas Scot (in whose justification the father vented himselfe with so much passion against me in Parlament); the reason of which favour is expressed to be the service he did in the restitution of his Majesty, in the opposition which he made to me at Duncanon forte.

That apostate Middleton, being constituted Charles Steward's principle agent in Scotland (a fit servant for such a master), gets a Convention, which he calls a Parlament, to be chosen, consisting of

such members as were wholy devoted to his service. The Earle of
Argile and the Laird Swinton, who were seized as aforementioned,
are sent by sea to Scotland, to be there butchered under a forme of
justice.

About the latter end of January, that famous patriot Sir Arthur
Haslerigg, who brought in the bill for setling of the militia by Parlament, one of the five members that was accused of by the King of
high treason and endeavoured by him to be forced out of the Howse,
who continued a faithfull and hearty wel-wissher to the interest of
the Commonwealth from the beginning of the troubles (though not
so happy alwayes to light upon the best meanes conducing thereto),
being seized and imprysoned in the Tower (as hath bin related), finding himselfe disappointed of the hopes he had in relation to the
publique good, and of his owne particcular concernements, and that
(by reason of his too much credulity) he had bin made use of by
Monke to be greatly instrumentall therein, with the sad and mellan-
cholly thoughts thereof he was so affected, that it proved so great a
burthen to   **902**   his spirit that he sunke under the weight, and there
ended his dayes. A shipp was provided, before the coming in of
Charles Steward, for my couzen Wallop, Sir Arthur Haslerigg and
Mr. Love, to have transported them. But the night before they intended
to sett sayle, Sir Arthur (I know not upon what vaine hopes), declaring he knew not anythinge he had done which he durst not justify,
resolved to stay; which was also the resolution of my couzen Wallop
(it may be by reason of the temptation of their great estates); so that
Mr. Nicholas Love was constrained to hold on his voyage alone, he
being resolved not to trust the mercey of enraged beastes of prey.

And as the goodness of the Lord was seene in directing him thereto,
so was it eminently in protecting him therein. For going as a merchant
of a shipp laden with corne for Norway, he was seized by a man of
warr of Ostend; who coming aboard his shipp, and discovering he
was a fugitive of England, notwithstanding, the Lord so overruled
his heart that he layd no hands on him, nor anythinge that he had,
though he daily seized all English shipps he could. Yea, when two
more of his companions were come to him, the master of the vessell
(wherein Mr. Love was) overheard the captaine of the first vessell
that came up to him, pleading with the other two captaines within
the cabbin, and disswading them from seizing the vessell or the carrying of him prysoner; urging, as a reason against doing of the latter,
that thereby they might ruyne him, and doe themselves no good. Thus
was he preserved from this eminent danger, presenting the said captaine only with some tobacco and a tobacco box which he liked, and
with some busshels of malt which he desired for his poultrey which
he had on board. This deliverance was so great, that when he related

it in Norway he was hardly beleeved. And when from thence, some monthes after, he arrived at Hamburgh, being tossed upon the seaes in a great storme (the same in which so many Dutch vessells and nine thousand of their marineers were cast away), a shipp which had but ten marryners in her sinking before their eyes, the Lord made them instrumentall to save the lives of those men, and soone after made use of those very men to save the shipp, and the lives of those who preserved theirs; the storme encreasing to such an height, and the shipp growne so leaky, that without supply of men it had bin imposs-ible to have preserved her, or themselves.

This allarum given by the 29 Fifth Monarchy men, and that of the plot which was of their owne framing, served them for three pur-poses. First, for the securing and imprysoning of many thousands, which they called phanaticques, to the filling of all prysons, hospitalls and halls about London, and in the country; where they for a long tyme refused to dischardge them, before they tooke the oaths of alle-giance and supreamacy, and gave security for their **903** peaceable living and appearance when called; which conditions, though some submitted themselves too, yet others refused, and afterwards were dis-charged without it. Secondly, for the searching for and seizing of the armes of all those who were judged disaffected to the present usurpa-tion. Thirdly, for the denying of liberty to any congregationall meet-ings, alleadging the last rising to be a product of that indulgence.

And the presbyterians by this tyme discover that all the priviledge they were like to have was to be last [devoured?]. For though their King had published a Declaration in favour of them, yet, the last Con-vention refusing to put it into a law, what the episcopall party for-merly said, touching the invalidity of a proclamation when opposite to an established law, now is put in execution. And by discountenanc-ing theyr rivalls, they make appeare how inconsistent two suns are in one horison, and that they thought it their interest much rather to close with the popish then with the presbyterian party; Dr. Heylin one of their King's chaplins, *in a booke which he lately published, chardgeing Mr. Calvin with laying the foundation of the warr in England, and with owne-ing principles destructive to monarchy.* And a booke intitled Philanax Anglicanus, first written in Latin and then in English, asserting that rebell and presbyterian are inseparable, is dedicated to Dr. Shelden, then called Bisshop of London, after Archbisshop of Canterbury, lycensed to be printed, and commended, by his chaplin; the subject matter of which is takeing for graunted that kings are unaccountable, and to blame Swinglius, Calvin, Beza, Pareus, Melanchton, Luther, Buchanon, Knox, etc. for what they have sayd in opposition thereto; condemning the States of the Low Countryes for casting off the Span-ish yoke, and popish religion, and clearing Rome from such *dangerous* principles (the kinges and powers of the earth being at present, as it seemes, constituted according to their desire and interest). And Mr. Dureus, who had for many yeares endeavoured reconcilliation betweene the Calvinist and Lutheran against their common enemy the papist, that he might have a full taste of the principles and resolution of the Bisshop of London, who was looked upon as the intellectus agens of their King *in matter of religion*, acquaints him with certeine propositions lately put forth by the popish party in Germany for the accomodating of the difference betweene the papist and Protestant; one whereof being that auricular confession should not be imposed, but left ad libitum. The Bisshopp blaming that moderation, as a duty *judgeing that confession* absolutely necessary to be used, Mr. Dureus *thereby becomeing satisfyed in their intentions, and being* thereby destitute of all hopes for the promoting of his interest for the present in England, betakes himselfe to his work of accomodation beyond the seaes.

The 30th of January was appointed by an act of the last Convention to be kept annually a day of fast and prayer, that the sin of the nation may be pardoned for the murther (as they call it) of the late King, etc. At the observation of it, the publique meetings **904** were very thinne, those who understood what praying and fasting meant refusing to appeare there on that occasion, many of them seeking the Lord together that day for the making of them sensible of the cause of his judgements that were upon them, and for the removall both of the one and the other. And the prophane party, who spent their tyme in drinking and whoring, could not spare so much tyme from their debauchery. This was the day when the bodyes of President Bradshaw, Deputy Ireton and Oliver Cromwell (according as was ordered by the late Convention) were taken out of their coffins, and hangd at Tyburne about two of the clock; being first carryed to the Sessions Howse in the Old Baily, and there condemned. The popish party now begin to talke high. A Romish preist had the confidence to say to a relation of myne, who was prysoner in the Gatehowse, that no king had power over the conscience, but the church had; and that he beleeved within a month or little more all Christian churches would be reconcyled to them, and then their church goverment would soone regulate all manner of sectaryes in the world, who had begot such confusions in goverment, and rebellions against princes and monarchs.

To further this designe, a popish wife must be had for Charles Steward, for the driving on and strengthning of this confederacy. The Lord Digby, now Earle of Bristoll, is sent (as is supposed for that purpose) into Italy, to demaund in marriadge the Duke of Parma's daughter, as being a match of Spaine's proposing, whose interest it was then adjudged advisable to close with. And in his way it's sayd he was to give satisfaction to a count's daughter in Flaunders, by whom Charles Steward had two bastards, and unto whom (as was sayd) he had given an engagement of marriadge. But whilest he was about his embassy, Chancellour Hyde taking advantadge of Digby's absence, and wrought upon as is reported by the present of a considerable some of money, engageth the King to enter into a treaty of marriadge with the King of Portugal's sister; where was neither mony nor freinds to be had, he being at enmity with the Low Countryes, and the King of Spaine having already entred his teritoryes with a considerable army.

And, seeing the entry of the Queene of France into Paris was with great sollemnity, that the Court of England may appeare to be as vaine as they, this usurper wanting the reall propertyes of a majestrate, viz. *either a call from the Lord, or* a holy, just, and righteous spirit *to act for him*, it must be made up in ceremony and outward pompe. And therefore great preparations are for the crowning of him, whose honour the Lord was every day more and more laying in the dust. That superstitious order of making Knights of the Garter, to make the shew the greater, as also that of Knights of the Bath, must be cellebrated. The King is to ryde from the Tower through the citty of London to Westminster. The Citty amongst other thinges, for feare rather then love, contribute towards this pageantry the buylding of fower triumphall arches, the making of which by computation cost **905** them eight thousand pounds. And that there might not be [anythinge wanting?] to disobleidge all who were not infatuated like themselves, the ready mony which the courtiers had raked out of the bowells of the poore people must be sent to France, for the furnishing them with such accomodations for this Mashacado as were most costly and fantasticall, and little bought of the citty of London except what was taken up on trust.

And that they may not be behinde in Ireland to contribute towards the building up the Tower of Babell, the old vitious person the former Bisshop of Derry, now called Archbisshop of Armagh, at the consecration as they tearme it of some of their bisshops, doth it with as many superstitious and idolatrous ceremonyes as if he had received particcular direction therein from the Pope himselfe, causing such light and vaine songes to be sunge as *are hardly* found on a publique theatre. And these holy fathers, together with Sir Theophylus Jones and the rest of the Privy Councell, and the Justices, Sir Maurice Eustace, the Lord Broghill and Sir Charles Coote, set forth a proclamation against the meeting of presbyterians, independents, Quakers, and other phanaticall persons; in which it's observable that the presbyterians now leade the van amongst the phanaticall persons, and that the two last of the Justices having changed their additions (the one being now intituled the Earle of Orrery, the other Earle of Mountrath), they thinke it convenient to chandge their interests. In the body of this proclamation, that they may not be thought partiall in their proceedings, they joyned the papists with those other phanaticques who are prohibited to meete. The Convention declare also, seeing they are satisfied that there is a present want of mony for the army, over and above the custome and excise and the certeine and casuall revenue, they doe agree to rayse a some of mony towards the present supply.

The Spanish Embassadour endeavours to breake off this confederacy with Portugall, and proffers to give better conditions, and greater summes of mony, with the Duke of Parma's daughter, then he was to have with the King of Portugal's sister. But the French faction beares sway, the King being altogether Frenchifyed (not only being so by birth of the surer side, but also by education and inclynation), so as those of that nation are the persons principally promoted, and their fasshions and customes cheifly imitated; upon which account the common people express great hatred to the Court and that nation, and those who lately cryed, Hosanna, seeme now as ready to *cry*, Crucify. And that which gave a demonstration of the affection to the good old cause was the sympathy that was expressed by an assembly of people who were auditours of Dr. Wilkinson (formerly reputed a presbyterian), in their contributing, towards the supply of the necessityes of those who lay condemned in the Tower for having judged the late King to death, the summe of an hundred and fower score pounds, as they passed out of the publique meeting place; the reporte of which gave a great allarum **906** to the Court, and put them upon the renewing of their dilligence, for the strengthning of their party, for the choosing of members for that Parlament which was to meete in May next, for the citty of London; well knowing how much it concerned them to have such chosen as might favour their present designe, and how much the whole nation was guided by their example. Yet notwithstanding all they could doe of that kinde for the choyce of Browne, though then Mayor of the Citty, and Robinson the Leiftennant of the Tower, and some others of the same spirit, they were refused with scorne; and fower persons, viz. Alderman Foulke, Alderman Love, Mr. Jones, and *Mr. William Thompson*, two independents and two presbyterians, were chosen, all of them such as had adheared to the Parlament party, and were now by the courtiers reputed phanaticques. This choyce was so dissatisfactory to the Court, that notwithstanding the great expense the Citty had bin at for the erecting of the tryumphall arches and other extraordinary preparations for the coronation, the King would have gone from the Tower of London by water to Westminster, had not his owne vaine pomp bin more concerned therein then the satisfaction of the Citty. And least the choyce of the Citty should influence the country to doe the like, they seize the common pacquet to prevent the publication thereof, and hasten away dispatches to their owne party, to get themselves chosen per fas aut nefas; so that what betweene threats and bribes, and the power that sheriffs and other officers had in the elections who were of the King and gisshops' owne making, scarse any were permitted to be retorned who had ever owned the cause of the Parlament.

That which at the sollemnity of the coronation was most remarqueable that I heard of, was that at the chapple of Wyndsor, when the superstitious ceremonyes were performing, one of the fellows named declyned bowing to the altar: but the King demaunding who had preferred that person, it being told him the Lord Lotherdale, the sayd Lord importuned the poore man to streine his conscience in complyance with that ceremony, which notwithstanding he did he was soone after displaced. Another was, that Mr. Knightly a member of the Great Parlament, and Colonell Richard Ingoldsby one of the late King's judges, who sate at the Courte at the tyme of pronouncing the sentence against him, and signed and sealed the warrant for his execution, were two of those who with severall others performed those popish and superstitious ceremonyes that were accustomed to be used at the making of Knights of the Bath; observing foolish and vaine fasts, wearing the cordiallier's habits, offering at **907** the comunion table (which they call the high altar), bathing themselves in a superstitious manner, swearing to love the King above all earthly thinges (nor excepting their wives), and calling on the Lady Mary to assist them in the performance of the said oath. Mr. Knightly, having some remaynder of conscience, scrupled for a while the bowing at the altar, and, being prevayled with to doe it, was so troubled for having done it that (as it was supposed) it was a meanes to shorten his dayes, he dying soone after.

At the sollemnity of the riding from the Tower to Westminster Abby, the place of coronation, the bisshops' places were voyd, it being sayd they durst not ride in their habits for feare of the people. After the superstitious ceremony of annoynting their idoll (and the mocking of the people, in asking in a formall way, when they administered the oath to him, whether they would have this man to reigne over them) was passed, the coronation dynner was in Westminster Hall; where the champion Mr. Dimmock, armed de cap à pied, enters on horseback, challendging to fight with any person who should deny Charles Steward to be lawfull King of England. Many thousand persons would without doubt have entred the list, had not the Lord thought fit to permit that he should be backt with more then a just title, his champion, or his owne manhood to deffend it. The dinner was not halfe ended, before this mocke King was enforced to rise and run away to Whitehall, by reason of the unheard-of thunder, lightning and raine; which though his owne flatterers prophanely applyed to the greatning of their sollemnity, as if heaven itselfe exprest its joy thereat by the dischardge of their cannon, yet others, more understanding in the dispensations of the Lord, supposed it rather a testimony from heaven against the wickedness of those who would not only that he should rule over them, but were willing to make them a captaine to leade them into Egiptian bondage; from which the Lord by his providence plainly spake his desire to have delivered them.

CHAPTER SEVEN

The Queene, shortly after her retorne into France, marryes her daughter to the Duke of Anjou, brother to the King of France. The match with the King of Portugal's sister is resolved upon; which resolution Charles Steward, at the first meeting of his Convention which he calls a Parliament, acquaints them with, not as desiring their advice therein, or a probation thereof (thinking that below him), but in order to their providing of monyes for her reception, and for setling of his revenue. Those in the Howse of Comons order the sacrament of the Lord's Supper to be taken by all their members kneeling, which Colonell Norton **908** and Mr. Hampden, son to that famous patriot Mr. John Hampden, scrupled to doe. Alderman Love, one of the members in parlament for the citty of London, was voted out of the Howse for having spoken against the Booke of Common Prayer. And Gunning that popish preist (though passing under the name of prelaticall), pressing in a sermon he preached before the Howse to a reconcilliation with the church of Rome, speaking favourably of them, had the thankes of the Howse given him of his sermon, notwithstanding Mr. Morris one of the King's Secretaryes publiquely opposed it, saying he thought he expected none from them as yet before he had wonne the Howse to his oppinion, and therefore moved he might be sent to Rome for this thankes, for for his parte he had none to give him. Yea such hopes had the popish party now conceived of carrying the day, that the Lady Abbess of Fountarabeau, base daughter to Henry the 4th, sent into England to demaund the restitution of the lands there belonging to her nunnery, it being founded by one of our kinges who endowed it with lands in England. And an intimate freind of myne, going to see the English convent of monkes in Paris, found them full of hopes concerning England.

But it's not yet tyme to discover the bottom of the designe. For the present worke is to dash the hopes, and to suppresse the interest, of the presbyterians. And to this end the Marquess of Argyle, who upon that score, when their King tooke the Covenant to roote out prelacy and popery, did with his owne hand set the crowne upon his head in Scotland, is thought adviseable to be taken off. A Parlament of that nation, which Middleton that perfidious and apostate person had packed of interested members, must be instrumentall therein. They chardge him with many thinges he had done against the late King. But supposing all the world would crye out upon them, should they put him to death for what he did before the accord which he

had made with the present King, looking upon his crowning of him
as a sufficient indemnity for what was past, they chardge him for joyning with Cromwell in his usurpation, and for assisting of him in the
late chandge of goverment. But though he made it appeare he was
only passive therein, as the whole nation were (being necessited
thereto for the preserving of himselfe from ruyne), yet, because their
great master would have it so, they declare him guilty of high treason.
And so full of revendge the Court creatures shewed **909** themselves,
that they pressed to have him executed in the same [manner?] as
was the Marquess of Montrose. But the major parte of the Parliament would not consent thereto, but ordered that he should be
beheaded.

There was one minister whose name was   Gatterick, who
had opposed Middleton when he was in rebellion against that state, and
a Captaine of that nation, who were put to death by them at the same
tyme; the former sayd to be for having spoaken in justification of the
putting of the late King to death, the other for having bin on the
scaffold at the tyme of his execution. All three of them bore a full
and cleare testimony as to the justice of the cause in which they had
bin engaged against the King, and layd downe their lives therein with
much cheerefulness and satisfaction; the Marquess of Argile possitively bearing his testimony against the King's being head of the
church, saying that though he was put to death for the said witness,
yet, the word of the Lord being most cleare therein, the Lord by his
providence would continue to testify on the behalfe of those who
should owne that witness, as he had begun to doe against those who
had so done. Sir Archibold Johnston is proscribed, and some others,
and Major Generall Holborne, Middleton's old comrade, imprysoned; which said Middleton, having sacrificed his conscience to his
master's service, makes no scruple to violate the bonds of humanity
and freindship. Yea, it's a principle and usuall practice with such instruments of tyranny to engage themselves in horrid and irreconcileable acts, that they may render themselves the fitter to be trusted,
according to the advice of Achitophell given to Absolon for the lying
with his father's concubines.

And now to such an height of wickednesse is their party growne
in England, that they enact the Covenant for the rooting out of prelacy and popery in England and Scotland (which was so sollemly
taken by the generallity of people in both nations, even by their King
himselfe) to be burnt by the hand of the Comon Hangman; which
was put in execution accordingly, both in Westminster and London.
The Parliament of Scotland follow their example, disowning that
which had its originall from themselves. That of Ireland doth the like.
The Howse of Commons in England prepare an act for the restoring

of the bisshops to their place in Parlament, from whence they were excluded by the consent of the late King. It's now thought fit to adjourne till November following. *According to humain appearance, Monke might now (with the foole in the gospell) say, his barnes being full and built wider, Soul take thine ease. But that you may see the contrary, I thinke fit, for the takeing notice of the just hand of the Lord, heare to insert the very words of Gumble, his creature and historiagrapher, [which are in page?] 262. [Hee?] General Monke, in the end of the yeare 1661, falls extremely sicke, which did so consume his body that by his owne confession hee never was well after; his body being ever since given to . . . ., and those swellings that in the end caused his death, and was ever after more heavy and lethargique. Yea, it was sayd that his appetit was soe depraved with the gout that hee found noe difference of tast in whatever hee eate or dranke. And he adds, For my part I assure myselfe that it's difficult to find anyone, who was elevated in soe high degree of fortune, that enjoyed lesser pleasure therein, for hee had noe satisfaction therein, and hee made use of all those things, as neglecting them, and [without?] delight. Thus farr Gumble, hereby participating of the punishments the poets . . . Tantulus to bee condemned, and seemes an earnest of what (is to be feared) is deserved for [him?] heereafter.*

Bisshops are sent out of England into Scotland; by reason of which proceedings, and the deadness of trade, the people grow discontented, and talke so high, that the King puts off his intended progress for feare of tumults, and rayseth men in England, Scotland **910** and Ireland for to enforce obedience to his will. It's observed, that the King's Councell and Counsellours are divers, the latter being most papists, and many of them of Ireland; that of three regiments of foote, and one of horse, which is about London, more of the souldiers goe to the French, Spaniard's, and Portugal's chapples, then to our churches; and that the papists wore their beades publiquely in London. And such a jealousy is conceived of the citty of London, not long since most zealous for his Majestie, that it was moved (during the last sessions) that the Mayors of London for the future should be chosen by the Parlament, and consequently in the intervals by the King; the debate of which, though put off to their next meeting, much enraged that great Citty. A bill was also brought into the Howse for the execution of those 17 of the King's judges who, being under the sentence of death, were prysoners in the Tower, and by the act of indemnity not to have the sentence executed as to their lives but by act of parliament. The King finding, by the pulse of those who call themselves a Howse of Commons, that they were a councell devoted to his service, and for episcopacy, countenances the scoffing of the presbyterians upon the publique stage. And in a play made of the late warr, the English and Scots presbyters are brought in, giving thancks for the severall victoryes, as Mr. Marshall, Calamy, Baxter etc., with which representation the King expressed himselfe *highly* pleased.

And as they contynued their old trade of scoffing at religion, and the professours thereof, so of carrying on their mischeiveous designes by lyes and fictions. For it being now resolved to crush the presbyterian interest, and, contrary to all honour and honesty, that those poore innocent lambes, the 17 prysoners in the Tower formerly spoken of, should be sacrificed to the lusts of the tyrant, fearing that so villanous an act might provoake those who had any sense of publique callamatyes, and any love to comon justice, or to themselves (theise 17 having in effect the faith of the nation for the security of their lives), to make opposition thereunto, for the prevention thereof, under pretence of a plot of severall united interests (which they make to be nyne, viz. Citty, Commonwealthsmen, Rumpers, purchassers, casheired officers, presbyterians, independents, anabaptists and Quakers), most of those throughout England who had either heads or hands for carrying on their pretended conspiracy were imprysoned. Mr. James Harrington, Mr. John Wildeman, Mr. Ireton, Mr. Samuell Moyer, Mr. Barebone and others were clapt up in the Tower of London. **911** Yet in some countryes the royall party, themselves looking upon this designe to be feigned, would not needlesly vexe their poore neighbours by imprysoning them as they were directed. But so obdurate were the Court party growne that, at the adjournement of the two Howses for the twelve dayes which they call holy dayes, their Chancellour, by order of Charles Steward his master, acquaints them therewith, and desired them to appoint a Comittee of Both Howses to enquire into it, and to take care of the peace of the nation; which was done, and the newes bookes for severall weekes after tooke occation to speake of the horridness of this plott, without mentioning any particculars. But as the comittee made no discovery, so the greatest cavaleers gave no credit to what was said about it.

However, the innocent prysoners are not permitted to have their liberty. And least Sir Henry Vane's head, and Major Generall Lambert and the other military officers' hands, who were prysoners in the Tower, should upon a rising of the Citty (which they feared, the discontents growing very high) be made use of against them, they remove Sir Henry Vane, Major Generall Lambert, Sir Hardress Waller, Colonell Cobbet and Major Creede into some islands, where they were kept prissoners. And it's pretended to their freinds that it's done out of respect to them. But it's well knowne what kindness they bare to Sir Henry Vane, and will shortly appeare more vissibly; for the Howse is no sooner met againe, but they are moved and often pressed by some Court instruments that Sir Henry Vane and Major Generall

Lambert should be brought to their tryall. And for the better coulour-
ing of this cruelty, the tenants of Sir Henry Vane are made use of,
who being sued by him for his rents (which they deteyned in their
hands by virtue of an order of those which formerly sate in the Howse
of Commons, which was in force only during their continuance) apply
themselves for releefe to those now sitting in the same Howse; which
motion of theirs put them into such a heate, that they were even upon
passing a vote for the sequestring of his estate, unconvicted or unheard, but in fine agreed upon moving their King to have him brought
to his tryall; which though he was fully resolved upon, yea and his
execution also, it's not yet thought convenient to hearken to them.

In Worcestershire, an intercepted letter was pretended for the clapping up of many there. And though it be well knowne that one of
themselves writ it, yet are the prysoners still reteyned. Many strange
apparitions were seene since the retorne of their King to this tyme,
in the ayre, water and earth, as may be seene in a booke published
in print, expressing the places where, the tyme when, and the persons
by whom they were seene; amongst which, mention is made of severall
troopes of horse marching with coulours flying neere **912** Mont-
gomery Castle, where some of the prysoners were, which gave occasion
to many of the country, who saw them, to beleeve they were of those
comonly called fanaticques, advancing for the releefe of the prysoners,
upon which they followed them till they saw them vanish. The
reporters heereof were at first troubled by the Justices of Peace,
till so many countrymen made oath of it that they graunt it to be
true.

Those in the Commons Howse (at their meeting after the twelve
dayes adjournement), having bin heated with the wyne and good
cheere they had devoured during this holy season, finding their
master's appetite desired more blood (the naturall food of tyrants),
fall feircely upon the prysoners in the Tower, against whom the sentence of death was passed by the pretended Court of Justice. And
though they were agreed what to doe with them, yet for forme sake,
or rather for tryumph, they will have them brought before them, to
say what they could why sentence passed upon them should not be
executed. Enough was without doubt said by them to satisfy any unprejudiced persons that they, who would be thought to represent the
nation, ought not to imbrue their hands in the blood of those who
had their lives secured to them by those who were owned to have
the power of the publique faith of the nation. But what particcularly
was sayd to that effect I have not bin informed; save what Mr. Henry
Martyn, that faithfull servant of the Comonwealth, and one of the
said prysoners, observed to them, to wit, that about ten of his countrymen had bin already put to death for having bin instrumentall

in the death of the late King the father, and if he or any of those his countrymen now before them should be adjudged to dye, it must and would be sayd to be for that they had too much confided in the word of his sonne. But whatever was or could be said, conscience, honour and honesty having quitted for the present their station within those walls, they pass an act for the execution of all of them, except Colonell Downes, Colonell George Fleetwood, Mr. William Hevin-ingham, Sir Hardress Waller, Colonell Robert Lilborne and Colonell Harvey; the last three of which are reserved to have the sentence exe-cuted upon them as shall be declared by a particcular act to be passed for that purpose. This act, and that sacred one for uniformity in reli-gion, with their King the head of their church, are carryed up by them to their Lordes together.

In the meanetyme they order Mr. Robert Wallop that eminent patriot, Sir Henry Mildemay, Sir James Harrington, and the Lord Mounson, and Mr. Phelps, who **913** were excepted out of the act of indemnity, and reserved for such punishment as should be heere-after thought fit (not extending to life), shall be carryed to Newgate, and from thence drawne on the sledd to Tyburne with ropes about their neckes, and so to be brought againe to the Tower of London, and there to remaine. Mr. Wallop, Sir Henry Mildemay, and the Lord Mounson, being in custody, were brought to the barr in the Howse of Comons, and there received this sentence. The other two had withdrawne themselves, and the sentence was ordred to be executed upon them when taken. This sentence was executed upon the former three on the 17 of January, Mr. Wallop and Sir Henry Mildemay deporting themselves with much patience and Christian resolution. And the keeneness of the people's rage being now blunted towards those kind of sufferers, and turned another way, they carryed themselves towards them with much temper and moderation, express-ing their pitty and sorrow to see their countrymen thus treated for having bin faithfull to their trust.

The Court-engines had, before this, passed an act for the confisca-tion of their estates, together with the estate of Sir Arthur Haslrerigg, and those of the King's judges whom the Lord had taken to himselfe by death; which, as it had bin always a supercedeas to a procedure against any, be the cryme what it would be (it being most unjust to condemne any unheard, as these were put out of capacity to be), so it would have bin now, had these men any sense of justice towards others, or any love to themselves or their posterity (whom they preju-dice, not only in giving judgement against those who were their reall and faithfull freinds, but by giving it unheard). And after death, they prescribe a president for the pulling of their owne bones out of their graves, and depriving of their children, it may be their grandchildren,

of the lands and goods they leave them. For this, and other such barbarous acts of theirs, yea that they may be sure to make this president
strong enough against themselves by this pretended act of parlament,
they voyd all trustes for any of those whom they thus condemne, or
for any of their children. Yea, that they may make their injustice comprehensive of strandgers as well as relations, they voyd their last wills
and testaments, and so render their executors (who it may be were
strangers to them) to be liable to the repayment of any legacy they
have payd by virtue of the said executorship.

As the Lord witnesseth against this sort of men by giving them over
to such blyndness, so by his contynued prodigies; and particcularly
about this tyme by a very great storme, which did harme in many
places, killing many people in the streetes and howses, by the fall of
howses, tyles and chimneys; great parte of the pageants, set up in
the streetes for the King's coronation, which were to stand till the
Queene's entry, being blowne downe, together with many weathercockes and fanes on the Tower, which was judged by some as ominous
to single persons lifted up above their *proper* stations. The weather
being very bad and unseasonable, the feare of a famine puts them upon
the enjoyning of **914** a publique fast for the prevention thereof. But
the presbyterians and independents made the famine of the word
more their subject then that of bread; for which there appeared but
too much ground, the great doctrine of the tymes being for blind
obedience to the comands of those in power. Take for this one
instance. The Bisshop of Worcester's chaplin, preaching in that
cathedral upon the first of Jan.   , told the people they were to
beleeve as the church beleeved. And if, sayd he, your superiours
should command you to be circumcised, you ought to submit. For
though it would be bad in them to comand it, yet would it be a sin
in you to refuse it if comanded, for that our Saviour was circumcised
in obedience to command, which they ought to imitate. This man's
master is well knowne to be one of the two who are cheife in church
affaires. Severall such repetitions might be made, but by this may
be calculated the rest. The aforesaid Bisshop had sylenced Mr. Baxter
(who was one of Charles Steward's chaplines for a while since his
retorne) as to his diocese, and in a paper in prynt gives these two
reasons for his so doing: first, he preached without his leave, secondly,
he had blowne the trumpet of sedition, which though the King could
pardon as to the fact, the church could not as to the scandall without
publique repentance; whereby was vissible what this sorte of men had
gained by this chandge, which they impatiently longed after and
unweariedly contended for.

The common reporte and expectation was that those poore lambes
in the Tower who had the bloody sentence pronounced against them,

and already put in execution as farr as the unnaturall and perfidious Howse of Comons could contribute thereto, should be sacrificed the same day of January that the late tyrant was executed; there wanting nothing to the compleating of that worke but the concurrence of the Howse of Lordes (the most of which were their King's absolute creatures, and the whole Howse his councell, depending as much on monarchy as the shadow on the substance), and the consent of Charles Steward, who was the primum mobile of this barbarous procedure, and according to the nature of his constitution thirsted more after the blood of the innocent then his appointed food. But the Lord to shew his prerogative, and that he can when he pleaseth worke by un-likely, yea contrary meanes, appeares in the Mount. And after the aforesaid prysoners (being brought to the barr of the Howse of Lords, to speake for themselves, as they had done in the Howse of Commons) had offered what they had to say on their behalves, and Mr. Henry Martin had to this purpose delivered himselfe, to wit——

I now stand condemned by an Howse of Commons. My life lyes at your mercy, or rather before your justice. The Howse of Comons I alwayes adored, you I have opposed. But this is not the same Howse of Commons I served and honoured; nor that which invited us to render ourselves upon promise of security   **915** as to our lives, and which gave us in effect the fayth of the nation to that end. You are the same Lords whom, though I opposed in relation to the constitution (it being inconsistent, as I humbly supposed, with the good of the publique), yet not as to your persons, knowing that there are among you many of singular worth and honour. And therefore (though con-trary to all faith and common honesty) we are delivered to the slaughter by those from whom, as we deserved, so we expected better dealing. Yet cannot we have such unworthy thoughts of this Howse, to suspect that, contrary to the faith given, they will concurr with that which is proposed to them for the putting of the bloody sentence passed upon us in execution, and thereby contract the blood of the innocent on their head, and render such a blemish in the escussion of their potesterity as can never be defaced——

the Lord so wrought with what was offered that it inclyned the Howse of Lords to put a stopp to this barbarous and cruell act, in which (as is reported) the Earle of Northumberland to his great honour was very instrumentall.

At this tyme also a checque was put to the act for uniformity, not out of favour to the fanaticques (under which notion are included all those who were not of the episcopall, viz. the King's religion), but severall accidents concurring thereunto, as in parte the power of pap-ists (who had about thirty votes, besides those of their freinds in that Howse), no provission being made for them therein. But that which

swayed principally was the occation the King had for the borrowing
of mony for the supply of his pressing occasions, for which end it's
thought adviseable for the present to cajole the citty of London. And
therefore Hyde and severall of the bisshops are against the passing
thereof, and for laying it aside. It's pretended to clash with the act
of indemnity, of which they must seeme to be very tender, in that
with a retrospect it outs all those of their livings and parsonages who
had not bin ordained by the bisshops before such a day then passed.
But the Citty being (by this subtilty) gulled into the loane of mony,
and the papists having received satisfaction as to their scruple, the
act soone after passeth with as much strictness and severity against
the godly party as the bisshops themselves could desire. But by reason
of this little delay in the passing of the act, Charles Steward takes
occation in his speech to the Commons (after he had acquainted them
with the expectation he had of his Queen's arrivall shortly, and
desired them to prepare a complement for her in giving order for the
mending the highwayes and streetes) to tell them he had bin unhappy
in being taken for a papist when beyond sea, and for a presbyterian
since his being in England. But his maine designe was to let them
know that he intended shortly to adjourne them, and to desire them
therefore to lay aside all private business till they had setled his
revenue and the militia; he wanting mony **916** exceedingly, all that
he receives seeming to be put into an bottomless bagg.

It was now confidently reported in Normandy, that two million
of livers are sent from New Haven to England in two English men
of warr, for which it's supposed Dunkirk is to be delivered; neither
of which then seemed likely. The Parliament being so devoted to their
master's service (in hopes he would be as forward to gratify every
one of them) that whereas he demaunds a supply of eight hundred
thousand pounds, they give him what they computed to amount to
twelve hundred thousand pounds; which, besides other wayes, they
order to be payd by the passing of two shillings for every chimney;
which occationed Alderman Fowke, one who served for the citty of
London, to express his feares least this imposition would set the chimneys, and so the citty of London, in a flame not easily to be quenched;
the execution of which act was so displeasing to the people, that from
thence they nominated Charles Steward, the chimney-sweeper; who,
finding this society of men so absolutely devoted to his service,
appeares more open-faced to owne the papists. Mass is publiquely
said in London, and severall partes of the country; the Irish interest
begins to be owned; the lands of many of the cheife rebells restored;
and others of them, till the generall restitution shall be thought seasonable, are by order of their great and gratious master payd pensions
out of the Exchecquer, whilest the English Protestant souldiery are

ready to starve for want of pay. And for the better carrying on of this worke, the Earle of Ormond, whom they now call Duke (Irish by nation, and whose parents are not only Irish but papists, and who was engaged by articles which he made with the Irish in 1648 on the behalfe of Charles Steward his master to restore unto them their lands), is appointed Viceroy there. One Ewen, also a papist, was appointed Agent for Hamburgh, but dyed before he could get thither.

Notwithstanding which vissible demonstrations that it was in designe to advance popery and tyranny in England, and to destroy libertyes religious and civill (whereby the justice of our cause, and the necessity of our engaging therein, became more and more evident), *two of those who judged the late King to death, viz. Collonell Barkestead and Collonell Okey, comeing from Hanno (a towne in Germany, where they, with two more in the like condition, viz. Collonell Walton and Collonell Dixwell, had beene admitted burgesses, and received into protection) to Delfe, in Holland, for receiveing and conducting their wives (whose arrivall they attended out of England) to Hanno aforesayd, the place of their intended residence, Mr. Corbet, another of the sayd judges, giveing them a visit, these three were apprehended at Delfe aforesayd, by order from the States Generall,* upon the sollicitation of Downing (now Agent there for Charles Steward, **917** and formerly, as a greate pretender to the Parlament interest, was enterteyned by them in severall imployments, first as a chapline to Colonell Okey's regiment in the army, and then as Scoutmaster-Generall of the army, in which he contynued severall yeares, and arrived to the atteyning of a great estate, to wit of about 7 or 800 li. a yeare, who before, when retorning from New England, was not worth a groat). Yet contrary to the profession of religion, and his function as a minister, yea and engagement to his former colonell, Colonell Okey, and assurance given to him that he had no comission for the looking after him, the sayd colonell, having by a private hand (as relying on his ingenuity) sent unto him to be informed whether he had or no, the said Downing, resolving with Demas to embrace the present world, quits conscience, religion, morality, humanity and all obligations to God and good men, and treacherously embrews his hands in the blood of the aforesaid innocent persons; which was little supposed the States of Holland would ever have appeared in, haveing cast off the yoake of tyranny and popery themselves, and looking upon it as their interest to give all sortes of persons liberty and freedome, in reference to commerce and other advantadges, to cohabite with them.

Yet, contrary to their owne principles and publique interest, they impower and authorize persons for the seizing of the aforesaid gentlemen (*one whereof residing amongst them, and the other two only* passing through their country), contrary to the law of nations, *the lawes of humanity*, and these express texts of scripture, Deut. 19. 34, But the stranger that dwelleth with you, shall be as one borne amongst you, and thou shalt love him as thyselfe, etc.; with Deut. 10. 19, and Deut. 23. 15, 16, Thou shalt not deliver unto his master the servant which is escaped from his master unto thee. He shall dwell with thee, even amonge you, in that place which he shall choose, in one of thy gates where it likes him best; thou shalt not oppress him; as also Obadiah vers. 14, and Heb. 13. 1, 2; yea, and that for doing the same things, and in order to the same ends, as the States of the Low Countryes had done, and this without any previous engagement obleiging or constrayning them thereto, or any warning given by them for any in their condition to avoyd their country; they thereby rendring the abode of all others within their teritoryes alike unsafe unto them, and their trading with them hazardous; yea   **918** and all this contrary to the engagement of some of the States Generall. *I have heard that the great Turke, rideing abroad, protected a poore larke which sheltered itselfe in his bosome from the pursuite of a bird of prey. But neither lawes of humanity or divinity, of nature or nations, will serve for bounds to the rage of Sathan and his instruments in the prosecution of Christ in his cause and faythfull members; a cleare evidence to me that the reigne of Sathan is to bee but short, and that the day of the Lord's appearance to judgement is not farre of.* But! A peace must be made with Charles Steward, yea though the foundation thereof be layd in blood, in the blood of innocents, and they run not only the hazzard of the loss of trade, but bid defiance to God and good men.

And as the Lord Jesus seemes at this tyme to be coming in these clowdy dispensations for the setting up of the scepter in nations, as well as persons, so must there be a falling away of the one as well as the other. And the faithfull witnesses of Christ are to be betrayd by both, and brethren Comonwealths shall deliver up one another to death, as well as naturall and Christian brethren. But so it is that (though this monstrous generation of men had sent some of their owne members, with their ministers, to be further informed of this matter of fact for which they were seized, and the cause wherein they had engaged, from the gentlemen themselves, and that the said ministers, upon conference with them seeming to have a better oppinion of their persons and cause then they had before, had given them assurance they should be further heard before anythinge were resolved touching their being sent away), so active and dilligent was this bloodhound Downing, in his master the devill's service, fearing the people would have rissen and rescued them, that they were prevayled with by him to be hurryed into one of Charles Steward's men of warr, chained like rogues, and kicked by footemen; much to the trouble and dissatisfaction of the meaner but better sorte of people, one of whom, a grave ancient man, was heard to say he thought the child unborne would have cause to bewayle that action. The wife of Colonell White, being then in Holland, did what she could for the getting of their liberty, appearing publiquely on their behalves; whose endeavours I doubt not but the Lord accepted.

In a few dayes they arrived in England, and being committed to the Tower of London, were disposed by order of the Leiftenant to their severall pryson lodgings; where they continued in a very comfortable condition, in respect of the peace, joy and patience in which they possessed their soules, untill the 16 April 1662; upon which day they were carryed by water to the Upper Bench barr, now called the King's Bench barr, to receive judgement; having bin before, by that which in this day of usurpation is called an act of parlament, atteynted of high treason for compassing the death of the late King Charles. After a very short dispute whether the prysoners at the barr were the persons named in the aforementioned pretended act of atteinder, yea or no, witnesses being produced who made full proofe in the affirmative, and the prysoners themselves confessing it, the jury gave in their verdict that they were the persons named in the sayd act; whereupon the Court gave judgement accordingly, overruling what they said for the arrest of judgement, as they would have done without doubt whatever had bin said by them, though they might have **919** urged, and that upon the highest reason imaginable, the pretended act by which they were said to be atteinted was no act of parlament, for that those who made it were no parlament (not because they were called by the writ of the Comonwealth and not by that of the King, as some would have it, but for that the Parlament which began in 1640, and by act of parlament not to be dissolved but by its owne consent, is still in being, it never having consented to its owne dissolution, and therefore whatever was done by any other subsequent to that, though it carryes the title of an act of parlament, is nothing so, two parlaments being inconsistent at the same tyme, and those who obeyed the act of the said lawfull Parlament (whereof one of those three was a member), especially during the said Parliament, ought not to be questioned by any inferiour power for what they did in obedience thereto). But inter arma silent leges. The clubb prevayles instead of right reason, and under the forme of law the highest wickednesses are now perpetrated. Sentence being given, they are remanded to the Tower; where they remaine, from the day of their tryall to the day of their suffering, in a frame of spirit full of joy and peace in beleeving, sweetely, patiently and profitably (both to themselves and others) spending that little tyme which remained.

Mr. Myles Corbet was a gentleman of an ancient familly in the county of Northfolke, bred up to the law in the society of Lincoln's

Inn, yet not neglecting to search after the knowledge of the law of God, and to conforme his life thereto. And to that end, with severall other gentlemen of the Innes of Court whose hearts the Lord had wrought upon by the power of his spirit, he frequented the ministry and company of Dr. Preston, that famous instrument in the Lord's hand, and afterwards of Dr. Ussher, knowne afterwards by the name of Primate of Ireland. He was aged 67 yeares when he suffered; the greatest parte of which tyme the Lord was pleased to use him more or less in publique services, having for thirty seaven yeares bin still a member in the severall parlaments that had bin called, joyning constantly with those who most eminently appeared for the cause of God and their country, being named of the High Courte for the tryall of the late King. He having many tentations upon him, forbore to appeare therein till the day the sentence was pronounced, at which tyme that word in Revelation 21. 8, viz. the fearefull and unbeleeving shall have their parte in the lake that burnes with fire and brimstone, being set upon his heart by the Lord, did so worke upon him and powerfully prevayle with him that he durst not any longer absent himselfe, but made haste to come and sit amongst them, least the threatned punishment of the fearefull should be his portion. And being demaunded by some freinds, the day before his execution, what inward peace and satisfaction he had in his conscience touching that for which he was condemned, and to suffer death, he replyed, that considering he judged that the blood of Ireland lay at the King's doore, and that he leavyed warr against the Parlament, he was fully satisfyed of the lawfulness of the fact, as well as of the power by which the late King   **920**   was tryed and adjudged to death, and that if all that had bin done were to be acted over againe, he would doe as he had done, and would not abate an inch of it.

He was imployed by the Parlament for many yeares together as one of their Comissioners for the goverment of civill affaires in Ireland; in which imployment he manifested himselfe a great freind to justice, a favourer of good people, especially of good ministers, and a great husband of the treasure of the Comonwealth; in the meanetyme trusting the Lord to make provission for his familly, wasting his owne estate in the service of the publique. He rejoyced that he was thought worthy to lay downe his life in so glorious a cause; professing that the overflowing wickednesses of all kindes he had lived to see and heare of since the late amazing change, rather to be trembled at then reckoned up, did give no small confirmation and justification to those former proceedings which are now so much condemned. He departed this life in much assuredness of the blessedness of his estate to all eternity, and of the Lord's speedy appearing for his people.

Colonell John Barkstead was a cittizen of London, a goldsmith by profession; and being sensible of the encroachments made upon the libertyes of the nation, spirituall and civill, when the Lord raysed up the Parlament in the yeare 1640 (as his Gideon for the releeving of them from the hands of their enemyes), he contributed what he could to their assistance; had at first the command of a company of foote in the regiment of Colonell Venne; and was afterwards Major of foote, and Governour of the garrison of Redding, and afterwards preferred to the comand of a regiment; and was very instrumentall for the raysing of recruits for the service of Ireland and Scotland; and was constituted by the Parlament Leiftenant of the Tower of London, which command he held for many yeares. When the Lord called him forth to witness to the justice of that act for which he suffered, he did it with much cheerefulness and satisfaction, declaring himselfe ready and willing to be offred up, as being very cleare in his conscience that what he was accused of and condemned for was done by him in obedience to the call of God, and the authority of the nation; and was often heard to say, and particcularly the day before his execution to an emynent minister, that his great burthen then was that he ever lifted up a finger against any of the people of God who were of a contrary oppinion to him; and desired them to love the image of Jesus Christ wheresoever they found it.

Colonell Okey was a cittizen of London, appeared with the first on the behalfe of the Parlament, was a Captaine of foote, and after a Captaine of horse in the regiment of Sir Arthur **921** Haslerigg, and then Major of the said regiment. Upon the new modell of the army in 1645, he was appointed Colonell of a regiment of dragoons, which was afterwards converted into a regiment of horse; in all which commands he behaved himselfe with much faithfulness and courradge. During the tyme of Cromwel's usurpation, he was dismissed the army for appearing on the behalfe of the publique and civill authority of the nation. And when Richard Cromwell his Convention was summoned to meete, he was chosen by the gentry and good people of the county of Bedford to represent them there. The Great Parlament being after restored to the exercise of their authority, they reestablished him in his comand in the army. He always manifested much zeale to their interest. And when by the providence of God he was called to witness to the justice of the cause, by the powring out of his blood, he professed, that if he had as many lives as he had haires on his head, he would willingly expose them all therein; and that as to the judging of the King to death (for which he was now called to suffer), although he had oft sought the Lord to discover to him, and make knowne whether he had done ill therein, he was still more and more confirmed in the justice and necessity of that undertaking, and that he had done therein what was his duty to doe.

On the 19 of April 1662 this bloody sentence was ordered to be put into execution, and to that end three sleds were prepared to draw them from the Tower to Tyburne. Colonell Barkstead was drawne on the first sled, Colonell Okey on the second, and Mr. Myles Corbet on the third. The savouriness of their expressions, and the sweete and Christian frame of spirit they were found in, together with the refreshment and satisfaction they had from the consideration of the excellency of the cause which they had acted in, and which now they suffred for, being elsewhere and particcularly expressed, I shall not heere insert. Mr. Miles Corbet (with whom I had acted for many yeares in the Parlament, and as their Comissioner in the managdement of their civill affaires in Ireland), observing a well-wissher of myne neere him whilest he was setling himselfe on the sled, calls to him, and desires him to remember his affectionate love to my deare wife, and to thanke her for her intended vissit, and to tell her that he both prayed and hoped that the Lord would preserve and keepe her husband for some further worke. They all three layd downe their lives cheerefully, being assured to take them up againe. And if any expressions fell from them at the tyme and place of execution that might seeme to owne the authority and the present posture of affaires in England as a mercey, considering the eminent testamony they bore to the justice of the cause which they engaged in under the Parlament against the King, and the satisfaction they declared they had in that for which they suffred, it must certeinly be intended by them to be only as they were a power permitted by the Lord, and the restoring of them to the exercise thereof to   **922**   be a mercey only in the sense of those who were the constant adhearers to that interest, and not that it was so in itselfe.

The bloody sentence was executed upon all three of them, their soules being thereby set free to take their flight to their brethren under the altar, to cry with them for vengeance. The heades and quarters of Colonell Barkstead and Mr. Corbet were disposed of as the rest of their brethren's were, their lymbes on fower gates of the Citty, Colonell Barkstead's head on the Tower, and Mr. Corbet's on the bridge. Colonell Okey's body, after it was masecrated, was given to be disposed of as his wife should thinke fit, without any application or seeking of hers; who appointeing him to be buryed at Stepney (his first wife lying there in a vault which he had purchased for a burying place for him and his familly), the rumour of his funerall being spread abroade, many thousands of sober substantiall people were assembled at and about Newgate Market, where the body lay, to attend its interment, and some thousands more were coming thither to that purpose; so that there were in veiu about twenty thousand people attending that sollemnity, who though they behaved themselves with all manner of civillity, yet Charles Steward, allarumd thereat, revoaked his first

graunt to Mrs. Okey, and ordered the Sheriff to disappoint and disperse the company attending the funerall, which the Sheriff did with
much harshness, and many bitter expressions; but the people, no less
couragious then before in manifesting their affection to this their
butchered fellow cittizen and countryman, affirmeing, when the
Sheriff demaunded how they durst shew such respect to a traytour,
and where their tickets of invitation were, They are heere, clapping their hands
on their breasts. But so soone as they saw there was no other remedy,
they left the mangled body to the dispose of them who had imbrued
their hands in its blood, the company leaving many thousand sighes
to accompany him to his unknowne grave; who that night was carryed
to the Tower of London, and there interred with the Service Booke
(whereby, as farr as in them lay, he was wounded afresh), where
(according to the wordes of the sayd booke in a formall manner then
repeated) *his body* lyes in sure and certeine hope of a joyfull resurrection, *as his soul rests in assurance of the* [reviving of the?] cause itselfe,
in the Lord's owne tyme and way.

The newes of this barbarous and inhumane act of the States being
now made publique at Geneve, who were much affrighted with the
deportment of the King of France towards them, and not knowing
but that a desire from him, who stood neerely related to our great
adversary, might worke the like effect upon this little Comonwealth
in relation to us, wee thought fit to get what assurance we could of
our safety whilest we stayed here, and if that would not be given us,
to make provission for ourselves elsewhere; to which end we imployed
Mr. Perrot, our landlord, to Mr. Voisin, then the first Centique,
desiring him to deale freely and clearely with us as to what we might
expect, should we be demaunded. And as we understood from him,
he expressed a great simpathy with us in our condition, promissed
to doe for us to the utmost of his power, and in particcular that if
any letters came to him concerning us (which he said they must doe
before they came to the Councell, it being according to their constitution to convey them by   **923** his hand) he would give us timely notice
thereof, and if it were in the night we should have the water-gate
opened for our escape (he having the keeping of that key), and if it
were in the day we should goe out at which gate we pleased (which
we had againe confirmed to us by Mr. Lisle, when he went on our
behalves to express an acknowledgement of this favour); adding withall, that when his brother Centique Mr. Dupaine was retorned from
Berne, where he then was, they would consult together how they
might make it more sure unto us, either by giving it under their hands
or otherwise.

With this I rested wholy satisfyed, being as much as I could rationally expect. But Mr. Lisle, making many objections against our stay,

and being resolved upon a removall, upon lettres he received from
his relations, at least for some tyme (and Mr. Cawley not willing to
quit me, and yet unfree to stay with me upon those tearmes), presseth
Mr. Perrot, upon the retorne of Mr. Dupaine, to put him upon a
conference with his brother Centique upon this affaire. Whereupon
Mr. Perrot (moved partly out of affection to us, and partly out of
respect to his owne gaine), upon conference thereof with Mr. Dupaine
the Procurer Generall of the said towne (coussen to Mr. Perrot, and
nephew to Mr. Dupaine the Centique), resolves on petitioning the
Councell for their publique protection; which he acquainting me
with, I opposed, as that which was not fit for them to doe, and was
as unfit for us to desire, least thereby we should bringe them into
trouble upon our account; they already strugling for life under their
owne weight. But Mr. Perrot telling us that the Procurer Generall
was fully of oppinion that it was both easy and fit to be done, and
that his brother, who was a leading man of the Councell, was of the
same judgement with him therein, conceiving them to be better
acquainted with the state of their affaires then myselfe I resolved to
be passive therein.

But upon their attempt to put this result in execution, they found
the success I expected. And the business being brought before the
Councell, Mr. Lett, one of the Centiques whom the first Centique
had endeavoured to conceale it from (knowing the expectation he
had of the payment of a great debt owing by the King of England
to himselfe in the right of his wife, and it may be also enclyning in
his affections to that interest), comming to be acquainted therewith,
not only obstructed the same, but threatned those who had a hand
therein, supposing they intended to have surprised the Councell. But
the Councell being unwilling to deny, and fearefull to graunt, the
request, deferr the consideration thereof, and by some of their
members advise the withdrawing thereof, which was done accordingly before it was publiquely read (as we were informed). In the
meanetyme (that we might make sure our retreate), we being recco-
mended by our true and sincere freind Mr. Delabady to some whom
he had an interest in amongst their Excellencyes of Berne, we make
our application to them for their protection, and particcularly for our
naturalization, and to that end employ a messenger on purpose, by
the helpe of some freinds from Lausanne; wherein the Leiftenant
Bailivall showed much affection and freindshipp, he being our choyce
freind, and this very yeare brought into the place of one *Mr. Godward*,
whom God removed out of **924** the world, the only freind to
monarchy and enemy *to us* in that towne *wee knew then of*; which providence I could not omit heere to insert.

Mr. Lisle and Mr. Cawley, meeting with this rubb at Geneve, continue their resolution to remove thence; where some tyme after I resided, as relying on the word of the Centique which he had given for our security. They having hyred a boate to carry them to Lausanne, I accompanying them to the water side, had a letter seasonably delivered us from him whom we had imployed to their Excellencyes of Berne, assuring us that they had graunted our requests; which was an encouragement to me to continue my former resolution of staying at Geneve, supposing they would the rather owne us because we were now countenanced by their best freinds and allyes. And therefore, after a day or two, I thought it adviseable to feele the pulse of the first Centique as to the continuance of the first engagement he had given us, and for that end tooke an occasion to excuse unto him Mr. Lisle's and Mr. Cawley's leaving the towne without wayting on him, and to let him know that the application to the Councell was not advised by me, but that I rested before, as now, well satisfyed with the verball engagement he had given us for our security; which I had no sooner imparted to him, but he with some discomposedness of spirit, and as I judged some feare, anwered he could now no longer looke upon himselfe obleiged to what he formerly had promissed, he having made it in expectation what was done therein should be kept secret, whereas now he thought the King of England had notice thereof before this.

Finding myselfe thus plainly dealt with, looking on it as my duty to use all probable meanes for my preservation, that so if the Lord should permit me to fall into the hands of my enemyes I might be found in his way, and might have his blessing and assistance in such a dispensation, I quitted Geneve the next day; and with Mr. Phelpes, one of our fellow sufferers (and who by an especiall providence some weekes before came into our company, and entred into pension with us), went after our two freinds, whom we found at Lausanne, having received the protection which their Excellencyes of Bearne were pleased to favour us with, which they graunted unto us severally by our owne propper names (an argument of their couradge and faithfulness to the cause of God and his people, in that they so openly owned his poore persecuted witnesses, when they had bin so lately delivered up to the slaughter by those whose true interest was the same for which they suffred). Mine and Mr. Cawley's name being somwhat mistaken in the transcript, we sent them back to be amended, which they ordred to be done without the least chardge. I trust the Lord will recompence this their labour of love an hundredfold into their bosome.

The Portugall being much pressed by the Spanish forces (Don John of Austria taking many townes, and treating the Governours thereof as rebels against his master, and drawing towards Lisborne itselfe), they grew much discontented at the delay of the sollemnization

925 of the marriadge betweene their Infanta and Charles Steward the pretended King of England; insomuch that, to appease the people, she appeared publiquely in quality of the Queene of England, having bin formerly espoused to him by proxy. And after some tyme she was received by Montague into a vessell sent for the conveighing her to England. And though she met with great stormes at sea, and were like to rayse more at land, yet was it the will of the Lord that she should land safe at Portsmouth; which Charles Steward having notice of went to receive her, but found her not answerable to his expectation, yet, being resolved to use his accustomed liberty in making use of those he best liked and could corrupt, tooke little notice thereof. The weomen she brought with her, being not handsome, were soone dismissed and sent into Portugall, that so roome might be made for those who might more fit Charles Steward's pallate; amongst which Mrs. Palmer (whose husband must be called Earle of Castlemaine) being his principle favourite, hath not only a place reserved, but a power to displace the Countess of Portsmouth from being Groome of the Queene's Stoole (though she had a full graunt thereof), for saying that when the Queene came Mrs. Palmer must quit the Courte, and to put the Countess of Suffolke her aunt in the place of the said Countess.

Thus is this poore nation, wherein the Lord had wrought such wounderfull thinges, now governed and disposed by the vilest and basest of the sonnes and daughters of men, whose deeds being altogether evill, and that continually, they therefore, hating the light, endeavour to suppress (and as much as in them lyeth to roote out) those who hold forth this light, either in word or conversation. But the Lord, who never wants meanes to witness to his owne truthes and cause, doth it now in this evill day, not only by the constant and patient sufferings of his owne people, but eaven out of the mouths (or rather by the sylencing) of his enemyes. For instance take this one of many, the Chancellour's chaplin preaching before their King upon these wordes, Eccles. 7. 10, Say not thou what is the cause that the former dayes were better then these, for thou dost not enquire wisely concerning this; at the hearing of which, the chappell was more then ordinarily full, the text and sermon being knowne beforehand, in that it had bin preached before his master, and by him recomended to their King. The prohibition in the text he laboured to enforce by an induction of particculars. The first was, that the pagan tymes were not better then these; next, he said the popish tymes were not; and the last he insisted on was the tymes of the late rebellion. And whilest he was endeavouring to evince that which was indeed the maine thinge he intended to handle, it pleased God he was suddenly taken with a qualme, drops of sweat standing in his face as bigg as pease, and ime-

diately he lost the use of his speech, only he uttered   **926** some few
words to this effect, O Lord we are all in thy hands, be mercyful unto
us; and then came downe. But our enemyes, who refuse to have the
Lord Christ raigne in them or over them, will not heare nor understand till he come, whose right it is, and command that they be
brought forth, that they may be slaine before him.

In the meanetyme our relations were so afflicted with what had
befallen our three freinds, especially my deare and tender wife, that
(fearing least the majestrates of Geneve should deale with us as those
of Holland had dealt with them) they send a messenger on purpose
to us to caution us, and to desire us to remove to some place of greater
suerty; which, by reason of his lying sixe weekes sick at Paris, we had
done before he reached us, which he did at Lausanne; where we were
much refresshed by the account we had of the health and welfare of
our freinds and relations; by whom I had an opportunity to comuni-
cate myselfe more freely unto them, then I had since my parting from
them. Amongst other letters which I writ by him, I sent one to our
freinds upon the publique account, the effect whereof was as followeth.

The Lord hath appeared in our dayes to doe great thinges, such
as our fathers had not seene, nor eares scarse heard of. He raysed up
the poore, foolish, unexperienced and weake ones of the earth, to con-
found the rich, the wise, and the mighty thereof, speaking clearely,
as well by his providence as his word, that his designe is to advance
himselfe, and the riches of his grace in his sonne, and to give him
the necks of all his enemyes who would not that he should reigne over
them. And as in all ages he hath bin making way for this glorious
reigne of his, so did the wheele hasten to that end in our dayes. But
the Tobias and Sanballats, having an enmity thereunto, did what they
could to obstruct the same, and under pretence of furthering that
structure did more accomplish their designe then they could have
done any other way. Yet was the Lord so mercyfull to us that he made
those montaines plaine before him, and put a prize into our hands,
which had we wisedome we might have made a wounderfull improvement of. But so it was, that having through the assistance of the Lord
subdued all those enemyes who publiquely opposed the liberty due
to us as men and Christians, our enemyes began to be those of our
owne howse; amongst whom the lust of power and domination prevayling, much art was used by them for the drawing in of many zealous, well-meaning and pious Christians (who earnestly desired to see
those good thinges which the Lord had promised, and their soules
thirsted after, accomplished) to joyne in destroying the civill authority
of the nation; the unwarrantableness and unseasonableness of which
undertaking was, by the sad consequences thereof, soone after discovered; those whose hearts were upright to what was pretended unto

being trodden under foote, and such only promoted to ride in the
charret with Jehu who with Jehonadab had their hearts right with
his heart, who were for him and his interest,   **927** which was to make
his will the rule of obedience both in church and state.

This horrid and detestable impiety is promoted by ballancing of
interests, sometymes by closing with an imposing spirit, in that which
they call an Howse of Commons, consisting of such Court vermin as
were packt for that purpose, and another while with those who were
sayd should be a ballance to that spirit, in that which they called
an Other Howse. But all is under these specious pretences to keepe
up a selfe and carnall interest, to the great scandall of the gospell,
and the reproach of its professours, amidst those many formes that
were then owned and practiced scarse anythinge of the power of
godlyness remayning, that principally consisting in a faithfull witness
to the worke the Lord had upon the wheele in that our day; which
to me seemed to be the establishing of such a righteous frame of goverment under which men may enjoy their civill liberty, and not be
imposed upon by the lust of any person or party, and the word of
the Lord may be freely published, and the Saints and churches live
in the exercise of its ordinances without interruption; the whole duty
of man, contained in the law and prophets, being to love God above
all, and our neighbour as ourselves, our love to God being manifested
in our obedience to the voyce of his servant, who would have us to
doe unto others as we would that others should doe unto us, and that
his desciples should not lord it over one another (our love to our
brother being an evidence of our love to God); it being against reason
that men should either constreyne to, or restreyne from, that which
is neither in their power to give, or take away, faith being the pure
gift of God heerein. Therefore to wit in establishing officers that are
peace, and exactours that are righteousness, and by removing all vyolence out of the land, we manifest our love to our naturall brother
by providing for his civill libertyes to which he hath a right, and to
our Christian brother in procuring such a magistracy whose interest
it is to countenance him in the preaching of the word, and the practice
of all gospell ordinances, they tending to the strengthning of the said
goverment. And all conscientious persons, whose doctrine tends not
to lycentiousness, would finde themselves reciprocally obleiged to
strengthen the sayd goverment, from which they receive protection;
whereas should men of the most pure perswasion, having got the
power into their hands, endeavour to impose their beleefe in spirituall
thinges by outward force on others (besides the contrariety of such
a procedure to the tenure of the gospell), as their sword would be
against all others, so would that of all others be against them. And
all who differ from them would (as in interest bound) be united both

in heart and hand against them, by which meanes whether they were not like rationally to be prevayled against, I leave to all indifferent persons to judge; no one conscientious principle being owned by one of forty throughout the nation.

As well therefore from the consideration of prudence, as of duty and conscience (which tells us we ought to obey the higher powers, and content ourselves with our share in goverment relating to the outward man, submitting to, or at least **928** not opposing, those in whom the Lord by his providence declares the power to be, who though it may be are not so righteous and just as were to be wisshed, yet by praying *for them* we may lead *quiet and peaceable lives, in all godlynesse and honesty,* and blessing the Lord for the libertyes and priviledges they permit us to enjoy, and by *accompanying the* preaching *the word* with an holy and righteous conversation), let us endeavour to wynne them to be of the same perswation in spirituall thinges with ourselves. In the meanetyme let us not impose our beleefe on them, as we desire not to be imposed on by them, it being no less reasonable that the majestrate should enjoy the liberty of his conscience as we that of ours. Now therefore, seeing such a righteous goverment is aggreable to the word of God and the rule of right reason, the true interest of men and Christians (who understand not of what spirit they are, if they would lord it over their brethren, and have fire from men to consume those who differ from them), let us learne to doe to others, as we would they should doe to us, with plaine trueth. Though no one party whilest uppermost would owne so as to practice, the God of this world blynding their eyes, yet now being under a persecuting and AntiChristian power, who for the setting up of carnall pollicy would roote out the forme of godlyness itselfe, all may see it their wisedome and interest to submit unto, that they might put it in practice when they have an opportunity so to doe; which who can tell how soone the Lord would give, were we fitted with a spirit for the promoting a forme of goverment for the upholding of which the interest of all men and Christians would concenter? This would be an happy effect of the hand of the Lord that hath bin upon us, and would soone put us in posession of what is most desirable; it being the great designe of our adversaryes to keep up their Nimrodian power by dividing the languages of the people of God, *whose happynesse and perfection consists in their being one with Christ, as hee and the Father are one.* The Lord therefore unite us in his feare, that by suffering we may be fitted for the doing of his will, and give us wisedome to know when to goe forward and when to stand still, that by making hast we may not strengthen the hand of the enemy, nor by standing still neglect the opportunity he puts into our hands, but that, being on our Watch Tower, and living by faith, we may see our duty so plainly, that when the Lord's tyme is come we may up and be doing, and the Lord may appeare to be with us and to owne us.

At the retorne of the messenger, he was not less welcomb to our freinds and relations, in that he brought with him not only an account of our health and welfare, but of the mercey of the Lord in enclyning the hearts of both majestrates and people, amongst whom he had cast our lot, to owne and favour us; this being some refreshment to them amongst those butcheryes and crueltyes of which they were daily spectatours, poore England being become now the slaughterhowse of the lambes of Christ; the next of which that is to be brought on the stage is that renowned patriot Sir Henry Vane, who had bin the cheife steeresman of publique affaires during the late warrs, and whom the Lord owned as an emynent instrument in his worke. And therefore our bloody and treacherous enemy, as well to take revendge for what was past, especially in relation to Strafford, **929** as to secure themselves for the future in their usurpation and tiranny (there being no person living whose councells and interests they more dreaded), conclude it necessary to imbrue their hands in his blood (contrary to the request of the two Howses, who called in the King for the sparing of his life in case he should be found guilty, and the sayd Charles Steward's promise upon the said request), at least if he could not be prevayled with to betray that cause wherein he had bin so emynently instrumentall, and to which he had bin so faithfull.

In order heereunto, he and Major Generall Lambert, who were in the same qualification in the act of amnisty, are brought from the isles unto which they had bin sent, to the Tower of London, whither the Attorney Generall, Palmer, was sent to take their examination in order to their tryall; upon whose retorne from the Tower, he reported that he found these two in a very different frame, declaring that they deserved to be differently treated (if a lawyer of the Temple of an unspotted reputation may be credited, who said that the same night the Attorney retorned from the examination, he heard him say, that Major Generall Lambert alleadged for himselfe that his designe was alwayes to bring in the King, and to doe the same thinge that Monke had done, but that having such about him as were highly principled against it, he durst not move it to them for feare of having his throat cut; and that he was satisfyed upon the whole he understood from him that he was not principled against his Majestie, but rather for him, and that he had never acted for the Parlament, but for his pay, being alwayes in his principle for monarchy, and for having it setled in the right lyne, if it might have bin; but Sir Henry Vane was of such strandge principles (viz. for the advancing of the will of God, as the rule of man's obedience, and for opposing the lusts and carnall corrupt interests of men, a principle destructive to the Diana by which Mr. Palmer got his great gaine), that he judged he would dye, and the other receive favour).

What Sir Henry Vane said at his tryall on behalfe of the publique, and his owne particcular, was so rationall and convincing that his adversaryes (who for twenty yeares past would have cut his throate at any tyme, and therefore not likely to spare him now they had an opportunity to destroy him), unwilling to have their workes of darkness discovered, suppress the notes which were taken of what he sayd in his justification; wherein he so highly owned the authority of the Parlament, that some of his freinds thereupon told him he had cast away his life; whereunto he replyed, I as little vallew my life *in a good cause*, as the King doth his promise; Sir Henry perceiving, *notwithstanding the engagement for his life*, by all the circumstances of his tryall, that they intended nothing more then to butcher him. Though what he sayd be supprest, yet, the heades of what he would have sayd being published at lardge, I shall forbeare to particcularize it, save only what was sent in the generall in a publique manuscript from London to Geneve, dated the 22 June 1662, whereby may be seene the sense men had of that affaire.

What was written is as followeth.   **930** The last Friday, being the 16th of this month, Sir Henry Vane pleaded for his life, and Major Generall Lambert for his. But it may be rather said, the first pleaded for the life of his country and the libertyes thereof, and the other for his owne; the issue whereof in all appearance will be, that Vane will be put to death, and Lambert pardoned, although they are both under the sentence of death; the reason of this difference being no other then the manner of their defence; the one alleadging the authority of the Great Parlament for his justification, and that he was indemnifyed by the act of amnesty, and the other lessening and excusing what he did against Sir George Booth, and Monke, which were the cheife heades of his chardge, by the ignorance of their intentions; neither the one nor the other having declared that they had a designe to restore the King, and Monke having to the contrary declared for the restitution of the Great Parlament. Vane spake fower howres following, and much perplexed the Court and councell, having acquired to himselfe the reputation of a most emynent patriote (if ever there was any) in pleading for the dying libertyes of his country. It being cleare that all the party which seemed to be indemnifyed by the act of amnesty shall be punished in his person, and that for this only cause, that in his pleading he undertooke by the authority of the said Parlament to justify what he had done (holding forth and mainteyning that the Howse of Commons (representing the whole body of the people), in case of difference betweene the authority royall and pollitique, posesseth a just power to defend the rights of the people against the King, and to authorize all the people of England and every one of them to defend them; and adding that by the law of England, the lawfull king being disposest, every subject that acts under and for the king in posession, though an usurper, shall be indemnified, and not looked upon as guilty of any treason against the king who is out of posession), notwithstanding all which, and much more alleadged by him very materially, he is condemned to dye.

Lambert on the other hand having received renewed promises of favour, in the meanewhile the Court will not advantadge themselves by putting of Vane to death; all discerning men playnly seeing that their designe is to overthrowe the fundamentals of the libertyes of England. After Sir Henry Vane was under the sentence of death, this that foloweth came from other hands. He comported himselfe with such an even, composed, Christian and cheerefull frame of spirit, that it was to the astonishment of all who came neere him, hoping that the shedding of his blood might prove a meanes of gathering together into one the disperssed interests and remnants of the adhearers to this cause, of whatever differing perswasions, declaring that he should thinke ten thousand lives (if he had them) well spent in such a service. He refused to hearken to those of his freinds who advised him to aske his life, judging the King so highly obleiged to spare his life that it was fitter for him to doe it then for himselfe to seeke it. My deare wife going to take her leave of him the day before his death, when none but his neere relations came to him, he (perceiving her out of his chamber wyndow) desired she might be admitted, and deported himselfe   **931**   towards her as wholy unconcerned in that bloody sentence under which he was; telling her he was now only to put in execution the lesson which he had through grace long since learned, to wit to dye, declaring as greate a confidence in the resurrection of the cause as of his owne body, of which he doubted not, and that he hoped the Lord would preserve me for some other worke; but yet advising her to resigne up all into the hands of God, who would not fayle to doe his worke and to raise up instruments when his tyme should come. He found death rather shrinking from him then he from it. Some of his freinds prevayled to have his sentence exchanged from hanging and quartering to beheading. It was told him he should goe on foote to the Tower Hill, the place of execution. But being afterwards acquainted by one of the Sheriff's men that there must be a sled, he replyed, Any way how they please, for I long to be at home, to be dissolved, and to be with Christ which is best of all.

As he was drawne on the sledd, the people cryed alowd from the tops of howses, and out of wyndows, The Lord goe with you, the great God of heaven and earth appeare in you, and for you. And being asked by some how he did, he answered, Never better in all my life. Another asking how should he doe ill who suffered in so glorious a cause, he replyed, This cause hath given life in death to all the owners of it, and sufferers for it. When he passcd within the rayles on Tower Hill, there were many lowd acclamations of the people, crying out, The Lord Jesus goe with your deare soule, etc. The undaunted couradge, together with that meeke and Christian frame of spirit wherewith he appeared on the scaffold, was to the astonishment of all the spectatours. The majesty of his presence, the reputation of his person, and power of his reason were so great, that they saw it convenient to use the same method towards the interrupting him in his speech on the scaffold as they had done in his pleadings before the Courte, Robinson (the jaylor of the Tower) answering, to what was said by him touching the judges' refusing to set their seales to his bill of exceptions, that it was a lye, and that he was there to testify it was false.

And the trumpets being ordred to sound in his face to hinder his being heard, Sir Henry Vane replyed, God will judge betweene you and me in this matter. But seeing you cannot beare matter of fact, I shall only say this, that whereas the judges have refused to seale that with their hands that they have done, I am come to seale that with my blood that I have done. But proceeding to the justification of the cause wherein he was engaged and for which he suffred, from the Remonstrance of the Howse of Commons, the Sollemne League and Covenant, the trumpets sounded againe, and the Sheriffe catched at the paper in his hand. Robinson called for the written bookes, and searched his pocquets, to the great dissatisfaction of many of their owne party; Sir Henry deporting himselfe without the least discomposure, only saying, My usuadge from man is no **932** harder then was my Lord and master's, and all that will live his life this day must expect hard dealing from the worldly spirit. He would not, after he had finished his prayer, encouradge the executioner to butcher him by giving him any signe when he would have him to strike, but chose to be altogether passive, telling him he was alwayes ready. A little before the stroake he spake to this effect. I bless the Lord who hath accounted me worthy to suffer for his name. Blessed be the Lord that I have kept a conscience voyd of offence to this day. I bless the Lord I have not deserted the righteous cause for which I suffer. His last words were, Father glorify thy servant in the sight of men, that he may glorify thee in the dischardge of his duty to thee and his country.

This choyce martyr of Christ, and eminent champion for his country's liberty, was a gentleman of an ancient familly, eldest son of Sir Henry Vane, Secretary of State, and Comptroler of the Howse of the late King. It pleased the Lord to call him to the knowledge and love of him in his youth, when he was about the age of fowerteene yeares; since when he encountred with many difficultyes, having

manifested great abillity as well as zeale in the witness he bore against
the superstitious innovations which the episcopall hierarchy did intro-
duce; upon which account he was constreyned, for the enjoyment of
the liberty of his conscience, when about the age of eighteene yeares,
to withdraw himselfe into New England; where he remained during
the space of five or six yeares, the two last of which he was chosen
Governour of the said country. In the beginning of the Parlament
he was without his seeking chosen a member of it, and there made
it appeare that the Lord had qualified him, with will and ability, for
the promoting of his glory and the good of mankind. He had a quick
apprehension, a strong memory, a deepe and peircing judgement, a
great foresight and copious expression, a free and gracefull utterance,
an emynent and singular zeale and affections for the cause of Jesus
Christ and the weale publique, a noble and high couradge and resolution to put those meanes in execution which he judged tended to a
subserviency to his great end, making the Lord and not man his feare.
In briefe he was a polititian truely pious, and a Christian truly
politique.

After his retorne from New England, he was by the interest of his
father constituted one of the Treasurers of the Navy; from which being
removed by the late King, for that he imployed his talent in the Parlament faithfully, the Howse of Comons restored him thereto, out of
which he freely gave the halfe of the proffits (which amounted in the
whole to fower thousand pounds per annum) for the maintenance
of the warr against the King; which sayd warr being ended, he put
that receipt in such a way, that by the order of the Parlament that
duty was discharged for the sallary of a thousand pounds per annum,
to the advantadge of the publique many thousand pounds, though
to his owne loss; for the which the Parlament thought fit to give him
some consideration.   **933** After Cromwell's defection, he looking on
him as having betrayed the cause of God, and sacrificed it to his lust,
he would never cast in his lot with him, though he might have sate
at his right hand, but bore a constant witness against his usurpation,
and suffered imprisonement in his person, and much damadge in his
estate, for his so doing. After the retorne of Charles Steward the
present usurper, his conscience bearing him witness he had done nothing in relation to the publique for which he could not cheerefully
suffer, he abode at his hyred howse with his familly at Hampstead
neare London; where, under false and unworthy pretences of his
being engaged in councells with some of the army for the driving out
of Charles Steward againe, he was seized by souldiers who were sent
by the said Charles Steward's directions, and by them carryed to the
Tower, and so from place to place for about two yeares; after which
tyme it was thought convenient by this confederacy of butchers, under

a forme of law, to put him to death for words spoken by him, and orders issued from him, as a member of parlament, and for promoting their interest and service (as hath bin before rehearsed, and as is more fully to be seene in the publication of his said tryall at the Upper Bench in Westminster, June the 2nd and 6th anno domini 1662, together with what he intended to have spoaken the day of his sentence, June 11, etc.).

The Lord had blessed him with a consort verry godly and virtuous, and in all other respects very desirable, with a very hopefull issue, with a parentage very noble, with a revenue very lardge and plenty-full, having of what was left him by his ancestours betweene fower and five thousand pounds' rent by the yeare. But he chose to quit all, rather then to wound his conscience by deserting the cause of God and his country. Since the tyme of his conversion, he was much in prayer and searching the scriptures both publiquely and privately, encouradging others both by word and example so to doe, being him-selfe of a pious and exemplary conversation. *In comparison of the cause wherein he was engaged, and for which he suffered,* he despised his life, laying it downe freely and cheerefully in full assurance of his taking it up againe, and that the Lord would suddainly appeare to owne his cause and people.

Some monthes before, this confederacy of wicked men imbrued their hands in the blood of a precious servant of the Lord, one John James, a cittizen of London, who was accused for having affirmed, in his prayer at a publique meeting, that Charles Steward the present usurper was a tyrant, and guilty of the blood of the Saints. The witness who was to be made use of in this tragedy, being checqued by his owne conscience, resolved to fly beyond the seaes, and being to that end got as farr as Dover, was sent for back by Robinson, the jaylor of the Tower. And when the sceane was prepared, Foster that blood-thirsty wretch, and the rest of his brethren, being on the Bench, and Palmer, Finch, Glyn, and Maynard, fower of the tyrant's blood-hounds, at the barr for the worrying of this poore innocent lamb, this witness, being produced, could not say he (the said John James) then prysoner at the barr, was the person who spake those wordes whereof he was accused; the said witness not seeing the person accused at **934** the tyme the words were spoaken. Whereupon they so threatned this witness in the Court, and the councell so handled him in private, that being againe brought into the Court, he confidently affirmed that he was the man who spake those wordes. But John James denyed the words in the manner they were testifyed against him, and alleadged that if any such words were spoken, it was before the act of indemnity passed; and using the words of Jeremiah the prophet, sayd to them, As for me, behold I am in your hands, doe with me as seemeth good and meete to you; but know ye for certeine that if ye put me to death, ye shall surely bringe innocent blood upon yourselves. He professed himselfe to be one who wayted for the advancement of the scepter of Jesus Christ over nations as well as over Saints, and that, in relation to himselfe, death was more to be desired by him then life; he being with very hard labour scarse able to furnish himselfe with bread for the day, whereas in his Father's howse there were many mansions, and bread enough. But he was a preaching and a praying Saint, and looked upon as an acceptable sacrifice to the bloody tyrant, and therefore must be offered, though some of those who were of this confederacy had not their consciences so fully seared as not to repent them for having had their hands therein. Yet such was the obdurateness of the tyrant himselfe, that when the wife of this poore man now under a sentence of death made her application by petition to him for the life of her husband, he threw the petition over his shoulder, saying, He is a rogue and shall be hanged. Thus this poore man (scarse able to get a livelyhood by his trade of ribbon weaving, yet rich in faith), having finished his testimony, being hanged for the same, and his quarters given for meate to the fowles of the ayre, is gone to make up the cry of those his brethren and fellow servants under the alter, for vengeance on those who dwell on the earth. Major Generall Lambert having altered his pleading (as I have bin informed) from what he intended not long before his tryall, in consideration thereof was repreived during the pleasure of the King.

Heere is the fifth period of this narrative.

APPENDIX A: LUDLOW'S TABLE OF CONTENTS

Bound into the Bodleian manuscript is Ludlow's table of contents from 1660 (the beginning of part five) to 1685, drawn up (in Ludlow's own hand) after the Bodleian manuscript had been composed. The portion of the table which covers the Bodleian manuscript (1660–77) is reproduced below.

A Voyce from the Watch Tower
In Severall Passages of Providence relating [to?]
Publiq, and Privat Concernes
Discovering the Vision of Duty, etc.
Divided into   Parts

The Fifth Part, containeing in the generall the betraying of the publiq cause and the faythfull assertours thereof by Monke in confederacy with the secluded members: divided into seven chapters.

Associat yourselves, and yea shall bee broken in pieces, take counsell together and it shall come to nought, for God is with us, 8 Isaiah 9, 10.

The prophets prophesy falsly, the priests beare rule by their meanes, and what will ye doe in the end thereof, 5 Jeremiah 31.

They have forsaken me the fountaine of liveing water, and hewed them out cisterns broken cisters that can hold noe water, 2 Jeremiah 31.

They have healed the hurt of my people slightly saying, peace, peace, when there is noe peace, 8 Jeremiah 11.

Hee feedeth on ashes, a deceived heart hath turned him aside, that hee cannot, etc. Say is there not a lye in my right hand, 44 Isaiah 20.

The Lord takes away from Judah the stag, and the staffe, etc., and gives children to bee their princes, etc., and the base shall behave themselves proudly against the honorable, 3 Isaiah 1, 5.

They say in the pride and stoutnes of their heart, the brickes are fallen downe, but wee will build with hewen stones, etc., 9 Isaiah 9, 10.

I was wroth with my people, etc. and have given them into thy hand, thou didst shew them noe mercy, 47 Isaiah 6.

I am verry sore displeased with the heathen, etc. for I was but a little displeased and they helped forward the affliction, 1 Zechariah 15.

For thy violence against thy brother Jacob, shame shall cover thee, and thou shalt bee cut off forever, etc., Obadiah 10 etc.

How is the faythfull citty become an harlot? It was full of jugement, righteousnes lodged in it, but now murtherers, 1 Isaiah 21 [etc.?].

Shall evill bee recompensed for good? For they have digged a pit for my soul, etc., 18 Jeremiah 20.

Woe to him that buildeth a towne with blood, and stablisheth a citty by iniquity, 2 Habbakuk 12.

They turne aside the poore in the gate, etc. therefore the prudent shall hide themselves, for it is an evill time, 5 Amos 12, 13.

Yea shall bee brought before kings and rulers for my name's sake, and some of you they shall cause to bee put to death, etc., 21 Luke 12, 16.

And their dead bodyes shall ly in the streete of the great citty which spiritually is called Sodom, and Egypt, etc., 11 Revelations 8.

Sanctify the Lord of Hosts himselfe, and let him bee your feare, and hee shall bee for a sanctuary, 8 Isaiah 13, 14.

When thou passest through the watters I will bee with thee, and when thou walkest through the fier, thou shalt not be burnt, 43 Isaiah 2.

It became him, for whome are al things, etc. to make the captaine of their salvation perfect through sufferings, 2 Hebrews 10.

Who now rejoyce in my sufferings for you, and fill up that which is behind of the affliction of Christ in my flesh for his body's sake, which is the church, 1 Colossians 24.

Yea, and if I bee offered upon the sacrifice, and service of your fayth, I cry, and rejoyce with you all, 2 Philippians 17.

Whosoever will save his life shall loose it, and whosoever will lose his life for my sake shall find it, 16 Matthew 25.

Others were tortured not accepting of deliverance, that they might obtaine a better resurrection, 11 Hebrews 35.

They rejoyced they were counted worthy to suffer shame for his name, 5 Acts 41.

And they overcame him by the blood of the lamb, and by the word of their testimony, and they loved not their lives unto the death, 12 Revelations 11.

And I saw the soules of them that were beheaded for the witness of

Jesus, etc. and they lived and reigned with Christ a thousand yeares, 20 Revelations 4.

The first chapter begining at the 26th line of the 721 page containes

[The second chapter?] begining at the 14th line of
the 752 page containes

...., and his declaration from Bredagh presented to his Parliament
by Sir John Greenvill 752; .... monarchical government, and the
army's submission thereto both sent to their King 753; .... Lords'
[proclamation?] 754; the nomination of commissioners to fetch the
King 757; .... the various temper of its members 759; the officiousnes
of Coote and Jones 760; .... to have bound the King to previous
tearmes on his restitution 760; .... his owne confession, the seizure
of Major Generall Harrison 761; .... of indemnity with its limitations,
with the injustice of them 762; the justice .... Parliament's cause 763;
that the King is guilty of the blood shed in the warre 764; that those
who are guilty of blood are to bee put to death 767; kings as well
as others 768; that the ... of the people, and execution of justice, are
to bee preferred to the priviledge of Parliament or person of the King,
even of the Covenant itselfe 775; that .... proceedings of the Commons could not bee avoyded, without betraying the cause and contracting the guilt of blood 777; the blacknes of the sinne of the secluded
members in betraying the publiq cause, and sacrifycing the faythfull
assertors thereof 778; the prudentiall reasons that prevayled with
some not to oppose this great change though not desiered by them
780; the order of the assembly for the taking into custody such as
had signed the warrant for the execution of the late King, and the
issue thereof 781; their arbitrary order for seizing their reall and personall estate, and the issue of that 782; the issue of the election of
the bourrough of Hinden, the sending of Major Generall Harrison
and Justice Cooke prisoners to the Tower 783; heats amongst the
commissioners, the sending of mony to Charles Steward, etc. and his
treatment at the Hague 784; the exception of 7 from pardon, the
seizure of Colonell Jones and Mr. Gregory Clement, and the eminent
deliverance of others 785.

The third chapter begining at the 12th line of the 786 page containes

Charles Steward his landing at Dover, etc. 786; his entrance of London, his reception, and the joy at his arrivall 787; the proclamation
against drinking of healths, the nomination of the 7 persons excepted,
and 3 more, and proclamation for others to render themselves 788;
this assembly claimeing the benefit of the King's declaration on the
behalfe of the people, twenty more excepted as to their estates 789;
some of the King's judges rendring themselves 789; the malice and
falshood of Colonell Theophilus Jones 790; reasons induceing to

reasons that moved to the following thereof 814; the protection, direction and deliverance the Lord was pleased to vouchsafe to give one
of the King's judges 815; the issuing forth a proclamation forbiding
to entertaine one of the King's judges, and requiering the seizing of
him 818; the priviledge of following the pillar of fier in a darke day
819; the rewards held for the seizing of three of the King's judges
822; the jugling of the episcopall party with the presbyterian, and
of their King with the purchasers 823; the seizure of Mr. Hugh
Peeters, and the disbanding of the army, to governe by force, and
fraud 824.

The fifth chapter begining at the 20th line of the 824 page containes

The slaying of ten of the Lord's witnesses, and a short narrative of
the life and death of Major Generall Harrison 824; a demonstration
of the partiallity of the common law as to pleas of the crowne and
particularly of the commit for tryal of the King's judges 825; the contrariety of Sir Orlando Bridgeman his speech to itselfe and to all
truthe, divine and morrall 827; the proceedings against Sir Hardres
Waller, Major Generall Harrison, and Mr. Heningham, with their
manner of pleading, and several answers 830; the verdict against
Major Generall Harrison, the sentence against, and the inhumanity
of the Court towards him 838; his deportment after sentence and in
prison, his couragious testimony in his way to, and at, the place of
execution 840; a short narrative of the life of Mr. Carew, his eminent
testimony for the Lord before the Court, etc. 842; the issue of Mr.
Carew's processe, and the bringing of Colonell Adrian Scroope to
their barre, with his plea 844; the unparalelled basenes of the apostat
Browne, with the isssue . . . .; the charge against Mr. Scot, the witnesses against him 845; his plea . . . .; the issue of Mr. Scot's processe,
the charge against Colonell Jones and Mr. . . . .; the appeale of Mr.
Carew on the pronounceing of sentence against him . . . .; the testimony Mr. Carew bore from the time of his condemnation, to . . . .;
a short narrative of the life of Justice Cooke 853; his charge . . . .; his
answere to the charge 855; the contradictorinesse of the reply 857
. . . .; the charge against Mr. Hugh Peeters 858; his plea, and answere
with . . . .; a demonstration of the spirit and principle of Justice Cooke,
during his imprisonment, before, and . . . .; the testimony of an enemy
as to Justice Cooke, Mr. Peters his good confession, and the . . . .; the
narrative of the life of Mr. Scot 864; the witnes hee bore after his
. . . .; a demonstration of the badnesse of the King's cause 867; a narrative of Mr. Clement . . . .; a narrative of the life of Colonell Adrian
Scroop, and the faythfull testimony hee bore in [prison?] . . . .;

The sixth chapter begining at the 38th line of the 888 page containes order aforesayd 904; endeavours to procure a popish wife for their King, preparations for his coronation 904; the adoration of the hierarchy in Ireland and suppression of presbytery, the Court being swayed by the French faction 905; the Citty's chooseing of members for the Parliament disaffected to the Court, their jugling with the country elections 906; the prophane and superstitious ceremonyes at the coronation, the Lord's witnese against it by thunder, as [foretold?] 1 Samuel 12. 17, 907.

The seventh chapter begining at the 34th line of the 907 page containes

The boldnes of the popish party, the favour shewen them by this assembly, and witnesse against it, the death and witnes of the Earle of Argile 908; the execution of Mr. Guttericke, and another at the same time in Scotland, and their witnesse, the burning the Covenant in England, Scotland and Ireland 909; the eminent hand of the Lord against Monke 909; the sending of byshops to Scotland, and the issue thereof 909; jealousys betweene the citty of London and this assembly, the jeering of presbyterians, the pretense of plots, and why 910; the sending of Sir Henry Vane and other prisoners out of England, and injustice of this assembly in Sir Henry Vane's case 911; apparitions in the aire, the trechery of this assembly in the case of the King's judges, and the issue thereof 912; their cruelty towards Mr. Wallop, Sir Henry Mildmay and Lord Mounson, and their injustice towards Sir Arthur Haslerig and the King's judges 913; the beating downe of the tryumphall arches, and weathercockes 913; the publishing of popish tenents and wounderful preservation of the King's judges 914; the putting a stop to the act of uniformity, and the reasons thereof, the King's speech to his assembly 915; the prodigality of this assembly, the taxe of chimney mony, the countenance of papists, Earl of Ormond being [Viceroy?] of Ireland 916; the seizeing of Mr. Miles Corbet, Colonell Okey and Colonell Barksteed at Delfe by the Stats' order, and sending them into England 917; the peace betwene England and Holland founded in blood, the inhumane treaty of those 3 prisoners, their charge 918; their plea, answere, and issue thereof 918; the frame of spirit they were in, a narrative of the life of Mr. Miles Corbet 919; Mr. Corbet his faythfull witnesse, Colonell Barkstead his life, with his faythfull testimony, and his good confession 920; the execution of these 3 martyrs with the assistance they had from the Lord at the time and place of their execution 921; the great appearance at Colonell Okey's intended funerall, their disappointment, the ground of Mr. Lisle etc. remove from Geneve 922;

the Lord's enclineing their Excellencyes of Berne to receive them into their protection, and the issue thereof 924; the landing of the Infanta of Portugall in England, the viciousnes of the Court, the Lord's hand against its chaplin 925; a witnes on the behalfe of the publique cause, what it is, wherein instruments were waunting, and what's conceived to bee duty for the future 926; the preparations for the tryall of Sir Henry Vane, and Major Generall Lambert, their charges, their severall pleas, and answers, and their issue 929; the blessed frame of spirit Sir Henry Vane was in at his tryall, and after sentence, and the eminent testimony he bore at all three 930; a narrative of the life, and death of Sir Henry Vane 932; of the charge, and answere, bloody treatement of John James cittyzen of London 933.

[The Sixth Part containeing?] in the generall the lying of the dead bodys of the witnesses . . . . being permitted to bee put into their graves, and the Lord his . . . . [heaven?] for the setting them on their feete, during the usurpation of . . . . : divided into seven chapters.

. . . . see their dead bodys three days and an halfe, and shall not suffer, etc., 11 Revelations 9.

. . . . the earth shall rejoyce over them and make merry, and send gifts, etc., 10 verse.

. . . . they are full of the fury of the Lord, the rebuke of thy God, 51 Isaiah 20.

. . . . indignation of the Lord because I have sinned, etc. untill he plead my cause, and execut jugement, 7 Micah 9.

. . . . to see what hee will say unto mee, and what I shall answere when I am reproved, 2 Habakkuk 1.

. . . . in righteousnes wilt thou answere us O God of our salvation, who art the confidence, etc., 65 Psalms 5.

. . . . Lord, etc., that the people shall weary themselves, etc., for the earth shall be filled with the knowledge, etc., 2 Habakkuk 13, 14.

. . . . destroy me, being myne enemyes wrongfully, are mighty, then I restored what I tooke not away, 69 Psalms 4.

. . . . and thou shalt goe even to Babylon, there shalt you bee delivered, 4 Micah 10.

. . . . peace with the Assyrian shall come into our land, etc., and the remnant of Jacob shall be a dew from the Lord, 5 Micah 5, 3.

Although I have scattered them among their countrys, yet I will bee to them a little sanctuary, etc., 11 Ezekiel 16.

He shall smite thee with a rod, etc., for yet a little while, and the indignation shall cease, and mine anger in their destruction, 10 Isaiah 24, 25.

Come my people [to hide?] thyselfe as it were for a little moment, etc., for behold the Lord comes out of his place, to punish, etc., 26 Isaiah 20, 21.

I know his wrath sayth the Lord, but it shall not be soe, his lyes shall not effect it, 48 Jeremiah 30.

And whosoe falleth not downe, and worshippeth, shall the same hower bee cast into the might of the fiery furnace, etc., 3 Daniel 6, etc.

Yea have condemned, and killed the just, etc. Be patient therefore unto the comeing of the Lord, whose coming draweth nigh, 5 James 6, 7, 8.

        hee that believeth maketh not hast

And Moses sayd unto the people, feare ye not, stand still, and see the salvation of the Lord, etc., 14 Exodus 13, 14.

The Lord is well pleased for his righteousnes sake, he will magnify the law, and make it honorable, 42 Isaiah 21.

After 3 days and an halfe, the spirit of life from God entered into them, etc., and they heard a great voyce from heaven, etc., 11 Revelations 11, 12.

Now will I arise sayth the Lord, now will I be exalted, etc., yea shall conceive chaff, yea shall bring forth stubble, 33 Isaiah 10, 11.

When thy hand is lifted up, they will not see, but they shall see, and bee ashamed for their envy at the people, etc., 26 Isaiah 11.

For lo I begin to bring evill on the citty, which is called by name, and should ye bee utterly unpunished? Ye shall not bee, etc., 25 Jeremiah 29.

Behold I have taken out of thy hand the cup of trembling even the dregs of the cup of my fury, etc. and put into, etc., 51 Isaiah 22, 23.

I will overturne, overturne, overturne, and it shall bee noe more, untill hee come, whose right it is, etc., 21 Ezekiel 27.

The first chapter begining at the 32d line of the 934th page containes

The heightening of persecution, the Queene's coming into England with the King's natural son, objections against the Portugal match 934; the sending of forces to Portugal, the effect of Sir Henry Vane's plea, the presbyterians' disappointment, and requitall 935; Mr.

find protection, and friendshipp, from their Excellencyes of Berne, etc. 964; the proceedings against those engaged in the Irish deseigne, the witnesses, juges, and issue of their tryall 966; the persons who suffered and the hand of the Lord therein 967; the banisshing of priests, and their insolence 968; the backwardnes of the House to give mony, and the reason thereof, Charles Steward accusing Sir Richard Temple, and the issue thereof 969; the Earle of Bristol his speech in the Commons House, the King's sense thereof, the Earle's resolution thereupon 970; the Earle's accusing the Chancellour Hide of high treason, the articles themselves, and the Lords' proceedings thereon 971; the Earle's reply, their King's threats by letter, and the issue thereof, their King's jugement of the acts to bee presented to him 972; the acts themselves, the Court's jugling about that for religion, etc. and the issue thereof 973; the King's speech to his two Houses 974; some observations upon that speech 975.

The second chapter begining at the 17th ....

The people's discontents in England, Ireland and Scotland ....; the feares and divisions of enemyes, with the hopes of friends ....; the occasion of an addresse to their Excellencyes of Berne by the ....; the King of England his present resolutions, his juggle with ....; the reasons induceing Mr. Sheldon the present Archbyshop to bee [popish?] ....; the slaying of the Lord Warriston in Scotland and his [testimony?] ....; Mr. Hollis his complaint to Mr. Lullin, the Geneve agent at Paris ....; the giveing in of a suitable and seasonable mercy, and the ....; the Lord's eminent hand in rayseing up friends, and discovering ....; the prosequution of nonconformists, a Quaker's testimony, ...; the prosequution of the Earle of Bristoll 996; the ground of ....; the death of Mr. Blackborne, the imprisonment of Mr. Nevill ....; an eminent deliverance formed against some ....; the care taken by the magistrats for their future preservation ....; some passages relating to the Queene of England, and touching the ....; the jealousys and discontents of the French ambassadour, the policy of the ....; the King's dissatisfaction with the bill for the triennial Parliament, the zealous ....; preparations for tryall of the northerne conspirators, a mercy in the midst of .... designe ...; the conjuration against those engaged therein, the persons accused, their charge, and .... 1006; their plea, and answere, and the issue thereof, the judge's cruelty, the partiallity of the jury, and the issue thereof 1007; Mr. Rayner's charge, and answere, the unjustice of the proceedings of the bloody execution of their sentences, the martyrs' witnes 1008; the Duchesse of Savoy's death, the execution of Colonell Turner and man-

The third chapter begining at the 38th line of the 1016 page containes of the English in France and Spaine, and the issue thereof 1041; the prosequution of the act of uniformity, the severall effects thereof, the violation of the act of indemnity 1042; the Emperour's truce, and peace with the Turke, and besiedging and takeing of Erford, the prosequution of nonconformists 1043; renewed experience of the Lord's goodnes, and the successe of the English at Guiny 1044; the policy of the Duch for relieving the fort, Charles Steward's rage thereat, and their answere 1045; Duprea's murdering Mr. de la Flecher, and the reasons thereof, the slight prosequution of the murderer 1046; Mr. de la Flecher's letter, expressing his care for the preservations of some of the King's judges 1047; the English seizing the Dutch shipps by way of reprisall, and the issue thereof 1048; the little effect of Charles Steward's rage against the nonconformists, the fining of a jury, and the hope of friends 1049; the Convention's forwardnes to assist their King, De Ruiter his successe at Guiny, Holmes his imprisonement 1050; the death of Count William of Nassaw 1050; workes of darkenesse brought to light, and the Lord's protecting his witnesses 1051.

The fourth chapter begining at the 9th line of the 1052 page containes

The English [attacqueing?] the Duch in the Mediterranean sea, the French defeat at Grigerey, the reason of Ormond's purchasinge Charlemont 1052; Colonell Hutchinson's death, etc., the King's being furnished with mony, the proclamation of warre with the Duch 1053; the Lord's witnesse against Lawson's shipp, the shipwracke of the Royall Oake, London's zeale for their King 1055; invitations to engage on behalfe of the Duch, with the reasons offered against it 1056; the tearmes proposed by the Duch 1058; the discovery of new designes against some of the King's judges, and the Lord's directions to meanes for their prevention 1059; .... murder 1060; the apparition of commets, and other prodigies 1061; .... of some neighbour potentats, the counterfeiting the King's and the Duke's Seale 1062; .... the cowardlynesse of two English shipps, the injustice of men and the Lord's justice 1063; .... fleete being at sea, and some passages relating to the Duch fleet's putting forth 1064; .... London, the discontents of the presbyterians in England and Scotland, and their designe 1064; .... to bee made use of, and their ground of their hopes, and their call 1065; .... of Vevey, and others on the behalfe of the King's judges 1065; and of Boursier Steiger 1068; .... the various reports of the fight betweene English and Duch, and the certainty thereof 1069; .... and their punishing of those who fayled in their duty 1070; .... and particcularly of Vice Admirall Lawson 1071; the King of France his mediation, and demands 1072; .... meanes he used to prevent

The fifth chapter begining at the 37th line of the 1087 page containes thereof 1099; the Duch fleet's returning home, and why, the divisions amongst the English officers, the miserys of the people and greatnes of their taxe 1100; the enmity against the Lord's people, and their divisions, the hand of the Lord against his enemyes 1101; the uniting of the French army with the Duch, their jealousys of Brandenbourg and Prince of Orang his party 1101; Mr. Drelinquort's enmity to, and ignorance of the Lord's worke, and his witnesses, discovered 1102; reasons for not embarqueing with the Duch 1105; the death of Queene Mother of France, that King's declaring warre with England, his carryage towards the Queene Mother of England 1106; the grounds of some freinds' hopes, and stirrings, the death of Mr. William Cawley and his witnes 1107; the King of Danmarke, and Marquis of Brandenbourg's joyning with the Duch 1107; the King of Portugall's marriage with a French woman 1108; the English proclaiming warre with France, Mr. Stoop's invitation to correspondence against England 1108; the discourse held with Mr. Stoope and Mr. Constance, sent by the Count of Donnah on Pensioner Dewit his desier 1109; the Bishop of Munster his peace with the Duch, the posture of affaires at Vienna, Madrid, Stockholme, and Paris, etc. 1110; an invitation from Pensioner Dewit, etc. and some friends in Holland to treat at Paris about publique affaires 1111; the ground of some friends' hopes, and others' fears 1112; the reasons for not confiding in the assistance offered 1113; the arrivall of two messagers from friends, the discourse held with them, and the issue thereof 1114; Mr. Lockier his letter of invitation 1115.

The sixth chapter begining at the 40th line of the 1116 page containes

The King of England's pollicy for the strengthening his fleete, their conjuration against 7 friends, and the bloody issue thereof 1117; a more full discovery of this conjuration, the improbability of the designe, and the use made of it 942; the tryall and quittall of the Lord Montegle, the proclamation requiering severall persons to appeare under paine, etc. 1117; an offer of assistance, the Duch and English treaty of prisoners, a designe to assasinat Pensioner Dewit, etc. 1118; the two fleetes being at sea, the division of the English fleete, Monke's engageing the Duch, etc., and the issue thereof 1118; preparations for renforcing the fleets, and for the English secureing their coals 1120; the defeat of the English at Christopher's, the rising at Carrickefergus, and issue thereof, the Duch fleet at sea 1121; the boggling of the French with the Duch, the propositions from the Duch to the Parliament's party 1122; divisions among Parliament's friends that are at Paris, further invitations to engage with the Duch 1123; an answere to that invitation 1124; a reply to that answere, with the issue of the whole 1125; the reasons of Mr. Hollis his returne from France, the holding forth liberty of conscience, dissatisfaction with popish commanders 1126; another fight betwene the English and Duch, with the issue 1126; the state of affaires in Polonia 1127; Colonell Desbourough his treatment for his landing in England, Colonell Nangle his rising in Ireland, and issue thereof 1127; the dissolution of the Parliament in Ireland 1127; endeavours to set Major Generall Lambert at liberty, with the issue thereof 1128; prodigies in England, the questioning of Tromp, the fiering of Duch shipps in the Uli, and issue thereof 1128; the conspiracy of Buat, the cashiering of Tromp, new experiences of the goodnes, and faythfulnes of the Lord 1129; the murder of Mr. Tornello by de Fargus, the two fleets at sea . . . . ; the dreadfull fier of London and the emminent hand of . . . . ; the French's favouring the King of England, the poursuit of som . . . . ; the falling of 3 French men of warre into the hands of the English, the . . . . ; the condemnation of Mr. Buat, etc., his execution and excuse, the . . . . ; the providence relating to Major Warren's son, the difference between . . . . ; Hubert's confessing the fiering of London, his processes and issue thereof, the . . . . ; the riseing of the presbyterians in Scotland, and issue thereof . . . . ; the Duch answere to the King of England's justification of the warre, his . . . . ; the defeate of the presbyterian party in Scotland, their . . . . ; the hand of the Lord on their enemys, and against the . . . . ; a great storme in Linclonshire, with its effects, the jealousys the [Convention have?] . . . . ; the Speaker's harrange on the presenting of the act forbiding the . . . . ; the correspondence of the King of France and England, Dewit's excuse for not treating . . . . ; the King of England his complementing the Duch, and his relying thereon, the prosequution . . . . ; the prosequution of some freinds to the publique [with the offer of?] . . . . 1143.

The seventh chapter begining at the 20th line of
the 1144 page containes

The King of France his entering Flaunders with an army, ... Stat's jealousy 1144; the Duch fleet's putting to sea, the renewed hopes of friends with their . . . . 1145; the King of France his possessing himselfe of Charleroy, Doway and Tourney, the landing of . . . . under the . . . . 1146; the Lord's hand against some English shipps, the parade and division of English commissioners at Bredagh, the Hollander's offers and pretenses 1147; the resolution taken therein, the Parliament's sitting proposed to bee hastened, on the Duch fleete being at sea and

an army raysed 1148; the Lord's hand against the family of the Burgo-
master of Lausanna, the Duch fleet's attaqueing the English in the
Thames, and the issue thereof 1149; the divisions of the English Court,
the dissatisfactions of the people, and the affronting of Chancellier
Hide 1150; the accusation of Mr. Pet, the nations being alarumd by
the Duch, the further hopes of friends, and grounds thereof 1151; jealousys of the Duch's intentions, their attaque of Harwich fort, and the
event thereof 1152; the conclusion of the treaty at Bredagh, the confirmation of the peace, the principall articles thereof 1153; observations on this peace, and some privat articles thereof 1154; the losse
the English sustained during this treaty, etc. 1156; the taking of Lisle
by the French, and their defeating 2000 Spaniards 1156; Hamburge
not being included in the treaty 1157; the Parliament's adjourne-
ments 1157; their King's speech to them, the ground of Parliament
and people's discontent 1158; the rescue of Captaine Mason 1158;
the Privy Counsell declaring for the army's disbanding, their ordering
the Great Seale from Hide, the Lord's hand .... 1158; Hide's excuse,
and yet submission, one cause of his disgrace his policy in relation
to his grandson, the Duch's successes at Syrinam 1159; the King of
France his jealousys of the Convention 1159; the Duke of Buckingham's
readmition to favour, the discountenance of ..., the murder of Mr.
Lisle etc. 1160; the disbanding of the Scotch army, Sir Orlando
Bridgeman made Keeper of the Seale, Rushworth his secretary,
Bridgman's speech to the Convention 1160; the two Houses' thankes
to their King, the Lord's voyce from heaven for the raysing of his
witnesses, the Stats' pollicy for giving their liberty 1161; the field
officers of the Stats' land army, Hide's pollicy for his preservation,
the chardge of high treason by the Commons 1162; the Lords'
answere, Hide's champions, his flight, his letters to King and Lords'
House, and issue of them 1163; the articles preferred against him
1163; the Lords' resolution thereon, with the opinion and desier of
the Commons 1165; the ejecting of Mr. Ashburnham out of the
House, the release of severall prisoners, and death of Mr. Robert
Wallop 1165.

Secondly the Lord's continuening to speake from heaven by his providences, in order to the seting his witnesses on their feete dureing the
usurpation of Charles the 2d under the administration of the Duke
of Buckingham, Secretary Binet, Sir Anthony Ashly Cooper, and
Treasurer Clifford: divided into seven chapters.

I will shake all nations, and the desier of nations shall come, 2 Haggai
7.

And they shall drinke, and bee moved, and bee mad because of the sword I will send amongst them, etc., 25 Jeremiah 16, etc.

Thou shalt even drinke it, and sucke it out, and thou shalt breake the shreds thereof, and pluck off thine owne brestes, 23 Ezekiel 34.

Babylon, etc. made all the earth drunken, the nations have drunke of her wine, and therefore the nations are mad, 51 Jeremiah 7.

And I will call for a sword against him, etc. Every man's sword shall bee against his fellow, etc. Thus will I magnify myselfe, 38 Ezekiel 21, etc.

And the three hundred blew the trumpets, and the Lord set every man's sword against his fellows, 7 Judges 22.

In the hand of the Lord there is a cup, etc. but the dreggs thereof all the wicked of the earth shall wring out, etc., 75 Psalms 8.

The children of Moab, and Amnion stood up against those of Mount Seir, etc. and then everyone helped to destroy another, 2 Chronicles 20. 23.

They shall bee as when a standard bearer fainteth, and the rest of the trees of his forrest shall be few, that a child may write them, Isaiah 10. 18.

As I prophesyed there was a noyse, and behold a shaking, and the bones came together bone to his bone, etc. but there was no breath in them etc., 37 Ezekiel 7.

[The first chapter begining?] at the first line of
the 1166 page containes

.... enjoy more liberty then formerly, Dr. Owen's jugement and desiers, etc. 1166; .... passing of severall acts, the punishing some officers of the navy 1167; .... a peace betweene Spaine and France, the imprisoning the King of Portugall, and their peace with Spain 1168; .... England and Holland, the King of France his possessing the county of Burgundy, and manner how 1169; .... [opposition?] thereunto, the King's speech, and the Commons' dissatisfaction 1169; .... [entitled?] Vox et Lachrymae Anglorum 1170; .... the giveing of mony, the zeale of the Convention against indulgence 1171; .... [Earle?] of Shrewsbury's duell, the cause and issue thereof 1172; the ... and dissimulation thereof, the rage of the Commons House against nonconformists 1172; .... especially against bawdy houses, etc., the Lord's witnessing against false prophesying, etc. 1173; .... in searching out the author of the fier of London, the peace betwene Spaine and France, and tearmes [on which?] 1174; .... the King of France,

his greatnes, his resolutions to succour the Isle of Candie 1175; ....
Lords, and Commons 1175; the Parliament's adjournment, the difference betwene Ormond and Broghill 1176; .... Lord's faythfulnes,
and goodnes in feeding with bread from himselfe 1176; [one?] ....
1177; the contest touching the meeting of the Parliament, the enlarge-
ment of some prisoners 1178; [King of England?] .... vengeance
1178; new designes against some of the King's judges, instruments,
meanes, and issue of all 1179; reasons .... [of a mixt?] congregation,
of the sacrament of the Lord's Supper 1184; the [issue?] .... Mr.
Hommel 1186; Boursier Steiger's resolution to adhere to the King's
judges 1187; Gevene's being ... by the Duke of Savoy, and the canton
of Berne endeavoured to bee divided from the other cantons 1188;
the propositions from the Stats to the Protestant cantons, the Prince
of Orange his party getting ground, Turene's turning papist 1189;
the carrying on workes of darknes, Mr. Trever in the place of Secretary
Maurice, etc., defensive betwene Duke of Lorraine and Prince Palatin
1189; the King of Polonia's resigning his crowne, differences amongst
the grandees of Spaine, alsoe those of England 1190; Roun his
renewed proposition, the difficultys touching not communicating in
the Lord's Supper, in the jugement of friends 1191; arguments against
imposing in matters of fayth 1192; objections answered 1203; questions resolved 1204; meanes for removeing the roote of bitternes proposed 1206; what is the duty of magistrat and people in religion to
the maintenance of a gospell ministery, with submission humbly
offered 1212; the conclusion of the whole 1214.

The second chapter begining at the 49th line of
the 1215 page containes

Resolutions for the succour of Candy, the peace betwene the Prince
Palatin and Duke of Lorraine, Pere Nitard's retreate, and state preparations 1216; Colonell Delbou's designe, the Lord Roberts being
Deputy of Ireland, the prorogation of the Parliament, Prin's appearing against episcopacy 1217; the severall designes of the Court party
1217; the renewed designe of Roun, and the Lord's hand in bringing
him to justice 1218; the dispensation of the Lord, in relation to one
Mr. Thomas Schugar an Englishman 1221; the King of France his
prosequution of Mr. Balthasar, King James his opinion of those called
Puritans 1222; the prosequution of nonconformists, and the Lord's
overruling providence therein 1223; Mr Delabady his witnes at
Geneve, the grounds of his leaving them and his reception at Middle-
bourg in Zeland 1224; his persecution by the formall clergy, the
grounds thereof, and the issue of that contest 1225; the election of

The third chapter begining at the 8th line of the 1249 page containes

French's successe in Lorraine, endeavours to seize Coronet Joyce, and reasons of it, fresh experiences of the Lord's goodnesse 1251; the complyance of some nonconformists with the King, their weaknesse therein manifested by a treatise for athisme, owned in print 1254; some remarques on the sayd treatise 1255; Mr. Kiffin not permitted to serve as Sheriffe, and Sir Edward Ford Mayor of London 1257; the two Houses' complyance with their King, his correspondency with the Prince of Orange 1257; his demand of the Scots' ministers, etc. 1258; Mr. Delabady his retiering from Amsterdam, the great mortality in England, the little sense thereof in Court, Citty, or Parliament 1258; the attempt on the Earle of Ormond, and that on Sir John Coventry, with the reasons, and issue thereof 1259; the mocke justice on the assassinats of Sir John Coventry, the murther committed by Sir Anthony Vincent and others 1260; the fall of the playhouse at Dublin, etc., the murther of a watchman by the King's naturall son, Monke's son, and others 1261; the recruiting of the House of Commons, the death of the Duke of Yorke's son, and his Duchesse 1261; the kindnesse of Mr. Oldisworth, the hopes at Rome of England's returning to them 1261; their opinion of the late King 1262; a further discovery of Mr. Lisle's murther, who Riardo is, his .... the Stats' jealousy of the King of France, their sending men to Cologhen, the .... the policys, and debaucherys of the Court, a fier at Oxford, ... the attempt to seize the crowne, etc. in the Tower of London, death of the ....; the funeralls of Browne and Glin, transactions betwene forraigne princes ....; a witnesse against making a trade of warre, a further evidence of ....; Mr. Cornelius Holland leaveing Switserland, and why 1267; his disappointment ....; the forbidding to export the marchandise of France or Holland by each ....; the execution of the Count of Serrin, etc., the divisions at the Court of ....; transactions betweene Spaine and France, Cologhn's agreeing with their Byshop ....; the King of France his congratulation of Berne, the Stats' addresse to ....; the King of England's shutting up the Exchequer, the issue of Downing's embassy to the ....; the posture of Spaine, and resolution of Sweden 1273; the Lord's rebukes of ....; the favour held forth to some English, and why, the death of Mr. Edward Bagshaw ....; the mutuall succour given by the Spaniard and Stats, Grotius the Stats' ambassadour ....

The fourth chapter begining the first line of the 1276 page containes

The English fleet's attaqueing the Stats' Smyrna fleete, before any warre ....; some remarques of the King of England's trechery 1277; a fast proclaimed in England, ...; the King of France his declaration

of the Duch East India fleete, and the losse of the English 1308; the
French quitting some garrisons about Amsterdam 1309; Monmouth's
entering of Bruxels, etc., the seidge of Groninghen, and delivery of
the fort of Ronkler, the advance of Brandenbourg 1309.

The fifth chapter begining the first line of the 1310 page containes

Seditions in Polonia, and the Turke marching against them, Mr.
Delabadie, etc. sitting down at Altena being driven from Erford 1310;
the King of France his dissatisfaction with the canton of Berne 1310;
the cloud betwene Geneve and Duke of Savoy diverted by his breach
with Genoa 1311; the Genoa's victory 1311; their taking of Arbinglio,
the union of the Suisse, Utreche, and other places' too late repentance
1312; the princes of the Empier being requiered to quit their allyance
with France, persecution in Hungary, the Swedish embassys 1313;
the King of France discharg of prisoners, libells at Vienna, the harrangue of the Prince of Orange to the Stats, Mr. Cornelius Dewit's
explanation 1313; the Court's severity against Mr. Dewitt, the barbarous murther of Mr. Cornelius Dewitt and his brother the Pensionary 1314; some remarques on the murther of the Dewitts 1315;
the sentence against Montbas, the injustice of Pensionary Dewitt's
accusation 1316; the Duke of Savoy's answere to the canton of Berne,
the Prince of Orange his pollicy to advance his tyranny, the madnes
of the people 1317; an advertissement to the Suisse, the Emperour's
arming, as alsoe Brandenbourg's and Swede's, the raysing the siedge
of Groninghen 1318; Turen's march towards the Rhine, the confirmation of the treaty betwene the Emperour, Spaine, Elector of Brandenbourg, and Stats 1318; Trump in the place of Vice-Admirall Ghent,
the insurrection at Amsterdam against de Ruiter, the divisions in that
city 1319; the beheading the late governours of Wesel, and of Rhine-
bourg, demonstrations of the Prince of Orange being guilty of the
blood of the Dewitts 1320; the posture of the armys of the Stats', Brandenbourg's, Emperour's, the French, the King of Damark's answere
to the English, their losse at sea 1320; the posture of the English and
Duch fleets, and of the forces raysed in England, the prorogation of
the Parliament 1321; the confusions in Holland, and severall rencontres betweene French, and Duch, the French fortifying Vaert, and
Worden 1322; Turene his message to Cologhne, and their answere,
the Duke of Bavaria's sending succours to the Duke of Savoy 1322;
the Emperour's message, and propositions to the cantons of Swisse,
the victory of the Portugalls in the Indies 1323; severall rencontres
of the English and Duch, Montbas his challenge, the siedge of
Woerden and the shamefull raysing of it 1324; a meeting at Middle-

1343; the seizing of the 2 Duchmen in France, the Emperour's demand of the Duchesse of Insbruck's daughter, the Duke of York's discharge of his Protestant servants 1343; the casting away of a French ship richly loaden about Lisborne, the taking the Isle of St. Thomas, the taking of St. Helen from the English 1344; the dispute about repayring the bridge of Strasbourg, and issue thereof; the march of forces from Millan to Burgundy by Suisse 1344; the disput about the [Governour?] of Neufchattel, and issue thereof 1345; reasons for the Elector of Brandenbourg his treaty with Mareschal Turene, the siedge of Couverden, the union in Polonia, their preparations against the Turke 1346; the addresses of the Turke and Muscovite to the King of France, his leaveing Paris and taking the field, preparations to withstand him 1347; the posture of Stats', and 2 Kings' fleets, the King of France his preparations to besiedge Mastrich, the Emperour's raysing forces 1347; the Duchesse of Orleance delivered of a son, the two Kings' fleete putting to sea 1347; a demonstration of the Lord's overruling hand 1348; the siedge of Mastrich, the fight at sea betweene the fleets and issue thereof, the Governour of Mastrich his resolution 1349; the second fight at sea, and issue thereof, the King of France his summoning of Mastrich, the Governour's answere 1350; the manner of the attaque, and its defense, its rendition, the reasons thereof, and conditions on which 1351; the taking of Navigne, the advertisment to the King of France from heaven, his fortifying of Nancy 1352; Brandenbourg's complyance with the French, the advance of the Emperour's army, the taking of New Sconse 1353; some previous discourses to the treaty, the King of France, and the King of England's demands, and the issue thereof 1353; the posture of the fleets, the disappointment of the English landing at the Brill, the fier at Wapping, dissatisfaction of the Prince of Orang, the taking of Colmar 1354; the delivery of Schlestad, transactions betwene the Suisse and King of France, the French and Imperial army, the taking of Treves 1355; the treaty of marriage betwene the Duke of Yorke and the Duchesse of Modena's daughter, the fight betwene the fleets, and issue thereof 1356; the retaking St. Hellen, etc., the Stats' gratifying their sea commanders, divisions betwene Prince Robert and D'Estres, Count Ossery commands the English fleete 1357; the league betwene Spaine and the States, the Emperour's declaration for raysing forces 1358; the Emperour's oath 1359; some passages relating to the Emperour's and French army, and to the Byshop of Wurtsburg 1359; the taking of Naerden 1360; the punishing of severall French officers for delivering of Naerden, before necessitated thereto 1360.

The seventh chapter begining at the 24th line of
the 1360 page containes

The French drawing out of severall places in Holland, on the
Emperialist's advance, the takeing of Freebourg and esteme of
Colonell Rabenhaupt 1360; the affronting of the Portugall ambassadour at Madrid, the warre breaking forth betwene Spaine and
France 1360; the publishing of it at Paris 1361; the Princess of
Modena's arrivall at Paris, the intercourse betwene the two courts,
the motions of the French, Duch, and Imperialists' army 1361; the
fight betweene the Muscovits, Turkes, and Tartars, with its issue
1361; the alliance betwene England and France renewed, etc. 1362;
the Parliament declaring against the Duke of Yorke's marriage, etc.,
the taking of Bon, the marriage of the Emperour, the King of England's speech to the Parliament 1362; the two Houses' dissatisfaction
with their King's answer touching the Duke's marriage, their resolutions, and adjournement 1363; the demand on the behalfe of the Duke
of Lorraine, the demarches of both armys, Mr. Hummel's farewell
letter 1364; renewed experience of the Lord's goodnes, the taking the
Seale from Sir Anthony Ashley Cooper, the proclamation against
papists, Finch mad Keeper 1364; the marriage of the Duke of York,
Turen's complaints to the King, and issue thereof 1364; the quitting
of Utrech, the death of the King of Polonia 1365; the Polonians' victory over the Turkes, the taking of Orange cittadel 1365; the King's
offer to the Stats, etc., the French quitting Emerick 1366; the French
army in streights, the publishing libells at London, the articles offered
by the Stats to King of England's answere to them 1366; discontents
in Scotland, the losse of two English men of warre, differences betwene
Montery and Prince of Orange, and about the raysing men in Suisse
1367; the French cruelty at Ach 1367; preparatifs to the meeting of
the Parliament, their King's speech to them, the Earl of Shrewsbury
the manager [of that buisinesse?] 1368; the Commons' resolutions
to have greivances redressed, etc., about the militia, touching the
Lord Lauderdale, and Duke of Buckingham 1368; the Duke's appearing before the Commons, the questions proposed to him, his answere,
and their resolution thereupon 1369; the proceedings of the Commons
against Secretary Binet qualifyed Earle of Arlington, the articles
against him 1369; Secretary Binet his answere, the resolution of the
Lords touching their members, the Commons' seeming zeale against
popery, etc. 1370; the Commons' inclination to peace, the Court's
pollicy to prevent them, their pressing for a peace, and for many good
lawes 1370; the King's dismission of the Duke of Buckingham, etc., the
King's French mistresse retiering into France, the peace concluded
betwene England and Holland 1371; Mr. Bagnall's information

of the Court caball, the King's speech to his Parliament, the French march into Bourgogne 1372; the taking of Pesme, the Spaniard's preparations for the Mediterranien sea 1372; the proceeding of the Commons against Secretary Binet 1373; the present temper of the Lords House, the progresse of the French in the county of Burgundy 1373; the French falling into the Palsgrave's country, the enmity of the English against the French, reasons for adjournement of the Parliament 1374; the King's speech to the Parliament, some observations thereon, the advisers to this prorogation, and the meanes of procuring it 1375; the dismission of Duke Hammilton, and other Scots commissioners from Whitehal, the adjournement of the Scotish Parliament 1375.

Thirdly the .... heaven by his providences in order to the .... during the usurpation of Charles the 2d under the administration of the Lord Lauderdale, ... Finch, and Secretary Binet, qualified Earle of Arlington: .... chapters.

The first chapter begining the 44th line of the 1375 page containes

The recalling the English plenipotentiarys from Cologhne, the seizing Prince William of Furstembourg, and issue thereof 1375; the death and funerall of Mr. Hummel, the death and last testimony of Mr. Delabady 1376; the Lord's blessing the House of Obededom for the arke's sake, the death of Mr. William Say and Mr. Edward Dendy, with their testimony 1378; the King of England's correspondence with the Prince of Orange, the preparations for attaquing and defending the French County, severall renconters about the Rhine 1379; the King of France his propositions at Nimegue, preparations for warre, Major Generall Rabenhaupt his successe against Bishop of Munster 1379; the King's deciding the disput about the Governour of Newcastle 1379; the burning the Duke of Bavaria's pallace, the siedge of Beçanson, etc. 1380; the dispute about the abasing the pavillion, the King of England his jugling, etc., the Elector of Cologhne and Bishop of Munster quitting the French party 1380; the drawing of the French out of Zutfen, Arnhem and Nimegue, articles agreed on betwene some of the confederats 1380; the Duch preparations by land and sea, Mareschal Bellefont his disgrace, the burning of some villages in France by .... 1381; the Spanish claime, some renconters betweene the Spaniard and French in Catalogne, the taking of Beçanson 1381; the blocking of Dole and Salines, murmurings against the Prince of Orange, his pride, and pollicy, the Court of England endeavours to satisfy the people 1382; the Queene Regent of Spaine

of Dinant, etc. 1398; rencounters in Catalogne, the French being possessed of Messine, Don Afonso resigning the Portugall crowne, rencounters on the Rhine 1399; the delivery of Grave, etc., the Prince of Orange his pretexts for raysing the siedge of Oudenard, the Lord's hand against such as are called by his name 1400; the siezing of Prince Lobovitski by the Emperour, the King of England his pressing the Stats to a peace, and effect thereof 1401; Monterry his justice in restoring Prases, the taking of Waslenheim, the discovery and prevention of a design on Nancy 1401; the routing of the French Riereban in Lorraine, the killing of the Duke of Carsol, the posture of Brandenbourg and Turene's army 1402; the imprisonment of Leiftenant Colonell Stoope, the Imperialists' possessing of Huy 1402; and retaking of Dinant 1403; the Turke's taking of Human, etc. 1403.

The second chapter begining the 29th line of the 1403 page containes

The Swedes . . . . in Pomerania, their dissimulation, and the jealousyes of them 1403; preparations to resist the Swede, jealousys of the Bishop of Munster 1403; the Duch boreing their eares to the . . . his doore posts 1404; reports concerning Chevalier Rohan his designe, his examination, sentence, and execution, and of Mr. de Preaux, Madame de Villars and Vander Enden 1404; the King's gratifying the garrison of Grave, the French and Spanish Indian fleets, the freightening of Brisac, the fight about Mulhusen 1405; the reasons for the Elector of Brandenbourg's drawing off his army, Duke de Villaharmosa being made Governour of Flaunders 1406; the death of Hide, the taking of Dachstein, Captaine Contarini's death, the Swede's trechery, the Stats' embassy to the Emperour 1406; . . . . 1406; the difficulty betwene the Elector of Mayene and the Elector Palatine, the Polonia's successe in Ukrain 1407; . . . . Messine, the death of the Barron of Liosla, the ambassadour's complaint against Cardinal Altier 1407; . . . . being made Barron in England, the Count's preparations against the meeting of the Parliament 1408; . . . . to the supposed royall reliques, the citty of London's present to their King 1408; . . . . [accepting?] the souveraignty of Gueldres, Nimegue, the place of treaty for a generall peace 1408; . . . . the sicknes, and recovery of the Prince of Orang, the beheading the Governour of Phare 1408; . . . . to the death of the Earle of Mayence, the insurrection at Bordeaux, the . . . [favour?] . . . [then the reforme?] 1409; . . . . agreement betwene the English and Holland East India Companys, the persecution of the nonconformists 1410; . . . . their King, and his Chancellour's speechs to the two Houses, and the issue thereof 1410; . . . . [for calling?] their English [out?] of France, etc., the commitment of articles against the

The third chapter begining the 23d line of the 1436 page containes the King's dissatisfaction therewith, the popish clergy prefered before the reform in the Bishop test 1440; the burning of the pamphlet by the hangman that arraignes that test, the severity against those of Bourdeaux, the King of England's policy 1441; the Imperialist drawing to winter quarters, the Lord's hand against the Swedish fleete, the taking of Wolgast, Don John appearing at court, etc. 1441; a designe to surprise Bellegard, and another to seize Huy, and the issue of both, officers of France preferred, the plenipotentiaries of Nimegue 1442; the adjournement of the Parliament 1442; the reason thereof, the dissatisfaction of Citty and people, and the King's pollicy to appease them 1443; the taking of Wismar, some rencontres betweene the Swede and confederats, the taking of ..., and besidging Wolgast 1444; Duke of Narailles commanding in Catalogne, the contest about Deux Ponts, and issue thereof; the taking of Fames, and Dorsex 1444; the agreement about Carlstad, the killing of Colonell Hageldorne, the contest about Kekelein, and issue thereof 1444; the delivery of Carlstad, the exchange of Mareschal de Crequi, Tromp his commanding the Danish fleete 1444; the Swede's repulse at Wolgast 1444; the Stats' embassy to Muscovy, transactions in Hungary and Polonia 1445; the King of Polonia his coronation, differences betwene the Spanish sea officers, de Ruiter his riding before Messine 1445; the fight betwene the Duch and French fleets in Sicile, and issue thereof, De Ruiter his reception at Naples 1446; the King of England's proposition to the Emperour, the confederats' demands, the losse of the English marchants 1447; the fight betwene the natives and English in New England, the putting out of Privy Counsellors in England 1447; the forbiding coffy houses, the imprisonment of Colonell Danvers, etc., the great change of the people's affections in England 1448; the King of France his impowering the King of England to give passes, the French successe in Flanders, and repulse at Herbeins 1448; a monster borne at Mastrich, the Suisse's union, some rencontres betwene Swede and confederats, and releiving of Wolgast 1449; the seizing the Hamburgers' goods at Magdlebourg, etc., the change of commanders both in French and confederats' armys 1449; the French losse at Bukolt, the Barron of Quinzy quitting the Spanish service, the pillage of Duke of Wertembourg's country 1449; the demands of Arragon, Duke Mortimer's death, the generall officers of the French army for this campagne 1449; advertisments of mortality to the King of France, the death of the Duke of Muscovy, and of the Elector of Bavaria 1450; the seizure of Chancellier, Griffenfield, etc., the Swedes attacquing Altena, death of Major General Werts 1450; the blocking of Phillipsbourg, the burning of Ham, etc., a designe against Messine, and issue thereof 1450; the slighting of Huy, Leige, Dinant, etc., the Elector of Cologhne, and Duke of Newbourg's declaring for the Emperour, and .... 1450; jealousys of the Common-wealths of Genoa, and Venice, King of England's endeavours for peace, divisions at his Court, etc. 1451; Mrs. Palmer's going for France, Mr. Duras a Frenchman's favour at the English Court 1451; Sir Horatio Townsend by the people 1452; some passages at Tangers, Jamica, Teapoli, New England, and Liege, the taking of 8 bylanders by Dunkirquers 1452; the promoting of severall generall officers by the allys, and the quarters of their forces, the harquebusing Mr. Golts 1452; the seizing of the Marquesse de Brinvillars, her confession, the execution of the Count Blancard, transactions in Polonia 1453; the French wasting of the Waas, the killing of Colonell Massietts, and issue thereof, the taking of Condé 1453; the siege of Bouchaine, the trechery of the Prince of Orange, the sea fight before Augusta, and issue thereof 1454; the rencontre in Rossilion, the encamping of the 2 armys, and the taking of Bouchaine 1454.

APPENDIX B: THE CONCLUSION OF
PART FOUR

The concluding lines of part four of 'A Voyce from the Watch Tower' are preserved on the opening page of the Bodleian manuscript (p. 721), and are reproduced below.

not being so mad-headed as the rest, and [being?] .... enemy to their proceedings, upon the [account?] .... bisshops' lands, thought fit to make his [peace?] .... to declare his willingness, not only to parte .... but with what other estate he had, to [prevent?] .... of the nation to the satisfaction of the .... pass betweene the secluded members .... who upon their declaring to lend the [somes?] of them, ordered a petition to be delivered .... members; wherein, whether by order of the .... or direction of Monke, I know not, but .... that Alderman Fowlke, by whose hand it was delivered (many others accompanying him), in his harrangue, after he had spoake to the particculars of the petition (the scope whereof was to lay open the misseryes that had bin amongst them for many yeares past, and the hopes they had by their meanes to come to a settlement), which he in conclusion pressing them to limited them not to any particcular forme, but declared their acquiescence either with a monarchy or a Comonwealth, as it should seeme most convenient to them.

INDEX

(Page numbers are those of the present volume. Appendix A is not indexed. The term 'regicide' is used broadly.)